CALIFORNIA
STATE PARKS
FOUNDATION

Dedicated to protecting, enhancing, and advocating
for California's magnificent state parks.
Find out more by calling (800) 963-7275
or visit www.calparks.org

California's State Parks

A DAY HIKER'S GUIDE

John McKinney

 WILDERNESS PRESS · BERKELEY, CA

California's State Parks: A Day Hiker's Guide

1st EDITION June 2005
  2nd printing April 2006

Copyright © 2005 by The Trailmaster, Inc.

Front cover photos copyright © 2005 by Ed Cooper
Interior photos, except where noted, by John McKinney
Interior maps: Hélène Webb
Cover design: Larry B. Van Dyke
Book design: Emily Douglas
Book production: Lisa Pletka
Book editor: Cheri Rae

ISBN 0-89997-386-8
UPC 7-19609-97386-7

Manufactured in the United States of America

Published by: **Wilderness Press**
               1200 5th Street
               Berkeley, CA 94710
               (800) 443-7227; FAX (510) 558-1696
               info@wildernesspress.com
               www.wildernesspress.com

Visit our website for a complete listing of our books and for ordering information.

Previously published as *Day Hiker's Guide to California's State Parks* by Olympus Press.
Portions of this book have appeared in the author's hiking column in the *Los Angeles Times*,
as well as in *Sunset* and *Westways* magazines.

Cover photos: Waterfall at Julia Pfeiffer Burns State Park *(top left)*
                 Desert Sand Verbena and Coyote Peak, Anza-Borrego Desert State Park
                 (top right)
                 Chapel, Fort Ross State Historic Park *(bottom right)*
                 McArthur-Burney Falls Memorial State Park *(bottom left)*

SAFETY NOTICE: Although Wilderness Press and the author have made every attempt to ensure that the information in this book is accurate at press time, they are not responsible for any loss, damage, injury, or inconvenience that may occur to anyone while using this book. You are responsible for your own safety and health. The fact that a trail is described in this book does not mean that it will be safe for you. Be aware that trail conditions can change from day to day. Always check local conditions and know your own limitations.

ACKNOWLEDGMENTS

A heartfelt thank you goes to the California State Parks Foundation and its staffers and supporters, who contribute so much to our wonderful parks, including Foundation Board Chairman and legendary hiker Don Robinson. The author would like to express his sincere appreciation for the enthusiasm and guidance offering during the preparation of this guide by California Department of Parks and Recreation field personnel. A special thanks goes to all rangers, district superintendents, and the many park employees who were unfailingly courteous and helpful to me during my visits to the 200-plus parks mentioned in this book. Another thank you goes to the California Park Rangers and the interpretive association members who field- and fact-checked the information in this guide.

PHOTO CREDITS

Cristine Argyrakis 92; Frank Balthis 149; Roslyn Bullas/Michael McKay xvii, 206; California Coastal Commission 302, 304; California Department of Parks and Recreation 3, 4, 31, 54, 104, 136, 160, 165, 194, 209, 227, 262, 275, 312; Delaware North Companies Parks & Resorts 188; Jon Foster 64; Bob Howells 33. All other photos by John McKinney.

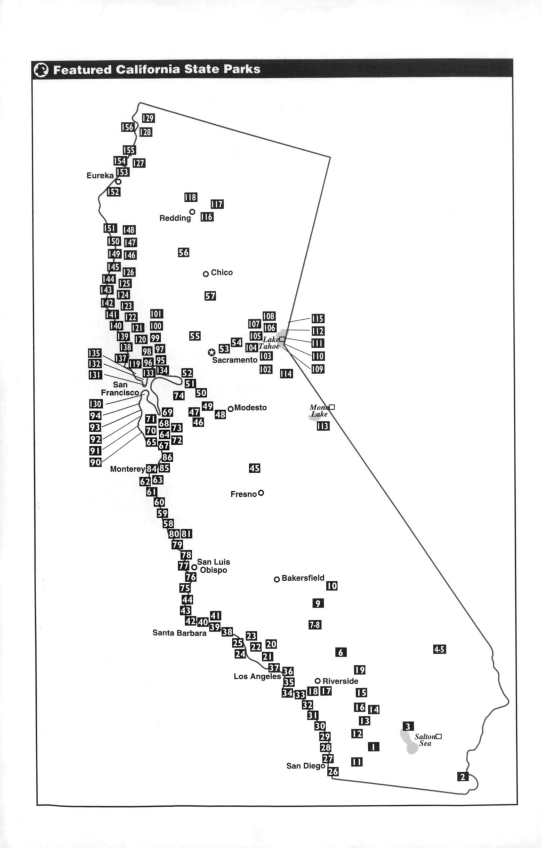

⊙ Key to Locator Map

SOUTHERN CALIFORNIA DESERT
1 Anza-Borrego Desert State Park
2 Picacho State Recreation Area
3 Salton Sea State Recreation Area
4 Mitchell Caverns Natural Preserve
5 Providence Mountains State Recreation Area
6 Saddleback Butte State Park
7 Antelope Valley California Poppy Reserve
8 Arthur Ripley Desert Woodland State Park
9 Tomo-Kahni Village Site
10 Red Rock Canyon State Park

SOUTHERN CALIFORNIA MOUNTAINS
11 Cuyamaca Rancho State Park
12 San Pasqual Battlefield State Historic Park
13 Palomar Mountain State Park
14 Mount San Jacinto State Park
15 San Timoteo Canyon State Park
16 Lake Perris State Recreation Area
17 California Citrus State Historic Park
18 Chino Hills State Park
19 Silverwood Lake State Recreation Area
20 Santa Susana Mountains State Park
21 Will Rogers State Historic Park
22 Topanga State Park
23 Malibu Creek State Park
24 Leo Carrillo State Park
25 Point Mugu State Park

SOUTHERN CALIFORNIA COAST
26 Border Field State Park
27 Silver Strand State Beach
28 Torrey Pines State Beach
29 Torrey Pines State Reserve
30 San Onofre State Beach
31 San Clemente State Beach
32 Doheny State Beach
33 Crystal Cove State Park
34 Huntington and Bolsa Chica State Beaches
35 Santa Monica Bay State Beaches
36 Malibu Lagoon State Beach
37 McGrath State Beach
38 San Buenaventura State Beach
39 Emma Wood State Beach
40 Carpinteria State Beach
41 El Capitan State Beach
42 Gaviota State Park
43 La Purisima Mission State Historic Park
44 Point Sal State Beach

CENTRAL VALLEY
45 Millerton Lake State Recreation Area
46 San Luis Reservoir SRA
47 Pacheco State Park
48 Turlock Lake State Recreation Area
49 Great Valley Grasslands State Park
50 Caswell Memorial State Park
51 Brannan Island State Recreation Area

52 Delta Meadows State Recreation Area
53 Folsom Lake State Recreation Area
54 Auburn State Recreation Area
55 Colusa-Sacramento River State Recreation Area
56 Woodson Bridge St. Recreation Area
57 Lake Oroville State Recreation Area

CENTRAL CALIFORNIA MOUNTAINS
58 Limekiln State Park
59 Julia Pfeiffer Burns State Park
60 Pfeiffer Big Sur State Park
61 Pt. Sur State Historic Park
62 Andrew Molera State Park
63 Garrapata State Park
64 Forest of Nisene Marks State Park
65 Henry Cowell Redwoods State Park
66 Big Basin Redwoods State Park
67 Fall Creek
68 Castle Rock State Park
69 Portola Redwoods State Park
70 Butano State Park
71 Burleigh-Murray State Park
72 Fremont Peak State Park
73 Henry W. Coe State Park
74 Mt. Diablo State Park

CENTRAL CALIFORNIA COAST
75 Oceano Dunes State Recreation Area
76 Los Osos Oaks State Reserve
77 Montaña de Oro State Park
78 Morro Bay State Park
79 Morro Strand State Beach
80 San Simeon State Park
81 William Randolph Hearst State Beach
82 Point Lobos State Reserve
83 Carmel River State Beach
84 Asilomar State Beach
85 Marina State Beach
86 Salinas State Beach
87 New Brighton and Seacliff State Beaches
88 Natural Bridges State Beach
89 Wilder Ranch State Historic Park
90 Año Nuevo State Reserve
91 Bean Hollow State Beach
92 Pescadero State Beach
93 Half Moon Bay State Beach
94 McNee Ranch State Park

NORTHERN CALIFORNIA MOUNTAINS
95 Jack London State Historic Park
96 Annadel State Park
97 Sugarloaf Ridge State Park
98 Bothe-Napa Valley State Park
99 Robert Louis Stevenson State Park
100 Anderson Marsh State Historic Park
101 Clear Lake State Park
102 Calaveras Big Trees State Park
103 Indian Grinding Rock State Historic Park
104 Marshall Gold Discovery State Historic Park

105 South Yuba River State Park
106 Empire Mine State Historic Park
107 Malakoff Diggins State Historic Park
108 Plumas-Eureka State Park
109 Washoe Meadows State Park
110 D.L. Bliss–Emerald Bay State Parks
111 Sugar Pine Point State Park
112 Burton Creek State Park
113 Mono Lake Tufa State Reserve
114 Grover Hot Springs State Park
115 Donner Memorial State Park
116 McArthur-Burney Falls Memorial State Park
117 Ahjumawi Lava Springs State Park
118 Castle Crags State Park

NORTHERN CALIFORNIA REDWOODS
119 Armstrong Redwoods SR, Austin Creek State Park
120 Hendy Woods State Park
121 Montgomery Woods State Reserve
122 Standish-Hickey State Recreation Area
123 Richardson Grove State Park
124 Benbow Lake State Recreation Area
125 Humboldt Redwoods State Park
126 Grizzly Creek Redwoods State Park
127 Prairie Creek Redwoods State Park
128 Del Norte Coast Redwoods State Park
129 Jedediah Smith Redwoods State Park

NORTHERN CALIFORNIA COAST
130 Candlestick Point State Recreation Area
131 Angel Island State Park
132 Mt. Tamalpais State Park
133 China Camp State Park
134 Benicia State Recreation Area
135 Samuel P. Taylor State Park
136 Olompali State Historic Park
137 Tomales Bay State Park

NORTH COAST
138 Sonoma Coast State Beach
139 Fort Ross State Historic Park
140 Salt Point State Park
141 Kruse Rhododendron State Reserve
142 Manchester State Beach
143 Van Damme State Park
144 Greenwood Creek State Beach
145 Mendocino Headlands State Park
146 Big River State Park
147 Mendocino Woodlands State Park
148 Russian Gulch State Park
149 Jug Handle State Reserve
150 MacKerricher State Park
151 Sinkyone Wilderness State Park
152 Azalea State Reserve
153 Trinidad State Beach
154 Patrick's Point State Park
155 Humboldt Lagoons State Park
156 Tolowa Dunes State Park

CONTENTS AT A GLANCE

CONTENTS

1   SOUTHERN CALIFORNIA DESERT   11

2   SOUTHERN CALIFORNIA MOUNTAINS   33

3 SOUTHERN CALIFORNIA COAST   65

SANTA MONICA MOUNTAINS

4 CENTRAL VALLEY   105

SAN JOAQUIN VALLEY (SOUTH)

SACRAMENTO VALLEY (NORTH)

5 CENTRAL CALIFORNIA MOUNTAINS 131

6 CENTRAL CALIFORNIA COAST 169

7 NORTHERN CALIFORNIA MOUNTAINS 207

WINE COUNTRY

Top left: Twining virgin's bower in the springtime at Mt. Diablo State Park.

Top right: Rock formations at Anza-Borrego Desert State Park.

Bottom: Throwing a line in at Henry W. Coe State Park.

The first major project undertaken by the California State Parks Foundation was the reconstruction of the chapel at Fort Ross State Historic Park that had been destroyed by fire. The project was completed in 1972.

In addition to providing funding for major "structural" restoration projects, the Foundation also facilitates the hands-on involvement of thousands of volunteers through its annual "Earth Day Restoration and Cleanup" program.

Land acquisition is also a focus for the California State Parks Foundation. China Camp State Park in Marin County was established when the Foundation deeded 1,500 acres, including two miles of shoreline, to the State Parks system.

ABOUT THE
CALIFORNIA STATE PARKS FOUNDATION

From the red rock desert to the redwood coast, and from Hearst Castle to the High Sierra, California State Parks are as diverse as the California landscape. Individually and collectively, California's parklands reflect the natural and historical legacy of the Golden State. Each park protects a unique place, expresses a unique part of the California experience, and preserves the state's legacy.

For more than 35 years, the California State Parks Foundation has partnered with the California Department of Parks and Recreation to ensure that the grandeur of this astonishing state continues for generations to come. In project after project, in park after park, the Foundation contributes immeasurably to this great park system, the nation's finest.

The Foundation has acquired funding for hundreds of vital programs that the State of California could not support on its own. Since its inception, the Foundation has supported the protection and enhancement of our parks.

A recent survey of Californians revealed a great appreciation for, and commitment to, California's park system; however, this same survey also indicated that respondents were little aware of the extent of the state's parklands or the true number of state parks in the system. Two dozen parks, guessed some, 50 said others. About 100 parks was the greatest number of parks they estimated to be in the system.

Actually, California is blessed with 278 state parks—and the number is growing! John McKinney's lively and comprehensive new *California's State Parks: A Day Hiker's Guide* puts you on the trail to adventure in every state park that has a walk or hike. Enjoy! And as you hit the trail, consider helping us support California State Parks by joining the California State Parks Foundation. Please join 50,000 other Californians dedicated to protecting our glorious parks and become a Foundation member.

ELIZABETH GOLDSTEIN
President

Dedicated to protecting, enhancing, and advocating
for California's magnificent state parks.
Find out more by calling (800) 963-7275
or visit www.calparks.org

Left: Bighorn sheep roam Anza-Borrego, the largest state park.

Middle left: Ancient woodlands are a highlight at Henry W. Coe, second largest state park.

Middle right: State historic parks interpret history, from oranges to gold mines.

Bottom: The matchless grove at Bull Creek Flat forms the heart of Humboldt Redwoods, one of the first state parks established in the 1920s.

INTRODUCTION

All of us own this land—more than a million acres of it. This land has names like Anza-Borrego, Castle Rock, Grizzly Creek and Richardson Grove.

This land with the colorful names is the California State Park System, widely regarded as the nation's finest.

Other states have high mountains, vast deserts, and scenic shorelines, but only California contains all of these natural features, and preserves examples of them in its park system.

The multitude of intriguing state park environments, and the many fine paths that explore them, add up to some world-class walking adventures —certainly some of the best walks in the West.

It's been my pleasure, as an author and hiking expert, to send my readers tripping afoot all over the West, all over the world. Time and time again, readers report that among the hikes I've chronicled, the most pleasurable and popular hikes they've taken are those in California's state parks.

Ancient redwoods grow along the mist-covered edge of the continent. The alpine beauty of the Sierra Nevada towers above Emerald Bay and Sugar Pine Point state parks on the shores of world-famous Lake Tahoe. Warm, sandy state beaches from San Clemente to Refugio beckon visitors to Southern California. The state's unique history comes alive at the Franciscan mission at La Purísima, the Old Customs House in Monterey, the Russian chapel at Fort Ross.

State parks preserve a cross-section of California ecology from the bottom of the Central Valley at Caswell Memorial State Park to the top of alpine peaks at Mt. San Jacinto State Park; from uncommonly dry desert lands, where Joshua trees thrive, such as Saddleback Butte State Park to the near-rainforest environment of Del Norte Redwoods State Park.

State parks showcase a fabulous array of Nature's handiwork: giant Sequoias in Calaveras Big Trees State Park; the rare Torrey pines making a last stand in a reserve near San Diego; palm oases in Anza-Borrego Desert State Park; some of the tallest trees on earth at Humboldt Redwoods State Park.

State parks highlight California's history—and offer visitors the opportunity to follow the trails of the forty-niners, Spanish missionaries and Native Americans. Hike into history where the Gold Rush began (Marshall Gold State Historic Park), where a famed writer found inspiration (Jack London State Historic Park), where a lonely lighthouse-keeper lived and worked (Pt. Sur State Historic Park).

Park pathways are as varied as the parks themselves. Some trails are easy—a "walk in the park." Leg-stretchers along the Sacramento River at Woodson Bridge and Colusa state recreation areas allow motorists a break from Interstate 5; beach walks from Border Field State Park to MacKerricher State Beach provide a similar break from Coast Highway 1. Take short walks into history, past the Immigration Station on Angel Island, up Fremont Peak, named for the famed pathfinder.

Many state park walks are suitable for the whole family—slow paced-adventures with much to see on a short hike. These family hikes, by utilizing described options, can usually be extended to half-day or all-day outings.

The avid hiker will find challenges aplenty in the parks, too—long day hikes that offer grand tours and great workouts.

This guide is your invitation to adventure. You'll learn about the history and natural attractions of California's state parks, as you walk some of California's best trails.

"The Best of California Forever" is the slogan of the California Department of Parks and Recreation. State parks preserve many stunning examples of California's varied landscape; they are yours to protect and enjoy.

CALIFORNIA'S STATE PARKS

The California Department of Parks and Recreation administers some 278 state park "units," as park officials call them. Don't be surprised if you see or hear a number greater or lesser than 278 ("nearly 300" and "more than 250" are popular descriptions) because there's debate even within the Department about what to count where. When counting parks, does one count state parks administered and operated by a city or county parks department? Should parks acquired by the Department, but not yet open to the public, be counted?

In 1993, the Department began to introduce some "user-friendly" terms to describe itself. The "California Park System" is now often used instead of the redundant "California State Park System." And the Department of Parks and Recreation (or DPR as its often known) has slowly been introducing the term "California Park Service" to the public.

We usually refer to the state's 200-something units as state parks, but they actlly go by a half-dozen different descriptions:

State Parks, by definition, are major areas with outstanding scenic, scientific, natural or cultural values. They are managed for both recreation and preservation.

State Historic Parks preserve structures and lands of historic interest. These parks may also commemorate a person or historic event.

State Wilderness is an area managed to best preserve the primeval character of the land. No permanent structures are permitted.

In **State Reserves,** too, ecology comes first. They protect flora, fauna and geology adjudged to be of statewide signficance.

State Recreation Areas, often centering around a lake or river, provide large-scale outdoor recreation opportunities and usually host a large number of visitors.

State Beaches, fronting California's bays and ocean shores, also offer many recreational opportunities, though some beaches beckon vistors to quieter, more nature-oriented pursuits.

California State Parks: A Brief History

Truly, with 278 state parks, there are 278 stories to tell. Each "unit" has a unique story. Each park contributes a page to the whole story—a story-in-the-making, really, because new parks, preserves, recreation areas and historic sites are added to the system every year.

While walking the parks, you'll learn some of these stories. Maybe you'll saunter Colusa-Sacramento River State Recreation Area and learn the "rags-to-riches" story of a stretch of river that was transformed from a dump site to a park site. Or maybe you'll hike through the heart of Humboldt Redwoods State Park and learn how the economically and politically powerful Rockefeller family saved a magnificent redwood forest for the state and nation.

The tale of the park system as a whole is fascinating as well—a saga that includes politics, conservation battles, both noisy and quiet, some Californians with great vision and some with very little, and a public that has consistently supported the parks with its enthusiasm, votes, and funding.

As a matter of historical record, the first state park was Yosemite, given to California by President Lincoln's proclamation in 1864. Early in the 20th century, California returned Yosemite to the federal government and began creating its own parks.

In 1902, the California state park system was born with the establishment of California Redwood Park in the Big Basin area of the Santa Cruz Mountains. Perhaps it is only fitting that one of the state's proudest possessions—the magnificent redwoods—should have provided the inspiration for the creation of the Golden State's park system.

California's first state park—and the establishment of a state park system a quarter-century later—were certainly aided by two strong social movements in America: the conservation movement and the historic preservation movement. While conservationists acted to preserve the natural scene from

Early park ranger revels in his work.

Mt. San Jacinto in Southern California to Mt. Diablo in Northern California, historical preservationists championed the chapel at Fort Ross, the Old Customs House in Monterey, and a memorial to the Donner Party.

With the founding of the national park service in 1916 and its blossoming in the 1920s to become something Americans pointed to with great pride, California had a working model from which to fashion its own park service and park system.

"California is growing in population more rapidly than any other state," early parks advocate Duncan McDuffie said in 1925. "Unless a comprehensive plan for the preservation of recreational and scenic areas is set in motion, our children and our children's children will want for the opportunity of out of door life that makes for sound bodies, clear brains and good citizenship."

Not everybody agreed. Ultra-conservative Governor William Friend Richardson (who somewhat ironically would one day have a state park named for him) was hostile to the state park movement and vetoed park legislation.

"Plain stupid and entirely void of vision," fumed conservationist and Republican Congressman William Kent in response to Richardson's veto. "A blind porcupine could write just as good commentary on the question."

Pro-park forces prevailed, and in 1927 a state park system was established. The following year was really a landmark year for California's parks. Pamphlets were circulated, window stickers stuck in Model A's, a motion picture short released to movie houses—all in support of the park and recreation bond act of 1928. The public voted overwhelmingly to approve the bond and finance a state park system.

But it was not much of a park service or park system at first; it consisted of little more than the original California Redwood Park, a couple of north coast redwood parks, Mt. Diablo and some historic sites and structures. The entire field staff numbered just fifteen.

The other major event of 1928 was the commission of distinguished landscape architect Frederick Law Olmsted, Jr., son of the famed Central Park designer, to conduct a survey of the state to locate and describe possible parks. Olmsted and his staff evaluated 330 sites, and found 125 of them sufficiently worthy for consideration as state parks. Olmsted turned in his lengthy survey report on the last day of 1928 and promptly collapsed from exhaustion.

Is there a grander sight than sunlight streaming through a redwood forest?

Olmsted's survey was not only a practical plan, but a heartfelt expression of the value of state parks to the physical and mental well-being of Californians.

It was the job of the new state park staff, Olmsted believed, to teach the populace how to enjoy the great outdoors while at the same time preserving it for future generations. A second important mission was to defend the parks against all forms of commercial exploitation.

While the Great Depression of the 1930s caused many Californians untold economic hardship, it did not suppress the rapidly growing state park system. Land prices sharply declined, thus enabling the state to make a number of purchases at bargain prices—particularly in the north woods and along Southern California's beaches. Pfeiffer Big Sur State Park, Castle Crags State Park and San Clemente and Santa Monica beaches, were among the many acquisitions of the 1930s.

During the hard economic times, the federal Civilian Conservation Corps contributed enormously to the nation's parks and forests. The CCC worked an estimated 10,000 "man-years" in California's state parks. Heavy, infrastructure-type projects such as bridges, roads, and campgrounds were the the specialty at the CCC. The Corps also built some spectacular structures that are much admired today, including the summit building atop Mt. Diablo and Mountain Theater atop Mt. Tamalpais.

World War II, accompanied by gas and tire rationing and park personnel shortages, meant fewer visitors to the state parks. Some parks, such as Anza-Borrego, were closed during the war. Other parks, including Calaveras Big Trees and Pfeiffer Big Sur, were used to house and train troops.

After the war came a travel boom and the beginning of a long period of prosperity. The legislature rushed to approve funding for more parks and more park facilities. Robert Louis Stevenson State Park, Samuel P. Taylor State Park and San Buenaventura State Beach were some of the units added to the park system in the late 1940s.

In 1951, Governor Earl Warren persuaded Californian Newton Drury, just completing a stint as national park director, to assume the post of state park director. The Drury years (1951-1959) were characterized by much park acquisition, fueled in part by offshore oil royalties to the state.

Drury figured the Department should fund as many land purchases as possible; modest facilities could always be developed later. Drury reasoned: "People have a right to use the parks of course. But no generation has a right to use them up."

Emerald Bay on Lake Tahoe, Leo Carrillo and El Capitan State Beaches, and Caswell Memorial State Park in the Central Valley were among the many acquisitions of the 1950s.

Governor Edmund G. Brown (1959-1967) will always and forever be known as the booster and builder of California's gargantuan State Water Project. All that water routed and stored for agriculture and the state's big cities might as well be used for recreation, too, Brown believed. The big "reservoir parks" were given to the park system to develop.

By the early 1960s, some 30 million visitors flocked to state parks. California's rapidly growing population needed more parks and more facilities. A 1964 state parks and recreation bond act earmarked $150 million for the system. Thanks in part to Walt Disney, who served as a parks spokesman, and his production of a short color film that dramatized the need for parks, voters overwhelmingly approved the bond measure.

Sugarloaf Ridge, Point Mugu, Malakoff Diggins and Montaña de Oro were some of the parks acquired during the 1960s.

Governor Ronald Reagan (1967-1975) was no park booster, but he appointed a park director who certainly was: William Penn Mott, Jr. Mott defended the parks from the budget axe and expanded the system; he also professionalized the department. He established a training center at Asilomar to educate park staff as naturalists. Modern times, he believed, called for modern law enforcement methods, and park rangers were required to become peace officers.

The year 1969 was a banner year for the spirit of voluntarism that has contributed so much for so long to California's state parks. The first "Trails Day" turned out hundreds of volunteers to work on the Skyline-to-the-Sea Trail in Big Basin Redwoods and Castle Rock state parks. This effort became the inspiration for California's annual statewide "Trails Day," which enlists the aid of thousands of volunteers to work on park trails.

The California State Parks Foundation was founded in 1969. This nonprofit organization has raised and donated millions of dollars to fund state park land acquisitions, facilities and programs.

Mott pioneered modern fund-raising methods. Under his direction, the department negotiated improved concessionaire agreements, and in 1970 launched the first computerized campsite reservation system.

Fueled by off-road vehicle licensing fees, the state park system continued its expansion in the 1970s: Huntington Beach, Empire Mine, Wilder Ranch. In 1974, California voters once again approved another park bond act, Proposition One, for $250 million.

As the 1970s progressed, the park's post-war expansion began to slow and the parks were increasingly beset by overcrowding, vandalism and environmental problems. In a 1978 speech commemorating the park system's 50th anniversary, then-director Russell Cahill warned: "I look around today and see a people out of touch: out of touch with nature, out of touch with their history, out of touch with each other."

During the 1980s, the parks began to face the first of ever-increasing budget cuts. The Department was required to earn some of the revenue needed for its ongoing operations—a reasonable requirement that most everyone supported.

However, this mandated fundraising accelerated during the 1990s to amounts the state park system couldn't possibly collect. The Department was placed in an untenable situation: If the Department failed to meet its revenue goals, it was penalized by cuts in personnel and programs. If it did meet its goals, state government required DPR to raise even more revenue.

Today, the Department faces several problems, including a financial situation that is becoming a true crisis in proportion, and deferred maintenance that is mounting. Because of the more-than-usual need for revenue, commercialization of the state park system from those who misinterpret the mission and purpose of state parks is a definite threat these days.

The Department's challenge in the 21st century is to provide for the recreation needs of a growing population that is increasingly ethnically and culturally diverse, while at the same time preserving and protecting the lands in its charge. Quite a challenge!

Fortunately, California state park visitors have a much better grasp of the value of parks than California state politicians, and understand that their value is more than the yearly revenue they generate. Since the beginning of the parks movement early in the 20th century, California's citizens have supported their parks, preserving priceless lands for future generations and supporting the parks with their votes and volunteer hours, admission fees and tax dollars.

Optimists hope that the present generation of Californians is as forward-looking as an earlier generation who took to heart the words of early parks advocate/ state parks director Newton Drury as he argued (successfully) for the state parks bond act of 1928: "The benefit to Californians will be many times the cost. State Parks will pay not only in increased revenue...but, what is more important, will pay rich dividends in the health and happiness of our people by assuring for them and for their successors, enjoyment of the scenic beauty and outdoor recreation which Californians have always looked upon as their heritage."

State of the State's Trails

By some estimates, the state park trail system includes more than 2,000 miles of trail. About 150 parks have at least one compelling walk or hike, and are thus included in this guide.

For the most part, park trails are in pretty good shape, particularly in comparison to paths in national forests or those of other land use agencies. While trails are all too often a low priority maintenance item at the parks, they have stayed in hike-able shape thanks to the hard work of many dedicated volunteers from trails and conservation organizations.

Keeping a watchful eye on the state's trails (including, but not limited to state park trails) are the seven members of the California Recreational Trails Committee. Members, representing various locales around the state and various trail constituencies (cyclists, equestrians, hikers, river-runners, etc.), advise the state parks director on trail matters.

The CRT Committee, formed in 1969, broadened its responsibilities during the 1970s and assumed an advisory and coordination role for trail development in city, county and regional park departments.

In 1977-78, the Committee spearheaded the development of the California Recreational Trails Plan, which examined the needs of hikers, cyclists, boaters and off-road vehicle users.

Ever since, the Committee has met quarterly in locales around the state. Meetings give trails enthusiasts a chance to discuss issues of both regional and statewide importance. Although the Committee's power is strictly limited to a sometimes frustrating advisory role, it does serve as a valuable source of trails information.

The Committee hosts an a trails conference each spring, usually at the state's Asilomar Conference Center. Trails advocates from all over the state gather to share information about trail projects, get briefed on the latest land use policy and legal developments, learn new trail building and trail publicizing techniques.

A very important Committee task, assumed in recent years, is the coordination of statewide Trails Days. This annual springtime event enlists volunteers to work on trail projects from the Southern California deserts to the northern redwoods.

Using this Guide

Hiking opportunities are detailed in more than 150 state park units mentioned in this book. The parks are grouped by geography into chapters, then further organized in rough south-to-north order.

Most of the parks clearly belong in their respective categories, but a couple of parks straddle geographical areas and I've made a judgment call as to which chapter to place these parks. For example: San Clemente State Beach clearly belongs to the Southern California Coast chapter. But what about Clear Lake State Park, located in that "other wine country" north of the Napa-Sonoma wine country?

Distance, expressed in round trip mileage figures, follows each destination. The hikes in this guide range from 1 to 15 miles, with the majority in the easy (under 5 miles) range and moderate (5 to 10 mile) category. Gain or loss in elevation follows the mileage in hikes with significant ups and downs.

In matching a hike to your ability, you'll want to consider both mileage and elevation as well as condition of the trail, terrain, and season. Hot, exposed chaparral or miles of boulder-hopping can make a short walk seem long.

Hikers vary a great deal in relative physical condition, but you may want to consider the following: An easy walk suitable for beginners and children would be less than five miles with an elevation gain of less than 700 to 800 feet. A moderate walk is considered a walk in the 5- to 10-mile range, with under 2,000 feet of elevation gain. You should be reasonably fit for these. Preteens sometimes find the going difficult. Hikes of more than 10 miles and those with more than a 2,000-foot gain are for experienced hikers in top form.

Season is the next item to consider. California is one of the few places in the country that offer four-season hiking. You can hike some of the trails in this guide all of the time, all of the trails some of the time, but not all of the trails all of the time.

Precautions: A few trails in this guide may be impassable in winter and spring due to high water. Relevant fire and flood information has been noted below the season recommendation.

An introduction to each hike describes what you'll see in a particular state park and what you'll observe along the trail: plants, animals, panoramic views. You'll also learn about the geologic and human history of the region.

Directions to the trailhead take you from the nearest major highway to trailhead parking. For trails having two desirable trailheads, directions to each are given. A few trails can be walked one way, with the possibility of a car shuttle. Suggested car shuttle points are noted.

After the directions to the trailhead, you'll read a description of the hike. Important junctions and major sights are pointed out, but I've left you to discover the multitude of little things that make a hike an adventure.

About the Maps

The maps in this book and the California Parks series support the author's mission, which is to provide an introduction for the day hiker to the state's best state, national, coastal and desert parklands.

Many of the Golden State's parklands are regarded by rangers, administrators—and most importantly by hikers—as true "hiker's parks." These footpath-friendly parks offer miles and miles of maintained trails, with plenty of options for great day hikes. For these adventures, in contrast with, say, easy "walks in the park," route descriptions are described in more detail and accompanying maps highlight more trails and park features.

It's a delight for me to share some of my favorite, often carefully selected, shorter California trails, too. Among these short but scenic paths are nature trails and history interpretation trails, as well as beach trails and informal footpaths along a river. These short hikes have correspondingly short route descriptions, and the accompanying maps chart a minimal number of features. A handful of the selected hikes are so short, and the on-the-ground orientation for the hiker so obvious, that mapping them would not add anything to the visitor's experience and, in a few instances, would be downright silly.

Fellow hikers, do give us a heads-up about any trail changes you notice or any discrepancies you observe between the map and territory.

For reasons I can't explain, during the 20-plus years that I've been chronicling hiking trails, you hikers have been lots more vigilant about pouncing on errant or out-of-date prose and telling me about it than you have about pointing out the need for any trail map updates. (Jeez, I can't even misidentify a rare plant or obscure bird without hearing about it from so many of you...) Anyway, your cartographic input is always welcome.

Anza-Borrego Desert, California's largest state park, beckons the hiker with hundreds of miles of intriguing routes.

CHAPTER ONE

1

SOUTHERN CALIFORNIA DESERT

Californians who have an affinity for the desert are fortunate to have portions of two vast deserts preserved in state parks: the Mojave (high desert) and the Colorado (low desert). The designations refer to altitude and latitude. There is (relatively) more rainfall in the high desert, and the hot season isn't as hot and severe as it is in the lower desert.

In the western Mojave Desert the hiker can explore the Joshua tree forests in Saddleback Butte State Park and Arthur Ripley Desert Woodland State Park. Red Rock Canyon State Park, recently greatly expanded, attracts visitors with its awesome cliffs and colorful rock formations.

Not to be missed is the state's ultimate spring flower show—the blankets of gold covering the slopes of Antelope Valley California Poppy Reserve. During a good wildflower year, California's state flower creates a stunning tableau on the reserve's hillsides.

Borrego Palm Canyon, one of California's largest palm canyons.

In the eastern Mojave, the park system includes Mitchell Caverns, intriguing limestone caves that can be explored on ranger-led walks. The caverns is part of Providence Mountains State Recreation Area, where hikers can wander through a great high desert environment and enjoy far-reaching vistas.

More than 600,000 acres of the Colorado Desert are protected by Anza-Borrego Desert State Park. California's largest state park includes virtually every feature visitors associate with a desert—washes, badlands, mesas, palm oases, and many more. It offers a remoteness, a desolation, a special beauty that brings back visitors seeking solitude year after year.

ANZA-BORREGO DESERT STATE PARK

■ BORREGO PALM CANYON TRAIL
To Falls is 3 miles round trip with 600-foot elevation gain; to South Fork is 6.5 miles round trip with 1,400-foot gain; Season: October-May

B orrego Palm Canyon was the first site sought for a desert state park back in the 1920s. It's a beautiful, well-watered oasis, tucked away in a rocky V-shaped gorge. The canyon's many charms, along with its easy access from the park visitor center, combine to make it the most popular sight-to-see in the park by far—at least for those willing to take a short hike.

With more than a thousand palms, the oasis once ranked number three among all the state's native fan palm gatherings. However, the palm population was decimated by a flash flood in September of 2004. A ten-foot-high wall of water washed away some 70 percent of the Borrego's palms.

The oasis-bound hiker will find many a toppled palm lying in or near the boulder-strewn riverbed. Fortunately, there are sufficient survivors to perpetuate the species.

The still-enjoyable trail makes its way to a much-reduced palm grove and seasonal waterfall. A longer option takes you exploring up-canyon.

In winter, the trail to the falls is mighty popular; get an early start to beat the crowd and for a better chance of sighting the bighorn sheep that frequently visit the canyon. In the summer, you'll probably have the oasis all to yourself.

DIRECTIONS TO TRAILHEAD The trail begins at Borrego Palm Canyon Campground, located one mile north of park headquarters. Trailhead parking is available at the west end of the campground near the campfire circle.

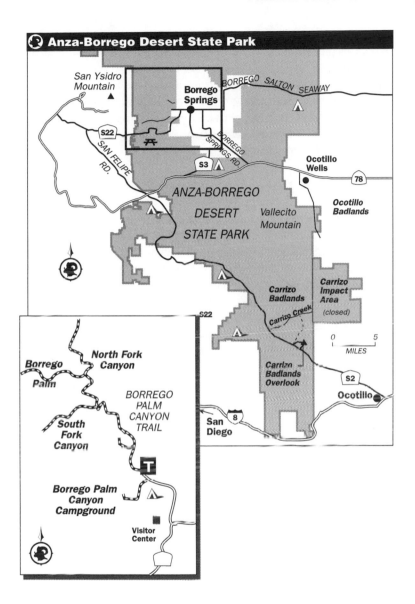

THE HIKE   Beginning at the pupfish pond, you walk up-canyon past many desert plants used by the Indians for food and shelter. Willow was used for home-building and bow-making; brittlebush and creosote were used for their healing qualities; honey, along with mesquite and beavertail cactus, was a food staple. You might also notice Indian grinding holes in the granite.

   The broad alluvial fan at the mouth of the canyon narrows and the sheer rock walls of the canyon soon enclose you as the trail continues along the healthy, but seasonal stream. Already surprised to learn how an apparently life-less canyon could provide all the Indians' necessary survival ingredients, you're surprised once more when Borrego Palm Oasis comes into view. Just beyond the first group of palms is a damp grotto, where a waterfall cascades over huge boulders. The grotto is a popular picnic area and rest stop.

From the falls, you may take an alternate trail back to the campground. This trail takes you along the south side of the creek, past some magnificent ocotillo, and gives you a different perspective on this unique desert environment. By following the optional route, you can continue hiking up the canyon. Hiking is more difficult up-canyon after the falls, with lots of dense undergrowth and boulders to navigate around.

To South Fork: From the "tourist turnaround" continue up the canyon. The creek is a fairly dependable water supply and is usually running late in the fall. The canyon is wet, so watch your footing on the slippery, fallen palm fronds. The canyon narrows even further and the trail dwindles to nothing. Parallel the streambed and boulder-hop back and forth across the water. The canyon zigs and zags quite a bit, so you can never see much more than a few hundred yards ahead. The hike is well-worth the effort though, because most of the 800 or so palms in the canyon are found in its upper reaches. Sometimes you'll spot rock-climbers practicing their holds on the steep red-rock cliffs above.

The canyon splits 1.75 miles from the falls. Straight ahead, to the southwest, is South Fork. The rocky gorge of South Fork, smothered with bamboo, is in possession of all the canyon's water. It's quite difficult to negotiate. South Fork ascends to the upper slopes of San Ysidro Mountain (6,417 feet). The Middle Fork (the way you came) of Borrego Palm Canyon is dry and more passable. It's possible to hike quite a distance first up Middle Fork, then North Fork of Borrego Palm Canyon, but check with park rangers first. It's extremely rugged terrain.

PICACHO STATE RECREATION AREA

■ STAMP MILL, ICE CREAM CANYON TRAILS
From Park road to Stamp Mill Ruins is 2 miles round trip; through Ice Cream Canyon is 4.5 miles round trip

Picacho State Recreation Area beckons the visitor with spectacular Colorado River and Colorado Desert scenery. Colorful canyons, rugged volcanic peaks and isolated backwater lakes are among the diverse landforms of this obscure park located in the Colorado River Basin on the California-Arizona border.

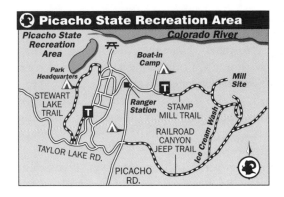

Picacho State Recreation Area

Picacho State Recreation Area
Colorado River
Park Headquarters
Boat-in Camp
Mill Site
STEWART LAKE TRAIL
Ranger Station
STAMP MILL TRAIL
RAILROAD CANYON JEEP TRAIL
Ice Cream Wash
TAYLOR LAKE RD.
PICACHO RD.

In spring and fall, Picacho is the place to view migratory waterfowl, including egrets, blue herons and a multitude of ducks. Perhaps the showiest of the winged congregants along the Colorado River is the Canada goose— a stirring sight and an unmistakable sound.

Hikers often spot large animals roaming the park: mule deer, coyotes and feral burros. Some lucky hikers even get fleeting glimpses of the elusive big horn sheep. Three park inhabitants always seem to be in a hurry, even in the heat: quail, raccoons and roadrunners.

For most visitors, Picacho is a nine-month park. During the mid and late summer months, Picacho is extremely hot place. Its low elevation and southerly positioning means temperatures routinely reach 105 to 115 degrees in high summer.

Rangers report that mosquito season extends from April through July. The pesky bugs are particularly thick and annoying on the shores by the area's still backwater lakes.

The park's main dirt road twists through ironwood-filled washes and offers vistas of the mighty Colorado River. Towering above it all is park namesake 1,942-foot Picacho Peak, a plug-dome volcano.

Picacho was a bustling boomtown in the 1890s. Some 700 men worked the mine and Picacho's population soared to 2,500 in the early 20th century. Steamboats chugged up and down the Colorado, bringing life's necessities to the town, and taking the ore to market. When the Colorado River was dammed, the historic hamlet was flooded.

For the hiker, Picacho offers several signed trails plus numerous opportunities to trek cross-country up beckoning washes. Stamp Mill Trail (2 miles round trip) crosses the park's volcanic slopes and visits Picacho's stamp-mill sites. Ice Cream Canyon Trail tours the tuff and winds among the odd ironwood trees. Above, cacti-dotted canyon walls soar higher and higher and the feeling is that of entering a very special world.

Stewart Lake Trail (2.5 mile loop) crosses an intriguing volcanic landscape as it skirts the shore of (usually dry) Stewart Lake. An interpretive brochure describes the desert flora to be found along this trail, named for early Picacho prospector Clyde Stewart.

DIRECTIONS TO TRAILHEAD From Interstate 8 on the California-Arizona border, exit on Winterhaven Drive/Fourth Avenue and proceed north 0.5 mile to County Road S-24. Turn right and 0.25 mile later, turn left on Picacho Road.

(Yuma is located on the Arizona side of the river. Get provisions here and check out Yuma Territorial Prison State Historical Park.)

Follow Picacho Road (paved for just 4 miles). Near the All-American Canal, Picacho narrows and de-evolves into a sometimes bumpy, washboard dirt road and leads another 18 miles to Picacho State Recreation Area.

To reach the Stamp Mill trailhead, take the road to Lower Dock and soon turn right (east) on the spur leading very shortly to the trailhead and a parking area for a couple cars.

THE HIKE Stamp Mill Trail makes a modest descent over beavertail-cactus-dotted slopes. Enjoy vistas of Picacho Peak and of the Colorado River shore where the town of Piacacho once stood.

About 0.5 mile out, a short side trail leads to the Picacho Jail; actually it's a hillside hollow used by the sheriff to incarcerate the local bad guys and the miners to store explosives.

At 0.75 mile, you'll reach a junction with the right-forking path to Railroad and Ice Cream canyons. Continue another 0.2 mile to the rock walls and rusted ruins of Upper Mill, then a short distance farther to trail's end just above the ruins of Lower Mill.

Ice Cream Canyon Trail explores a colorful canyon tinted with strawberry and spumoni hues. Various cacti—barrel and cholla—dot canyon walls.

"Tuff" is the word for this trail, which crosses beds of the porous volcanic rock. Bighorn sheep sometimes roam the narrow confines of the canyon.

Walk the first 0.75 mile of Stamp Mill Trail then fork right, south, onto Ice Cream Canyon Trail. The path traces the wash bank up-creek, then soon drops to the bottom of the wash. After 0.25 mile, the path meets Railroad Canyon Jeep Trail.

Return via the jeep road for a 4.5 mile round trip hike.

SALTON SEA STATE RECREATION AREA

■ IRONWOOD NATURE TRAIL
From Visitor Center to Mecca Beach is 2 miles round trip;
to Corvina Beach is 4.5 miles round trip

Between the desert and the sea is an intriguing, sun-baked shoreline, quite unlike any other locale in the California desert.

Some eighteen miles of Salton Sea shoreline within the Salton Sea State Recreation Area invites the camper, angler, swimmer and sunbather. Hikers will

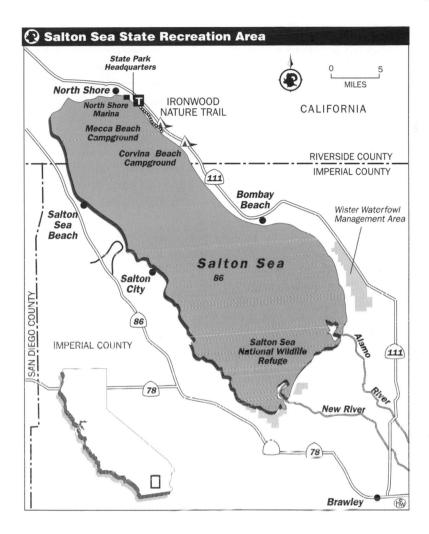

enjoy Ironwood Nature Trail which explores the shoreline between the visitors center and Mecca Beach.

The 15 mile wide, 35 mile long Salton Sea was formed in 1905 when Colorado River floodwaters overwhelmed an Imperial Valley dike during construction of the All-American Canal. For two years water poured into the Salton Sink, an ancient sea bed.

Surrounding rivers, washes and canals continue to refill the lake with a combination of rainwater and agricultural runoff. Fertilizers and other minerals contribute to the high salinity (more than 25 times "saltier" than the Pacific Ocean) of the Salton Sea. Scientists are researching the sea's odd chemistry and environmental conditions in order to determine why there are occasional massive bird die-offs along the shoreline. Researchers are investigating salt levels and seeking ways to stabilize them.

The Salton Sea's unusual combination of desert and aquatic environments attracts a wide variety (some 350 species have been counted) of birds. Most noticeable of the feathered visitors and residents are the geese, particularly the loud-honking Canada geese who fly here in their distinctive V-shaped formation.

Also easy to spot are the large snow geese and the Ross geese, white geese that are similar to, but smaller than, the snow geese.

Learn more about the origins, present dilemmas and possible ecological fate of the Salton Sea at the visitor center located near the park's harbor. Obtain a nature trail brochure and walk to the trailhead from here, or drive to Campsite 32 in the headquarters campground known as Los Frijoles Camp, now called New Camp or Headquarters Campground.

Plan to catch some rays or take a swim at trail's end. Sandy Mecca Beach is a popular swimming area. Showers are available to wash off the film of salt and plankton that coats the swimmer.

The Salton Sea's most intriguing trail isn't for hikers. A new kayak trail extends 14 miles along the shoreline, from behind the visitor center at Varner Harbor to Bombay Beach Campground.

Kayakers enjoy warm lake temperatures that range from the 60s in winter to the upper 80s in the summer. Two kayak camps—Salt Creek and Bombay Beach—beckon with kayak racks, picnic tables, restrooms, and showers.

During the winter months, rangers and volunteers lead interpretive hikes. Check at the ranger station or with camp hosts for scheduled walks.

DIRECTIONS TO TRAILHEAD Salton Sea State Recreation Area is located some 25 miles southeast of Indio via Highway 111.

THE HIKE From the campground, enjoy the thirty-stop nature trail that explores everything from salt to salt cedars to smoke trees. When you reach Mecca Beach, you can either return via the nature trail or by picking your own route closer to shore.

If you want to extend your walk, continue walking along the shoreline to undeveloped Corvina Beach Campground or as far as you choose.

MITCHELL CAVERNS NATURAL PRESERVE

■ CAVERNS TRAIL
1.5 mile guided hike of caverns

Trail trivia question: Where in Southern California can you explore some stunning scenery, be assured that it won't rain, and know that the temperature for your hike will always be a comfortable 65 degrees?

Hint: One of the overlooked gems of the California state park system.

If you're in the dark, then you're on the right path— the trail through Mitchell Caverns Natural Preserve, part of Providence Mountains State Recreation Area. Ranger-led walks through the dramatic limestone caves offer a fascinating geology lesson, one the whole family can enjoy.

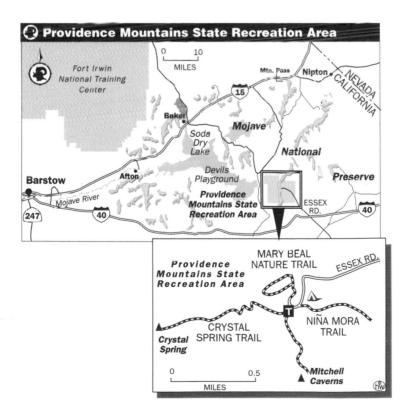

In 1932, Jack Mitchell abandoned his Depression-shattered business in Los Angeles and moved to the desert. For a time he prospected for silver, but his real fascination was with what he called the "Providence" or "Crystal Caves" and their potential as a tourist attraction. He constructed several stone buildings to use for lodging. (Today's park visitor center is one of these buildings.) Mitchell and his wife Ida provided food, lodging, and guided tours of the caverns until 1954. By all accounts, Jack Mitchell was quite a yarn-spinner. Old-timers still remember his tall tales of ghosts, lost treasure and bottomless pits.

Now that the caverns are part of the state park system, rangers lead the tours. They're an enthusiastic lot and quite informative. Visitors walk through the two main caves, which Mitchell named El Pakiva (The Devil's House) and Tecopa (after a Shoshonean chieftain). You'll get a close-up view of stalactites and stalagmites, cave ribbon, cave spaghetti and flow stone. And you'll learn about some of the caverns' former inhabitants—the Chemehuevi Indians and a Pleistocene ground sloth that stumbled into the darkness some 15,000 years ago.

During Jack Mitchell's day, visitors had to be nimble rock-climbers who waited for their tour leader to toss flares into the darkness. Nowadays, the caverns are equipped with stairs and special lighting.

Guided tours are conducted Labor Day through Memorial Day weekend, Monday through Friday at 1:30 p.m. On Saturday and Sunday, tours begin at 10:00 a.m., 1:30 p.m. and 3:00 p.m. In the summer, June 1 through August 31, tours are conducted on weekends only at 1:30 p.m. A tour takes 1.5 to 2 hours depending on your group's enthusiasm and collective curiosity, and a fee is charged.

THE HIKE   Because you can only tour the caverns with a park ranger, and because you wouldn't want me to spoil the many surprises of the cave walk with a step-by-step description, I won't further detail the Mitchell Caverns Trail. However, after exploring "the great indoors" allow some time to explore the park's outdoors pathways.

DIRECTIONS TO TRAILHEAD   From Interstate Highway 40, about 80 miles east of Barstow, exit on Essex Road and drive 16 miles to road's end at the Providence Mountains State Recreation Area parking lot. Sign up at the visitor center for tours.

PROVIDENCE MOUNTAINS STATE RECREATION AREA

■ NIÑA MORA, CRYSTAL SPRING, MARY BEAL TRAILS

0.5 to 2 mile round trip trails

Providence Mountains State Recreation Area, which includes Mitchell Caverns Natural Preserve, is a 5,900-acre island of state park land surrounded by the 1.6-million acre Mojave National Preserve.

DIRECTIONS TO TRAILHEAD See Mitchell Caverns Natural Preserve on previous page.

THE HIKE A trio of park trails offer an excellent introduction to the Providence Mountains, one of the dominant ranges in the eastern Mojave desert. For the Niña Mora Trail, join the signed path at the east end of the park's tiny campground; for the Crystal Spring Trail, join the signed trail ascending the slope near the beginning of the Mitchell Caverns Trail; for the Mary Beal Nature Trail, walk the road north of the visitor center to the signed start of the trail.

A cactus garden at the base of the Providence Mountains.

Experience the grandeur and isolation of the Providence Mountains, as well as grand vistas, by hiking the short (0.5 mile round trip) Niña Mora Trail. The path ascends the summit of one of a pair of hills known as Camel Humps.

Atop the hump, gaze out over some 300 square miles of desert. Clear-day views include Arizona's Hualapai Mountains, located about 100 miles to the east.

The trail was named for the niña (child) Mora, daughter of a Mexican silver miner who toiled in the region's diggings in the early 1900s. A miner's life—as well as that of his family members—was often a short one. And so it was with little Mora, who died at a very early age and lies buried in a grave near the trail that bears her name.

From the campground, the path leads over a barrel cactus- and yucca-dotted ridge, and past the grave marker of Niña Mora.

In no time you reach trail's end and a viewpoint which offers a good perspective on the weathered rhyolite crags of the Providence Mountains looming to the west. Below is Clipper Valley and to the east is Table Mountain.

Crystal Spring Trail (2 miles round trip with a 600-foot elevation gain) leads into the pinyon pine- and juniper-dotted Providence Mountains by way of Crystal Canyon. Bighorn sheep often travel through this canyon.

Crystal Canyon is walled with limestone and rhyolite, a red volcanic rock. High above the canyon, castle-like formations of this rhyolite crown the Providence Mountains.

The steep and rather rocky trail offers both an exploration of an inviting high-desert canyon and engaging vistas of the spire of Providence Mountains peaks and a slice of Arizona. Hikers enter a unique desert landscape framed by bold rhyolite outcroppings. Pinyon pine joins a veritable cactus garden of barrel, cholla and prickly pear varieties.

About 0.5 mile out, keen-eyed hikers may spy the pipeline Jack Mitchell built in the 1930s to supply his tourist attraction in-the-making. The path crosses to the canyon's right side and continues a last 0.25 mile to the end of the trail, just short of willow-screened Crystal Spring. Intrepid hikers may proceed on fainter trail to the spring and on to a viewpoint a short distance farther.

Pick up an interpretive booklet from the park visitor center and walk the Mary Beal Nature Trail (0.5 mile round trip), which offers a great introduction to high desert flora. Cliffrose and blue sage share the hillsides with cholla, catsclaw and creosote.

The trail honors Mary Beal, a Riverside librarian who was "exiled" to the desert by her doctor for health reasons. For a half-century this remarkable woman wandered through the Providence Mountains and other remote Mojave Desert locales gathering and classifying hundreds of varieties of wildflowers and other plants. The trail was dedicated in 1952 on Beal's seventy-fifth birthday.

The path meanders an alluvial plain. Prickly pear, cholla and assorted yuccas spike surrounding slopes. Benches offer restful places from which to contemplate the cacti, admire the volcanic boulders and county the speedy roadrunners often seem scurrying across the trail. Also savor views of the Providence Mountains and of Clipper Valley.

For the Niña Mora Trail, join the signed path at the east end of the park's tiny campground; for the Crystal Spring Trail, join the signed trail ascending the slope near the beginning of the Mitchell Caverns Trail; for the Mary Beal Nature Trail, walk the road north of the visitor center to the signed start of the trail.

SADDLEBACK BUTTE STATE PARK

■ SADDLEBACK BUTTE TRAIL
From Campground to Saddleback Peak is 4 miles round trip with 1,000-foot elevation gain; Season: October-May

Rarely visited Saddleback Butte State Park, located on the eastern fringe of Antelope Valley, is high-desert country, a land of creosote bush and Joshua trees. The park takes the name of its most prominent feature—3,651-foot Saddleback Butte, a granite mountaintop that stands head and shoulders above Antelope Valley.

The Richard Dowen Nature Trail is a good introduction to the Joshua tree and other plant life found in this corner of the desert. The trail to the boulder-strewn summit of Saddleback Peak takes a straight-line course, with most of the elevation gain occurring in the last half mile. From atop the peak, enjoy far-reaching desert views.

DIRECTIONS TO TRAILHEAD   From Highway 14 (Antelope Valley Freeway) in Lancaster, take the 20th Street exit. Head north on 20th and turn east (right) on Avenue J. Drive 18 miles to Saddleback Butte State Park. Follow the dirt park road to the campground, where the trail begins. Park (day use fee) near the trail sign.

THE HIKE The signed trail heads straight for the saddle. The soft, sandy track, marked with yellow posts leads through an impressive Joshua tree woodland. After 1.5 miles, the trail switchbacks steeply up the rocky slope of the butte. An invigorating climb brings you to the saddle of Saddleback Butte. To reach the peak, follow the steep leftward trail to the summit.

From the top, you can look south to the San Gabriel Mountains. At the base of the mountains, keen eyes will discern the California Aqueduct. To the east is the vast Mojave Desert, to the north is Edwards Air Force Base. To the west are the cities of Lancaster and Palmdale and farther west, the rugged Tehachapi Mountains.

ANTELOPE VALLEY CALIFORNIA POPPY RESERVE

■ ANTELOPE LOOP TRAIL
From Visitor Center to Antelope Butte Vista Point is 2.5 miles round trip with 300-foot elevation gain; Season: March-May

The California poppy blooms on many a grassy slope in the Southland, but only in the Antelope Valley does the showy flower blanket whole hillsides in such brilliant orange sheets. Surely the finest concentration of California's state flower (during a good wildflower year) is preserved at the

California's state flower is the star of the show in Antelope Valley.

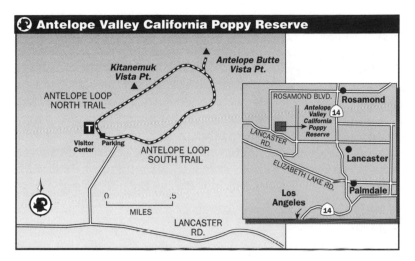

Antelope Valley California Poppy Reserve

Antelope Valley California Poppy Reserve in the Mojave Desert west of Lancaster.

The poppy is the star of the flower show, which includes a supporting cast of fiddlenecks, cream cups, tidy tips and gold fields. March through Memorial Day is the time to saunter through this wondrous display of desert wildflowers.

The poppy has always been recognized as something special. Early Spanish Californians called it Dormidera, "the drowsy one," because the petals curl up at night. They fashioned a hair tonic/restorer by frying the blossoms in olive oil and adding perfume.

At the reserve, you can pick up a map at the Jane S. Pineiro Interpretive Center, named for the painter who was instrumental in setting aside an area where California's state flower could be preserved for future generations to admire. Some of Pineiro's watercolors are on display in the center, which also has wildflower interpretive displays and a slide show.

Built into the side of a hill, the center boast an award-winning solar design, windmill power and "natural" air conditioning.

DIRECTIONS TO TRAILHEAD From the Antelope Valley Freeway (California 14) in Lancaster, exit on Avenue I and drive west 15 miles. Avenue I becomes Lancaster Road a few miles before the Poppy Reserve. The reserve (day use fee) is open 9 a.m. to 4 p.m. daily.

Spring wildflower displays are always unpredictable. To check on what's blooming where, call the park at (661) 942-0662 before making the trip.

THE HIKE Antelope Loop Trail—and all trails in the reserve—are easy walking and suitable for the whole family. Seven miles of gentle trails crisscross the 1,760-acre reserve; many hikers take every trail in the park without getting too tired.

Begin on the signed Antelope Loop Trail to the left of the visitor center. The trail passes through an orange sea of poppies and fiddlenecks, then climbs briefly to Kitanemuk Vista Point, 0.75 mile from the visitor center. Atop Vista Point are those flowery symbols of faithfulness and friendship, forget-me-nots, and an unforgettable view of the Mojave Desert and the snow-covered Tehachapis.

After enjoying the view, continue on to Antelope Butte Vista Point, where another lookout offers fine desert panoramas. From here, join the south loop of the Antelope Loop Trail and return to the visitor center.

After you've circled the "upper west side" of the Poppy Reserve, you may wish to extend your hike by joining the Poppy Loop Trail and exploring the "lower east side."

ARTHUR RIPLEY DESERT WOODLAND STATE PARK

■ RIPLEY NATURE TRAIL
0.5 mile interpretive trail plus a few miles of freeform walking.

B elieve it or not, Arthur Ripley Desert Woodland State Park hosts one of the last virgin Joshua tree forests in the Antelope Valley.

With its thriving Joshuas and junipers, accompanied by a thick undergrowth of buckwheat, beavertail cactus, sage and Mormon tea, the preserve is a reminder of how most of the Antelope Valley may have appeared to early travelers such as missionary Father Garces in 1776, or explorer John C. Frémont in 1848.

Located in far northern Los Angeles County, about three miles as the raven flies from the Kern County line, the park has yet to be plotted on most maps, and is all but unknown to most desert travelers. Poppy-lovers sometimes happen upon the park because it's located just seven miles down the road from the famed Antelope Valley California Poppy Reserve.

The Tehachapi Range, which separates the Antelope Valley from the San Joaquin Valley, forms the park's impressive mountain backdrop to the north. Mile-high Sawmill Mountain in the nearby Angeles National Forest, rises dramatically to the south.

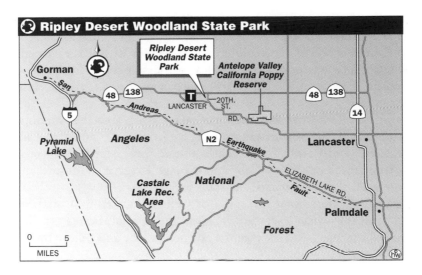

The State Department of Parks and Recreation seems content to leave well enough alone at Ripley. A single roadside sign (blink and you'll miss it) identifies the preserve, whose only visitor amenity is a rustic outhouse (very scenically situated, by the way, amidst the desert flora).

The park provides habitat for abundant Antelope Valley wildlife (except for the long gone antelope, of course). Quail, roadrunners, king snakes, rattlesnakes, kangaroo rats, coyotes and ground squirrels are commonly sighted within the park's boundaries. Lots of black-tailed rabbits and the occasional cottontail hop down the numerous bunny trails that crisscross the preserve.

The park's Joshuas are smaller than most; these *Yucca brevifolia* belong to the smaller than-average subspecies *Herbertii*. Struggling for nutrients in the preserve's sandy soil, these Joshuas rarely exceed 14 feet in height.

Joshuas have a well-deserved reputation for assuming grotesque shapes and the trees at the preserve are no exception; in fact, their twisted limbs and torsos appear all the more weird because of their bordering-on-dwarf stature.

Farmer Arthur Ripley (1901-1988) willed 560 acres of his property to the state. He and many other farmers and developers cleared hundreds of thousands of acres in the western Antelope Valley for crops and subdivisions. Ripley, however, cared enough about this particular pristine desert woodland to protect it for future generations.

The park's spring wildflowers in a good year include fiddleneck, scarlet bugler, coreopsis, goldfields, chia, blue dicks and filaree. Ripley's bigger plants are generally more dependable bloomers. In spring, the beavertail cactus produces attention-getting magenta-hued flowers while goldenbush puts forth yellow daisy-like blooms. Greeting hikers is the fragrant blue sage, which raises long spikey arms covered with blue flowers. Star of the spring show, though, is the Joshua tree with creamy white blossoms festooning its uplifted arms.

DIRECTIONS TO TRAILHEAD From Interstate 5, about 6 miles south of Gorman and 27 miles north of Valencia, exit on Highway 138 and head east 15 miles to Lancaster Road. Turn right (south). Follow Lancaster Road, which soon bends east, a bit more than 4 miles to the signed Arthur Ripley Desert Woodland State Park on the left (north) side of the road. Park carefully along the road.

If you're traveling from the Antelope Valley, you'll exit the Antelope Valley Freeway (14) in Lancaster on Highway 138 (Avenue D) and travel about 19 miles west to 210th Street. Turn south a mile to Lancaster Road.

From the Antelope Valley California Poppy Reserve, continue another 7 miles west on Lancaster Road to the state park.

The Mojave Desert State Parks Visitor Center, located in a small shopping center in Lancaster, has desert information and a small bookstore. From the Antelope Valley Freeway (14), take the Avenue K exit and follow the signs.

THE HIKE A twelve-stop interpretive trail, keyed to a pamphlet available from the state parks visitor center in Lancaster, leads past some of the preserve's featured flora. (A brochure is by no means necessary to enjoy the trail.)

Ripley's other rambles are of the do-it-yourself variety. Wander at will amongst the juniper and Joshua trees, inhale the sage-scented fresh air, and rejoice at the beauty of this wooded island on the land.

TOMO-KAHNI VILLAGE SITE

■ KAWAIISU TRAIL
Two to three-hour docent-led walk

For thousands of years the Kawaiisu roamed a vast territory from the Southern Sierra to the Tehachapi Range to the Mojave Desert. During the cooler months the tribe encamped at their "Tomo-Kahni," or Winter Village, nestled in the hills east of what is now the present-day town of Tehachapi.

Now thanks to a docent-led walking tour, a limited number of lucky visitors can explore the ancient land of the Kawaiisu, an intriguing preserve of wind-sculpted rock formations, pictographs and a pinyon pine forest. Tomo-Kahni is an unusual state parkland, created in the 1990s by tribal elders, anthropologists and state park officials who wished to protect this unique village site and the intriguing blend of High Desert and High Sierra environments that surrounds it.

Rangers and docents take pains to point out that Tomo-Kahni is not your basic state park, and that its purpose is education, not recreation. No visitor facilities have been constructed, no signs have been posted, and the preserve can be seen only on a guided tour. In Mission Impossible fashion, the location of Tomo-Kahni is not disclosed to tour members until just before departure from downtown Tehachapi.

The docents and rangers who lead the tours are an enthusiastic lot, and offer a compelling narration about the Kawaiisu during the three mile walk. The Kawaiisu, of Shoshonean lineage, call themselves Nuooah which, in their language, means "The People." Kawaiisu forebears may have lived in the desert-mountains environment some 3,000 years ago. The tribe has long been known for its creation of colorful and intricately designed baskets.

The Kawaiisu were hunter-gatherers who inhabited a very large territory ranging from the Southern Sierra to the Tehachapi Range to the western Mojave Desert. Such a diverse environment required the Kawaiisu to master the use of a multitude of plants. Anthropologists believe the Kawaiisu used more than 200 plants for foods, beverages and medicine.

On the trail through a pinyon pine woodland, it becomes obvious to the hiker where the Kawaiisu found pinyon pine nuts, as well as many other nuts, berries and plants for food. One tour highlight is an impressive sandstone rock outcropping pock-marked with more than 400 mortar holes where the Kawaiisu ground seeds and acorns.

Tour highlights for children are usually Rabbit Rock, a big, bunny-shaped boulder, and a very long rattlesnake pictograph found in an open-faced

Kawaiisu grinding holes.

cave. Glimpses of deer, rabbits, lizards and a variety of birds en route add more surprises to this very special exploration.

While their "Winter Village" suited the Kawaiisu just fine, we moderns find it too cold to visit in winter and too hot in summer. Tours of Tomo-Kahni are offered only on spring and fall weekends (weather permitting), and only by reservation. The slow to moderately paced walking tour (with some steep trail sections) lasts two to three hours. Wear sturdy boots and a hat for sun protection, and bring water.

A visit to Tomo-Kahni requires some planning. But once you enter a land so ancient and sacred, you'll be glad you made the effort.

DIRECTIONS TO TRAILHEAD   From Highway 14 in Mojave, turn west on State 58 and continue 20 miles to Tehachapi. Tours begin with an orientation held at the Tehachapi Museum Annex, located just across the street from the main Tehachapi Museum, at 311 South Green Street. After the orientation, visitors drive about 12 miles to the park. (High-clearance vehicles are recommended.)

Tomo-Kahni Walking Tours are available by reservation only and at a modest cost for adults and children. Call the California State Parks office in Lancaster for more information and reservations.

RED ROCK CANYON STATE PARK

■ HAGEN, RED CLIFFS TRAILS
1 to 2 miles round trip; Season: October-May

The view of Red Rock Canyon may very well seem like déjà vu. Cliffs and canyons in these parts have appeared in the background of many a Western movie.

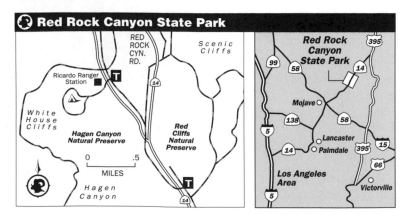

This bigger-than-life landscape has been the background for many Western movies.

A black-and-white movie of Red Rock Canyon would be dramatic: shadow and light playing over the canyon walls. Technicolor, however, might more vividly capture the aptly named red rock, along with the chocolate brown, black, white and pink hues of the pleated cliffs.

Gold fever in the 1890s prompted exploration of almost all the canyons in the El Paso Mountains. During this era, Rudolph Hagen acquired much land in the Red Rock area. He named the little mining community/stage stop Ricardo after his son Richard. The Ricardo Ranger Station is located at the site of the once-thriving hamlet.

Red Rock Canyon became a state recreation area in 1969; when it became obvious off-road vehicles were damaging the hills and canyons, Red Rock was upgraded to park status in 1982.

DIRECTIONS TO TRAILHEAD Red Rock Canyon State Park is located 25 miles north of the town of Mojave off Highway 14. Turn northwest off 14 onto the signed road for the park campground. Follow this road a short mile to Ricardo Ranger Station. The station has a small visitor center with nature exhibits.

THE HIKE Best places to hike are in the park's two preserves. You'll find some trails to hike, but this park lends itself to improvisation.

Hagen Canyon Natural Preserve is a striking badlands, with dramatic cliffs capped by a layer of dark basalt. A one mile loop trail explores the area. Red Cliffs Natural Preserve protects the 300-foot sandstone cliffs east of Highway 14.

The park nature trail, a 0.75 mile path tells the geologic story of the area, and points out typical desert flora. It's keyed to an interpretive pamphlet available at the trailhead. Join the nature trail at the south end of the park campground.

CHAPTER TWO

SOUTHERN CALIFORNIA MOUNTAINS

Southern California boasts a remarkably diverse collection of mountainous state parks from the Mediterranean-flavored flora of the Santa Monica Mountains to the alpine splendor of the San Jacinto Mountains.

For a memorable walk, trek through lodgepole pine country to the top of 10,804-foot Mt. San Jacinto, high point of the state park system. The great naturalist John Muir found the view from the summit "the most sublime spectacle to be found anywhere on this earth!"

Semi-circling the Los Angeles-Orange County metropolis are several lesser-known ranges with state parks that provide much-needed open space and recreation for big basins residents: Bernasconi Hills surrounding Lake Perris State Recreation Area; Chino Hills; Santa Susana Mountains, where hikers follow a stagecoach route known as Devil's Slide.

Take a look at the Santa Monica Mountains—on the wild side of Los Angeles.

Another highlight for the hiker is the Santa Monica Mountains, the only relatively undeveloped mountain range in America that bisects a major metropolitan area. The mountains stretch from the heart of Los Angeles to Point Mugu, 50 miles away. State park lands—Will Rogers, Topanga, Malibu Creek, Leo Carrillo and Point Mugu—have extensive networks of fire roads and footpaths that lead through native tall-grass prairies and fern-lined canyons, and up to rugged, rocky ridgetops that seem far removed from the city below.

CUYAMACA RANCHO STATE PARK

■ STONEWALL PEAK TRAIL

From Paso Picacho Campground to summit is 4 miles round trip with 900-foot elevation gain; return via California Riding and Hiking Trail; Cold Stream Trail is 5.5 miles round trip

Plentiful rain and the Cuyamacas' geographical location between coast and desert make these mountains a unique ecosystem. The 4,000- to 6,500-foot peaks host rich forests of ponderosa and Jeffrey pine, fir and incense cedar, as well as some wonderful specimens of live and black oak. In lower elevations, broad grasslands stretch toward the horizon.

Generations of hikers enjoyed these mountains as did birdwatchers, because desert, coastal and mountain species are all found in the range. The look of the mountains, the experience of the visitor is much different today.

In 2003, the Cedar Fire devastated the state park, burning black oak and pine forests, grassland and riparian corridors. It was the worst wildfire loss in state park history. However, nature's healing powers are truly miraculous. The park (except for its stands of pine) is recovering in extraordinary fashion.

More than 110 miles of hiking trails pass through the old rancho. The Cuyamacas offer four-season hiking at its colorful best: fall with its brown, yellow and crimson leaves; winter snows on the higher peaks; spring with its wildflowers; and sudden summer thunderstorms.

The forested shoulders of Stonewall Peak offer especially fine fall hiking. "Leaf peepers," as autumn tourists are called in New England, will enjoy viewing the brown, yellow and crimson leaves of the Cuyamaca high country.

Rounded Mount Cuyamaca (6,512 feet) is the highest peak in the range, but Stonewall Peak is more prominent. "Old Stony" is about 1,000 feet lower, but its huge walls of granite and crown of stone make it stand out among neighboring peaks. The popular Stonewall Peak Trail will take you to the top of the peak (5,730 feet) and give you grand views of the old Stonewall Mine Site, Cuyamaca Valley and desert slopes to the east. An optional route lets you descend to Paso Pichacho Campground via the California Riding and Hiking Trail and the Cold Stream Trail.

DIRECTIONS TO TRAILHEAD From San Diego, drive east on Interstate 8. Exit on Highway 79 north. The highway enters Cuyamaca Rancho State Park and climbs to a saddle between Cuyamaca and Stonewall peaks. Park near the entrance of Paso Picacho Campground. The trail to Stonewall Peak begins just across the highway from the campground.

THE HIKE From Paso Picacho Campground, the trail ascends moderately, then steeply through oak and boulder country. The black oaks display vivid colors in fall.

The trail switchbacks up the west side of the mountain. From the blackened forest, views from the north unfold. Cuyamaca Reservoir is the most obvious geographical feature. Before a dam was built to create the reservoir Cuyamaca Lake, as it was called, was a sometime affair. The Indians never trusted it as a dependable water source and the Spanish referred to it as la laguna que de seco, or "the lake that dries up." During dry years, the cows enjoy more meadow than reservoir and during wet years, have more reservoir than meadow.

Vegetation grows more sparse and granite outcroppings dominate the high slopes as the trail nears the top of Old Stony. A hundred feet from the summit, a guardrail with steps hacked into the granite helps you reach the top. Far reaching views to the east and west are not possible because a number of

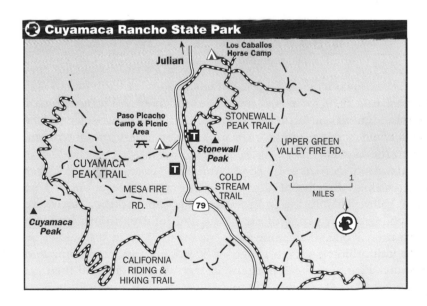

close-in mountains block your view. You can, however, orient yourself to Cuyamaca geography from atop Stonewall Peak. Major Cuyamaca peaks, from north to south, are North Peak, Middle Peak and Cuyamaca Peak.

It's exciting to be atop Stonewall Peak when a storm is brewing over the Cuyamacas, but beware that the peak has been known to catch a strike or two. Black clouds hurtle at high speed toward the peak. Just as they are about to collide with the summit, an updraft catches them and they zoom up and over your head.

Return the way you came or via the California Riding and Hiking Trail by backtracking 100 yards on the Stonewall Peak Trail to an unsigned junction. From here, bear right (north). The trail descends steeply at first, then levels off near Little Stonewall Peak (5,250 feet). It then descends moderately to the California Riding and Hiking Trail, which traverses the west side of the park. You travel for one mile on the California Riding and Hiking Trail, which is actually part of the Stonewall Peak Trail. It forks to the right and crosses Highway 79. Don't take the fork, but continue a half mile down the Cold Stream Trail, paralleling the highway, back to Paso Picacho Campground.

SAN PASQUAL BATTLEFIELD STATE HISTORIC PARK

■ BATTLEFIELD MONUMENT TRAIL
1 mile round trip

The Battle of San Pasqual had little military significance, historians surmise, but was nevertheless a pivotal event during the Mexican-American War—a conflict that brought California under American control and eventually into the Union.

At dawn on December 6, 1846, American troops, led by Stephen Kearny, peered through the fog at the Californios who were encamped in the San Pasqual Valley. Then they attacked. The Americans and their horses were in terrible condition (the result of an exhausting journey from New Mexico). To make matters worse, their gunpowder was wet.

The Californios, a superb group of horsemen under the command of General Andres Pico, met the Americans' charge with gunfire and their deadly long lances.

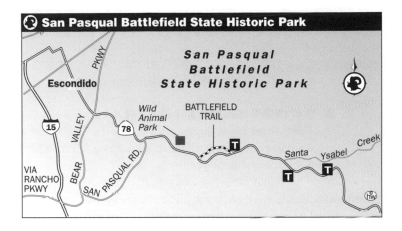

Some 21 Americans were killed and many more wounded, including General Kearny, in the short but intense battle. About a dozen Californios were wounded as well before both sides withdrew.

A four-day standoff followed. Kearny sent Kit Carson to bring back U.S. Army reinforcements from San Diego. The reinforced Americans, with overwhelming superiority, soon captured San Diego and Los Angeles as well.

The state historic park interprets the battle—the most severe one of the Mexican-American War fought in California. A visitor center and museum tell the story of the conflict with maps, displays and a video. Other exhibits feature the history and natural history of the San Pasqual Valley. The park's short nature trail and Battlefield Monument Trail are also good introductions to the life and lore of San Pasqual Valley.

Most visitors rush through the valley on the way to the San Diego Wild Animal Park, located adjacent to the park. But San Pasqual Valley and the state park are well worth a stop.

DIRECTIONS TO TRAILHEAD   From Highway 78, eight miles east of Escondido, take the turnoff to San Pasqual Battlefield State Historic Park. Leave your car in the lot by the visitor center.

THE HIKE   Join the nature trail, which begins on the hillside behind the visitor center. After 0.25 mile, join Battlefield Monument Trail and ascend a sloped bristly with prickly pear cactus. At a picnic ramada, enjoy an inspiring view of the wide San Pasqual Valley as well as a fine place to eat lunch. Return the way you came back to the visitor center or continue west on Battlefield Monument Trail to a historic monument next to Highway 78.

PALOMAR MOUNTAIN STATE PARK

■ SCOTT'S CABIN TRAIL

From Silver Crest Picnic Area to Scott's Cabin; Cedar Grove
Campground and Boucher Lookout is a 3.5 mile loop with
800-foot elevation gain

Palomar Mountain is a state park for all seasons. Fall offers dramatic color changes, and blustery winter winds ensure far-reaching views from the peaks. In spring, the dogwood blooms, and during summer, when temperatures soar, the park offers a cool, green retreat.

A mixed forest of cedar, silver fir, spruce and black oak invites a leisurely exploration. Tall trees and mountain meadows make the park especially attractive to the Southern California day hiker in search of a Sierra Nevada-like atmosphere.

The discovery of bedrock mortars and artifacts in Doane Valley indicate that native peoples lived in this area of the Palomars for many hundreds of years. The mountains' pine and fir trees were cut for the construction of Mission San Luis Rey. Remote Palomar Mountain meadows were a favorite hiding place for cattle and horse thieves, who pastured their stolen animals in the high country until it was safe to sneak them across the border.

This day hike is a grande randonnée of the park, a four-trail sampler that leads to a lookout atop 5,438-foot Boucher Hill.

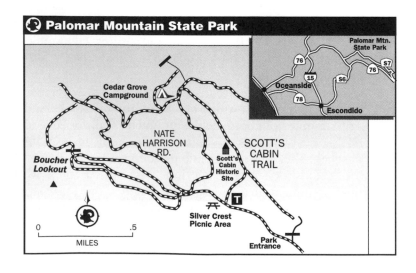

DIRECTIONS TO TRAILHEAD From Interstate 5 in Oceanside, drive northeast on State Highway 76 about 30 miles. Take County Road S6 north; at S7, head northwest to the park entrance. There is a day use fee. Park in the lot at Silver Crest Picnic Area just inside the park. Scott's Cabin Trail takes off from the right side of the road about 20 yards beyond the lot entrance.

THE HIKE A trail sign points the way to Scott's Cabin, a 0.5 mile away. Noisome Stellar's jays make their presence known along this stretch of trail. Scott's Cabin, built by a homesteader in the 1880s, is found on your left. The crumpled remains aren't much to view.

Descend steeply through a white fir forest and reach the signed juantion with the Cedar-Doane Trail, which heads right (east). This steep trail, formerly known as the Slide Trail because of its abruptness, takes the hiker down oak-covered slopes to Doane Pond. The pond is stocked with trout, and fishing is permitted. A pond-side picnic area welcomes the hiker.

Continue past the Cedar-Doane Trail junction a short distance to Cedar Grove Campground. Follow the trail signs and turn left on the campground road, and then right into the group campground. Look leftward for the signed Adams Trail, which cuts through a bracken fern-covered meadow. Once across the meadow, you'll encounter a small ravine where dogwood blooms during April and May. The trail winds uphill past some big cone spruce and reaches Nate Harrison Road.

The road is named in honor of Nathan Harrison, a Southern slave who followed his master to the California gold rush—and freedom—in 1849. Harrison laid claim to a homestead on the wild eastern edge of what is now state parkland, and had a successful hay-making and hog-raising operation, despite numerous run-ins with bears and mountain lions.

Across the road, your path becomes Boucher Trail, which ascends a north-facing slope through white fir, then through bracken ferns and black oaks, to the summit of Boucher Hill. Atop the hill is a fire lookout and microwave facility. From the summit, you get a view of the surrounding lowlands, including Pauma Valley to the west.

Return to the parking area via Oak Ridge Trail, which descends one mile between the two sides of the loop road that encircles Boucher Hill. The trail heads down an open ridgeline to a junction of five roads, where it's a mere hop, skip and a jump back to the Silver Crest Picnic Area.

MT. SAN JACINTO STATE PARK

■ SAN JACINTO PEAK TRAIL

From Mountain Station to Round Valley is 4 miles round trip with 600-foot elevation gain; to San Jacinto Peak is 11 miles round trip with 2,300-foot elevation gain

The San Jacinto Mountain range is one of those magical places that lures hikers back year after year. Hikers enjoy the contrasts this range offers—the feeling of hiking in Switzerland while gazing down at the Sahara.

Palm Springs Aerial Tramway makes it easy for hikers to enter Mount San Jacinto State Wilderness. Starting in Chino Canyon near Palm Springs, a modern tram with rotating floors takes passengers from 2,643-foot Lower Tramway Terminal (Valley Station) to 8,516-foot Upper Tramway Terminal (Mountain Station) at the edge of the wilderness.

The day hiker accustomed to remote trailheads may find it a bit bizarre to enter Valley Station and find excited tourists sipping drinks and shopping for souvenirs. But the gondola rapidly leaves terra firma behind. Too rapidly, you think. It carries you over one of the most abrupt mountain faces in the world, over cliffs only a bighorn sheep can scale, over several life zones from palms to pines. When you disembark at Mountain Station, your ears will pop and you'll have quite a head start up Mount San Jacinto.

The wild areas in the San Jacinto Mountains are administered by both state park and national forest rangers. The middle of the region, including San Jacinto Peak, is part of the state park; most of it is managed as a wilderness area. On both sides of the peak, north and south, the wilderness is part of the San Bernardino National Forest.

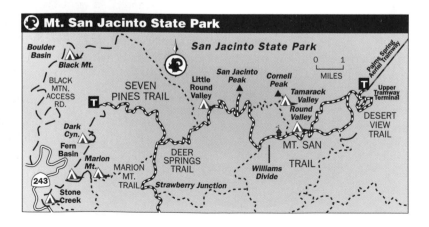

The meadows and High Sierra-like scenery can be glimpsed on a moderate hike to Round Valley; the ascent through the lodgepole pine forest to the top of Mt. San Jacinto is absolutely splendid, as are the views from the peak.

DIRECTIONS TO TRAILHEAD From Interstate 10, exit on California 111 (the road to Palm Springs). Proceed nine miles to Tramway Road, turn right, and follow the road 2.5 miles to its end at Mountain Station. Contact the Tramway office for information about prices and schedules.

THE HIKE From Mountain Station, walk down the cement walkway through the Long Valley Picnic Area and past a seasonal adventure center to the state park ranger station. Obtain a wilderness permit here.

Continue west on the trail, following the signs to Round Valley. The trail parallels Long Valley Creek through a mixed forest of pine and white fir, then climbs into lodgepole pine country. Lupine, monkeyflower, scarlet bugler and Indian paintbrush are some of the wildflowers that add seasonal splashes of color.

After passing a junction with a trail leading toward Willow Creek, another 0.3 mile of hiking brings you to Round Valley. There's a trail camp and a back-country ranger station in the valley, and splendid places to picnic in the meadow or among the lodgepole pines.

An alternative to returning the same way is to retrace your steps 0.3 mile back to the junction with the Willow Creek Trail, take this trail a mile through the pines to another signed trail north back to Long Valley Ranger Station. This alternative route adds only about a 0.25 mile to your day hike, and allows you to make a loop.

To Mount San Jacinto Peak: From Round Valley, peak-bound hikers follow the sign for Wellman Divide Junction. From the Divide, a trail leads down to Humber Park. At the divide, you'll be treated to spectacular views of Tahquitz Peak and Red Tahquitz, as well as the more-distant Toro Peak and Santa Rosa Mountain. You continue toward the peak on some vigorous switchbacks. The lodgepole pines grow sparse among the crumbly granite. At another junction, a half mile from the top, the trail continues to Little Round Valley but you take the summit trail to the peak. Soon you arrive at a stone shelter—an example of Civilian Conservation Corps handiwork during the 1930s—built for mountaineers who have the misfortune to be caught in winter storms. From the stone hut, you boulder-hop to the top of the peak.

The view from the summit—San Gorgonio Pass, the shimmering Pacific, the Colorado Desert, distant Mexico—has struck some visitors speechless, while other have been unable to control their superlatives. Helen Hunt Jackson's heroine Ramona found "a remoteness from earth which comes only on mountain heights," and John Muir found the view "the most sublime spectacle to be found anywhere on this earth!"

SAN TIMOTEO CANYON STATE PARK

Not yet open for public use pending necessary
planning, facility development, and staffing.

When San Timoteo Canyon State Park opens, it will bring some much-needed "breathing room" to the fast-growing Inland Empire. Park highlights include trails for hiking and horseback riding, a relatively untouched canyon and some important historical resources, including the San Timoteo Schoolhouse. One of San Timoteo's most famous residents was the teenaged Wyatt Earp, whose family lived in the canyon from 1864 to 1868.

Conservation groups have worked with the California Department of Parks and Recreation since 1999 to establish a state park in scenic San Timoteo Canyon. Movie producer Gale Ann Hurd donated her ranch land to the Riverside Land Conservancy, which purchased other property in the canyon. A good-sized park of some 10,000 acres is the goal.

San Timoteo Canyon extends from the mountain headwaters of San Timoteo Creek to its confluence with the Santa Ana River. The 14 mile long canyon, ranges from one-quarter to one-half mile wide, and slopes downward from 2,400 feet in elevation at its eastern end to 1,200 feet at its western end. The south side of the canyon is flanked by severely eroded hills known as the badlands.

During prehistoric times, San Timoteo Canyon served as a kind of border between the native Serrano to the north and the Cahuilla to the south. The canyon was later used by a number of Hispanic and Anglo ranchers. In 1873 a watering station was established at El Casco, where the first transcontinental railroad line passed through the canyon.

A seasonal creek flows through the canyon, which is lined with willows and cottonwoods. The canyon's north slopes are blanketed with chaparral, including chamise, ceanothus and scrub oak. California buckwheat and various sages predominate on the dry, south-facing slopes.

San Timoteo Canyon's natural attractions are many. Spring blooms include California poppy, lupine, popcorn flower and elderberry. Mule deer, coyote, black-tailed jackrabbit, deer mice and raccoons are among the mammalian occupants of the canyon.

Contact the park for information about access to the park and hiking possibilities.

LAKE PERRIS STATE RECREATION AREA

■ TERRI PEAK TRAIL

From Campfire Center to Terri Peak is 3.5 miles round trip with 800-foot elevation gain; to Indian Museum, return via lakeshore, is 6 miles round trip

Perris in the Spring. No need to battle the hordes of tourists flocking to that other similar-sounding place of romance across the Atlantic. No need to travel 6,000 miles and spend lots of money to have a good time.

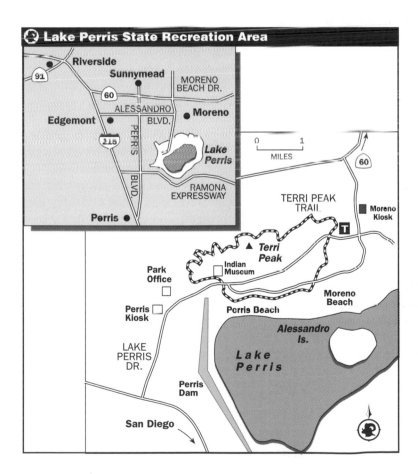

For just a few francs you can visit a manmade wonder, Lac de Paris, otherwise known as Lake Perris State Recreation Area. So pack du pain et du vin (actually alcohol is now prohibted in the park) and head for the most romantic Pomona Freeway offramp in all of Southern California.

Few nature lovers—or lovers of any kind—have discovered the romance of Perris. True, a million and a half visitors come to the lake each year, but most are interested in only the nature found wriggling on the end of a hook.

While the parc is oriented to les autos et les bateaux, there is a network of trails for those visitors who wish to explore Perris à pied. Perris pace-setters will enjoy the trek to Terri Peak, easily the most romantic spot in all of the surrounding hills. Springtime colors the hills with a host of wild fleurs, including goldfields, California poppy, fiddleneck, baby blue eyes and blue dicks. The view from Terri Peak on smog-free days is trés fantastique.

DIRECTIONS TO TRAILHEAD From the Pomona Freeway (60), a few miles east of its intersection with I-215, exit on Moreno Beach Drive and proceed 4 miles to the park. Immediately after paying your state park day use fee at the entry kiosk, turn right on Alta Calle. Look sharply right for the campfire center sign. Park in the center's lot and proceed up the concrete trail. The unsigned trail begins to the left of the campfire center.

THE HIKE The trail ascends gradually west and occasionally intersects a horse trail. The unsigned path is tentative at first but an occasional wooden post helps keep you on the trail, which climbs boulder-strewn slopes.

The coastal scrub community—sage, buckwheat, chamise and toyon predominates. Also much in evidence are weedy-looking non-native species, as well as mustard, prickly pear cactus, morning glory and Russian thistle.

The trail climbs to a small flat meadow then turns southwest and climbs more earnestly to the peak. From atop Terri Peak, enjoy clear-day views of the San Bernardino Mountains to the northeast and the Santa Ana Mountains to the southwest. Below is fast-growing Moreno Valley, checkerboarded alternately with green fields and subdivisions. You can see all of Lake Perris, Alessandro Island, along with hundreds of boaters, anglers and swimmers.

The trail from Terri Peak down to the Indian Museum is sometimes in poor condition. Beginning hikers may want to retrace their steps to the trailhead. The more experienced will begin their descent. You may lose the trail a couple of times; however you won't get lost because it's easy to stay oriented with the lakeshore on your left and the Indian Museum ahead.

After a steep descent, the trail bends sharply east and deposits you at the Indian Museum's parking lot. The museum includes exhibits interpreting the Luiseño, Cahuilla, Chemehuevi, Serrano and other desert tribes and how they adapted to life in the Mojave Desert region.

From the museum, you follow the asphalt road down to Alta Calle, cross this main park road and continue down to Perris Beach. Here you may cool off with a swim.

Improvise a route along the lakeshore using the sidewalk and bicycle trail until you spot the main campground entrance on your left. Enter the campground, pass the kiosk, then pick up the intermittent footpath that winds through the campground. This path and some improvisation will bring you to Alta Calle and back to the trailhead.

CALIFORNIA CITRUS STATE HISTORIC PARK

■ CITRUS INTERPRETIVE TRAIL
From Gazebo to Gage Canal is 1.25 miles round trip

Park visitors are greeted by a replica of an orange juice stand, located on the corner of Van Buren Blvd. and Dufferin Ave. In the days before interstate highways and reliable auto air conditioners, stands offering fresh squeezed orange juice and lemonade were a common sight and popular with thirsty motorists.

The brightly colored stand is an appropriate welcome to California Citrus State Historic Park, which tells the story of how "Citriculture" influenced the landscape—and culture—of Southern California, as well as how it helped shape public perception of the region.

Navel oranges, Valencia oranges, lemons and grapefruit are grown in the park, which boasts some 186 acres under cultivation by a nonprofit corporation. Check out the park visitor center, which resembles a packing house, and features exhibits that tell the story of California's citrus industry. Docents sometimes give talks and conduct walks.

Arts and Crafts aficionados will love the Sunkist Center and what's often referred to as "the park within the park." Visitors have the opportunity to walk through an old-fashioned park, created in the Craftsman/California bungalow motif of the first two decades of the twentieth century. Landscape architects of the era designed parks to provide gentle paths for strolling, areas (without equipment) for children to play, and plenty of picnic grounds. The idea was to offer park-goers a quiet place to relax and restore their spirits.

The park has an intriguing interpretive path, as well as other trails leading past the citrus groves. A palm lined gravel path leads to groves and past grove memorabilia to a knoll, which offers grand clear-day views of the San Gabriel Mountains and San Bernardino Mountains.

DIRECTIONS TO TRAILHEAD From Highway 91 (the Riverside Freeway), in the Arlington Heights area of Riverside, exit on Arlington Blvd. and travel 2 miles southeast to Dufferin Avenue. Turn left then make a right into the park and a left into the first parking lot. The interpretive path begins at the gazebo by the Sunkist Center. If available, pick up an interpretive pamphlet at the gazebo.

THE HIKE The five-stop tour includes a historical overview of the introduction of the orange to Southern California and a visit to the park's Varietal Collection, which numbers more than 100 kinds of citrus trees, including California's commercial species and exotics from around the world.

Other gentle lessons along the way help hikers learn about the three essentials for successful citrus production: good soil, suitable climate (different species thrive best in specific microclimates), and water. In rain-challenged Southern California, irrigation is truly the lifeblood of citrus production so it's fitting that the interpretive path offers a good look at the Gage Canal, a 20 mile waterway that tapped the Santa Ana River in San Bernardino and brought water to the groves now part of the state park. The canal, built by Matthew Gage between 1885 and 1889, is still used by area citrus farmers.

CHINO HILLS STATE PARK

■ HILLS-FOR-EVERYONE TRAIL
Along Ranch Road to McDermont Spring is 4 miles round trip
with 400-foot gain; to Carbon Canyon Regional Park
is 7.5 miles one way with 800-foot loss

Chino Hills State Park, located in Orange, San Bernardino and Riverside counties, preserves some much needed "breathing room" in this fast-growing area. Nearly three million people live within sight of the Chino Hills and more than 15 million people live within a 40 mile radius of the park!

The park is the state's most expensive ever, with an excess of $50 million spent by the time it opened for full time use in 1986. Some, but not too much development is in store for Chino Hills; mostly the park will continue to be the province of horseback riders, mountain bikers and hikers.

The 12,500-acre park is located near the northern end of what geologists call the Peninsular Ranges Geomorphic Province. The Chino Hills are part of the group of hills that include the Puente Hills to the northwest. These hills form a roughly triangular area of approximately 35 square miles of valleys, canyons, hills and steep slopes.

Extensive grasslands blanket the slopes. The hills are covered with wild oats, rye, black mustard and wild radish. On south-facing slopes is the soft-leaved shrub community, dominated by several varieties of sage.

High temperatures, often combined with heavy smog, suggest that a summer visit can be something of an ordeal. The park is much more pleasurable in the cooler months, and especially delightful in spring.

Hills-for-Everyone Trail was named for the conservation group that was instrumental in establishing Chino Hills State Park. The trail follows a creek to the head of

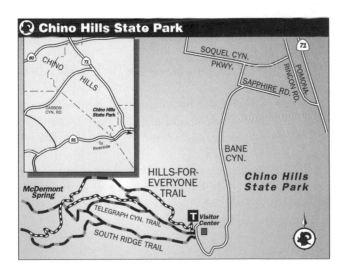

Telegraph Canyon. The creek is lined with oak, sycamore and the somewhat rare California walnut.

DIRECTIONS TO TRAILHEAD Chino Hills State Park can be a bit tricky to find. The park is located west of Highway 71 between the Riverside Freeway (91) and the Pomona Freeway (60). From the Riverside Freeway (91) in Corona, go north on Highway 71 for 8 miles and exit on Soquel Canyon Parkway. Make a left, proceed to Elvinar Road, turn left and proceed through a residential area. Just after Elvinar turns east and becomes Sapphire Road, you'll see the signed Chino Hills State Park dirt entrance road on your right. (This park entry road is closed for a period of 48 hours after a rainstorm.) Enter the park on this dirt road (which returns to pavement in 1.5 miles) and proceed to the park entry kiosk (information, fee collection). Once past the kiosk, continue to Rolling M Ranch Barn and the parking area for the Hills-for-Everyone and Telegraph Canyon Trails.

THE HIKE Hills-for-Everyone Trail descends to a small creek and follows the creek up canyon. Shading the trail—and shielding the hiker from a view of the many electrical transmission lines that cross the park—are oaks, sycamores and walnuts. Of particular interest is the walnut; often the 15- to 30-foot tall tree has several dark brown trunks, which gives it a brushy appearance.

The trail, which can be quite slippery and muddy after a rain, passes a small (seasonal) waterfall. The slopes above the creekbed are carpeted with lush grasses and miners lettuce.

Along the trail is found evidence of the park's ranching heritage, including lengths of barbed wire fence and old cattle troughs. For more than a century this land was used exclusively for cattle ranching.

Near its end, the trail ascends out of the creekbed to the head of Telegraph Canyon and intersects a dirt road. McDermont Spring is just down the road. Some of the livestock ponds, constructed during the area's ranching days, still exist, and hold water year-round. McDermont Spring—along with Windmill and Panorama ponds—provides water for wildlife.

To Carbon Canyon Regional Park: Telegraph Canyon Trail (a dirt road closed to public vehicular traffic) stays close to the canyon bottom and its creek. It's a gentle descent under the shade of oak and walnut trees. The walnuts are particularly numerous along the first mile of travel and the hiker not inclined to hike the length of Telegraph Canyon might consider exploring this stretch before returning to the trailhead.

The route passes an old windmill. Farther down the canyon, the walnuts thin out. A lemon grove, owned by the state park but leased to a farmer, is at a point where the dirt road intersects Carbon Canyon Road. Walk along the broad shoulder of the latter road 0.5 mile to Carbon Canyon Regional Park.

SILVERWOOD LAKE
STATE RECREATION AREA

■ MILLER CANYON TRAIL
To Serrano Beach is 3.5 miles round trip;
to Marina is 6 miles round trip

Silverwood Lake has a noisy side and a quiet side, a developed side and a wild side. The lake has a split personality: On summer weekends, it's a place to water-ski, swim, and camp. During other seasons, people come for quieter pursuits—bird-watching, fishing, hiking.

The lake was created when Cedar Springs Dam was constructed and waters from the State Water Project filled a little valley that was formed long ago by the meandering West Fork of the Mojave River. Water for the lake comes more than four hundred miles from northern California through a truly astonishing maze of plumbing.

Early in the 20th century, at the bottom of what is now Silverwood Lake, about a hundred families worked the land and founded the town of Cedar Springs. Strawberries put the town on the map; tourists traveled for miles to buy jars of strawberry jam.

By the mid-1920s, Seventh-Day Adventists, who developed a small tuberculosis sanitarium in the area, were the pillars of the community. Cedar Springs

remained a popular weekend outing through the Depression years. The rustic community was razed, then covered when Silverwood Lake was filled in 1972.

Around the lake is a diversity of habitats. Thick chaparral—manzanita, ceanothus, chamise, mountain mahogany, plus oak and scrub oak—crowds the lakeshore. Alder, willow and sycamore line nearby creeks. On higher slopes is a thriving forest of ponderosa pine, fir and incense cedar.

A diversity of habitats means many different bird species. The serious birder will pick up a bird checklist at the park's entrance station.

Silverwood Lake's trail system surprises. Experienced hikers might figure the park's premier path is the Pacific Crest Trail, which crosses a portion of the recreation area; actually, this stretch of PCT offers a less-than-thrilling day hike. PCT fans will much prefer day hiking along the nearby Deep Creek section of the trail.

The walker might also figure that the lakeside bikepath is not for pedestrians; actually, walkers are welcome to use the paved path, officially known as "Bike and Hike Trail." The aesthetically pleasing trail gives access to portions of lakeshore that cannot be reached by auto.

Silverwood's best hike is the part footpath/part bikepath route through Miller Canyon. Miller Canyon Trail leads to some woodsy retreats, grand views, and Serrano Beach, an inviting sand strand and picnic area.

DIRECTIONS TO TRAILHEAD From Interstate 15 at Cajon Junction, take the Highway 138/Silverwood Lake exit. Drive ten miles east to the main entrance of Silverwood Lake State Recreation Area. Continue four more miles past the entrance on Highway 138 to the signed Miller Canyon turnoff. Turn left. The actual signed trailhead is at the edge of the Miller Canyon Group Camp; however, parking is awkward hereabouts because parking is restricted to cars registered in the group camps.

THE HIKE From the signed trailhead at the Miller Canyon Group Camp, join the footpath dropping into the canyon. You soon begin sauntering along Miller Creek, one of the far-flung tributaries of the Mojave River.

First stop along the trail is Devil's Pit, a not-very-appropriate name for what can be a heavenly swimming hole in spring and summer. Above this "pit" is an observation platform, offering views down Miller Canyon and up at nearby peaks of the San Bernardino Mountains.

At Lynx Point (another inappropriate name; there aren't any lynx in the area) is another vista point. The panorama includes a view of Mt. Baldy, highest summit in the nearby San Gabriel Mountains.

Below Lynx Point, Miller Canyon Trail intersects the paved bike and hike trail. A short walk on the left fork of the trail brings you to a little-used hike-bike camp—perfect for a picnic. From the camp, you can continue on the Bike and Hike Trail along the south lakeshore to park's marina.

Taking the right fork of the trail leads to Miller Canyon Road. Follow the road a few hundred feet to its end, then resume walking on the paved Bike and Hike Trail. Serrano Beach is a short 0.25 mile up the trail.

After another 0.25 mile, the paved Bike and Hike Trail ends at Jamajab Point, which offers good views across the lake to the park's marina. A narrow trail, used mostly by fishermen, winds another 0.5 mile along the lakeshore.

SANTA SUSANA MOUNTAINS STATE PARK

■ STAGECOACH TRAIL

From Chatsworth Park South to Devil's Slide is 2.5 miles round trip with 500-foot elevation gain

One of the major obstacles to stagecoach travel between Los Angeles and San Francisco was a route out of the west end of the San Fernando Valley over the Simi Hills. About 1860, a steep road was carved out of the rock face of the hills. The steepest stretch, a peril to man and beast, was known as Devil's Slide.

The slide, the old stage road and a portion of the Simi Hills are preserved in a park in-the-making located just west of Chatsworth. In 1989, the state pur-

As you hike up this trail, imagine stagecoaches making the same journey years ago.

chased 400 acres in the Santa Susana Pass area and added it to another 400 acres of state-owned parkland. The park represents two decades by San Fernando Valley and Simi Valley environmentalists, spearheaded by the Santa Susana Mountain Park Association.

Santa Susana as a park name is confusing because the Simi Hills, not the nearby Santa Susana Mountains, are protected by the park. Visually, the Simi Hills with their sky-scraping sedimentary rock formations are quite different from the rounder, taller Santa Susana Mountains to the north of Chatsworth.

The reddish-orange sandstone outcroppings of the Simi Hills, dating from the Tertiary and Mesozoic periods 60 to 80 million years ago, form a dramatic backdrop for the park. It's easy to see why these rugged hills were a popular setting for Western movies.

The hills overlook Chatsworth, named after Chatsworth, England. Founded in the 1880s, it became a community of vegetable patches, orchards, cattle and horse ranches. Although one of the west San Fernando Valley's oldest towns, it's managed to hang on to its rural character somewhat better than most valley communities.

A network of trails loop through the park, but the trails are unsigned and more than a little confusing. During your first visit to the park, expect to improvise a bit. Once you get the lay of the land, subsequent visits will be easier.

As you drive up Devonshire you'll notice signed Stagecoach Trail, an equestrian trail. Leave your car and pick up this trail if you wish, but it's more convenient continuing to the ample parking area in the main part of Chatsworth Park South.

DIRECTIONS TO TRAILHEAD   From the Ventura Freeway (101) in Woodland Hills, exit on Topanga Canyon Boulevard and drive 6.2 miles north to Devonshire St. Turn left and proceed 0.75 mile to Chatsworth Park South, a city-owned park with wide lawns and picnic areas, located next to the new state park. If you're coming from the Simi Valley-San Fernando Valley Freeway (118), take the Topanga Canyon Boulevard exit in Chatsworth, drive 1.5 miles to Devonshire and turn right to the park.

THE HIKE   From the parking lot, walk across the wide lawn (or take one of the dirt paths that border the lawn). With the park recreation center directly behind you, navigate toward a couple of oaks and join a gravel path that begins just below a water tower on your right.

Begin a moderate ascent. When presented with confusing choices and unsigned junctions, try to keep ascending straight up the hill. Don't drift too far to the south where there's a line of electrical transmission towers, or too far to the north where the Southern Pacific railroad tracks penetrate the mountains.

A half mile from the trailhead you'll intersect a paved road, which winds up to a small hydroelectric pumping plant. You, however, will almost immediately abandon this road at a break in a chain link fence by two telephone poles. Here you'll find the old stage road and begin to climb more earnestly toward Devil's Slide.

A century ago, the road was in much better shape. Erosion has carved wagon-wheel-sized potholes into the soft rock. The Devil's Slide is more like the Devil's Stairs these days.

Near the top of the slide is a historical marker placed by the Native Daughters of the American West commemorating "Old Santa Susana Stagecoach Road, 1859-90." This is a great place to pull up a rock, sit a spell and survey the San Fernando Valley, which spreads south and east. Just below is Chatsworth, a mixture of old ranchland and new townhouses. If you're lucky, you'll sight a freight or passenger train snaking through the Simi Hills and disappearing into the Santa Susana tunnel.

After enjoying the view, you can continue another 0.25 mile up the Stagecoach Trail and inspect the rest of Devil's Slide. Or you can retrace your steps and take one the side trails leading southeast over to the park's intriguing rock formations.

WILL ROGERS STATE HISTORIC PARK

■ WILL ROGERS TRAIL
To Inspiration Point is 2 miles round trip
with a 300-foot elevation gain

Will Rogers, often called the "Cowboy Philosopher," bought a spread in the Santa Monica Mountains in 1922. He and his family enlarged their weekend cottage to 31 rooms. The Oklahoma-born Rogers toured the country as a trick roper, punctuating his act with humorous comments on the news of the day. His roping act led the humorist to later fame as a newspaper columnist, radio commentator and movie star.

Today, the ranch and grounds of the Rogers Ranch is maintained as Will Rogers State Historic Park, set aside in 1944. You can see a short film on Rogers's life at the park visitor center and tour the ranch house, still filled with his prized possessions.

America's cowboy philosopher at home in the Santa Monica Mountains.

Rogers himself designed the riding trails that wind into the hills behind his ranch. The path to Inspiration Point is an easy walk for the whole family.

DIRECTIONS TO TRAILHEAD   From Sunset Boulevard in Pacific Palisades, 4.5 miles inland from Sunset's junction with Pacific Coast Highway, turn inland on the access road leading to Will Rogers State Historic Park. Park your car near the polo field or near Rogers' house.

THE HIKE   Join the path near the tennis courts west of park headquarters and begin ascending north into the mountains. (You'll see a couple of different trails; join the main, wide bridle path.)

Rogers Trail ascends a ridge overlooking nearby Rivas Canyon and leads to a junction, where you take the turnoff for Inspiration Point. Not really a point at all, it's actually more of a flat-topped knoll; nevertheless, clear-day views are inspiring: the Santa Monica Bay, the metropolis, the San Gabriel Mountains, and even Catalina Island.

TOPANGA STATE PARK

■ EAGLE ROCK LOOP TRAIL (BACKBONE TRAIL)

To Eagle Rock via Eagle Rock/Eagle Springs Loop is 6.5 miles round trip with 800-foot elevation gain; to Will Rogers SHP via Eagle Rock, Fire Road 30, and Rogers Road is 10.5 miles one way with a 1,800-foot loss

Topanga Canyon is a quiet retreat, surrounded by L.A. sprawl but retaining its rural character. The state park is sometimes billed as "the largest state park within a city limit in the U.S."

The name Topanga is from the Shoshonean Indian dialect. These Indians and their ancestors occupied the canyon on and off for several thousand years until the Spanish evicted them and forced them to settle at the San Fernando Mission.

Until the 1880s, there was little permanent habitation in the canyon. Early settlers tended vineyards, orchards, and cattle ranches. In the 1920s, the canyon became a popular weekend destination for Los Angeles residents. Summer cabins were built along Topanga Creek and in subdivisions in the surrounding hills. For one dollar round-trip fare, tourists could board a Packard auto stage in Santa Monica and be driven up Pacific Coast Highway and Topanga Canyon Road to the Topanga Post Office and other, more scenic spots.

Most Topanga trails are good fire roads. On a blustery winter day, city and canyon views are superb.

In the heart of the state park, the walker will discover Eagle Rock, Eagle Spring and get topographically oriented to Topanga. The energetic will enjoy the one-way journey from Topanga to Will Rogers State Historic Park.

The Topanga State Park to Will Rogers Park section of the Backbone Trail has been finished for quite some time and has proved very popular. The lower reaches of the trail offer a fine tour of the wild side of Topanga Canyon while the ridgetop sections offer far-reaching inland and ocean views.

DIRECTIONS TO TRAILHEAD From Topanga Canyon Boulevard, turn east on Entrada Road; that's to the right if you're coming from Pacific Coast Highway. Follow Entrada Road by turning left at every opportunity until you arrive at Topanga State Park. The trailhead is at the end of the parking lot. (For information about the end of this walk, consult the Will Rogers State Historic Park write-up and directions to the trailhead on the previous page.)

THE HIKE From the Topanga State Park parking lot, follow the distinct trail eastward to a signed junction, where you'll begin hiking on Eagle Springs Road. You'll pass through an oak woodland and through chaparral country. The trail slowly and steadily gains about 800 feet in elevation on the way to Eagle Rock. When you reach a junction, bear left on the north loop of Eagle Springs Road to Eagle Rock. A short detour will bring you to the top of the rock.

To complete the loop, bear sharply right (southwest) at the next junction, following the fire road as it winds down to Eagle Spring. Past the spring, you return to Eagle Spring Road and retrace your steps back to the trailhead.

Three mile long Musch Ranch Trail, which passes from hot chaparral to shady oak woodland, crosses a bridge and passes the park pond, is another fine way to return to the trailhead.

To Will Rogers State Historic Park: Follow the loop trip directions to the northeast end of Eagle Rock/Eagle Spring Loop, where you bear right on Fire Road 30. In one-half mile you reach the intersection with Rogers Road. Turn left and follow the dirt road (really a trail) for 3.5 miles, where the road ends and meets Rogers Trail. Here a level area and solitary oak suggest a lunch stop. On clear days enjoy the spectacular views in every direction: To the left is Rustic Canyon and the crest of the mountains near Mulholland Drive. To the right, Rivas Canyon descends toward the sea.

Stay on Rogers Trail, which marches up and down several steep hills, for about two more miles, until it enters Will Rogers Park near Inspiration Point.

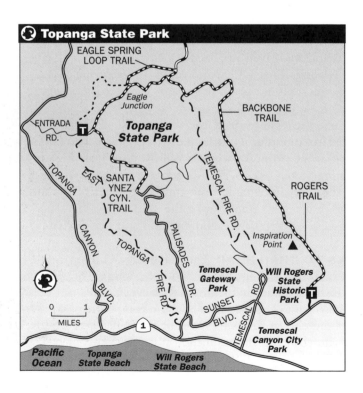

MALIBU CREEK STATE PARK

■ MALIBU CREEK TRAIL

To Rock Pool is 3.5 miles round trip with 150-foot elevation gain; to Century Lake is 4.5 miles round trip with 200-foot elevation gain

Before land for Malibu Creek State Park was acquired in 1974, it was divided into three parcels belonging to Bob Hope, Ronald Reagan, and 20th Century Fox. Although the park is still used for moviemaking, it's primarily a haven for day hikers and picnickers.

Today the state park preserves more than 7,000 acres of rugged country in the middle of the Santa Monica Mountains. Malibu Creek winds through the park. The creek was dammed at the turn of the century to form little Century Lake.

The trail along Malibu Creek explores the heart of the state park. It's an easy, nearly level walk that visits a dramatic rock gorge, Century Lake and several locales popular with moviemakers.

DIRECTIONS TO TRAILHEAD From Pacific Coast Highway, turn inland on Malibu Canyon Road and proceed 6.5 miles to the park entrance, 0.25 mile south of Mulholland Highway. If you're coming from the San Fernando Valley, exit the Ventura Freeway (101) on Las Virgenes Road and continue four miles to the park entrance.

THE HIKE From the parking area, follow the wide fire road. You'll cross the all-but-dry creek. The road soon forks into a high road and a low road. Go right and walk along the oak-shaded high road, which makes a long, lazy left arc as it follows the north bank of Malibu Creek. You'll reach an intersection and turn left on a short road that crosses a bridge over Malibu Creek.

You'll spot the Gorge Trail and follow it upstream a short distance to the gorge, one of the most dramatic sights in the Santa Mon-

Malibu Creek gorge.

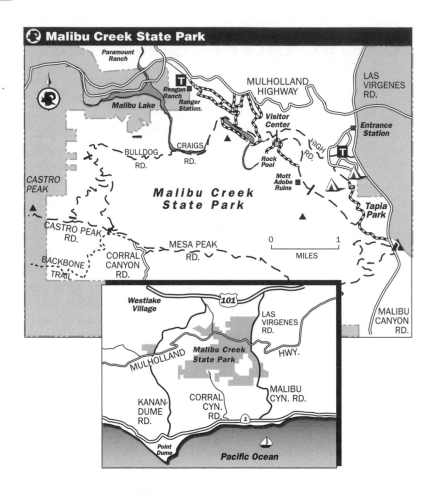

ica Mountains. Malibu Creek makes a hairpin turn through 400-foot volcanic rock cliffs and cascades into aptly named Rock Pool. The "Swiss Family Robinson" television series and some Tarzan movies were filmed here.

Return to the trailhead or retrace your steps back to the high road and bear left toward Century Lake. As the road ascends you'll be treated to a fine view of Las Virgenes Valley. When you gain the crest of the hill, you'll look down on Century Lake. Near the lake are hills of porous lava and topsy-turvy sedimentary rock layers that tell of the violent geologic upheaval that formed Malibu Canyon. The lake was scooped out by members of Crag's Country Club, a group of wealthy, turn-of-the-century businessmen who had a nearby lodge.

You can call it a day here, or continue on the fire road past Century Lake. You'll pass the location of the now-removed set for the "M*A*S*H" television series. The prominent Goat Buttes that tower above Malibu Creek were featured in the opening shot of each episode.

LEO CARRILLO STATE PARK

■ NICHOLAS FLAT TRAIL

From Leo Carrillo State Beach to Nicholas Flat is 7 miles
round trip with 1,600-foot elevation gain

Leo Carrillo State Beach has always been a popular surfing spot. Surfers
tackle the well-shaped south swell, while battling the submerged rocks
and kelp beds. In recent years, the state added a large chunk of Santa Monica Mountains parkland, prompting a name change to Leo Carrillo State Park.

The park is named after Angeline Leo Carrillo, famous for his TV role as
Pancho, the Cisco Kid's sidekick. Carrillo, the son of Santa Monica's first
mayor, was also quite active in recreation and civic affairs.

DIRECTIONS TO TRAILHEAD From the west end of the Santa Monica
Freeway in Santa Monica, head up-coast on Pacific Coast Highway about 25
miles to Leo Carrillo State Beach. There's free parking along Coast Highway,
and fee parking in the park's day use area.

THE HIKE The park's Nicholas Flat area is one of the best spots in the Santa
Monica Mountains for spring wildflowers because it's a meeting place for four
different plant communities. Chaparral, grassland, coastal scrub and oak woodland all converge near the flat. Another reason for the remarkable plant diversity
is Leo Carrillo's elevation, which varies from sea level to nearly 2,000 feet.

Along park trails, look for shooting star, hedge nettle, sugar bush, hollyleaf
redberry, purple sage, chamise, blue dick, deer weed, burr clover, bush lupine,
golden yarrow, fuschia-flowered gooseberry, and many more flowering plants.
Around Nicholas Pond, keep an eye out for wishbone bush, encelia, chia,
Parry's phacelia, ground-pink, California poppy, scarlet bugler and goldfields.

Even when the wildflowers fade away, Nicholas Flat is worth a visit. Its
charms include a big meadow and a pond patrolled by coots. Atop grand boulders you can enjoy a picnic and savor Malibu coast views.

Nicholas Flat Trail can also be savored for one more reason: In Southern
California, very few trails connect the mountains with the sea. Get an early start.
Until you arrive at oak-dotted Nicholas Flat itself, there's not much shade en
route. Signed Nicholas Flat trailhead is located a short distance past the park
entry kiosk, opposite the day use parking area.

Soon the trail splits. The right branch circles the hill, climbs above Willow
Creek, and after a mile, rejoins the main Nicholas Flat Trail. Enjoy this interesting option on your return from Nicholas Flat.

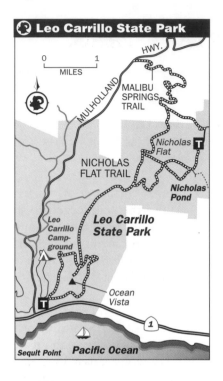

Take the left branch, which immediately begins a moderate to steep ascent of the grassy slopes above the park campground. The trail switchbacks through a coastal scrub community up to a saddle on the ridgeline. Here you'll meet the alternate branch of Nicholas Flat Trail. From the saddle, a short side trail leads south to a hilltop, where there's a fine coastal view. From the viewpoint, you can see Point Dume and the Malibu coastline. During the winter, it's a good place to bring your binoculars and scout the Pacific horizon for migrating whales.

Following the ridgeline, Nicholas Flat Trail climbs inland over chaparral-covered slopes. Keep glancing over your right shoulder at the increasingly grand coastal views, and over your left at the open slopes browsed by the park's nimble deer.

After a good deal of climbing, the trail levels atop the ridgeline and you get your first glimpse of grassy, inviting Nicholas Flat. The trail descends past a line of fire-blackened, but unbowed, old oaks and joins an old ranch road that skirts the Nicholas Flat meadows. Picnickers may unpack lunch beneath the shady oaks or out in the sunny meadow. The trail angles southeast across the meadow to a small pond. The man-made pond, used by cattle during the region's ranching days, is backed by some handsome boulders.

Return the way you came until you reach the junction located 0.75 mile from the trailhead. Bear left at the fork and enjoy this alternate trail as it descends into the canyon cut by Willow Creek, contours around an ocean-facing slope, and returns you to the trailhead.

POINT MUGU STATE PARK

■ SYCAMORE CANYON TRAIL

From Big Sycamore Canyon to Deer Camp Junction is 6.5
miles round trip with 200-foot elevation gain; return via
Overlook Trail is 10 miles round trip with 700-foot gain

Every fall, millions of monarch butterflies migrate south to the forests of
Mexico's Transvolcanic Range and to the damp coastal woodlands of
Central and Southern California. The monarch's awe-inspiring migration and
formation of what entomologists call over-wintering colonies are two of
nature's most colorful autumn events.

All monarch butterflies west of the Rockies head for California in the fall;
one of the best places in Southern California to observe the arriving monarchs
is the campground in Big Sycamore Canyon at Point Mugu State Park.

The monarch's evolutionary success lies not only in its unique ability to
migrate to warmer climes, but in its mastery of chemical warfare. The butterfly
feeds on milkweed—the favored poison of assassins during the Roman Empire.
This milkweed diet makes the monarch toxic to birds; after munching a
monarch or two and becoming sick, they learn to leave the butterflies alone.

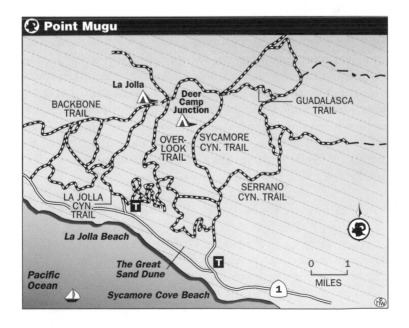

The butterflies advertise their poisonous nature with their conspicuous coloring. They have brownish-red wings with black veins. The outer edge of the wings are dark brown with white and yellow spots. While one might assume the monarch's startling coloration would make them easy prey for predators, just the opposite is true; bright colors in nature are often a warning that a creature is toxic or distasteful.

Sycamore Canyon Trail takes you through a peaceful wooded canyon, where a multitude of monarchs dwell, and past some magnificent sycamores. The sycamores that shade the canyon bearing their name are incomparable. The lower branches, stout and crooked, are a delight for tree-climbers. Hawks and owls roost in the upper branches.

The trail follows the canyon on a gentle northern traverse across Point Mugu State Park, the largest preserved area in the Santa Monica Mountains. This trail, combined with Overlook Trail, gives the hiker quite a tour of the park.

During October and November, Sycamore Canyon offers the twin delights of falling autumn leaves and fluttering butterflies. (Ask park rangers where the monarchs cluster in large numbers.)

DIRECTIONS TO TRAILHEAD   Drive up-coast on Highway 1, 32 miles from Santa Monica, to Big Sycamore Canyon Campground in Point Mugu State Park (day-use fee). Walk past the campground entrance through the campground to a locked gate. The trail begins on the other side of the gate.

THE HIKE   Take the trail up-canyon, following the creek. Winter rains cause the creek to rise, and sometimes keeping your feet dry while crossing is difficult. Underground water keeps much of the creekside vegetation green year-round—so this is a fine hike in any season.

One-half mile from the campground you'll spot Overlook Trail, which switchbacks to the west up a ridge and then heads north toward the native tall grass prairie in La Jolla Valley. Make note of this trail, an optional return route.

A second half mile of nearly level canyon walking brings you to another major hiking trail that branches right—Serrano Canyon Trail, an absolute gem.

Another easy mile of walking beneath the sycamores brings you to a picnic table shaded by a grove of large oak trees. The oaks might be a good turn-around spot for a family with small children. The total round trip distance would be a little over four miles.

Continuing up the canyon you'll pass beneath more of the giant sycamores and soon arrive at Wood Canyon Junction, the hub of six trails which lead to all corners of the park. Bear left on signed Wood Canyon Trail and in a short while you'll reach Deer Camp Junction. Drinking water and picnic tables suggest a lunch stop. Oak trees predominate over the sycamores along Wood Canyon Creek; however, the romantic prefer the sycamores, some of which have large clumps of mistletoe in the upper branches.

You can call it a day here and return the way you came. As you hike down the canyon back to the campground, the large and cranky scrub jay population will scold you, but don't let the squawking birds stop you from enjoying one of California's finest sycamore savannas.

To return via Overlook Trail: Continue past the junction with Wood Canyon Trail and Deer Camp Junction on the Wood Canyon Trail, which becomes Pumphouse Road. You'll climb over the divide between Sycamore Canyon and La Jolla Valley. Upon reaching a junction, you'll head south on the Overlook Trail, staying on the La Jolla Canyon side of the ridge. True to its name, Overlook Trail offers good views of grassy mountainsides, Boney Peak and Big Sycamore Canyon.

You'll pass an intersection with Scenic Trail, a rough path that hugs the ridge separating La Jolla and Big Sycamore Canyon, where you'll bear right and follow the fire road one-half mile back to the trailhead.

SOUTHERN CALIFORNIA COAST

an Diego, Orange, Los Angeles, Ventura and Santa Barbara county shores have long served as resort areas for Californians, as well as visitors from across the country and around the world. Though some state beaches are crowded blanket-to-blanket with sun worshipers, many offer a much more relaxing, even remote environment for a day at the beach.

The state beaches begin at the Mexican border with Borderfield State Park and continue past "America's Riviera" (Santa Barbara) to Refugio and El Capitan state beaches.

Each Southern California beach has its own character: best surfing, clearest water, panoramic view, most birdlife. The air and water temperatures are Mediterranean, the place-names Spanish.

The coast includes not only such sand strands as the "Sans"—Elijo, Onofre, Clemente and Buenaventura—but some nature preserves as well. Monarch butterflies migrate to a woodland on the bluffs above El Capitan State Beach. Birds and bird-watchers flock to the mouth of the Santa Clara River at McGrath State Beach. On the bluffs south of Del Mar grows the rare Torrey pine, set aside in a state reserve that shelters a rich native plant community.

BORDER FIELD STATE PARK

■ BORDER FIELD TRAIL
From Border to Tijuana River is 3 miles round trip;
to Imperial Beach is 6 miles round trip

At the very southwest corner of America is a monument marking the border between Mexico and California. When California became a territory at the end of the Mexican-American War, an international border became a necessity. American and Mexican survey crews determined the boundary and the monument of Italian marble was placed in 1851 to mark the original survey site. Today the monument stands in the shadow of the Tijuana Bull Ring and still delineates the border between the United States and Estádos Unídos Mexicanos.

During World War II, the Navy used Border Field as an airfield. Combat pilots received gunnery training, learning to hit steam-driven targets that raced over the dunes on rails called Rabbit Tracks. Despite a variety of real estate schemers, the Navy retained control of Border Field until the land was given to the state in the early 1970s.

Before you walk down the bluffs to the beach, take in the panoramic view: the Otay Mountains and the San Miguel Mountains to the east, Mexico's Coronado Islands out to sea, and to the north—the Tijuana River floodplain, the Silver Strand, Coronado.

Much of the Tijuana River Estuary, one of the few salt marshes left in Southern California and one of the region's most important bird habitats, is within Border Field State Park's boundaries.

Stop in at the visitor center and check out the natural history exhibits that interpret this unique environment.

This walk explores the dune and estuary ecosystems of the state park and takes you to wide, sandy Imperial Beach. Wear an old pair of shoes and be prepared for the soft mud of the marsh.

DIRECTIONS TO TRAILHEAD Border Field State Park is located in the extreme southwestern corner of California, with Mexico and the Pacific Ocean as its southern and western boundaries. From Interstate 5 (San Diego Freeway) south, exit on Hollister Street, proceed to a T-intersection, bear west (right) 2 miles on Monument Road to the state park. The park closes at sunset.

THE HIKE Follow the short bluff trail down to the beach, which is under strict 24-hour surveillance by the U.S. Border Patrol. The beach is usually deserted, quite a contrast to crowded Tijuana Beach a few hundred yards to the south. As you walk north on Border Field State Park's 1.5 mile long beach, you'll pass sand dunes anchored by salt grass, pickleweed and sand verbena.

On the other side of the dunes is the Tijuana River Estuary, an essential breeding ground, feeding and nesting spot for more than 170 species of native and migratory birds. At Border Field, the salt marsh is relatively unspoiled, unlike so many wetlands encountered farther north, which have been drained, filled or used as dumps.

Take time to explore the marsh. You may spot a marsh hawk, brown pelican, California gull, black-necked stilt, snowy egret, western sandpiper and American kestrel—to name a few of the more common birds. Fishing is good for perch, corbina and halibut, both in the surf along Border Field Beach and in the estuary.

A mile and a half from the border you'll reach the mouth of the Tijuana River. Only after heavy storms is the Tijuana River the wide swath pictured on some maps. Most of the time it's fordable at low tide, but use your best judgement.

Continue north along wide, sandy Imperial Beach, past some houses and low bluffs. Imperial Beach was named by the South San Diego Investment Company to lure Imperial Valley residents to build summer cottages on the beach. Waterfront lots could be purchased for $25 down, $25 monthly and developers promised the balmy climate would "cure rheumatic proclivities, catarrhal trouble, lesions of the lungs," and a wide assortment of other ailments.

In more recent times, what was once a narrow beach protected by a seawall has been widened considerably by sand dredged from San Diego Bay. There's good swimming and surfing along Imperial Beach and the waves can get huge. The beach route reaches Imperial Pier, built in 1912 and the oldest in the county.

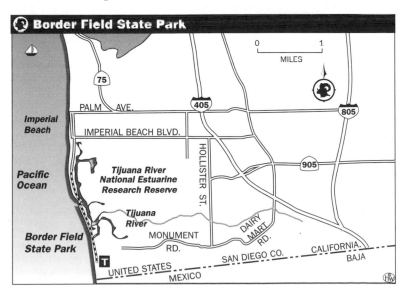

SILVER STRAND STATE BEACH

■ SILVER STRAND TRAIL

To park boundary is 2.5 miles round trip; to Coronado is 6 miles one way with a return by bus or 12 miles round trip

While a state beach boasting 2,000 parking spaces might seem the last place on earth to seek solitude, San Diego's Silver Strand remains remarkably uncrowded. By virtue of its great length (5 miles), the strand disperses visitors over its sparkling sands so that coastal congestion of the kind found at other Southland beaches is rare.

Truly, first impressions aren't everything. Silver Strand, as viewed from the windshield on busy Highway 75, appears dominated by four aircraft carrier-sized parking lots and the Navy's Star Wars-style communications equipment.

But beyond the steel and asphalt is a strand perfect for a saunter, short or long. Silver Strand, with millions of tiny shells mixed with its sands, sparkles in the sunlight. Wonderful waves, ideal for boogie boarding, arrive in set after dependable set.

The strand has been popular with beach-goers for more than a century. From the early 1900s to 1941, a beachside resort flourished on Silver Strand, better known in those days as "Tent City" for its predominant style of accommodation. A boardwalk, bowling alley and bandstands were some of the retreat's attractions. A highway-widening project and the outbreak of World War II put an end to Tent City.

The state beach (2.5 miles of the strand) hosts a multitude of such waterfowl as Brandt's cormorants, gulls, terns, sanderlings and loons. California sea lions are numerous offshore and an occasional school of porpoises visits the area.

The park includes a portion of San Diego Bay shoreline on the other side of the peninsula. From the ocean side of the strand, take one of the pedestrian underpasses beneath Highway 75 to Bayside Picnic Area. Ramada-covered picnic tables dot the bay shore and the crescent of Crown Cove. The calm, warm waters of the bay invite a swim.

This hike offers a mellow beach-comb north across Silver Strand State Beach. More ambitious walkers will saunter onward to Coronado City Beach in front of that rambling red-roofed queen of Victorian-era hotels, the Hotel Del Coronado.

Beach hikers can saunter up the strand to Coronado and return to the trailhead by bus. Catch a red, white and blue San Diego MTS bus (#901, Imperial Beach) from stops along Orange Boulevard (Highway 75) and ride back to the entrance of Silver Strand State Beach. Bus stops await just north of Hotel del

Coronado at the corner of Orange Boulevard and R.H. Dana Place and just south of the main hotel entrance on Orange Boulevard.

DIRECTIONS TO TRAILHEAD From Interstate 5 in San Diego, take the San Diego-Coronado Bay Bridge exit (State Highway 75). Cross over the bay to the peninsula and make a left on Orange Boulevard. Follow the Highway 75 signs through Coronado. The highway bends south (assuming the name Silver Strand Boulevard). From downtown Coronado, proceed 4.5 miles south to Silver Strand State Beach. Park (fee) in the most southerly lot and space you can find.

THE HIKE From the parking lot, hit the beach and start walking up-coast. Point Loma is the predominant view to the north; the Imperial Beach Pier and the Coronado Islands make up the engaging southern vista.

You soon reach the Navy Amphibious Base, which occupies much of the northern sand spit. The Navy permits beach hiking, but the base is off limits to the public.

North of the state park the tide tosses up a lot of junk and beach-combing artists fashion it into driftwood and plastic sculptures. It's also a good beach to look for shells.

At the north end of the Silver Strand, you'll step onto North Island. North Island is what this extension of the Silver Strand-Coronado peninsula is called today. You may puzzle over this enigmatic name. Its directional name, "north" offers no clue to its meaning. What is it north of? Nor is it an island. Yet Coronado

Beach is an unhurried, quiet place, so self-contained that it is commonly thought of as an island

You'll encounter modern architecture at its most utilitarian—the blocky style of the Coronado Shores condominium development as you walk Coronado Shores Beach—and a half mile later approach architecture at its most droll, the wondrous Victorian-era Hotel Del Coronado.

You'll hike along the beach south of the hotel known as South Beach, then in front of the hotel Central Beach. North of the hotel is, you guessed it, North Beach.

TORREY PINES STATE BEACH

■ TORREY PINES BEACH TRAIL
From Scripps Pier to Torrey Pines State Beach is
10 miles round trip

This beach hike begins at Scripps Pier, passes along Torrey Pines City Beach, known locally as Black's Beach, once swimsuit-optional, now enforced suits-only. After walking below some spectacular cliffs and along Torrey Pines State Beach, you'll arrive at Torrey Pines State Reserve, home to the rare and revered *Pinus torreyana*. Plan your hike for low tide.

Occupying a spectacular perch above Scripps Institution of Oceanography and the wide blue Pacific, the Birch Aquarium offers a great introduction to the wonders of the deep and insights into the many global research projects conducted by the institution. Check it out before or after your hike.

The aquarium features a Hall of Fishes with dozens of tanks. My favorite is the Hall of Oceanography, with well-crafted displays of the history of oceanographic sciences. Kids love the demonstration tidepool and touch-tanks.

DIRECTIONS TO TRAILHEAD   Exit Interstate 5 on La Jolla Village Drive, traveling west past UC San Diego to North Torrey Pines Road. Turn right, then make a left on La Jolla Shores Drive, follow it to the Aquarium turnoff on your right. Metered street parking is sparse, available on weekends only. Additional parking is available in the Aquarium parking lot up the hill with the purchase of a day permit.

THE HIKE As you look south from Scripps Pier, you'll see long and flat La Jolla Shores Beach, a wide expanse of white sand where the water deepens gradually. This is a family beach, popular during the summer with swimmers.

Walking north, the going is rocky at first; the surf really kicks up around Scripps Pier. Soon the beach widens, growing more sandy, and the spectacular curry-colored cliffs grow higher and higher.

A glider port once stood atop the bluffs. Manned fixed-wing gliders were pulled into the air, and they rode the currents created by onshore breezes rising up as they meet the cliffs. Nowadays, hang-gliders leap off the cliffs and, unless the wind shifts, come to a soft landing on the beach below.

The 300-foot cliffs tower over Black's Beach, named for William Black, Sr., the oil millionaire who owned and developed most of the land on the cliffs. During the 1970s, Black's Beach enjoyed fleeting notoriety as the first and only public beach in the country on which nudity was legal. Called "a noble experiment" by sun worshipers and "a terrible fiasco" by the more inhibited, the clothing-optional zone was defeated at the polls.

After passing a few more handsome bluffs, you'll spot a distinct outcropping called Flat Rock. Here you may join a bluff trail that leads to Torrey Pines State Reserve.

TORREY PINES STATE RESERVE

■ PARRY GROVE, GUY FLEMING TRAILS
From 0.4 to 1 mile nature trails

Atop the bluffs of Torrey Pines State Reserve lies a microcosm of old California, a garden of shrubs and succulents.

Most visitors come to view the 3,000 or so *Pinus torreyana*, which grow only here and on Santa Rosa Island, but the reserve also offers the walker a striking variety of native plants.

Be sure to check out the interpretive displays at the park museum and the native plant garden near the head of Parry Grove Trail. Plant and bird lists, as well as wildflower maps (February through June) are available for a small fee.

DIRECTIONS TO TRAILHEAD From Interstate 5, exit on Carmel Valley Road and head west to North Torrey Pines Road (also known as old Highway

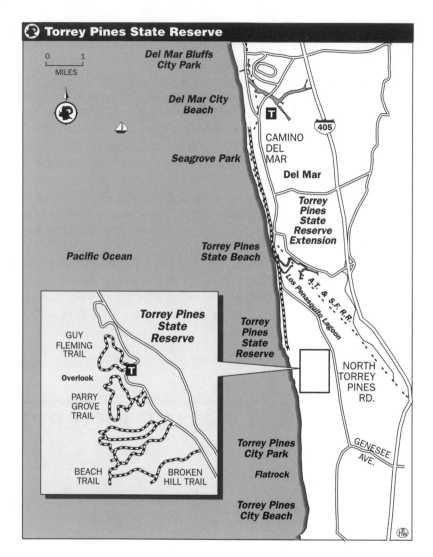

101). The main entrance to the reserve is at the base of the bluffs, where the park road climbs to a parking area near the reserve visitor center. You can also leave your car along the highway next to Torrey Pines State Beach and walk up the reserve road.

THE HIKE   Parry Grove Trail was named in honor of Dr. C.C. Parry, a botanist assigned to the boundary commission that surveyed the Mexican-American border in 1850. While waiting for the expedition to start, Parry explored the San Diego area. He investigated a tree that had been called the Soledad pine for the nearby Soledad Valley. Parry sent samples to his teacher and friend, Dr. John Torrey of Princeton, and asked that, if it proved to be a new species, it be named for Torrey. The Soledad pine became *Pinus torreyana*,

Some 3,000 *Pinus torreyana* thrive in the state reserve.

or Torrey pine, in honor of the famous botanist and taxonomist.

The 0.4 mile loop trail leads past toyon, yucca, and many other coastal shrubs. A five-year drought followed by an infestation of the Ipis bark beetle devastated Parry Grove. Only a handful of mature Torrey pines remain, accompanied by saplings planted in 1998.

Broken Hill Trail visits a drier, chaparral-dominated, landscape, full of sage and buckwheat, ceanothus and manzanita. From Broken Hill Overlook, there's a view of a few Torrey pines clinging to life in an environment that resembles a desert badlands.

Beach Trail leads to Yucca Point and Razor Point and offers precipitous views of the beach below. The trail descends the bluffs to Flat Rock, a fine tidepool area.

Guy Fleming Trail is a 0.6 mile loop that travels through stands of Torrey pine and takes you to South Overlook, where you might glimpse a migrating California gray whale.

SAN ONOFRE STATE BEACH

■ BLUFFS BEACH TRAIL
From Beach Trail 1 to Beach Trail 6 is 5.6 miles round trip.

San Onofre is a place of steep bluffs overlooking a narrow beach with patches of cobblestone. The beach, named for Egyptian Saint Onuphrius, is a joy to walk. But be aware that some sections are impassable at the highest tides. Check the tide table before you hike this beach!

Aptly named Bluffs Beach, part of San Onofre State Beach, is a three mile long sand strand with a backdrop of magnificent, 100-foot high bluffs. The dra-

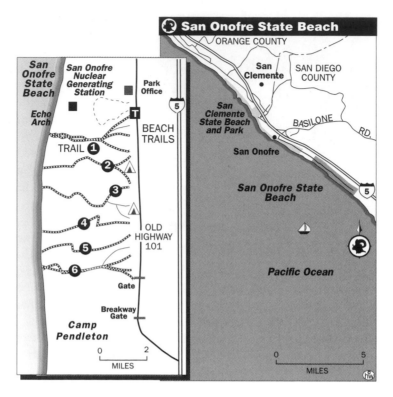

matically eroded sandstone cliffs, a kind of Bryce Canyon by the sea, effectively shield the beach from sight and sound of two parallel transportation corridors—the railroad tracks and Interstate 5.

Unfortunately, something of the peaceful ambiance of the park's coastline is diminished by the giant twin spheres of the San Onofre Nuclear Power Plant located just north and Camp Pendleton Marine Base to the south. The nuke and the marines are still very much present, but public access to the splendid beach has loosened up some of late. It's possible to walk a considerable distance both north and south of the power plant.

South of San Onofre State Beach is Camp Pendleton. The camp's beaches are officially off-limits, even if the no trespassing sign is removed, as it often is. However, the prevailing sentiment among beach goers is that the military is considerably less proprietary about its surf and turf these days.

San Onofre State Beach Campground is actually a length of old Coast Highway with some pull-outs. Charmless it is, but it's popular with surfers and other coastal recreationists who rate beach access over amenities.

And the beach access is first rate. A half-dozen signed trails (Beach Trail 1, Beach Trail 2 . . .) descend from the bluffs to the beach. The paths vary in length from 0.1 to 0.3 mile.

Walk for miles along aptly named Bluffs Beach.

DIRECTIONS TO TRAILHEAD From Interstate 5, a few miles south of San Clemente, exit on Basilone Road. Head west, then south, following the signs to San Onofre State Beach. Park in the first day-use area near the signed trailhead for Beach Trail 1.

THE HIKE I prefer starting with Beach Trail 1 and walking south along the state beach. From the beaches and bluffs, walkers sometimes spot dolphins, harbor seals and migrating California gray whales.

About three miles of beach-walking brings you to the end of state park property and onto Camp Pendleton's beach. The long sand strand south of the park is popular with nude sunbathers; while it's by no means a legally clothing-optional beach, be advised that many beach-goers opt for none.

SAN CLEMENTE STATE BEACH

■ TRESTLES TRAIL
To San Mateo Point is 3 miles round trip

"Our beach shall always be free from hurdy-gurdies and defilement. We believe beauty to be an asset as well as gold and silver, or cabbage and potatoes." This was the pledge of Norwegian immigrant Ole Hanson, who began the town of San Clemente in 1925. It was quite a promise from a real estate developer, quite a promise in those days of shameless boosterism a half-century before the California Coastal Commission was established.

Thanks in part to Hanson's vision, some of the peaceful ambiance of San Clemente, which he regarded as "a painting five miles long and a mile wide" has been preserved. And some of its isolation, too. Most everyone in the real estate community thought Hanson crazy for building in a locale 66 miles from

San Diego, 66 miles from Los Angeles, but today this isolation attracts rather than repels. This isolation was one of the reasons President Richard Nixon established his Western White House in San Clemente.

San Clemente State Beach is a great place for a walk. The beach is mercifully walled off from the din of the San Diego Freeway and the confusion of the modern world by a handsome line of tan-colored bluffs. Only the occasional train passing over Santa Fe Railroad tracks (located near the shore) interrupts the cry of the gull, the roar of the breakers. The trestles located at the south end of the beach at San Mateo Point give Trestles Beach its name.

Trestles Beach is one of the finest surfing areas on the west coast. When the surf is up, the waves peel rapidly across San Mateo Point, creating a great ride. Before the area became part of the state beach, it was restricted government property belonging to Camp Pendleton Marine Base. For well over 25 years, surfers carried on guerrilla warfare with U.S. Marines. Trespassing surfers were chased, arrested and fined, and on many occasions had their boards confiscated and broken in two. Find a veteran surfer and he'll tell you about escapes from jeep patrols. Many times, however, the cool marines would charitably give surfers rides while out on maneuvers.

This walk's destination, San Mateo Point, is the northernmost boundary of San Diego County, the beginning of Orange County. When the original counties of Los Angeles and San Diego were set up in 1850, the line that separated them began on the coast at San Mateo Point. When Orange County was formed from southern Los Angeles County in 1889, San Mateo Point was established as the southern point of the new county.

The enthusiastic, with the time and inclination can easily extend this beachwalk several miles south to San Onofre State Beach. Another option worth considering is to take the train to San Clemente and walk south from the Amtrak station.

DIRECTIONS TO TRAILHEAD From the San Diego Freeway (I-5) in San Clemente, exit on Avenida Calafia and head west a half mile to Calafia Beach Park, where there is metered parking. You can also park (for a fee) at San Clemente State Beach. A limited amount of free parking is available in the residential area near the state beach.

North-bound motorists on I-5 will exit at Cristianitos Road, turn left and go over the freeway onto Ave. Del Presidente and drive a mile north to Calafia Beach Park.

THE HIKE From Calafia Beach Park, cross the railroad tracks at the newly erected stairway and head south. As you'll soon see, San Clemente State Beach is frequented by plenty of shorebirds, as well as plenty of surfers, body surfers, and swimmers.

At distinct San Mateo Point, which marks the border of Orange and San Diego counties, you'll find San Mateo Creek. The headwaters of the creek rise way up in the Santa Ana Mountains above Camp Pendleton. A portion of the creek is protected by the Cleveland National Forest's San Mateo Canyon Wilderness. Rushes, saltgrass and cattails line the creek mouth, where sand-pipers, herons and egrets gather.

You can ford the creek mouth (rarely a problem except after winter storms) and continue south toward San Onofre State Beach and the giant domes of San Onofre Nuclear Power Plant. Or you can return the same way.

Or here's a third alternative, an inland return route: Walk under the train trestles and join the park service road, which is usually filled with surfers carrying their boards. The service road takes you up the bluffs, where you'll join the San Clemente Coastal Bike Trail, then wind through a residential area to an entrance to San Clemente State Beach Campground.

Improvise a route through the campground to the park's entry station and join the self-guiding nature trail (brochures available at the station). The path descends through a prickly pear- and lemonade berry-filled draw to Calafia Beach Park and the trailhead. The wind- and water-sculpted marine terraces just south of the trailhead resemble Bryce Canyon in miniature and are fun to photograph.

If you want to walk the whole nature trail, you'll walk up to site #70 in the campground, then retrace your steps (100 yards or so) back to the Calafia Beach parking lot.

DOHENY STATE BEACH

From Doheny State Beach to Capistrano Beach is 2 miles
round trip; to San Clemente Pier is 10 miles round trip

San Juan Capistrano attracts swallows and tourists while Capistrano Beach, which bounds the old mission town, attracts sanderlings and locals. Capistrano Beach, along with Doheny Beach to the north and San Clemente Beach to the south, offers the beach hiker a mellow saunter along the strand.

This beach hike begins just north of Dana Harbor at Doheny State Beach, a good place for family-style swimming and boogie-boarding because the harbor jetties gentle the surf here. Doheny attracts a lot of happy campers, though some seekers of peace and quiet complain that the campground is a bit too close to the highway.

Be sure to visit the Doheny State Beach Interpretive Center, which features an impressive tidepool exhibit, some aquariums and a photo gallery that highlights Orange County's long-board surfing era during the 1950s and 60s. The interpretive center (open 10 a.m. to 4 p.m. daily) is located close to the park's entry station.

DIRECTIONS TO TRAILHEAD   From the San Diego Freeway (5) in San Juan Capistrano, exit on Camino Las Ramblas and drive a mile westward to Highway 1. Turn north and very soon reach an intersection and make a left on Harbor Drive, then another quick left into Doheny State Beach. There is a state park day use fee.

THE HIKE   Walk down to the shoreline and saunter south along the white sand beach. After 0.25 mile, you'll reach the mouth of San Juan Creek. In summer, a sandbar closes off the creek mouth and forms a small lagoon patrolled by ducks and egrets. During the wintertime, or if the sandbar has been breached by the creek and is too high to cross, detour inland to the park road and follow it over the creek. Walk through the campground back to the beach.

After a bit more than a mile, you'll reach the end of Doheny and the beginning of Capistrano Beach, easily identified by the long, uninterrupted row of houses facing the beach. Lots of rock has been dumped near the tideline in an attempt to stabilize the beach and protect the houses from the surging waves; this translates into awkward passage and a less-than-aesthetically uplifting experience for the beach hiker.

At 2.75 miles, you'll reach undeveloped Poche Beach, a county park, and continue 0.5 mile to a development-crowded point that makes beach walking a challenge and thwarts all passage at higher tides. Detour inland, walk south along El Camino Real, then return to the beach by the MetroLink Station.

Resume your shore walk southward across the brown sands of San Clemente City Beach. San Clemente Pier and nearby refreshment opportunities suggest a turnaround point. Gung-ho hikers can continue another two miles or so down-coast across San Clemente State Beach to San Mateo Point and the Orange County/San Diego County line.

CRYSTAL COVE STATE PARK

■ MORO CANYON TRAIL

From Park headquarters to top of Moro Canyon is 7 miles round trip with 700-foot elevation gain

Extending three miles along the coast between Laguna Beach and Corona del Mar, and inland over the San Joaquin Hills, 3,000-acre Crystal Cove State Park attracts bird-watchers, beachcombers and hikers.

The backcountry of Crystal Cove State Park is part of the San Joaquin Hills, first used by Mission San Juan Capistrano for grazing land. Cattle raising continued under José Sepúlveda when the area became part of his land grant, Rancho San Joaquín, in 1837. In 1864, Sepúlveda sold the land to James Irvine and his partners and it became part of his Irvine Ranch. Grazing continued until shortly after the state purchased the property as parkland in 1979.

Former Irvine Ranch roads now form a network of hiking trails that loop through the state park. An especially nice trail travels the length of Moro Canyon, the main watershed of the park. An oak woodland, a seasonal stream and sand-

stone caves are some of the attractions of a walk through this canyon. Bird-watchers may spot the roadrunner, quail, Cooper's hawk, wrentit and many more species.

After exploring inland portions of the state park, allow some time to visit the park's coastline, highlighted by grassy bluffs, sandy beaches, tidepools and coves. The Pelican Point, Crystal Cove, Reef Point and Moro Beach areas of the park allow easy beach access. An offshore area adjacent to the park has been designated an underwater park for divers.

DIRECTIONS TO TRAILHEAD   Crystal Cove State Park is located off Pacific Coast Highway, about two miles south of the town of Corona del Mar or one mile north of Laguna Beach. Turn inland on the short park road, signed El Moro Canyon. Drinking water, restrooms, interpretive displays and plenty of parking are available at the ranger station.

Pick up a trail map at the ranger station. At the station, you can consult the schedule of ranger-led interpretive walks, which explore both inland and coastal sections of the state park.

THE HIKE   Below the ranger station, near the park entry kiosk pick up the unsigned Moro Canyon Trail, which crosses the grassy slopes behind a school down into Moro Canyon. At the canyon bottom, you meet a fire road and head left, up-canyon.

The walker may observe such native plants as black sage, prickly pear cactus, monkeyflowers, golden bush, lemonade berry and deer weed. Long before Spanish missionaries and settlers arrived in Southern California, a Native American population flourished in the coastal canyons of Orange County. The abundance of edible plants in the area, combined with the mild climate and easy access to the bounty of the sea, contributed to the success of these people; anthropologists believe they lived here for more than four thousand years.

The canyon narrows, and you ignore fire roads joining Moro Canyon from the right and left. You stay in the canyon bottom and proceed through an oak woodland, which shades a trickling stream. You'll pass a shallow sandstone cave just off the trail to the right.

About 2.5 miles from the trailhead, you'll reach the unsigned junction with a fire road. If you wish to make a loop trip out of this day hike, bear left on this road, which climbs steeply west, then northeast toward the ridgetop that forms a kind of inland wall for Muddy, Moro, Emerald and other coastal canyons.

When you reach the ridgetop, unpack your lunch and enjoy the far reaching views of the San Joaquin Hills and Orange County coast, Catalina and San Clemente Islands. You'll also have a raven's-eye view of Moro Canyon and the route back to the trailhead. After catching your breath, you'll bear right (east) along the ridgetop and quickly descend back into Moro Canyon. A 0.75 mile walk brings you back to the junction where you earlier ascended out of the canyon. This time you continue straight down-canyon, retracing your steps to the trailhead.

HUNTINGTON AND BOLSA CHICA STATE BEACHES

■ HUNTINGTON BEACH TRAIL

From Huntington State Beach to Bolsa Chica State Beach is 6 miles round trip; to Bolsa Chica north boundary is 7.5 miles one way

Huntington and Bolsa Chica are the Bonneville Salt Flats of beaches: Wide. Long. With more fire pits than Fiji. The state beaches (with Huntington City Beach sandwiched in the middle) extend some 9 miles along northern Orange County's coast, from the Santa Ana River to just-short of the San Gabriel River.

In many ways, Huntington/Bolsa Chica has always been a kind of blue-collar beach. Until Bolsa Chica beach came under state control in 1961, nobody did much to keep the beach clean—hence its once-popular name of Tin Can Beach. Despite a couple of boutiqued blocks where Main Street meets the shore, and some upscale subdivisions more in keeping with O.C. inland 'burbs, Huntington Beach still has rough edges, including bad-boy surfers and shoulder-to-shoulder oil wells.

Before Huntington Beach received its present name, the long shoreline was a popular camping spot. Millions of small clams were washed up on its sands

Long and wide—plus more fire pits than Fiji.

and old timers called it Shell Beach. In 1901, a town was laid out with the name of Pacific City, in hopes it would rival Atlantic City. In 1902, Henry E. Huntington, owner of the Pacific Electric Railroad, bought a controlling interest and renamed the city after himself.

This hike takes you north along wide sandy Huntington State Beach to Bolsa Chica State Beach and adjacent Bolsa Chica Ecological Reserve. You can also make this a one-way jaunt by taking advantage of OCTD Bus #1 which makes several stops along Pacific Coast Highway.

This is an ideal beach trail to bike and hike. A bike path extends the length of Bolsa Chica Beach to the Santa Ana River south of Huntington Beach. You can leave your bike at Bolsa Chica State Beach and hike up to it from Huntington Beach.

DIRECTIONS TO TRAILHEAD   From the San Diego Freeway (405) in Huntington Beach, exit on Beach Boulevard and travel 5.5 miles south to the boulevard's end at Huntington State Beach.

THE HIKE Walk north along the northernmost mile of the three-mile-long sandy state beach.The state beach blends into Huntington City Beach just before the pier. The beach is best known as the site of international surfing competition. Eighteen-hundred-foot Huntington Pier was built in 1914.

Beyond the pier is Bolsa Chica State Beach, The southern end has steep cliffs rising between Pacific Coast Highway and the beach. Huntington Beach Mesa or "The Cliffs" is popular with surfers and oil well drillers.

The northern three miles of the beach pack in all the facilities: showers, food concessions, picnic areas and more.

SANTA MONICA BAY STATE BEACHES: REDONDO, MANHATTAN, DOCKWEILER, SANTA MONICA

■ SANTA MONICA BAY TRAIL
20 miles one way

Fringed by palm trees, with the Santa Monica Mountains as dramatic backdrop, the wide sandy beaches along Santa Monica Bay draw visitors from around the world. Locals tend to get a bit blasé about this beauty in their backyard, and often fail to take advantage of what is, in my opinion, one of the world's great beach walks.

Favorite bay walks enjoyed by tourists include Venice Beach and the Venice Boardwalk, the Santa Monica Pier and Palisades Park in Santa Monica. The long and quite wide state beaches—Redondo, Manhattan, Dockweiler and Santa Monica—are interspersed with a number of municipal beaches and lagoons. For a really ambitious beach walk or weekend hiking holiday, I'd suggest a walk around the entire bay.

Such a walk will surely be a very long day—or a weekend-to-remember. You'll get a real feel for the bay, not only as a collection of beaches and seashore sights, but as a living, dynamic ecosystem whose health and well-being depend heavily on government and citizen action.

Geographically, Santa Monica Bay is a mellow intrusion by the Pacific Ocean into the western edge of the Los Angeles lowlands. The bay's magnificent curving beaches are cooled by a prevailing ocean breeze, which protects the coast from the temperature extremes—and smog—that are characteristic of the interior.

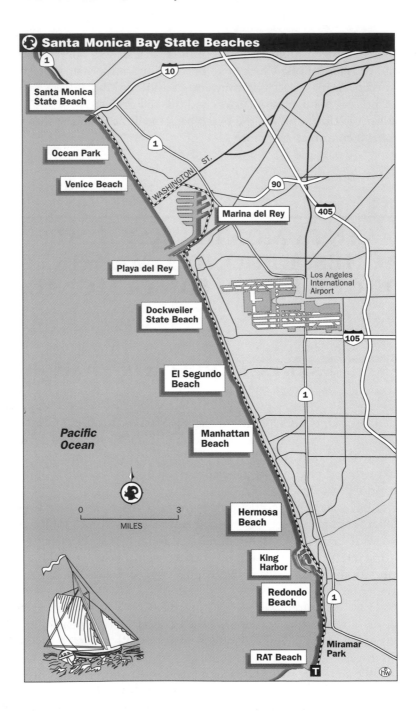

Santa Monica Bay State Beaches

Santa Monica State Beach

Ocean Park

Venice Beach

Marina del Rey

Playa del Rey

Dockweiler State Beach

El Segundo Beach

Manhattan Beach

Hermosa Beach

King Harbor

Redondo Beach

RAT Beach

Miramar Park

Pacific Ocean

Los Angeles International Airport

WASHINGTON ST.

0 3
MILES

Alas, all views along Santa Monica Bay are not picture-perfect; huge smoke-stacks from power plants tower over some South Bay beaches, while jets departing LAX fly low and loud over others. And the bay has its share of well-documented environmental problems, too. Sewers and storm drains empty into the bay. Organizations such as Heal the Bay have undertaken the Herculean task of educating the public and public officials that the bay is not merely a series of sand strands, but a complex ecosystem.

Pick a brisk fall or winter weekend to walk the bay and you'll be surprised at how much shoreline solitude you'll enjoy. It's possible to walk the bay from Torrance to the Santa Monica Pier in a very long day, but the 20 mile beach hike is more comfortably completed in two days.

If bay walking agrees with you, consider walking the rest of the bay-another 20 miles from the Santa Monica Pier to Pt. Dume.

You can arrange a car shuttle or use the bus system to return to your day's start point. Better yet, leave a bicycle at the end of your walk and cycle back to the trailhead along the South Bay Bicycle Path. Super-jocks will relish the challenge of what I call the Triathlon Trail: Walk the 20 miles from Torrance County Beach to the Santa Monica Pier, cycle the South Bay Bicycle Path, then take a long refreshing swim.

MALIBU LAGOON STATE BEACH

■ MALIBU BEACH TRAIL
1 mile round trip around Malibu Lagoon;
to Corral State Beach is 4 to 6 miles round trip

When Southern California natives say "Malibu Beach" this popular surfing spot is what they mean: the site of beach-blanket movies and Beach Boys songs. The state beach—formerly known as Surfrider—is a mixture of sand and stone. More than 200 bird species have been observed at Malibu Lagoon.

For Frederick Hastings Rindge, owner of 22 miles of Southern California coast, life in the Malibu of a century ago was divine. "The enobling stillness makes the mind ascend to heaven," he wrote in his memoir, Happy Days in Southern California, published in 1898.

Long before Malibu meant good surfing, a movie star colony and some of the most expensive real estate on earth, "The Malibu" was a shorthand name

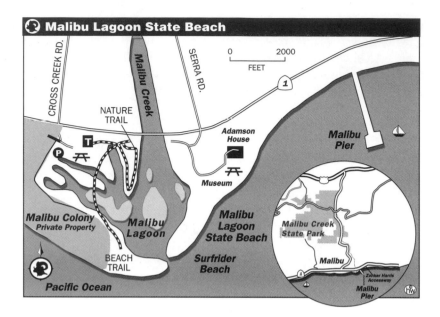

for Topanga-Malibu-Sequit, an early 19th-century rancho. This rancho extended from Topanga Canyon on the southeast to Ventura County on the northwest, from the tideline to the crest of the Santa Monica Mountains.

This beautiful locale attracted the attention of a wealthy Massachusetts businessman, Frederick Rindge, who was looking for an ideal spread "near the ocean, and under the lee of the mountains, with a trout brook, wild trees, good soil and excellent climate, one not too hot in summer."

Rindge bought the ranch and proceeded to divide his time between a townhouse in Los Angeles, from which he directed his business affairs—and his beloved rancho. The New Englander-turned-ranchero gloried in rounding up cattle, inspecting citrus groves and walking his St. Bernard along his many miles of private shoreline.

Alas for Frederick Rindge, his happy days ended rather abruptly when a 1903 fire burned his property. He died just two years later. His widow, May Rindge, decided to keep the rancho intact and to keep the public out of her coastal kingdom. Armed guards patrolled the dominion of the woman the newspapers called "The Queen of Malibu." For more than three decades, she not only stopped tourists and settlers, but blocked the state from completing Pacific Coast Highway. Eventually, however, the whole rancho was subdivided into ocean front lots and 100-acre "ranchos," as well as sites for hotels, yacht clubs and small summer homes.

Malibu Lagoon hosts many different kinds of waterfowl, both resident and migratory. The beach is rock cobble on the ocean side of the lagoon. To the landward side of the lagoon stretches the alluvial fill flatland deposited by Malibu Creek. The town of Malibu is situated here.

Across from the lagoon is a stunning California landmark, the Adamson House, a beautiful Spanish-style home built by Frederick Rindge's daughter, Rhoda Adamson. The house, built in 1929, makes lavish use of ceramic "Malibu Tile." The grounds have been restored to their former beauty with many ornamental trees and shrubs. Fountains and flagstone pathways wind through the landscaped grounds.

Adjoining the Adamson House is the Malibu Lagoon Museum, which contains a collection of artifacts and rare photographs that depict the various eras of "The Malibu," as this section of coastal Southern California was known.

DIRECTIONS TO TRAILHEAD Malibu Lagoon State Beach is located at Pacific Coast Highway and Cross Creek Road in Malibu.

THE HIKE First, follow the nature trails around the lagoon. Next, head down-coast to the historic 700-foot Malibu Pier, built in 1903. It's a favorite of anglers and tourists. Sportfishing boats depart from the pier.

Farther down-coast is Zonker Harris Accessway, long the focus of debate between the California Coastal Commission, determined to provide access to the coast, and some Malibu residents who would prefer the public stay out. The original sign read Zonker Harris Memorial Beach, honoring a character from the Doonesbury comic strip whose primary goal in life was once to acquire the perfect tan.

Up-coast, you'll pass Malibu Point; here the strong southwest swell refracts against a rock reef and creates the waves that makes Malibu so popular with surfers. Next you walk the narrow and sandy beach lined by the exclusive Malibu Colony residences, home to many a movie star. Toward the west end of The Colony, the beach narrows considerably and houses are built on stilts, with the waves sometimes pounding beneath them.

The beach is wider and more public at Corral State Beach, located at the mouths of Corral and Solstice Canyons.

MCGRATH STATE BEACH

■ MCGRATH BEACH TRAIL

From State Beach to McGrath Lake is 4 miles round trip; to Oxnard Shores is 8 miles round trip; to Channel Islands Harbor is 12 miles round trip

McGrath State Beach and McGrath Lake were named for the McGrath family, which had extensive coastal land holdings in the Ventura coastal area dating from 1874. Located on the western city limits of Oxnard, the two-mile-long state beach extends south from the Santa Clara River.

A small lake in the southern portion of the park helps to attract more than two hundred species of birds including black-shouldered kites, northern harriers, owls and herons. Such rare birds as ospreys, white wagtails, black skimmers and peregrine falcons have been sighted here. The lake, which is partially on private property, was damaged by a 1993 oil spill caused by a ruptured pipeline.

The Santa Clara Estuary Natural Preserve on the northern boundary of the park offers a haven for birds and habitat for weasels, skunks, jackrabbits, opossums, tortoises and gopher snakes. Near the state beach entry kiosk, a small visitor center features exhibits about the area's plants and wildlife.

This walk takes you on a nature trail through the Santa Clara River Estuary, visits McGrath Lake and travels miles of sandy beach to Channel Islands Harbor.

DIRECTIONS TO TRAILHEAD To reach McGrath State Beach from south-bound Highway 101, take the Seaward Avenue offramp to Harbor Blvd., turn south on Harbor and travel four miles to the park. Northbound visitors exit Highway 101 on Victoria Avenue, turn left at the light to Olivas Park Drive, then right to Harbor Blvd. Turn left on Harbor and proceed 0.75 mile to the park. The signed nature trail leaves from the day use parking lot. Signposts along the nature trail are keyed to a pamphlet, available at the entry kiosk.

THE HIKE From the parking lot, follow the nature trail through the estuary. The riverbank is a mass of lush vegetation: willow, silverweed and yerba mansa. In 1980, the Santa Clara River area was declared a natural preserve, primarily to protect the habitat of two endangered birds—the California least tern and Belding's savannah sparrow.

When you reach nature trail signpost 11, join a nearby trail that leads atop an old levee, first along the river, then down-coast along the periphery of the state beach campground. This trail joins a dirt road and continues down coast, but the far more aesthetic route is along water's edge, so trudge over the low dunes and walk along the shoreline.

Along the beach, visitors enjoy sunbathing or surf fishing for bass, corbina, or perch. In two miles, if you head inland a short ways, you'll spot McGrath Lake, tucked away behind some dunes.

As you continue south, more sandy beach and dunes follow. You pass a huge, old Edison power plant, and arrive at Oxnard Shores, a development famous for getting clobbered by heavy surf at high tide. The beach is flat and at one time was eroding at the phenomenal rate of ten feet a year. Homes were built right on the shoreline, and many have been heavily damaged. New homes are built on pilings, so the waves crash under rather than through them.

Past Oxnard Shores, a mile of beach walking brings you to historic Holly-wood Beach. The Sheik, starring that great silent movie idol Rudolph Valentino, was filmed on the desert-like sands here. Real estate promoters of the time attempted to capitalize on Oxnard Beach's instant fame and renamed it Hollywood Beach. They laid out subdivisions called Hollywood-by-the-Sea and Silver Strand, suggesting to their customers that the area was really a movie colony and might become a future Hollywood, but it never became a mecca for the stars or their fans.

This walk ends another mile down-coast at the entrance to Channel Islands Harbor.

SAN BUENAVENTURA STATE BEACH

■ BUENAVENTURA TRAIL
From Marina Park to the Ventura Pier is 4 miles round trip

When you walk San Buenaventura State Beach, you realize that this park didn't simply happen, it was designed—obviously during the state park system's pre-poverty era. Instead of the grungy tables stuck in the sand found at many beaches, San Buenaventura features wide, green picnic areas. It boasts volleyball nets, a fitness trail and even a pier.

The state beach offers plenty of room for all the popular beach activities: swimming, surfing, cycling, fishing and picnicking. It's one of Ventura County's safest spots for a swim because the sand slopes very gradually into the ocean.

Although San Buenaventura's sands are easily accessible (Harbor Boulevard extends along its inland border), the low sand dunes fringing the state beach give it a feeling of isolation from freeway traffic and sounds of the nearby city.

This San Buenaventura stroll begins at Marina Park, a family-friendly enclave perched just up-coast of Ventura Harbor's west channel. A little sandy beach, grassy hillocks and wooden windbreaks encourage spreading out the beach blanket and relaxing awhile. Children enjoy playing on the sand-locked, two-masted San Salvador, a boat load of fun, with plenty of places to climb.

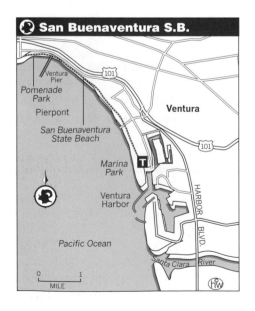

DIRECTIONS TO TRAILHEAD From Highway 101 in Ventura, exit on Seaward Avenue. Head briefly coastward and turn left (south) on Pierpoint Boulevard. Drive 0.7 mile to the boulevard's end and Marina Park.

THE HIKE From Marina Park, walk out to the end of the jetty, observe the many boats entering and leaving Ventura Harbor, then head up-coast. You can look across the harbor channel at an inviting sand strand, the southernmost segment of San Buenaventura State Beach.

The first mile of beach is fairly narrow and stabilized by a series of rock groins extending offshore. Houses line this length of shore. The second mile of beach, which sweeps toward Pierpont Bay and the Ventura Pier, is wider.

Stairs lead from the sand up to the Ventura Pier. The original pier was built way back in 1872. Today's recreational pier has a restaurant and a gift shop. Stroll past the anglers and enjoy great views of the coast and islands, as well as Ventura and its mountain backdrop.

If you want to extend your outing, promenade Promenade Park, which begins near the foot of the pier. You can continue to the Ventura County Fairgrounds or even the Ventura River.

EMMA WOOD STATE BEACH

■ OCEAN'S EDGE TRAIL

Emma Wood State Beach to Seaside Wilderness Park
is 1.3 miles round trip

Several ecological communities converge near the mouth of the Ventura River: sand dunes, a floodplain, cobblestone beach, riparian woodland and wetlands. Botanists have tallied some 300 plant species in the area; more than half of them are native.

This diversity of riverfront and oceanfront life is explored by Ocean's Edge Trail, a 12-stop interpreted nature trail.

In the early years of the last century, local naturalist E.P. Foster envisioned a world-class park like San Francisco's Golden Gate. He donated land at the Ventura River mouth to the county to create such a park. Alas, by the time the county began landscaping the area with Monterey pine, eucalyptus and palms, the Great Depression struck and the money ran out.

Instead of "Ventura's Golden Gate," the park became known as Hobo Jungle because of the many vagabonds who camped in the wetlands here. In bad weather, the hobos slept under the railroad bridge. Hobo Jungle now belongs to the city of Ventura, which renamed it Seaside Wilderness Park.

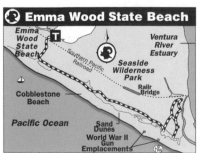

Emma Wood acquired large land holdings on the coast and coastal slope of north Ventura County, land that was originally part of Rancho San Miguelito. She died in 1944 and in the late 1950s her husband and heir gave to the state the beach west of the railroad overpass, a stretch of coast long popular with the public.

DIRECTIONS TO TRAILHEAD Emma Wood State Beach is located at the south end of old Pacific Coast Highway, north of West Main Street in Ventura. The turnoff for the Ventura River Group Camp area is just before the on-ramp to northbound Highway 101.

There's a fee for parking at the state beach. You can also park for free just outside the park and walk under the highway overpass to the group campground at the south end of the park. Signed Ocean's Edge Trail begins at an information display on the oceanside of the campground.

THE HIKE Ocean's Edge Trail takes you along Emma Wood's mixed rock and sand beach to Seaside Wilderness Park, where pine and palm trees rise above low sand dunes. The nature trail explores wetlands, including a second mouth of the Ventura River, a lagoon and sand bars.

CARPINTERIA STATE BEACH

■ CARPINTERIA BEACH TRAIL
From Carpinteria State Beach to Harbor Seal Preserve is 2.5 miles round trip; to Carpinteria Bluffs is 4.5 miles round trip; to Rincon Beach County Park is 6 miles round trip

"Safest Beach in the World," claim some Carpinteria boosters.

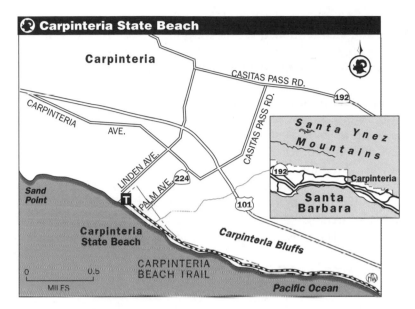

A long campaign to save the Carpinteria Bluffs, one of the last stretches of privately held, undeveloped coastline between Los Angeles and Santa Barbara, succeeded in 1998. Activists, local merchants, schoolchildren, and hundreds of Santa Barbara County citizens raised nearly $4 million to buy the bluffs from the property owner.

For more than two decades, a battle raged between development interests with plans to build huge housing and hotel projects and local conservationists who wanted to preserve the bluffs. Surfers, hikers, and birdwatchers have long enjoyed the bluffs, which rise about 100 feet above the beach and offer great views of Anacapa, Santa Cruz, and Santa Rosa islands.

Now that the bluffs are in the public domain, they are likely to add to Carpinteria's allure for coastal connoisseurs. Carpinteria residents boast they have "the safest beach in the world." Although the surf here can be large, it breaks far out and there's no undertow. As early as 1920, visitors reported "the Hawaiian diversion of surfboard riding."

The Carpinteria Tar Pits once bubbled up near the state beach. Spanish explorers noted that the Chumash caulked their canoes and sealed their cookware with the asphaltum. Around 1915, crews mined the tar, which was used to pave the coast highway in Santa Barbara County. In order to dig the tar, workmen had to heat their shovels in a furnace; the smoking tar would slice like butter with the hot blade. Long ago, the tar pits trapped mastodons, saber-toothed tigers and other prehistoric animals, Unfortunately, the pits, which might have yielded amazing fossils like those of the La Brea Tar Pits in Los Angeles, became a municipal dump.

On August 17, 1769, the Portolá expedition observed the native Chumash building a canoe and dubbed the location la carpinteria, the Spanish name for carpenter shop.

Carpinteria is one of the state park system's more popular beachfront campgrounds. A broad beach, gentle waves, fishing and clamming are among the reasons for this popularity. A tiny visitor center offers displays of marine life and Chumash history, as well as a children-friendly tidepool tank.

This beach hike heads down-coast along the state beach to City Bluffs Park and the Chevron Oil Pier. A small pocket beach contains the Harbor Seal Preserve. From December through May this beach is seals-only. Humans may quietly watch the boisterous colony, sometimes numbering as many as 150 seals, from a blufftop observation area above the beach.

After seal-watching, you can then sojourn over the Carpinteria Bluffs or contiue down the beach to Rincon Point on the Santa Barbara-Ventura county line.

DIRECTIONS TO TRAILHEAD   From Highway 101 in Carpinteria, exit on Linden Avenue and head south (oceanward) 0.6 mile through town to the avenue's end at the beach. Park along Linden Avenue (free, but time restricted) or in the Carpinteria State Beach parking lot (fee).

THE HIKE   Follow "the world's safest beach" down-coast. After a half mile's travel over the wide sand strand you'll reach state beach-bisecting Carpinteria Creek. During the summer, a sand bar creates a lagoon at the mouth of the creek. Continue over the sand bar or, if Carpinteria Creek is high, retreat inland through the campground and use the bridge over the creek.

Picnic at City Bluffs Park or keep walking a short distance farther along the bluffs past the Chevron Oil Pier to an excellent vista point above the Harbor Seal Preserve. Ambitious walkers may continue along the beach to Rincon Beach County Park, one of the area's top surfing spots on the Santa Barbara-Ventura county line.

EL CAPITAN STATE BEACH

■ EL CAPITAN BEACH TRAIL
From El Capitan to Refugio State Beach is 6 miles round trip

Monarch butterflies and mellow beaches are the highlights of this coast walk north of Santa Barbara. Autumn, when the crowds have thinned and the butterflies have arrived, is a particularly fine time to roam the coast from El Capitan State Beach to Refugio State Beach.

El Capitan is a narrow beach at the mouth of El Capitan Creek. Shading the creek is a woodland of coast live oak and sycamore. During autumn, monarch butterflies congregate and breed in the trees here. (Ask park rangers where the monarchs cluster.)

The butterflies have a distinctive coloring—brownish-red wings with black veins. The outer edges of their wings are dark brown with white and yellow spots. In October and November, the woodland of El Capitan Creek offers the twin delights of falling autumn leaves and fluttering butterflies.

"El Capitan" refers to Captain José Francisco de Ortega, a rotund Spanish Army officer who served as trail scout for the Portolá expedition. When he retired from service to the crown in 1795, he owed the army money and offered to square things by raising cattle. The government granted him his chosen land: a coastal strip, two miles wide and twenty-five miles long extending from just east of Pt. Conception to Refugio Canyon. He called his land Nuestra Señora del Refugio, "Our Lady of Refuge." Alas, Captain Ortega's retirement was short-lived; he died three years later and was buried at the Santa Barbara Mission.

After the death of El Capitán, the Ortega family continued living in Refugio Canyon for many years. The mouth of the canyon at the Pacific was the major contraband-loading point for Southern California during the early years of the 19th century when Spanish settlers were forbidden to trade with Americans. From the Ortega Ranch, hides, tallow, leather goods and wine were loaded onto Boston-bound sailing ships.

Smuggling activity came to an end in 1818 when French captain (some would say pirate) Hippoloyte de Bouchard sailed by. Bouchard, a mercenary hired by the Argentines, then struggling for independence against Spain, put ashore and burned Ortega's ranch buildings to the ground.

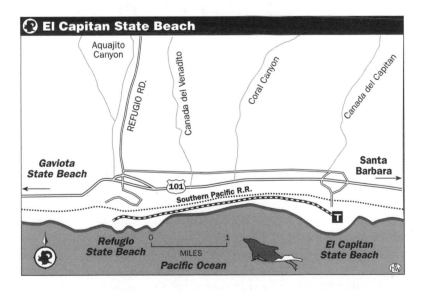

Beach, bluff and bike trails link El Capitan and Refugio state beaches. Depending on the tide, you can usually travel up-coast along El Capitan Beach as far as Coral Canyon Beach. Then you can join the bluff trails or the bike path, which is also open to hikers, for the balance of the trip to Refugio Beach.

El Capitan and Refugio are popular beach campgrounds and nice places to spend a weekend.

DIRECTIONS TO TRAILHEAD From Highway 101, 19 miles up-coast from Santa Barbara, take the El Capitan State Beach exit. Park in one of the day use areas; the park day use fee is also honored at Refugio and Gaviota state beaches.

THE HIKE Descend one of the paths or staircases to the shore, then head up-coast along the mixed sandy and rocky beach. Sea cliffs are steep here because they are constantly being cut back by wave erosion. You'll pass wide Coral Canyon, its walls covered with beds of highly deformed light-colored shales.

At Coral Beach, the tides often discourage beach-walking, so head up to the bluffs and follow the bike path.

Approaching Refugio State Beach, you'll see abundant kelp just offshore. If a breeze is blowing over the water, note how areas with kelp are smooth and kelpless areas are rippled.

Refugio State Beach, at the mouth of Refugio Canyon, is a rocky beach with tidepools. Turn around here, or continue beach-walking up-coast (it's 10 more miles to Gaviota State Beach) for as long as time and tides permit.

GAVIOTA STATE PARK

■ BEACH-TO-BACKCOUNTRY, OVERLOOK, HOLLISTER TRAILS

To Gaviota Pass Overlook is 5 miles round trip with 700-foot elevation gain; loop via Overlook and Hollister Trails is 8.5 miles round trip with 800-foot elevation gain

It would be unfair to say no one stops in Gaviota Pass. The pass hosts a Caltrans rest area, site of the only public restrooms along a 250 mile length of Highway 101 between Los Angeles and the hamlet of Bradley north of San Luis Obispo.

Most motorists who stop, and the multitudes who do not, remain oblivious to the area's historical importance and natural attractions. Too bad, because Gaviota Pass and its pathways are too good to pass up.

Most of the pass—the green scene on either side of Highway 101—is the rolling backcountry of 2,775-acre Gaviota State Park. Park trails meander across oak-dotted potreros and travel ridgetops that afford hikers grand vistas of Gaviota Pass and the wide blue Pacific.

Surely the most memorable view of the pass, to moviegoers anyway, occurs in The Graduate when lost soul Benjamin Braddock (Dustin Hoffman) drives a beautiful new Alfa Romeo through the mist and into the Gaviota Tunnel.

Explorer Gaspar de Portolá led his party through the pass in 1769. Expedition diarist, Father Juan Crespi dubbed the coastline here San Luis in honor of the King of France. However, Portolá's soldiers figured that La Gaviota, Spanish for seagull, was more appropriate.

Gaviota earned its small place in California history as a place to avoid. During the short Mexican-American War, General John C. Frémont and his 700 men were marching south toward Santa Barbara when they learned that the Spanish californio troops awaited in ambush at Gaviota Pass. American forces were led through nearby San Marcos Pass by rancher Benjamin Foxen on Christmas eve 1846. Thus, the Americans occupied Santa Barbara without bloodshed on Christmas day.

Gaviota State Park offers hiking on both sides of the pass. Eastside trail attractions include a hot springs and connections to Los Padres National Forest footpaths. On the west side of the pass, the park's trail network honeycombs a delightful backcountry and offers the hiker a number of loops of varying distances and difficulties.

DIRECTIONS TO TRAIL-HEAD From Santa Barbara, drive up-coast (west) some 30 miles on Highway 101. Just as the highway makes a dramatic bend north, you'll spot a sign for Gaviota State Park. Merge left into the left turn lane and

Don't pass on the chance to hike historic Gaviota Pass.

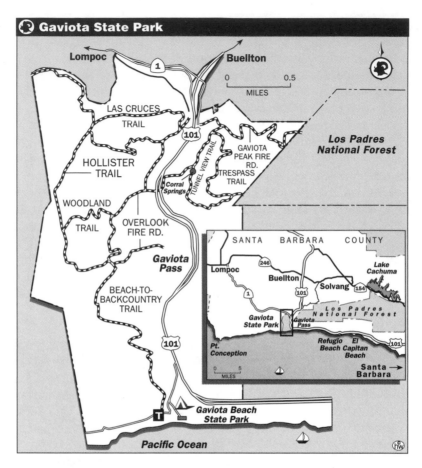

turn left across the highway onto the state park entry road. The park road leads to a kiosk (parking fee required) then down to the beach. You'll veer right before the kiosk and follow the unsigned road leading to the exclusive Hollister Ranch community. At the first bend in the road, you'll find the state park trailhead and a pullout for parking on the right.

THE HIKE Begin on the asphalt road (closed to vehicles), which leads 0.6 mile across thickets of sweet-smelling sage and fennel on a route parallel to Highway 101. Join the left-forking, signed ("Multi-Use Trail") path as it winds its way to the top of a mustard-splashed hillock. Here you can savor the first of many views of Gaviota Pass.

Next the path climbs more earnestly along a rocky ridge. Intriguing sandstone outcroppings protrude above chamise, ceanothus, manzanita and other members of the chaparral community. Just as your eye is drawn to some (inaccessible) caves across the canyon to your right, the trail deposits you at the mouth of a large cave on your left. The wind-sculpted cave is a large, open-faced recess in the rock where, it's easy to imagine, the native Chumash took shelter or early ranchers waited out the rain.

Beyond the cave, Beach-to-Backcountry Trail dips and rises another 0.5 mile or so before making a final dip to an unsigned junction with Overlook Fire Road.

A right on the fire road leads 0.5 mile to a viewpoint occupied only by a radio repeater antenna and a small concrete block building. Turkey vultures roost on nearby sandstone outcroppings, presumably taking in the same view as hikers.

A three-minute walk left on the fire road leads among grand old oaks to another unsigned junction. The fire road bends right (north) while Hollister Trail heads west. I prefer joining Hollister Trail which ascends west, then bends north along the boundary line between the state park and Hollister Ranch.

Hollister Trail travels a ridgetop and escapes the highway din that can irritate the hiker on other park trails. The trail offers great views over Hollister Ranch and the westward-extending coastline. After about 0.75 mile, the trail passes a junction (often very difficult to spot) with a right-forking connector trail that drops down to meet Overlook Fire Road.

Nearly two miles from its junction with Overlook Fire Road, Hollister Trail reaches a four-way junction. Hollister Trail ascends another 0.25 mile north to a viewpoint, then bends west to the park boundary line.

A right-forking fire road (Las Cruces Trail) descends steeply to a path near, and parallel to, Highway 101; Yucca Trail, signed on the ground but absent from park maps, also descends to this path.

Hikers can make a loop trip of this jaunt by descending on either the trail or the fire road to the footpath near Highway 101. Join an unsigned south-bound trail (overgrown in places) for 0.5 mile to meet Overlook Fire Road and ascend another 0.5 mile to a junction with Beach-to-Backcountry Trail.

LA PURÍSIMA MISSION STATE HISTORIC PARK

■ EL CAMINO REAL TRAIL
2 to 5 miles or more round trip

Of California's 21 missions, the most fully restored is La Purísima, located 4 miles north of Lompoc in northwest Santa Barbara County. La Purísima is the only mission with a sizeable amount of land preserved around it—and the only one with hiking trails.

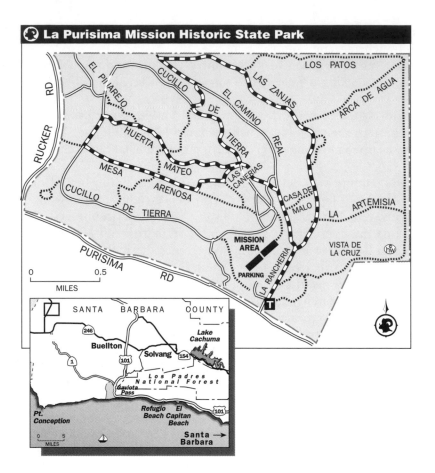

You could spend a fun day at La Purísima Mission State Historic Park in the Lompoc Valley—first heading for the Purisima Hills for a hike, then touring the mission. If you plan your visit for one of the park's "Mission Life Days" or "Purísima People Days," you'll find volunteer docents costumed as padres, soldiers and Indians and recreating mission life of the 1820s. Members of the volunteer group Prelado De Los Tesoros (Keeper of the Treasures) act out their parts well.

Wandering the thousand acres of hill and dale preserved in the state park will help you grasp that apart from the mission's religious purpose, it was a large commercial enterprise as well—early 19th-century agribusiness. You'll walk where crops were grown and cattle grazed, view the mission's far-flung waterworks system, and even see the ruts that are reminders of where the old El Camino Real passed through the mission compound.

Following secularization of the mission system, La Purísima was abandoned in 1834 and soon fell into ruin. In 1934, exactly 100 years after the padres left, the Civilian Conservation Corps began reconstructing the church and a whole complex of buildings. Other restoration projects continued intermittently ever since, and today La Purísima is the most completely restored of California's 21 missions.

Besides the church, you'll see the soldiers' barracks and the priests' quarters. On the mission grounds are reconstructions of the granary, bakery, olive press and soap factory. Pens and corrals hold Mexican sheep and cattle, similar to the breeds of the mission period. At the mission entrance is a small museum which displays historical information and artifacts recovered from the mission ruins. In a shady grove near the museum is a picnic ground.

The park trail system explores three different ecosystems. Los Berros Creek flows north-south through Purisima Canyon. West of Purisima Canyon is a large oak-dotted mesa that rises a hundred feet above the canyon floor. East of Purisima Canyon are the stream-cut Purisima Hills.

Local joggers and exercise walkers stick to the park's flatlands by joining El Camino Real, then rounding the barley fields and returning via Las Zanjas Trail. That's a circuit of about 3 miles. Hikers often use the narrower footpaths— Huerta Mateo and Mesa Arenosa Trails—and make a 2-mile loop. Add the 2 mile-loop and the 3-mile together for a fine 5-mile hike.

DIRECTIONS TO TRAILHEAD From Highway 101 in Buellton, exit on Highway 246 and head west 13.5 miles to Purisima Road. Turn right and proceed a mile to La Purísima Mission State Historic Park on your right. Limited free parking is available near the trailhead alongside Purisima Road or inside the park closer to the mission buildings (fee).

THE HIKE From Purisima Road, join La Ranchería Trail to the park museum, walk toward the picnic area, then join paved El Camino Real to signed Huerta Mateo Trail. This footpath leads over sandy terrain. Thriving in the sandy soil is coastal scrub vegetation that normally grows only on dune systems much closer to the coast. Occupying the slopes and ridge crests nearby is a flourishing oak woodland.

Stick with Huerta Mateo Trail past several signed junctions until you reach Cucillo de Tierra, a fire road. Turn left and walk a short quarter mile to signed Mesa Arenosa Trail. Down you go along this sandy trail until you reach a signed junction with Las Canerias Trail; join this path heading west 0.25 mile to wide Cucillo de Tierra Trail. You can turn right here and head back to the mission buildings; however, those hikers wishing to see more backcountry will turn left (north) and walk 0.4 mile to El Chaparral Trail, which provides a short connecting route to El Camino Real. Turn left and walk along the flat bottomland of Purisima Canyon, which has been cultivated since the construction of the mission and today supports an annual crop of wheat and barley.

El Camino Real runs out at the park boundary and you turn right (east) on Last Zanjas Trail. This path offers a lovely walk near Los Berros Creek. You'll pass a pond and portions of the old mission aqueduct as you enjoy the 1.25 mile walk back to the mission compound and the trailhead.

POINT SAL STATE BEACH

■ POINT SAL TRAIL
From State Beach to Pt. Sal is 5 miles round trip

When your eye travels down a matate beach—remote Point Sal, a nub of land north of Vandenberg Air Force Base and south of the Guadalupe Dunes. Windy Point Sal is a wall of bluffs rising 50 to 100 feet above the rocky shore. The water is crystal-clear, and the blufftops provide a fine spot to watch the boisterous seals and sea lions.

Point Sal was named by explorer George Vancouver in 1792 for Hermenegildo Sal, who was, at that time, commandante of San Francisco. The state purchased the land in the 1940s.

During the winter of 1998, portions of the 9-mile-long access road to the beach were washed out by winter rains. The road has not been repaired and remains closed to vehicles. At this writing, Point Sal State Beach is accessible only to visitors who mountain bike or hike to the beach.

Alternatively, the strong hiker can trek twelve miles (round trip) to the state beach from Rancho Guadalupe Dunes County Park located to the north of Point Sal. Bold cliffs, towering sand dunes and isolated beaches combine to offer a tableau to remember.

If you do manage to get to Point Sal State Beach, the walk north can be a challenging one–on the bluffs above rocky reefs. At low tide, you can pass around or over the reefs; at high tide the only passage is along the bluff trail. Both marine life and land life can be observed from the bluff trail. You'll pass a seal haul-out, glimpse tidepools, sight gulls, cormorant and pelicans, and per-haps see deer, bobcat and coyote on the ocean-facing slopes of the Casmalia Hills.

The trail system in the Point Sal area is in rough condition. The narrow bluff trails should not be undertaken by novice hikers, the weak-kneed or those afraid of heights. Families with small children and less experienced trekkers will enjoy beachcombing and tidepool-watching opportunities at Point Sal and the plea-sure of discovering this out-of-the-way beach.

DIRECTIONS TO TRAILHEAD (Remember to call about the road closure.) From Highway 101 in Santa Maria, exit on Betteravia Road. Proceed west past a commercial strip and then out into the sugar beet fields. Betteravia Road twists north. About eight miles from Highway 101, turn left on Brown Road. Five miles of driving on Brown Road (watch for cows wandering along the road) brings you to a signed junction; leftward is a ranch road, but you bear right on Point Sal Road, partly paved, partly dirt washboard (impassable in wet weather). Follow this road 5 miles to its end at the parking area above Point Sal State Beach.

THE HIKE From the parking area, follow one of the short steep trails down to the beautiful crescent-shaped beach. Hike up-coast along the windswept beach. In 0.3 mile, you'll reach the end of the beach at a rocky reef, difficult to negotiate at high tide. A second reef, encountered shortly after the first, is equally difficult. Descend carefully to the beach.

Unless it's very low tide, you'll want to begin following the narrow bluff trail above the reefs. The trail arcs westward with the coast, occasionally dipping down to rocky and romantic pocket beaches sequestered between reefs.

About 1.5 miles from the trailhead, you'll descend close to shore and begin boulder-hopping. After a few hundred yards, you'll begin to hear the bark of sea lions and get an aviator's view of Lion Rock, where the gregarious animals bask in the sun. Also be on the lookout for harbor seals, often called leopard seals because of their silver, white, or even yellow spots.

Your trek continues on a pretty decent bluff trail, which dips down near a sea lion haul-out. (Please don't approach or disturb these creatures.) You'll then ascend rocky Point Sal. From the point, you'll view the Guadalupe Dunes complex to the north and the sandy beaches of Vandenberg Air Force Base to the south. Before returning the same way, look for red-tailed hawks riding the updrafts and admire the ocean boiling up over the reefs.

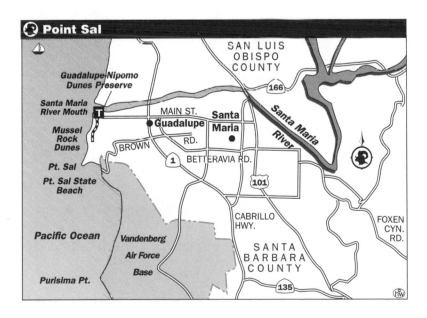

California's Water World: Caswell Memorial State Park on the banks of the Stanislaus River (above) and Brannan Island State Recreation Area (below).

CHAPTER FOUR

CENTRAL VALLEY

F ive hundred miles long, the Central Valley, or the Great Central Valley as it is known, is one of the richest agricultural regions in the world, some 25,000 square miles of farms and fields, levees and reservoirs, towns and cities.

Just how cultivated is the Valley? Fully 25 percent of all table food in the U.S. is grown here. If the Valley were a state it would rank fourth in farming behind Iowa, Illinois and Texas.

The Central Valley is commonly divided into the Sacramento Valley in the north and the San Joaquin Valley in the south. The Sacramento and San Joaquin rivers converge in the Delta, a complication of marshes, sloughs, channels and canals fed by trillions of gallons of water. Much of the Delta has been diked and dammed but like the rivers that nourish it, it has some places untamed by agriculture and waterworks projects.

The waters of the Sacramento River and its tributaries, which drain the Sacramento Valley, are collected in such mega-reservoirs as Lake Oroville and Folsom Lake; these lakes offer abundant water-oriented recreation, as well as some shoreline hiking.

The Sacramento River itself hosts a couple of parks with riverside trails, including Woodson Bridge State Recreation Area and Colusa-Sacramento State Recreation Area.

High Sierra snowmelt flows west in a network of rivers to the San Joaquin Valley. Supplying water for agriculture—and for a little fun, too—are Turlock and Millerton lakes.

Before the San Joaquin Valley was cleared for cultivation, it was dotted with woodland. Most of this woodland has disappeared, but at Caswell Memorial State Park, hikers can explore an oak woodland on the banks of the Stanislaus River.

The valley isn't all that easy for the hiker to explore. One consideration is the Valley's climate—too hot in the summer, too wet and cold in the winter; it's nearly perfect for agriculture of course, but much less so for walking. Along with the heat and cold, visitors and residents must contend in winter and spring with the radiation fog, more commonly called the tule fog or valley fog.

Some of the ecological essence of the valley remains in the form of state parks and preserves. You have to work a little harder to get to the heart of the Great Central Valley, but your efforts will be rewarded with some memorable vistas and superb waterbird-watching.

MILLERTON LAKE STATE RECREATION AREA

■ SOUTH SHORE TRAIL
From South Bay Picnic Area to the park marina is 4 miles round trip

Millerton Lake, seemingly located in the middle of nowhere but actually situated in what is almost the exact geographic middle of California, draws a lot of Middle America to its shores: boaters, fishermen, water-skiers, campers, and hikers. While millions rush by the lake on the way to Yosemite, as many as three quarters of a million folks a year visit this recreation area 20 miles northeast of Fresno.

The state park has Gold Tours, with a chance to pan for gold, on Saturdays during November and March. On December, January and February Saturdays, the park offers Eagle Tours; visitors board boats and glimpse wintering bald eagles, as well as dozens of other bird species.

Just as the San Joaquin River flows down from the High Sierra foothills into the Central Valley, it's dammed. Friant Dam was built across the river canyon in 1944, thus creating Millerton Lake.

The lake inundated the historic town of Millerton. The town evolved from an Army camp, Fort Miller, established to battle the local Yokut Indians, angered by the intrusion of settlers and 49ers on their territory. The small town of Millerton grew and served for awhile as the Fresno County seat, complete with an impressive courthouse built in 1867.

As Millerton Lake began to fill, preservationists rescued the courthouse by dismantling it and rebuilding it on higher ground. The courthouse, built of massive granite blocks, includes the reconstructed offices of the tax collector, sheriff, and assessor. It's open to visitors.

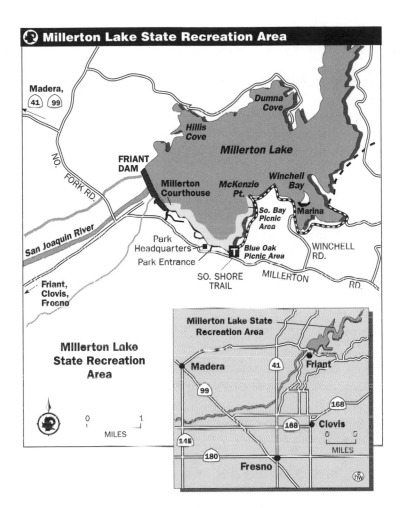

Millerton Lake measures about a mile wide near the damsite, three miles wide at its widest point. The lake backs up 16 miles into its river canyon.

Hikers heading for the hills surrounding the lake will find grassland, chaparral and oak woodland environments. The best hike is South Shore Trail, sometimes called Winchell Ridge Trail, which follows the contours of Winchell Bay on its way to the Marina at Winchell Bay. The trail extends some four miles from Blue Oak Camp Picnic Area to its end a bit past the marina. Because the first half of the trail closely parallels the road (on the inland side of the road no less), most hikers will find the second half of South Shore Trail more satisfying and begin the walk at South Bay Picnic Area.

DIRECTIONS TO TRAILHEAD From Highway 99 in Fresno, take Highway 41 north and proceed 20 miles to the Highway 145 turnoff. Follow the signs 5 miles east to the main park entrance on the south shore of Millerton Lake State Recreation Area. The park road follows the lakeshore to Blue Oak Picnic

Area, where there's trailhead parking. Start your hike here or, better yet, continue another two miles to South Bay Picnic Area.

THE HIKE From the picnic area, the trail turns east to round McKenzie Point. It's mellow walking with little elevation gain, as the path contours over oak-dotted grassy slopes.

The Upper Sonoran Life Zone around Millerton Lake is what botanists call the foothills: lots of oaks—blue, live and valley—plus the occasional grey pine and some chaparral.

You'll get fine vistas of the lake, as well as over-the-shoulder views of the Millerton Courthouse. After skirting Winchell Bay, you'll reach the marina, a no-nonsense facility that holds little interest for the hiker. Signs help walkers stay on the trail, which crosses Winchell Road just below another park entrance station and continues a bit farther along the lakeshore before passage is forbidden due to private property issues.

SAN LUIS RESERVOIR STATE RECREATION AREA

■ LONE OAK TRAIL, BASALT CAMPGROUND TRAIL, PATH OF THE PADRES
1.5 to 6 miles round trip

San Luis Reservoir, one of the mega-reservoirs of the California State Water Project, is actually three different bodies of water: the main reservoir, O'Neill Forebay and Los Baños Reservoir. The big reservoir's somewhat obscure claim-to-fame is that it's the largest reservoir in the U.S. that isn't an integral part of a river or creek. You can learn more about San Luis Reservoir and California's cyclopean waterworks system at Romero Visitors Center, just off Highway 152 on the northeast side of the reservoir.

Fishing is the state recreation area's most popular activity, followed by sailboarding, camping and picnicking. For hikers, the best time to visit is spring, when the usually brown hills turn green and are brightened by such wildflowers as California poppies, tidytips and larkspur. If you arrive in summer, expect

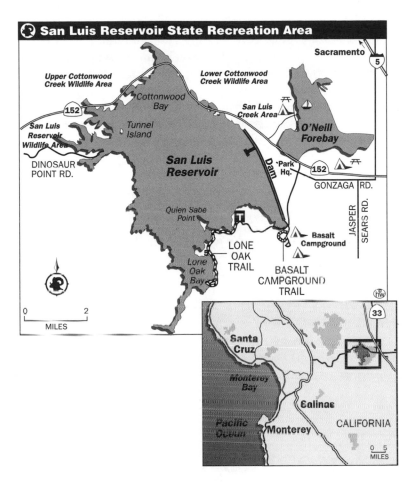

temperatures in the 90s, or even more than 100 degrees. In winter, frequent tule fogs blanket the area.

"Path of the Padres" is the name of a popular guided hike conducted during springtime weekends at San Luis Reservoir State Recreation Area. The boat tour and five mile hike retraces part of the trail taken by Spanish missionaries and soldiers who marched this way in 1805 gathering up the native Yokut to work on Mission San Luis Bautista lands.

Usually valley locals snap up all the tickets for these guided tours; visiting hikers, however, can embark on a self-guided tour of where the padres walked by joining the trail at North Rim Drive. The route utilizes a lakeshore trail around Salt Springs Cove, then heads alongside Los Baños Creek. Your self-guided tour, absent the boat ride up the creek, will be about double the five miles of the guided trip. The trail visits one of the state's largest sycamore groves and climbs to a ridgetop overlook for views of the western San Joaquin Valley.

Lone Oak Bay Trail (6 miles round trip) explores the oak-dotted lakeshore on the reservoir's south side. Golden eagles and red-tailed hawks are frequently sighted from this trail which offers excellent views of the lake. In spring, California poppies, bush lupine, tidytips, goldfields and Chinese Houses brighten the grassy slopes above the lake.

To begin this trail, follow the park road two miles from Basalt Campground. Just before the road ends at a boat launch site, turn onto a signed dirt road leading to the trailhead.

DIRECTIONS TO TRAILHEAD   The various units of the reservoir are reached off Highway 152, some two miles west of Interstate 5 and 10 miles west of the town of Los Baños.

THE HIKE   Basalt Campground Trail (1.5 mile loop) is a combination footpath/service road offering hilltop views. Join this trail near the entrance to Basalt Campground.

The path climbs grassy slopes for 0.75 mile to a viewpoint of the reservoir, San Joaquin Valley and Basalt Hill. An interpretive exhibit with a map points out the highlights visible from the viewpoint.

Millions of tons of basalt, the volcanic rock found hereabouts, was used in construction of San Luis Dam during the 1960s. You descend the hill to a park service road that returns you to the trailhead.

PACHECO STATE PARK

■ SPIKES PEAK, SOUTH BOUNDARY, CANYON LOOP, PIG POND TRAILS
To Spikes Peak is 5.5 miles round trip with 500-foot elevation gain

The trees are a tip-off that it gets mighty windy in Pacheco State Park. Squat, flag-shaped oaks bow to the east, sculpted by the prevailing winds into picturesque poses.

An even more obvious wind indicator than the stunted oaks are the multitude of wind turbines strategically placed on Pacheco's ridges. During the March through October "wind season," Pacheco Pass is a veritable wind tunnel that whirls the propellers of nearly 200 windmills.

Reflections of pastoral Pacheco.

Pacheco State Park earns a portion of the revenue from the 21 million kilowatts a year generated by the private utility that owns the windmills. Thanks to this revenue, Pacheco is a rarity in California's impoverished state park system—a park that actually has adequate funds for its maintenance.

Pacheco is located at an environmental crossroads of the coast range, Diablo Range and the San Joaquin Valley. Blue oaks and valley oaks dot the park's grassy slopes. Botanists have counted some 15 species of native grasses in the park.

Although Pacheco seems far removed from the coast, the Pacific plays a significant role in the area's odd weather. An indentation in Monterey Bay that puts the Pacific only 50 miles as the gull flies from the park, the park's location at a gap between mountain ranges, and strong westerly winds all combine to bring heavy coastal fog to the park during hot summer days.

Pacheco is a fairly dry park, though you might guess otherwise from the number of lakes depicted on the park map. Nun, Diamond, Bear's Hide, Wolf, Dinosaur, Mammoth and many more lakes are actually tiny reservoirs, originally created to serve as cattle watering ponds.

Hikers frequently spot mule deer, ground squirrels, black-tailed hares and feral pigs in the park. More elusive animals include badgers, skunks, gophers and voles.

The land around Pacheco Pass was originally part of a 48,000-acre Mexican land grant deeded to Juan Perez Pacheco in 1843. The Pacheco family soon built a tiny adobe fortress near a waterhole at the base of Pacheco Pass.

Rancho San Luis Gonzaga stayed in the family for a century. Paula Fatjo, a San Francisco debutante and fifth-generation descendant of the Pachecos, moved into the adobe fort-turned ranch headquarters in 1948. She desired to live the life of a rustic ranchero in emulation of her 19th-century relatives.

Unfortunately for Fatjo's pastoral way of life, the state of California began construction of the mammoth San Luis Reservoir and Fatjo was forced to sell her soon-to-be-underwater ranch to the state in 1963. She then relocated her ranch, historic adobe and all, 12 miles west from the top of Pacheco Pass.

Given the shabby treatment of Fatjo by state government, it speaks well of her character and generous spirit that, upon her death in 1992, she bequeathed her ranch to the state of California as a state park "for the protection, maintenance and fostering of natural flora and fauna."

Paula Fatjo's funky 1960s-era ranch house is a mixture of adobe and wood frame construction wrapped around a mobile home. Murals with wildlife themes decorate the walls. Nearby stand two crumbling walls (seriously damaged in Fatjo's forced move), all that remain of the Pacheco family's 1846 adobe.

An extensive network of former ranch roads comprises the park's trail system. Paths and junctions are well-signed. Rangers suggest that first-time visitors trek to the top of Spikes Peak, the park's 1,927-foot high point, for a good overview of the park. Reward for the climb is a 360-degree panorama from the San Joaquin Valley to the snowy crest of the Sierra Nevada.

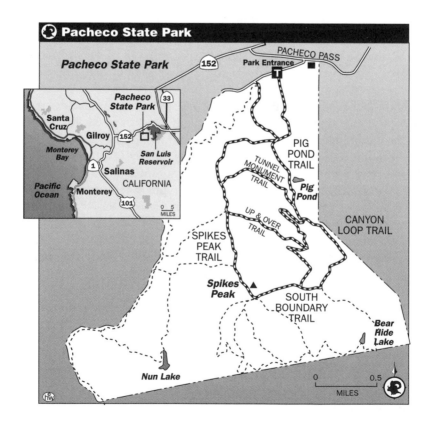

DIRECTIONS TO TRAILHEAD From Highway 101 in Gilroy, exit on Highway 152 and travel 24 miles east. Turn right (south) on Dinosaur Point Road and proceed 0.4 mile to the entrance for Pacheco State Park. Follow the park's short gravel road to a parking area and main trailhead.

From Interstate 5, you can also reach the park by taking the Highway 152 exit near Los Baños and traveling west to the state park.

THE HIKE Join signed Spikes Peak Trail (a dirt road) heading south. Pass through a gate and walk along a fence separating hikers from bovine park users and their pasture lands.

After 0.5 mile, Spikes Peak Trail bends west and soon passes signed junctions with both the north and south segments of Pig Pond Trail (your return route). The path climbs grassy hills, soon serving up views of historic Pacheco Pass to the north and a few dozen windmills positioned on breezy slopes to the east.

Keep climbing south with Spikes Peak Trail as it passes junctions with three east-west trending paths: Tunnel Monument Trail, Up & Over Trail and Spring Ridge Trail. A last 0.3 mile climb past the junction with Spring Ridge Trail brings you to the crest of Spikes Peak.

It's a modest promontory, but one with great clear day views: Fremont Peak to the southwest, Pacheco Peak to the west and Mt. Hamilton to the northwest, the snowy Sierra Nevada to the east.

From the summit, descend on signed South Boundary Loop Trail 0.4 mile east to a junction with Canyon Loop Trail and join this path as it drops north into a lovely oak-filled draw. The path zig-zags past junctions with Up & Over Trail and the eastern leg of the Canyon Loop Trail before joining Pig Pond Trail.

True to its name, the trail soon passes a pond named for the feral porkers and continues north to meet Spikes Peak Trail. (You can retrace your early steps by following this dirt road 0.7 mile back to the trailhead.)

For a different return route of about the same distance, briefly travel east on Spikes Peak Trail, then resume a northward course by getting back on Pig Pond Trail. As you approach park headquarters, you'll need to hop a low barbed wire fence, then walk through a cow pasture.

Stroll over to the historic ranch buildings and view Paula Fatjo's ranch house and the Pacheco family adobe. Hike 0.1 mile along the park access road back to the trailhead.

TURLOCK LAKE STATE RECREATION AREA

■ TUOLUMNE TRAIL
0.5 mile or so round trip

Bordered on the north by the Tuolumne River and on the south by Turlock Lake, the State Recreation Area offers many opportunities for outdoor recreation: boating, fishing, swimming, waterskiing on the lake; plus walking, camping, and blackberry picking along the river.

By the time the Tuolumne has flowed from Yosemite National Park into Hetch Hetchy Reservoir, then down the Sierra Nevada foothills into Don Pedro Reservoir, then finally to the San Joaquin Valley, it's a tame river indeed. But this tributary of the San Joaquin River still has places that display the kind of native plant life that was once common along the banks of the great rivers of the valley.

One such place is the mile of state property along the Tuolumne, where a tangle of blackberries and wild grape grow at the river's edge, accompanied by wildflowers and Woodwardia ferns.

It's not a completely natural environment, however; along the river and nearby slough are miles of piles of dredger tailings, the byproduct of a half-century of gold extraction on the river by La Grange Dredging Company. The company dredged about eight miles of the Tuolumne and extracted several million dollars worth of gold before shutting down operations in 1952.

Trails have been cut (and made by use) to the river's edge by blackberry fanciers, who enjoy picking the native fruit from July through October. The paths, which receive little or no maintenance and are overgrown, explore a woodsy environment around the campground, between the river and the lake. Not only are the paths poor, but access is difficult; there's no day use area on the river side of the park. Best bet is to ask rangers if you can leave your car near the park entrance station and walk into the campground where the trail begins.

DIRECTIONS TO TRAILHEAD From Highway 99 in Modesto, drive east on Highway 132 (Yosemite Boulevard) some 21 miles to Camp Road. Turn right, cross the Tuolumne River on an old iron bridge, fork left onto Lake Road, and drive 10 miles to Turlock Lake State Recreation Area. The lake is on the south side of the road; the campground, Tuolumne River, and the brief hiking trail are on the north side of the road.

THE HIKE You'll pick up the unmarked trail at Campsite 6. The hiking is improvisational; wander at will as far as your energy and the condition of the trail allow. Eventually your passage will be halted by blackberry thickets.

GREAT VALLEY GRASSLANDS STATE PARK

■ GRASSLANDS TRAIL
6 mile loop

The Great Central Valley is known nationally—even internationally as one of the world's most productive agricultural regions. It is not, however, known for its parks.

City-dwellers speeding along Interstate 5 or Highway 99 through the Central Valley often get the impression the region is one gigantic corporate farm, with every single acre under cultivation.

Yet some wild areas remain, reminders of days long gone when the deer and the antelope played on a vast grassland. A well-deserved pat on the back goes to the California Department of Parks and Recreation, whose Sacramento planners and field personnel have worked for several decades to set aside some pre-tractor terrain. The agency has acquired parkland in both parts of the Central Valley—the Sacramento Valley to the north and the San Joaquin Valley to the south—and tried to emphasize the region's unique natural attractions, as well as its special historic and cultural background.

One before-the-plow parcel well worth a visit is Great Grasslands State Park, located in the San Joaquin Valley some 25 miles west of Merced. A native bunchgrass prairie, vernal pools and a slow, lazy length of the San Joaquin River are highlights of the park. Great Grasslands seems even larger than its 2,700 acres because it's bordered by state and federal wildlife refuges.

The remote park, a combination of two heretofore obscure state units known as San Luis Island and Fremont Ford State Recreation Area, is visited mostly by locals who come to fish for bass and catfish from the banks and sand bars of the San Joaquin River.

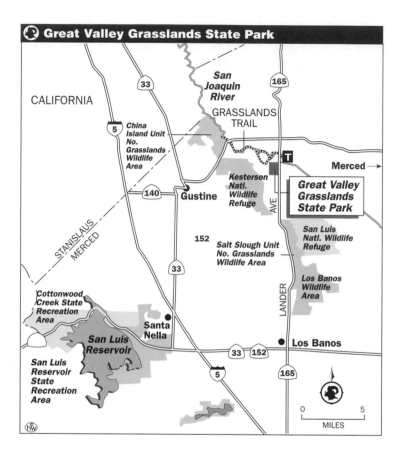

By linking a couple of levee roads (closed to vehicles), hikers can fashion a six mile tour of the great grassland, as well as the willow- and cottonwood-lined San Joaquin River that winds slowly, in a series of sloughs and oxbows, through it.

DIRECTIONS TO TRAILHEAD   From Interstate 5, 11 miles north of Santa Nella, take the Highway 140 exit. Drive 19 miles east to Highway 165. Travel 1.2 miles south on Highway 165 to the state park's fishing access on the San Joaquin River, then another 0.2 mile south of the San Joaquin River to a gate on the west side of the highway. The trail is the levee road beyond the gate.

THE HIKE   Walk the levee, overlooking the San Joaquin River to the north and sweeping grassland to the south. A half mile out, observe the large (in springtime) vernal pool, frequented by ducks and migratory waterfowl. One mile from the start is an unsigned junction. Head right, continuing to parallel the San Joaquin. After another mile and a half, the levee road turns south, away from the San Joaquin, then a mile farther still, turns east. The levee gets lower, the grass gets higher, and the hiker soon feels wrapped in very special world where the silence is broken only by the rustling of the grass.

Four-and-a-half miles out, you reach a junction and bear left on a flat gravel path back toward the San Joaquin River. After walking 0.5 mile, you reach this hike's first junction; bear right and retrace your steps a mile back to the trailhead.

CASWELL MEMORIAL STATE PARK

■ OAK FOREST TRAIL
1 mile or so round trip, plus optional longer walks

Before the San Joaquin Valley was cleared for cultivation, it was dotted with hardwood forests. Most of these woodlands have vanished, but at Caswell Memorial State Park, a remnant oak forest is preserved, a reminder of how the great valley appeared in days gone by.

Along the Stanislaus River banks is a thriving grove of valley oaks. Some splendid specimens stand 60 feet high and are 17 feet around.

Most visitors come to Caswell for the bass (striped, largemouth and smallmouth) fishing. The park's beach and swimming areas are popular on summer days.

The park also offers an opportunity to exit busy highways 99 and I 5 and stretch your legs. Walkers will find a historical plaque commemorating Indian leader Estanislaos (Stanislaus River and County namesake) who, in 1829, won a skirmish or two against a band of Mexican soldiers, before the full weight of the Mexican army crushed his insurrection.

Spring and fall are the most comfortable times to meander Oak Forest Nature Trail through stands of valley oak, then along the Stanislaus River. Heed all warning signs and stay well away from the nesting birds.

DIRECTIONS TO TRAILHEAD From Highway 99, some 10 miles north of Modesto, take the Ripon exit. Follow West Main Street through the little town, then past kiwi groves and produce stands to Austin Road. Turn left and travel 2.5 miles to the park. The trail departs from the park's day use area.

THE HIKE The nature trail once was an interpreted path, but isn't any longer. Instead, the walker will find a path that loop the loops through tangles of wild grape and blackberry bushes on the banks of the Stanislaus. Rangers conduct nature walks on Saturday mornings during the summer months.

The hiking is strictly improvisational; loop as long as you wish (you could actually get a few miles of hiking along the river and through the woods) before returning to the parking area or the park's swimming beach.

BRANNAN ISLAND
STATE RECREATION AREA

■ SEVEN MILE SLOUGH TRAIL
1 mile round trip

It's California's Waterworld, a thousand miles of rivers, sloughs, dams, dikes, lakes and levees. The Sacramento-San Joaquin Delta is both a region of rich farmland and a popular water sports recreation area.

Boating, fishing and water-skiing are popular Delta activities. Birdwatchers flock to the area and set their sights on the large wintering bird population.

One popular base for exploring the Delta is Brannan Island State Recreation Area, located some 40 miles south of Sacramento. The area is bordered by the Sacramento River, and Three Mile and Seven Mile sloughs.

Franks Tract, a large lake that's part of the state recreation area, also attracts the water sports crowd. Little Franks Tract is a protected wetland, crucial habitat for otters and waterfowl.

Brannan Island is typical of other Delta "islands." In an effort to create farmland from marshland, settlers channeled creeks and rivers and built dams and levees. In this way, many dry land islands were created. Some of these one-time marsh areas would be submerged if levee management ceased and nature was allowed to take its course.

A small visitor center has interpretive displays and publications that highlight Delta wildlife and history.

The walk through the state recreation area follows the levee above Three Mile Slough. For a longer (6 mile round trip) levee walk, head south along Seven Mile Slough to Three Mile Slough, and then on to the Sacramento River. The route, a combination of paved and dirt paths, leads to Highway 160 where Three Mile Slough merges with the Sacramento River.

DIRECTIONS TO TRAILHEAD From the intersection of Highways 12 and 160 on the east shore of the Sacramento River (across the river from the town of Rio Vista) head south on Highway 160 three miles to Brannan Island State Recreation Area. Drive past the campground and a boulevard of boat ramps to parking near the Seven Mile Slough swimming area.

THE HIKE Briefly join the bike path, leaving it to follow a dirt trail through the slough-side picnic area. You'll continue 0.25 mile above the willows and cattails to a fishing pier. Another 0.25 mile brings you to the end of the park road, the end of the slough (the path circles around to the other side) and ultimately the end of the trail.

DELTA MEADOWS
STATE RECREATION AREA

■ DELTA MEADOWS TRAIL
2 miles round trip

Tucked in the well-watered tail of Sacramento County near the Moke-
lumne and Sacramento rivers, Delta Meadows State Recreation Area
offers a quiet place to hike and canoe. The sleepy backwaters here attract
anglers, houseboaters, and those who just like to sit back and watch the river
flow.

Close to the park is the historic hamlet of Locke, built in 1915 by Chinese
workers who worked on the regions, farms, railroads and extensive levee system.
Chinese-Americans still make up most of the population of Locke.

DIRECTIONS TO TRAILHEAD From Interstate 5, some 20 miles south of
Sacramento, exit on Twin Cities Road and travel 5 miles west to intersect County Road E-13. Turn south and drive 2.5 miles to the hamlet of Locke (0.5 mile
north of Walnut Grove). Just before the road crosses Cross Channel Bridge,
turn left. Make another left onto the park's dirt road and proceed a short quarter mile to a primitive boat launch on the right. Parking is along the edge of the
park road.

THE HIKE The undeveloped park is a narrow corridor of land alongside Railroad Slough. Lively otters, beavers and muskrats inhabit the slough and shores.
Along the banks of the slough grow oaks, cottonwood and tules. Scads of trailside blackberries offer a summertime treat.

The park's dirt road follows an former railroad grade a bit more than a mile
through the park. A footpath parallels the road and extends alongside Railroad
Slough.

FOLSOM LAKE
STATE RECREATION AREA

■ WESTERN STATES TRAIL
From Rattlesnake Bar to Horseshoe Bar is 3 miles round trip

Closest to a metropolitan area of all the big reservoir parks, Folsom Lake attracts four million visitors a year. Situated in the Sierra Nevada foothills, just 25 miles from Sacramento, the lake is popular with those who like to camp, water-ski, boat, swim and fish.

Especially fish. Skillful anglers hook trout, catfish, large and small mouth bass, perch and Kokanee.

Folsom Lake, formed by Folsom Dam, has 75 miles of shoreline. The dam is located near the confluence of the North and South forks of the American River; this has created two long arms extending deep into the foothills with a peninsula in between.

In a popular state recreation area like Folsom Lake, rangers have lots of law enforcement duties; they've even been known to hold "VFW" reunions—that's Veterans of Folsom Wars.

Still, even the most law-and-order-style rangers like to point out the natural beauty of the 6,000 or so acres of land around the lake. Oak woodland and

Contemplate the long north arm of Folsom Lake from trailside vista points.

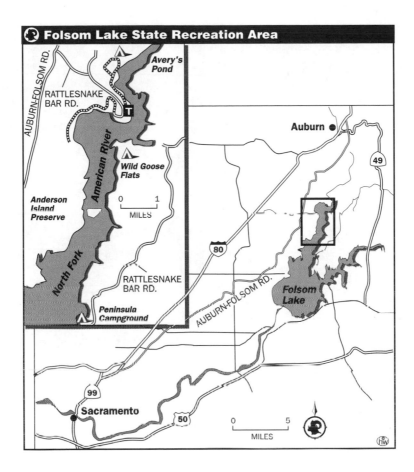

grassland sprinkled with spring wildflowers are part of the intriguing terrestrial habitat.

Hikers and horseback riders enjoy the park's 80 miles of trail. One stretch is part of the Western States Pioneer Express Trail between Carson City, Nevada and Sacramento. This path also connects Folsom Lake with Auburn State Recreation Area.

Folsom has a number of environmental camps that are only accessible by foot, boat or bicycle.

The more isolated hiking is along the North Fork and the South Fork of the America River, two long arms of Folsom Lake. Trails north and south from Folsom Dam also offer some good walking.

One fine stretch of Western States Trail is between Rattlesnake Bar and Horseshoe Bar. The "bars" refer to wide turns in the river where miners often found gold.

There's enough lake traffic to remind you you're hiking in a giant recreation area, but not so much that you can't enjoy a natural experience.

Horseback riders, too, enjoy Western States Trail.

DIRECTIONS TO TRAILHEAD   From Auburn-Folsom Road (which runs between its two namesake communities on the west side of the lake), turn east on Horseshoe Bar Road and follow it to its end at a gravel road, a parking area for horse trailers.

THE HIKE   Before entering the woods, the path meanders a meadowland and offers a curious sight: palm trees. On a humid day, you can imagine you're on a tropical isle.

The trail ascends into a woodland and crosses a wooden bridge over a creek flowing into the lake. Notice the tangles of wild grape hanging from the trees.

For the first mile and a half, the main trail (wider than a couple of confusing side paths along the way) rises and falls a few times, passing close to some private property and fence lines.

The trail reaches a somewhat level area by the water. Turn around here or continue with the lakeside trail for a few more miles.

AUBURN STATE RECREATION AREA

■ WESTERN PIONEER TRAIL
From Ruck-a-Chucky Campground to rapids is 4 miles
round trip

The dam builders didn't get their way on the American River.

In 1967, construction began on Auburn Dam, which would have turned the gorges and canyons along this stretch of the river into Auburn Lake. But a Montana dam, similar in design to the one under construction at Auburn, collapsed. This incident, along with conservation efforts by such groups as Friends of the River, put a halt to the project. The federal Bureau of Reclamation then allowed the state of California to use a portion of the river as a recreation area.

Since it's possible, though unlikely, the project could be revived (the dam was conceived in the 1940s and a few die-hard locals have been pushing for its construction ever since), no expensive roads or facilities have been constructed in the 30,000-acre recreation area; any such improvements would be covered by water if Auburn Lake came into existence.

Fishing, river-rafting, hiking and camping are popular activities at the park, which is located along more than 30 miles of the North and Middle Forks of the American River. Rafting excursions are available by commercial tour operators.

Folsom, one of the state's big reservoir parks and part of California's vast waterworks system, seems very much a part of the Central Valley; however, adjacent Auburn, sans dam, has a wilder vibe and seems more closely linked with the nearby Gold Country parks. Scenic Highway 49 winds through the recreation area and offers a glimpse of the sharp canyons and rugged countryside characteristic of the Mother Lode foothills.

A major part of the recreation area's 58 mile trail system is the Western Pioneer Trail, which travels from Sacramento to Lake Tahoe. Weekend backpackers can pitch a tent at a number of trail camps along the river.

Trail information and permits are available at a field office, located just off Highway 49, one-half mile south of the Auburn city limits.

Rangers recommend a stretch of trail along the river from Ruck-a-Chucky Campground to the Ruck-a-Chucky rapids. Early spring wildflowers brighten the pathway. Ruck-A-Chucky got its name from late 1800s gold miners, who found the "rotten chuck" served at most mining camps hard to digest. Over the years, this slang became the even more colorful ruck-a-chucky.

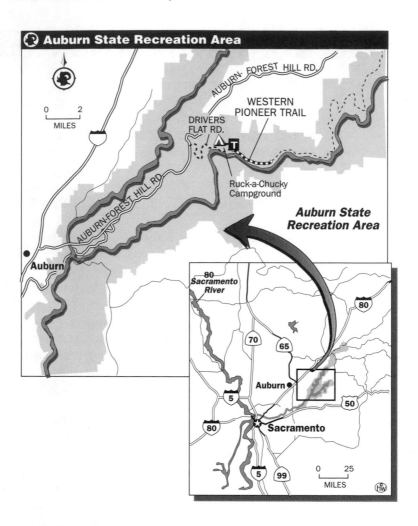

DIRECTIONS TO TRAILHEAD   From Interstate 80 on the outskirts of Auburn, exit on Auburn-Foresthill Road and head east eight miles. Turn right on dirt Drivers Flat Road (bumpy, but suitable for passenger cars with good ground clearance) and proceed 2.5 miles to Ruck-a-Chucky Campground and road's end at the trailhead. Note: Drivers Flat Road may be closed during inclement weather.

THE HIKE   From the signed trailhead, follow the closed road along the "warm side" of the river. The American River, which has its headwaters in the deep snows of the Sierra Nevada, has deposited quite a collection of sand, rounded cobblestones and great boulders en route, and carved an impressive canyon here as well.

The mighty American River broke off and carried away bits of gold from upstream quartz veins. It was this placer gold that brought 10,000 miners to the area, shortly after its discovery on the south fork of the river in 1848.

As you look down at the river, you might spot a merganser, one of those large diving ducks common on the American River. If you look up high above the river banks, you might see some little platforms marked by rock walls; Gold Rush-era miners lived way up there.

Ruck-a-Chucky rapids is not a stretch of river that sane river-rafters run, so there is a portage trail that leads along the banks to get around the rapids. A lookout point over the rapids is a good turnaround point. For a longer hike, you can continue another two miles to Fords Bar.

COLUSA-SACRAMENTO RIVER STATE RECREATION AREA

■ NATURE, LEVEE TRAILS
1 mile loop nature trail, plus 1.5 to 3 miles along levee

Campers, boaters, fishermen and hikers who enjoy this delightful park on the west side of the Sacramento River rarely can guess the previous use of the land now included in a state recreation area. It was—literally—a dump. The dump was filled, graded, and improved and in 1964 the area was opened as a park.

The area's climate, generous rains and fertile soil attracted scores of farmers, particularly after the Gold Rush when thousands of settlers homesteaded along the banks of the Sacramento River. One 19th-century writer, Charles Howard Shinn, enthused: "At Colusa, raisin plantations and stone fruit orchards appear like islands in an ocean of wheat." Today the Colusa area's foremost crop is rice.

The Sacramento, lined by cottonwoods and willows, wild grapes and figs, may look placid as a lake, but in winter the river often becomes a raging torrent. Great quantities of silt, which helps create some of the richest farmland in the nation, is left behind after flood season. Sometimes the park's boat ramp and picnic ground end up covered with mud. The park is a nice place for fishing off the riverbank or as a base for fishing expeditions up and downriver.

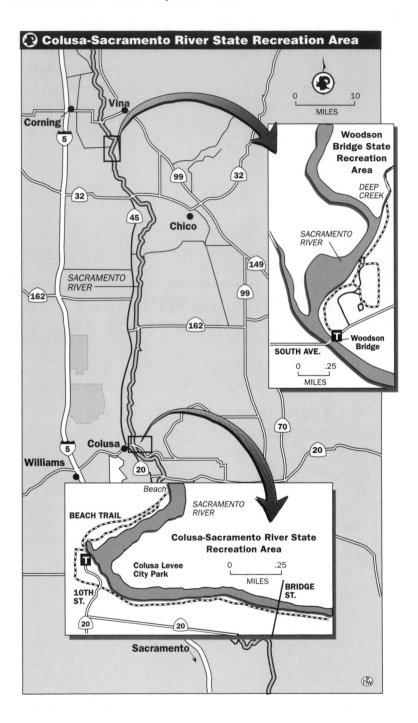

Colusa-Sacramento River State Recreation Area

DIRECTIONS TO TRAILHEAD   From Interstate 5 in Williams, some 60 miles north of Sacramento, exit on Highway 20 and drive east 9 miles to the quaint town of Colusa. As Highway 20 bends sharply south, you'll continue straight onto 10th Street and soon arrive at the state recreation area. The trail begins near a gate at the far side of the park.

THE HIKE   For hikers, Colusa is a walk in the park, an easy saunter down to the river and a sandy beach. During the summer, you can swim, if you don't mind cold water.

The trail is the old campground road; in 1980, the campground was moved to its present location to avoid the Sacramento River's annual flooding—and the subsequent rebuilding costs associated with the floods.

From the park's southern boundary, a levee extends up-river and down. Head down-river (south, then east) on the levee and you'll pass through a city park and get great views of Colusa, with its Victorian homes and historic buildings, as well as the ag-country beyond.

Take the right or left fork; the two paths link one-half mile later, just before the river. Make your way among the tall cottonwoods to the sandy beach on the river's edge. Loop back and join the levee, which passes through Colusa Levee City Park and offers views of Colusa's old buildings. Towering above the river to the east are the 2,000-foot Sutter Buttes; to the west are the more-than-a-mile-high peaks of the Coast Range.

A good turnaround point (0.75 mile from the park) is a bridge over the Sacramento and aptly named Bridge Street; however, you can continue walking the levee for several more miles past farms and fields.

WOODSON BRIDGE
STATE RECREATION AREA

■ SACRAMENTO RIVER TRAIL
1.5 miles round trip

Canoers, rafters and inner-tubers float down to Woodson Bridge State Recreation Area, located in an oak woodland on the Sacramento River between Chico and Red Bluff.

The park is often the day's-end destination for the above-mentioned flotilla, which puts in up river at Los Molino or Red Bluff. For fishermen, out for shad, striped bass, catfish and salmon, Woodson Bridge is not so much a destination as a departure point for launching a boat on the Sacramento.

Walkers stroll beneath the grand old oaks growing along the river. Joining the oaks are walnut, sycamore, and cottonwood. The park's trees muster quite a display of fall color. Beneath the trees grow a tangle of elderberry and wild grape.

The 428-acre park straddles both sides of the river; the west bank is undeveloped while the east bank offers 46 campsites amidst the oaks.

Immediately south of Woodson Bridge is Tehama County Park, which offers a boat-launching ramp and picnic ground. The county park's broad sand-and-gravel beach adjoins the state recreation area beach.

Woodson Bridge is open year-round, but the best times to visit are in spring and autumn, when the days are warm, but not scorching, as they are in summer.

The trail system is not extensive, but does offer a leg-stretcher of a walk along the Sacramento River. On a clear day in the North Sacramento Valley, you can look up and see the Trinity Alps, Mount Shasta and Lassen Peak towering in the distances.

DIRECTIONS TO TRAILHEAD From Interstate 5 in Corning, exit on South Avenue and head east 6 miles to Woodson Bridge.

From Highway 99 in Vina (about 15 miles north of Chico), exit on South Avenue and proceed 3 miles west to the park.

Best place to park and begin the walk is actually next door to the state park at Tehama County Park.

THE HIKE Below the bridge, you'll notice a gravel bar where local tubers put in and take out. Above the bar, on the river bank, two trails head into the thick undergrowth. Take either trail and you'll curve east with the river, soon joining the state park's nature trail. The nature here is willow, alder and cottonwood trees, along with wild grape and thickets of blackberry bushes.

Eventually you'll reach a small picnic area, a good turnaround point. You can extend your hike by walking 0.5 mile along the riverbank to the mouth of Deer Creek.

LAKE OROVILLE
STATE RECREATION AREA

■ LOAFER CREEK,
ROY ROGERS TRAILS
2 mile loop or 4.75 mile loop

Feather River-fed Lake Oroville offers lots to do, both on and off the water. Boating, water-skiing, fishing and swimming are popular forms of recreation on the big lake, while camping, picnicking, hiking and horseback riding are among the enjoyable pursuits along Oroville's lengthy, 167 mile shoreline.

The lake, located about 75 miles north of Sacramento, was created by higher-than-Hoover Oroville Dam in 1967. While it annually provides many thousands of Californians with a place to play, its main purpose is to hold water for distribution to the San Joaquin Valley, San Francisco and the Southland.

To learn about the lake and surrounding environs, check out the displays and observation tower at the visitor center. Here you'll find positively worshipful exhibits about western water-seekers, California's gigantic water system, and the role of water in our present-day civilization. My favorite exhibit is the one comparing the relative height of Oroville Dam in relation to the Statue of Liberty and the Eiffel Tower.

The state recreation area has a couple of short hiking trails that can be linked to provide a 2 mile jaunt, a more ambitious 4.75 mile loop, or something in between. An ambitious trail-building program over the past two decades has increased the park's network from nine to more than 50 miles of trail. Check out the new Potter Ravine Trail, which leads from Lake Oroville Dam along the west shore of the lake. The 14.5 mile-long Danbebee Trail extends from the town of Oroville to Loafer Creek.

DIRECTIONS TO TRAILHEAD From Highway 70 (Business), otherwise known as Oroville Dam Boulevard, in Oroville, head east to Highway 162 (Olive Highway) and continue five miles to Kelly Ridge Road. Turn left and drive a half mile. Just after the turnoff to the water treatment plant, turn right on the dirt road leading to a parking area.

THE HIKE Head back toward the water treatment plant and small dam. Ignore the signed trail beckoning you to hike to the visitor information center, and walk across the dam to the signed trailhead on the other side.

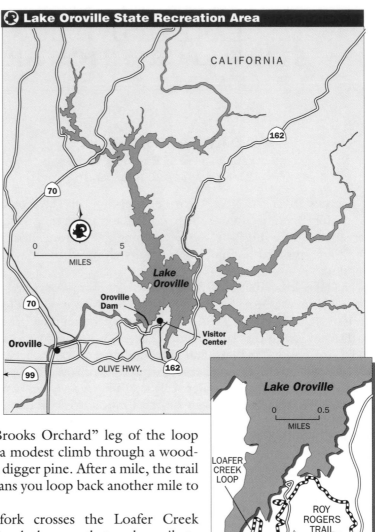

Take the "Brooks Orchard" leg of the loop trail and begin a modest climb through a woodland of oak and digger pine. After a mile, the trail forks. A left means you loop back another mile to the trailhead.

The right fork crosses the Loafer Creek Campground Road, then gently travels a mile to Brooks Orchard, a popular resting and watering place for the many horses and riders on Oroville's trails. A quarter mile past this rest stop, you'll cross a creek, then meander down toward the lakeshore. You'll skirt Loafer Creek Campground, then ascend oak- and ponderosa pine-covered slopes.

When you meet up with Loafer Creek Loop Trail, you'll swing right, hiking over grass slopes on a mellow descent back to the trailhead.

From Lake Oroville's visitor information center, you can join Chaparral Trail (an interpretive nature trail), then follow Kelly Ridge Trail to a lookout point above the lake; this lots-to-see loop is 2.75 miles.

CHAPTER FIVE

CENTRAL CALIFORNIA MOUNTAINS

Paralleling much of California's magnificent central coast is the equally magnificent Coast Range. The range rises to an extrordinary viewpoint—Mt. Diablo—near San Francisco Bay.

The Coast Range is better known by the names of its component parts, including the Santa Cruz Mountains and the Santa Lucia Mountains of Big Sur. In the young, geologically active Santa Cruz Mountains, generous rains support impressive redwood groves, some of which are preserved in state parks: Portola, Henry Cowell Redwoods and a forest undergoing restoration—The Forest Of Nisene Marks. The magnificent grove at Big Basin became California's first state park in 1902.

Linked to Big Basin by the superb Skyline-to-the-Sea Trail is striking Castle Rock State Park. This trail—and many local volunteers—made history when the first "Trails Day" event was held in 1969 to help restore the trail.

Fern-lined foot paths explore the redwood parks, centerpieces of the State Park system.

Ever since Highway 1 was constructed in 1937, dramatic Big Sur has been a magnet for visitors from around the world. Some of the southernmost stands of redwood, along with oak-studded portreros and wildflower-strewn meadows are preserved in the Big Sur state parks—Garrapata, Pfeiffer Big Sur, and Julia Pfeiffer Burns. Andrew Molera State Park in particular has an international flavor with many languages heard in its walk-in campground and along its trails.

LIMEKILN STATE PARK

■ LIMEKILN TRAIL
To Limekilns is 1 mile round trip

Inspiring redwoods, a sandy beach, and a trail into Big Sur history are some of the attractions of Limekiln State Park. The park opened in September of 1995 after the state acquired a privately held campground and 716 acres of land in southernmost Big Sur.

The isolated coastal canyon was named for its 1870–80s limekiln operations. Quarried limestone was "kilned" (smelted) in four huge wood-fired kilns. The product—powdered lime—was packed into barrels which were then attached to cable that was strung from the canyon wall down to the beach and some 50 yards out into the Pacific Ocean. Schooners slipped into tiny Rockland Cove, as the landing was known, and loaded the lime. The lime, a primary ingredient in cement, was used to construct buildings in Monterey and San Francisco.

The backwoods industry was hard on the woods. Surrounding redwoods were chopped down to fuel the limekilns and to make barrels to store the lime.

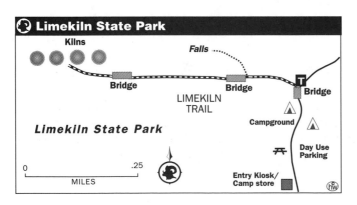

Much of Limekiln Canyon, however, escaped harm from this early industry and, after a quiet century, nature has healed most of Limekiln Canyon's wounds. Today the canyon shelters some of the oldest, healthiest, largest and southernmost redwoods in Monterey County. Some scientists speculate that these redwoods, along with those in other nearby steep canyons, may prove to be a special subspecies or variety of redwood that differs slightly from more northerly stands.

Not everyone thinks these southern redwoods are so unique. In 1984, a private landowner wanted to log the redwoods along the west fork of Limekiln Creek. Thanks to conservationists from around the state and the local Big Sur Land Trust, the trees were spared, and their habitat preserved in the public domain.

Limekiln Canyon is one of the Pacific Coast's steepest coastal canyons; it rises from sea level to more than 5,000 feet in elevation in about three and a half miles. This abrupt gradient means a tremendous diversity of flora. Botanists have identified twelve different plant communities within the confines of the canyon.

When the California Department of Parks and Recreation acquired Limekiln Canyon, it made some facilities improvements, but not many. The park's plumbing system remains problematic. Campsites are Big Sur funky, definitely not of the quality of those grand northern redwood park campgrounds designed by landscape architects.

Still, the park is very much undiscovered, and its family atmosphere and tranquil redwoods more than make up for any lack of facilities. The state park's campground and small camp store is managed by California Land Management, a private concessionaire.

Hiking is limited to the half-mile-long trail leading to the limekilns. It's possible that one day trail links will be developed to connect to the extensive trail system higher on Cone Peak

DIRECTIONS TO TRAILHEAD From San Luis Obispo, follow Highway 1 some 90 miles north to the signed turnoff for Limekiln State Park. The park is about 40 miles north of Hearst Castle, some 55 miles south of Carmel.

The turnoff is on the inland side of the highway, just south of the south end of the Limekiln Canyon bridge. Day-use parking is located just past the entry kiosk.

THE HIKE Walk through the campground to the first of three bridges and join the signed trail. Amble creekside to the next bridge, where you'll spot a signed, right-forking side trail that leads one-eighth mile to a pretty little waterfall.

The path continues among the tall redwoods and within sight of some lovely pools and cascades. After crossing a third bridge, the path ends at the limekilns. Four towering kilns, partially engulfed by the recovering redwood forest, stand as peculiar monuments to a long-gone industry.

JULIA PFEIFFER BURNS STATE PARK

■ MCWAY FALLS
0.5 to 0.75 miles each

For most visitors, "Big Sur" is synonymous with popular Pfeiffer Big Sur State Park. Often overlooked is a smaller slice of Big Sur located ten miles south—Julia Pfeiffer Burns State Park. It's a shame to overlook it. A redwood grove, dramatic coastal vistas, and the only major California waterfall to tumble into the Pacific are some of the park's attractions.

The park is a tribute to hardy pioneer Julia Pfeiffer Burns, remembered for her deep love of the Big Sur backcountry. Her father, Michael Pfeiffer, started a ranch in the Santa Lucia Mountains in 1869. In 1915, Julia Pfeiffer married John Burns, and the two ran a cattle ranch while living at their home located south of the present park.

You can easily sample the coastal charms of four-square mile Julia Pfeiffer Burns State Park by following the short Waterfall and Partington Cove trails. The park's coastal trails are great "leg-stretcher" jaunts to break up the coastal

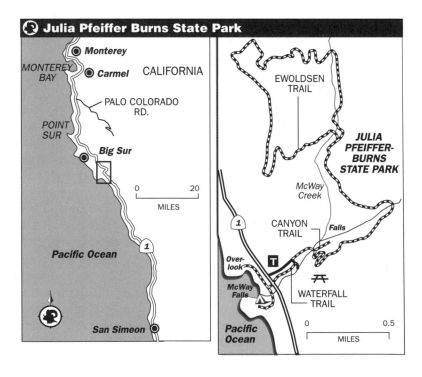

drive. In winter, the paths provide fine observation points from which to sight migrating California gray whales.

DIRECTIONS TO TRAILHEAD Julia Pfeiffer Burns State Park straddles Highway 1, about 36 miles south of Carmel and some 10 miles south of Pfeiffer Big Sur State Park. Turn inland into the park and proceed to the day use lot.

THE HIKE From the Julia Pfeiffer Burns State Park lot, take the signed trail toward Scenic Overlook. Along McWay Creek you'll spot some eucalyptus, quite a botanical contrast to the redwoods growing up-creek. (During spring, ceanothus and dogwood splash color along the trail.) The path leads through a tunnel under Coast Highway and emerges to offer the walker grand panoramas of the Big Sur coast.

You'll soon reach the overlook, where you can observe slender but dramatic McWay Falls tumbling a hundred feet from the granite cliffs into McWay Cove. On your return, you can take a side trail and meander over to the park's cypress-shaded environmental campsites, which are perched on the former site of Waterfall House.

PFEIFFER BIG SUR STATE PARK

■ VALLEY VIEW TRAIL
From Big Sur Lodge to Pfeiffer Falls, Valley View, is 2 miles round trip with 200-foot elevation gain

For most visitors, "Big Sur" means Pfeiffer Big Sur State Park. The state park—and its brief but popular trail system—is dominated by the Big Sur River, which meanders through redwood groves on its way to the Pacific Ocean, five miles away.

John Pfeiffer, for whom the park was named, homesteaded 160 acres of mountainous terrain between Sycamore Canyon and the Big Sur River. In 1884, he moved into a cabin perched above the Big Sur River gorge. (You can see the reconstructed "Homestead Cabin," which is located on the park's Gorge Trail.) John Pfeiffer sold and donated some of his ranchland to the state in the 1930s, and it became the nucleus of the state park.

Hike, swim, or just plain relax by the Big Sur River.

This walk, which follows the Pfeiffer Falls Trail and Valley View Trail, is an easy "leg stretcher" suitable for the whole family. It visits Pfeiffer Falls and offers a good introduction to the delights of the state park.

DIRECTIONS TO TRAILHEAD   Pfeiffer Big Sur State Park is located off Highway 1, some 26 miles south of Carmel and two miles south of the hamlet of Big Sur. Beyond the entry booth, turn left at the stop sign, then veer right (uphill). Very soon, you'll find some day use parking. A much larger parking area is located near the store and restaurant at the bottom of the hill.

THE HIKE   From the signed trailhead, follow the trail to Pfeiffer Falls. Very shortly, on your left, you'll spot a trail heading left to Valley View; this will be your return path. The walk continues under stately redwoods and meanders along with Pfeiffer-Redwood Creek.

You'll soon ascend a redwood stairway to a junction with Oak Grove Trail, which leads rightward 1.5 miles through oak and madrone woodland over to the Mt. Manuel Trail. Stay left at this junction and follow Pfeiffer Falls Trail through the forest and past a second branch of the Valley View Trail.

A stairway leads to an observation platform at the base of the falls. Pfeiffer-Redwood Creek cascades over a 40-foot precipice to a small grotto.

After enjoying the falls, descend the stairway and bear right on the Valley View Trail, which leaves behind the redwoods and ascends into a tanbark oak and coast live oak woodland.

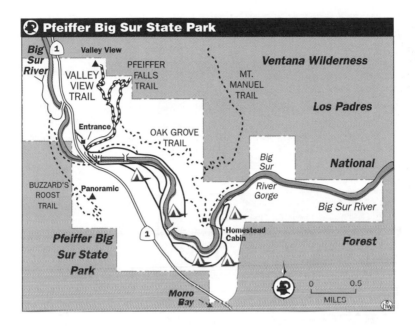

At a signed junction, turn right and follow the pathway along a minor ridge to a lookout. The Pacific Ocean pounding the Point Sur headlands and the Big Sur River Valley are part of the fine view.

Backtrack along Valley View Trail and at the first junction stay right and descend on Pfeiffer Falls Trail back to Pfeiffer-Redwood Canyon. Another right at the canyon bottom brings you back to the trailhead.

POINT SUR STATE HISTORIC PARK

■ POINT SUR LIGHT STATION TRAIL
0.5 mile guided walk

During the 19th century, when coastal roads were few and poor, most cargo was transported by ship. Ships traveled close to shore so that they could take advantage of the protection offered by bay and point. This heavy coastal trade—and its dangers—prompted the U.S. Lighthouse Service Board to establish a series of lighthouses along California's coast located about 60 miles apart.

Take a guided hike to the Point Sur Light Station.

Point Sur had been the death of many ships, and mariners had been petitioning for a beacon for many years when the government in 1885 appropriated $50,000 to construct a light station. The Point Sur light joined the one at Piedras Blancas situated 60 miles south and the one at Pigeon Point located 60 miles north.

The first light, which became operational in 1889, utilized one of the famed Fresnel lenses designed by French physicist Augustin Jean Fresnel. A whale oil lantern was the first light source. In later years, kerosene fueled the operation. Soot problems from the not-very-clean-burning kerosene kept the keepers busy polishing the glass and worrying about surprise visits from supervisors who conducted "white glove" inspections.

The lighthouse became fully automated in 1975. The original light, visible for 23 miles out to sea, is now on display in the Maritime Museum of Monterey.

The old stone buildings, when viewed from Highway 1, are intriguing; they're even more so when viewed up close on one of the tours conducted by volunteer docents. While the station undergoes restoration, the only way to see the facility—the only intact light station with accompanying support buildings on the California coast—is by guided tour.

The tour includes the lighthouse itself, the keepers' houses, the blacksmith shop and the barn, where livestock was kept. You'll learn the fascinating story of the isolated life lived by the four keepers and their families.

Docent-led tours are currently offered on weekends and on some Wednesdays: Saturdays 10 a.m. and 2 p.m., Sundays 10 a.m. and Wednesdays 10 a.m., weather permitting. There's a fee for the tours, which have a limited number of slots—available on a first-come, first-served basis. Suggestion: Arrive early. For more information: (408) 625-4419.

The walk to the lighthouse is interesting for more than historical reasons. Geology buffs will call the path to the light the "Tombolo Trail." A tombolo, rare on the California coast, is a sand bar connecting an island to the mainland.

The view from atop the 360-foot-high basaltic rock is superb. You're eyeball-to-eyeball with the gulls and cormorants. To the south is False Sur, named for its confusing resemblance to Point Sur, when viewed from sea.

In 1980, Point Sur Light Station was designated a state historic landmark, and in 1984 the U.S. Department of the Interior turned it over to the California Department of Parks and Recreation. The old Lighthouse Service Board was long-ago absorbed by the U.S. Coast Guard, and the kerosene lamp and steam-driven warning whistle have been replaced by a computer-directed electric beam and radio beacon, but Point Sur Light Station, as it has for a century, continues to warn ships of the treacherous Big Sur Coast.

DIRECTIONS TO TRAILHEAD Point Sur State Historic Park is located on the west side of Highway 1, some 19 miles south of Carmel and one-quarter mile north of Point Sur Naval Facility.

ANDREW MOLERA STATE PARK

■ BEACH, HEADLANDS TRAILS
3 miles round trip

Mountains, meadows and the mouth of Big Sur River are some of the highlights of a walk through Andrew Molera State Park, largest state park along the Big Sur coast. More than 20 miles of trail weave through the park, which has a diversity of ecosystems. You can hike along the bluffs overlooking three miles of beach, and climb through meadows and oak woodland. At the river mouth are a shallow lagoon and a beautiful sandy beach.

In 1855, Yankee fur trader Juan Bautista Roger Cooper acquired this land, formerly part of the Mexican land grant Rancho El Sur. Grandson Andrew Molera, who inherited the ranch, had a successful dairy operation. His Monterey Jack cheese was particularly prized.

A good leg-stretcher walk is to take Beach Trail to the beach at the mouth of the Big Sur River, then return via Creamery Meadow Trail. Beach Trail and a number of other park roads are old dirt roads, which allow side-by-side walking, thus appealing to sociable hikers. A longer tour of the park can be made via the Bluff, Panorama and Ridge trails. The coastal views from these trails are magnificent.

You may hear a number of foreign languages en route. The state park's walk-in campground is very popular with European visitors.

Note that the round trip loop described below relies on wading across the mouth of the Big Sur River. At times of high water, you'll have to make this trip an out-and-back or get your feet (and possibly much more) wet by crossing the river.

DIRECTIONS TO TRAILHEAD Andrew Molera State Park is just off Highway 1, some 21 miles south of Carmel.

Molera's bold headlands offer a hike to remember.

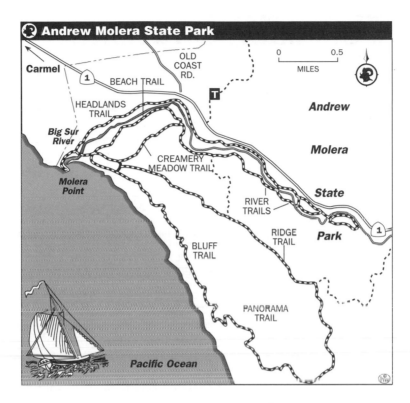

Andrew Molera State Park

Carmel
OLD COAST RD.
BEACH TRAIL
HEADLANDS TRAIL
Big Sur River
CREAMERY MEADOW TRAIL
Molera Point
RIVER TRAILS
Andrew
Molera
State
Park
RIDGE TRAIL
BLUFF TRAIL
PANORAMA TRAIL
Pacific Ocean
0   0.5
MILES

THE HIKE From the parking lot, cross the Big Sur River on the seasonal footbridge. Walk 100 yards or so along a broad path that soon splits. Bear right onto Beach Trail. (The left fork joins Creamery Meadow Trail, an ideal return route for those who like loop trails.) The trail stays near the river, whose banks are crowded with thimbleberry and blackberry, honeysuckle vines, willow and bay laurel.

At 0.3 mile, you pass through the park's campground. A side trail leads to Cooper Cabin, an 1861 redwood structure that's the oldest building on Big Sur's coast.

At the river mouth is a small beach and shallow lagoon, frequented by sanderlings, willets and many more shorebirds. A short path (Headlands Trail) leads above the beach to Molera Point, where you can watch for whales (January through April) or passing ships. The beach to the south is walkable at low tide.

Loop around the point and then return either the same way or via Creamery Meadow Trail on the south side of the Big Sur River.

GARRAPATA STATE PARK

■ ROCKY RIDGE, SOBERANES CANYON TRAILS
7 miles round trip with 1,200-foot elevation gain

Undeveloped and usually overlooked, Garrapata State Park offers a lot of Big Sur in a compact area. The park features two miles (probably closer to four miles counting the twists and turns) of spectacular coastline and a steep sampling of the Santa Lucia Mountains.

Rocky Ridge Trail quickly leaves Highway 1 behind and offers far-reaching views of the Santa Lucia Mountains and the sea. A grand loop of the state park can be made by returning to the trailhead via redwood-lined Soberanes Canyon.

The name Soberanes is linked with the early Spanish exploration of California. Soldier José María Soberanes marched up the coast to Monterey with the Gaspar de Portolá expedition of 1769. Seven years later, Soberanes served as a guide for Juan Bautista De Anza, whose party pushed north to San Francisco Bay. Grandson José Antonio Ezequiel Soberanes acquired the coastal bluff and magnificent backcountry that became known as the Soberanes Ranch.

Rocky Ridge Trail will be more enjoyable for the gung-ho hiker than the novice. The trail ascends very steeply as it climbs Rocky Ridge. Then, after gaining the ridge, hikers must descend an extremely steep mile (we're talking about a 20 to 30 percent grade here) to connect to Soberanes Canyon Trail.

The leg-weary, or those simply looking for an easier walk, will simply stroll through the redwoods of Soberanes Canyon and not attempt Rocky Ridge Trail.

DIRECTIONS TO TRAILHEAD Garrapata State Park is seven miles south of Carmel Valley Road, off Highway 1 in Carmel. There's a highway turnout at mileage marker 65.8.

THE HIKE From the gate on the east side of Highway 1, walk inland over a dirt road to a nearby barn, then a wee bit farther to cross Soberanes Creek and reach a trail junction. Soberanes Canyon heads east along the creek, but Rocky Ridge-bound hikers will keep with the closed road, heading north and dipping in and out of a gully.

Hikers rapidly leave the highway behind as the path climbs the rugged slopes, which are dotted with black sage, golden yarrow and bush lupine. The route uses few switchbacks as it ascends 1,435-foot Rocky Ridge. From atop the ridge are good views to the east of Soberanes Creek watershed, to the west of Soberanes Point, and to the north of Carmel and the Monterey Peninsula.

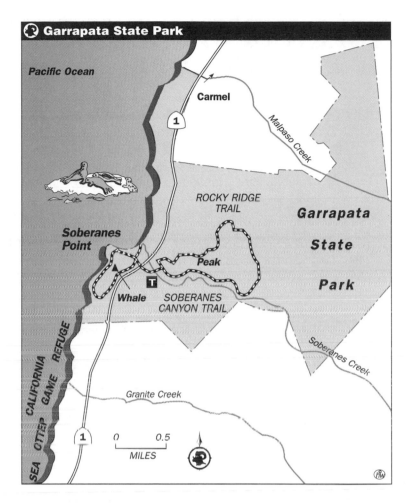

Garrapata State Park

Pacific Ocean

Carmel

1

Malpaso Creek

ROCKY RIDGE TRAIL

Garrapata

Soberanes Point

Peak

State

Whale

SOBERANES CANYON TRAIL

Park

SEA OTTER CALIFORNIA GAME REFUGE

Soberanes Creek

Granite Creek

1

0   0.5

MILES

The route contours eastward around the ridge. To the north is the steep canyon cut by Malpaso Creek. After leveling out for a time, the grassy path reaches a small cow pond, then descends over steep but pastoral terrain.

The trail is cut by cattle paths, a reminder of a century of grazing. The route plunges very steeply down the bald north wall of Soberanes Canyon. The mile-long killer descent finally ends when you intersect Soberanes Canyon Trail and begin descending, much more gently, to the west.

Soberanes Canyon Trail stays close to the creek and enters the redwoods. Western sword fern, redwood sorrel, blackberry bushes and Douglas iris decorate the path.

Near the mouth of the canyon, the trail becomes gentler. Willow, watercress and horsetail line the lower reaches of Soberanes Creek. Soon after passing some out-of-place mission cactus, brought north from Mexico by Spanish missionaries, hikers return to the trailhead.

FOREST OF NISENE MARKS STATE PARK

■ LOMA PRIETA GRADE TRAIL

From Porter Picnic Area to Hoffman's Historic Site is 6 miles round trip with a 400-foot elevation gain; several longer hikes are possible

One of the largest state parks in Central California, The Forest of Nisene Marks has few facilities, but it is this very lack of development that makes it attractive to anyone looking for a quiet walk in the woods.

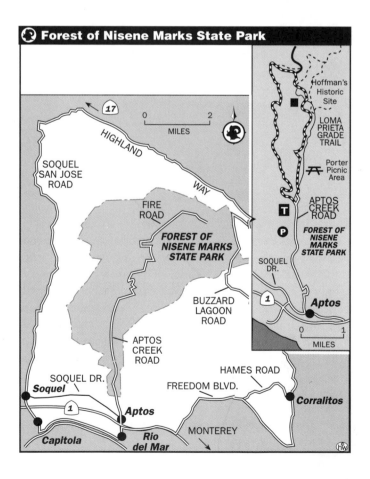

The woods, in this case, are second-growth redwoods. The park is on land near Santa Cruz that was clear-cut during a lumber boom lasting from 1883 to 1923.

Loma Prieta Lumber Co. had quite an operation. Using steam engines, oxen, skid roads and even a railway, loggers ventured into nearly every narrow canyon of the Aptos Creek watershed.

After the loggers left Aptos Canyon, the forest began to regenerate. Today, a handsome second generation of redwoods is rising to cover the scarred slopes.

The Marks, a prominent Salinas Valley farm family, purchased the land in the 1950s. In 1963, the three Marks children donated the property to the state in the name of their mother, Nisene Marks. As specified in the deed, the forest must not be developed and the natural process of regeneration must be allowed to continue.

Ferocious winter storms in 1982 and 1983 battered the canyons and ruined part of the park's trail system, in particular the paths in the upper reaches of Aptos Canyon. Railroad grades and trestles that had withstood a century of storms were washed away. Volunteers and the California Conservation Corps repaired the damage.

Loma Prieta Grade Trail follows parts of an old railway bed. A narrow-gauge steam railway ran from a mill to China Camp. A few ramshackle wooden buildings are all that's left of this lumber camp that once housed 300 workers.

DIRECTIONS TO TRAILHEAD From Highway 1 in Aptos, take the State Park Drive exit to Soquel Drive. Turn right (east) and proceed 0.5 mile into Aptos. Turn left on Aptos Creek Road and drive four miles to a locked gate at The Forest of Nisene Marks' Porter Picnic Area.

THE HIKE From the picnic area, follow Aptos Creek 0.4 mile to the Loma Prieta Grade trailhead. (An old mill site is a short walk up the road.)

For a short stretch, the trail stays near Aptos Creek. This creek, which rises high on Santa Rosalia Ridge, is joined by the waters of Bridge Creek, then spills into Monterey Bay at Rio Del Mar Beach. Silver salmon and steelhead spawn in the creek.

The old railway bed makes a gentle trail except for a few places where the old bridges have collapsed into steep ravines. Your destination of China Camp, now called Hoffman's Historic Site, has a few wooden structures.

You can return the same way or take the Ridge Connector Trail over to West Ridge Trail. This latter trail runs south and connects with Aptos Creek near the trailhead. Be warned that Ridge Trail is sometimes crowded by large amounts of poison oak.

HENRY COWELL REDWOODS STATE PARK

■ RIVER, EAGLE, PINE, RIDGE TRAILS
4 miles round trip with 500-foot elevation gain

H enry Cowell Redwoods State Park preserves first- and second-growth redwoods in a tranquil Santa Cruz Mountains setting.

Henry Cowell and Joseph Welch, who in the 1860s acquired the former Mexican land grant Rancho Cañada de Rincón, shared a similar commitment to protect the Big Trees Grove (now Redwood Grove). Welch's holdings were purchased by Santa Cruz County in 1930 and became parkland; in the 1950s this land was combined with 1,500 acres donated by Cowell's heirs to become a state park.

Thanks to the preservation efforts by these men, the "Big Trees" are as stirring a sight now as they were a century ago when railroad passengers bound for Santa Cruz from San Jose made a lunch stop amongst the tall trees.

The state park is hilly and with changes in elevation come changes in vegetation. Moisture-loving redwoods predominate on the lowlands while the park's upper ridges are cloaked with oak woodland and chaparral.

By connecting four of the park's trails, you can walk through all of the park's diverse ecosystems. You'll begin in the redwoods and ascend chaparral-covered slopes to an observation deck located in the middle of the park. Great mountain and coastal views are your reward for the ascent.

Be sure to stop in at the park interpretive center, which has exhibits and sells maps and books. Redwood Grove Nature Trail begins near the center.

DIRECTIONS TO TRAILHEAD Henry Cowell Redwoods State Park is located just south of Felton on Highway 9. You can pick up River Trail near the park entrance at Highway 9, or from the picnic area.

THE HIKE The short Redwood Grove Nature Trail, which visits one of the finest first-growth groves south of San Francisco, is a good place to start your exploration of

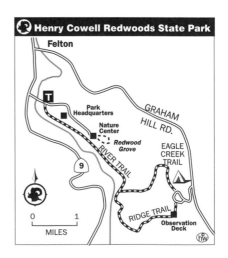

Wander amongst the "big trees," one of the finest first-growth redwood groves south of San Francisco.

the Santa Cruz Mountains. This popular trail, complete with interpretive leaflet, loops along the San Lorenzo Riverbank among the redwoods, some of which have been given names. One of the larger commemorative redwoods honors President Theodore Roosevelt, who enjoyed his 1903 visit to the grove.

River Trail meanders down river along the east bank of the San Lorenzo. You may hear the whistle of the Roaring Camp & Big Trees Railroad, a popular tourist attraction located adjacent to the park. The steam powered train takes passengers through the Santa Cruz Mountains on a narrow gauge track.

About 0.25 mile after River Trail passes beneath a railroad trestle, you'll intersect Eagle Creek Trail and begin ascending out of the redwood forest along Eagle Creek. Madrone and manzanita predominate on the exposed sunny slopes.

Bear right on Pine Trail (the pines you'll see en route are ponderosa pine) and climb steeply up to the observation deck. Enjoy the view of the Monterey and Santa Cruz coastline, the redwood forests, and that tumbled-up range of mountains called Santa Cruz.

On the return trip, take Ridge Trail on a steep descent to River Trail. Both River Trail and its nearly parallel path—Pipeline Road—lead back to Redwood Grove and the picnic area.

BIG BASIN REDWOODS STATE PARK

■ SKYLINE TO THE SEA, BERRY CREEK FALLS, SUNSET TRAILS

To Berry Creek Falls and beyond is 10.5 miles round trip with 600-foot elevation gain

In 1902, the California State Park System was born with the establishment of the California Redwood Park at Big Basin Redwoods State Park in Santa Cruz County. California preserved many more "redwood parks" during the twentieth century, but the redwoods at Big Basin remain one of the gems of the park system.

And one of the gems of the state's trail system—Skyline to the Sea Trail—explores Big Basin Redwoods State Park. As its name suggests, the path drops from the crest of the Santa Cruz Mountains to the Pacific Ocean. Views from the Skyline—redwood-forested slopes, fern-smothered canyons and the great blue Pacific—are superb.

This gem of a trail has many friends. During one weekend in 1969, dedicated members of the Sempervirens Fund and the Santa Cruz Trails Association turned out more than 2,000 volunteers to dig, clear, prune and otherwise improve the trail. Area volunteers put together an annual Trails Day that is now a model for trails organizations throughout the state.

The wildest and most beautiful part of the Skyline stretches from park headquarters at Big Basin to Waddell Creek Beach and Marsh. It winds through deep woods and explores the moist environments of Waddell and Berry Creeks.

Berry Creek Falls is one of Big Basin's top attractions.

Springtime, when the creeks are frothy torrents and Berry Creek Falls cascades at full vigor, is a particularly dramatic time to walk the Skyline to the Sea Trail. During summer, the cool redwood canyons are great places to beat the heat.

Tall trees and a trio of waterfalls make this trip through the Big Basin backcountry a hike to remember. The three falls—Berry Creek, Silver, and Golden—are enchanting, as are lesser cascades along Berry Creek.

The walk begins on the Skyline to the Sea Trail, but leaves this path well before the sea, detours to visit the waterfalls, then loops back to the main part of Big Basin. Paths alternate between wet and wild redwood-filled canyons and drier exposed ridges. This is a grand, clockwise tour of California's first state park, a most memorable walk.

DIRECTIONS TO TRAILHEAD From Santa Cruz, drive 12 miles north on Highway 9. Turn west on Highway 236 and proceed nine miles to Big Basin Redwoods State Park.

The walk begins on the Skyline to the Sea Trail, but leaves this path well before the sea, detours to visit the waterfalls, then loops back to the main part of Big Basin. Paths alternate between wet and wild redwood-filled canyons and drier exposed ridges. This is a grand, clockwise tour of California's first state park, a most memorable walk.

THE HIKE From park headquarters, walk west from the entry fee kiosk and follow signs for Skyline to the Sea Trail.

From the Redwood Nature Trail, cross Opal Creek and bear left on Skyline to the Sea Trail. First the route is in very tall redwoods, climbs over a ridge (and past a junction with Middle Ridge Road), then returns to the redwoods.

Two miles out, you cross the Kelly Creek footbridge, sticking with the Skyline Trail despite the temptations of several side trails. Kelly Creek merges with West Waddell Creek and three miles along travels a course above West Waddell Creek.

Four miles out you'll cross West Waddell Creek on a footbridge. A side trail leads 0.1 mile to a vista point for a closer look at the misty 65-foot falls cascading into the redwood-filled canyon.

Another 0.5 mile of travel brings you to an overlook of 60-foot Silver Falls and a bit farther Golden Falls, which spills over a reddish-gold cliff.

Five miles along, Berry Creek Falls Trail junctions with Sunset Trail, which you'll join, hiking for a time over more open, oak- and madrone-covered slopes before returning to the redwoods.

The path crosses Berry Creek, crests a ridge and descends to Waddell Creek. About 9.5 miles from the start, you'll cross Middle Ridge Road, descend 0.5 mile to Dool Trail, travel along redwood-lined Opal Creek and return to the trailhead via the Opal Creek footbridge.

FALL CREEK UNIT
(HENRY COWELL)

■ FALL CREEK TRAIL
Loop to limekilns is 3.2 miles round trip with 200-foot elevation gain; to Trail's End is 7.2 miles round trip with 900-foot gain

The forks of Fall Creek, a forest of second-generation redwoods and Douglas fir, are some of the attractions of a walk through this isolated area of Henry Cowell Redwoods State Park. Located on the slopes of Ben Lomond Mountain in a wild canyon northwest of Felton, this part of the park also boasts a lush creekside habitat of ferns, big-leaf maple and alder.

Hikers with a historical interest will enjoy traveling to old limekilns and a millsite. In the 1870s, IXL Company built three limekilns, producing nearly a third of the state's lime supply. Park namesake Henry Cowell took over the business at the turn of the century and under his guidance much of the lime used in the cement necessary to rebuild San Francisco after the 1906 earthquake was produced at the Fall Creek works. Fall Creek redwoods were logged in order to construct redwood barrels for storing lime and for logs to fire the limekilns.

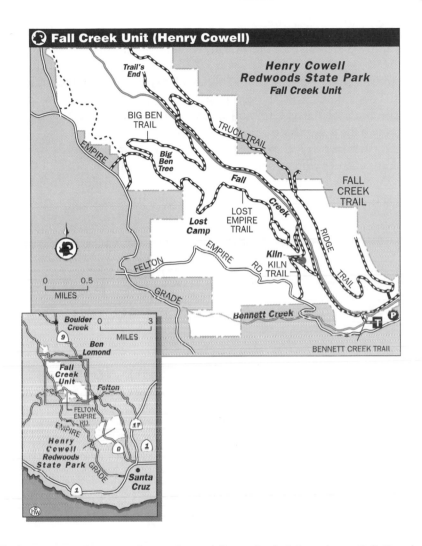

Fall Creek Unit (Henry Cowell)

Today a second generation redwood forest is thriving along Fall Creek, and the long-abandoned, moss-covered kilns with their arched opening, are a photographer's delight.

Old wagon roads, now park paths, travel along lovely Fall Creek and lead to the old kilns and barrel mill site.

DIRECTIONS TO TRAILHEAD From Highway 1 in Santa Cruz, turn north on Highway 9 and drive five miles to Felton. Turn left (west) on Felton Empire Road and proceed 0.5 mile to the small Fall Creek parking area.

THE HIKE Join switchbacking Bennett Creek Trail for 0.25 mile to its junction with Fall Creek Trail, staying left and heading up-creek. About 0.8 mile out, you'll cross the South Fork Bridge, pass an intersection with South Fork

Trail (your return route) and continue along the north fork of Fall Creek through a mixed woodland of redwood, fir, tanoak and maple.

Another 0.6 mile walk brings you to Cape Horn Trail junction. (Those inclined toward a shorter (3.2 mile) Fall Creek exploration should go left here.)

North Fork hikers cross the creek on twin logs and enter redwood forest. Regard the ruins of Barrel Mill and continue through the redwoods to trail's end at a tiny dam 3.6 miles from the trailhead.

Retrace your steps to Cape Horn Trail, a dirt road which soon leaves the creek, climbs a short while, then descends to the South Fork of Fall Creek and the limekiln area. Next you'll join South Fork Trail and follow it 0.4 mile back to North Fork Trail, turn right and walk 0.8 mile back to the trailhead.

CASTLE ROCK STATE PARK

■ SARATOGA GAP, RIDGE TRAILS
To Castle Rock Falls and Interpretive Center is 5.5 miles round trip

Perched high on the western slope of the Santa Cruz Mountains, among frequent fogs (and just above occasional smogs) Castle Rock State Park offers dramatic rock formations and quiet forest paths.

Castle Rock, the park's 3,214-foot high point, is a sandstone formation that appeals to rock climbers, geologists and photographers. A thick evergreen forest obstructs the view from Castle Rock.

Much better panoramas are to be had atop Goat Rock, a sandstone outcropping that offers hikers clear-day views of the San Lorenzo Valley and Pacific Ocean.

By the early 1900s, Castle Rock was already a tourist attraction. InterUrban streetcars carried visitors from the Santa Clara Valley up to Congress Springs (just above the present-day town of Saratoga). Intrepid travelers then hiked (or hired a horse and buggy to carry them) to Castle Rock.

For a pleasant loop through the park, join Saratoga Gap Trail, which visits Castle Rock Falls and leads to Castle Rock Trail Camp. Your return is via Ridge Trail, which parallels Saratoga Gap Trail at higher elevation and offers grand clear-day views.

DIRECTIONS TO TRAILHEAD From Highway 17 just north of Los Gatos, exit on Highway 9, winding through the town of Saratoga and ascending the

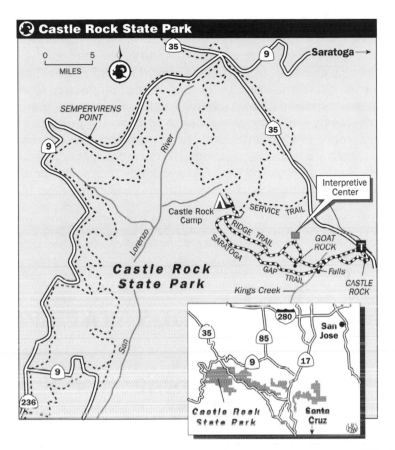

Santa Cruz Mountains to meet Highway 35. From the junction of Highway 9 and Highway 35 (Skyline Blvd.) drive south on 35 for 2.5 miles to the signed state park lot on the right. The signed trail begins at the west end of the lot.

THE HIKE Begin descending on Saratoga Gap Trail under the shade of oaks and ferns, soon passing the side trail leading to Castle Rock.

The main path follows a creek and crosses on a footbridge. You'll pass a signed trail (your return route) leading to Goat Rock, and continue to Castle Rock Falls, 0.75 mile from the trailhead.

Judging by the substantial looking observation platform, you might expect a more overwhelming spectacle than the hundred-foot Kings Creek cascade known as Castle Rock Falls. Ah, but never mind the falls located just up-canyon, take a look down-canyon to the San Lorenzo River watershed and the wide blue Pacific; this view may have been the main reason for the erection of an observation platform.

The path ascends wooded hillsides and, 0.5 mile beyond the waterfall, leaves behind the trees and climbs into the chaparral. From this elfin forest, hikers get clear-day views of Monterey Bay.

The trail alternates between brushy hillsides and madrone- and oak-filled canyons on the slope of Varian Peak, named for physicist-conservationist Russell Varian, who was instrumental in the creation of the state park.

Russell Point Overlook offers a good view, but a nicer rest/lunch stop is 0.25 mile farther at Castle Rock Trail Camp. The camp, located in a knobcone pine forest, has water and picnic tables.

From the camp, you'll retrace your steps as far as the junction with Ridge Trail, which you'll join on an ascent of oak- madrone-, and boulder-dotted slopes. This path leads a mile to another observation point and to a terrific interpretive center, a collection of outdoor exhibits that really show the lay of the land. (The geography lesson is particularly valuable when fog blankets the Santa Cruz Mountains, as if often does.)

On the final segment of this day hike, you'll loop past Goat Rock, a favorite of local climbers, then descend to rejoin Saratoga Gap Trail. Turn left and return to the trailhead.

PORTOLA REDWOODS STATE PARK

■ IVERSON, SUMMIT, SLATE CREEK TRAILS

6 miles round trip; longer and shorter options possible

You could call this tranquil park, perched on the opposite side of the Santa Cruz Mountains from Big Basin Redwoods State Park, "Little Basin Redwoods State Park." Like its well-known cousin, this park is a natural basin forested with coast redwoods. Portola Redwoods State Park it is, however, its name honoring explorer Don Gaspar de Portolá, who led an expedition in search of Monterey Bay in 1769.

The California landscape has changed immeasurably since Portolá's time, but places like this park still evoke the feeling of wild California. This wild feeling begins outside the park boundaries as you travel Alpine Road. The view is of wide-open spaces, of uncluttered valleys and ridges topped with nothing more than grass and cows.

The park centers around two creeks—Peters and Pescadero—which meander through a basin. Douglas fir and oaks cloak the ridges while redwoods, accompanied by huckleberry and ferns, cluster in cooler bottomlands.

Most redwoods in the area are second-growth trees; this land, like most in the Santa Cruz Mountains, was logged during the 19th century. However, most of "logging" at Portola was for shingle production; trees needed a very straight grain and were selectively cut. Thus, many large trees escaped the ax and may be seen today inside the park.

The Islam Temple Shrine of San Francisco used the property as a summer retreat for its members from 1924 until 1945, when the state acquired the land. During the 1960s, Portola had an amusement park-feeling. Pescadero Creek was dammed, providing a large fishing and swimming area. One year, 150,000 people poured into the small park. In 1974, the dam was removed and Portola reverted to quieter pursuits—camping, hiking, nature study. Rangers sometime refer to Portola as a "neighborhood park," meaning thus far only locals have discovered this ideal-for-a-family outing small redwood forest. My favorite day hike is a six mile "walkabout" that utilizes five different trails. Drop

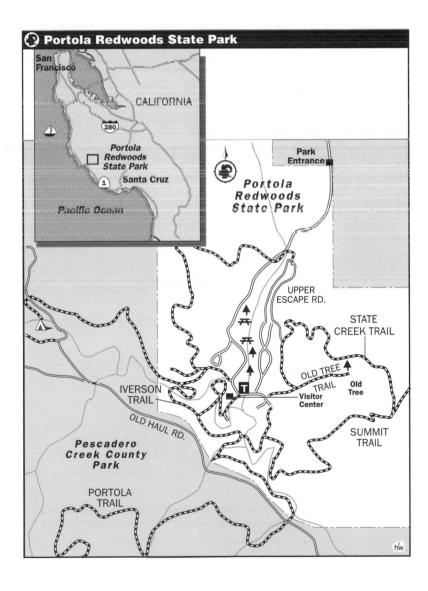

in at the park visitor center to view the nature and history exhibits. Interpretive programs are conducted during the summer and on some weekends.

DIRECTIONS TO TRAILHEAD   From Interstate 280 (Junipero Serra Freeway), about six miles north of San Jose, exit on Saratoga Avenue and head south, joining Highway 9 in the town of Saratoga. Highway 9 ascends west into the mountains to a junction with Skyline Boulevard (Highway 35). Turn right (northwest) on Skyline and follow it to a junction with Alpine Road and the signed turnoff to Portola Redwoods State Park. Turn onto Alpine Road. After 3.5 miles, turn left on Portola State Park Road and continue 3 more miles to the park. Leave your car at Tan Oak or Madrone picnic areas just across the road from the visitor center.

THE HIKE   Join Sequoia Nature Trail, which begins behind the park visitor center. Tramp through the redwood forest, cross Pescadero Creek, and loop around Louise Austin Wilson Grove, site of the Shell Tree.

Next join Iverson Trail, which meanders along Pescadero Creek. A short side trail leads to diminutive, fern-framed Tip-Toe Falls.

Iverson Trail visits the ruins of Iverson Cabin as it meets a park service road. A right leads to Old Haul Road which in turn leads five miles to San Mateo Memorial County Park. You turn left, cross Pescadero Creek on a bridge, and soon arrive at a signed junction with Summit Trail.

True to its name, Summit Trail ascends some 600 feet in elevation to a rather undistinguished summit. It then dips briefly to a saddle and a signed junction with Slate Creek Trail. It's another mile east to the park's trail camp, a pleasant, though waterless, rest stop.

From the saddle, Slate Creek Trail descends a pleasant mile west, then contours south to Old Tree Trail and the park's campground. Walk through the campground, then join the park road for a brief walk back to the park visitor center.

BUTANO STATE PARK

■ MILL OX, GOAT HILL, AÑO NUEVO TRAILS
4 miles round trip with 700-foot elevation gain

According to Native American lore, butano means "a gathering place for friendly visits." Visitors who find out-of-the-way Butano State Park will no doubt agree with this assessment.

On the map, Butano State Park seems rather close to the bustling Santa Clara Valley, and to the Bay area. But this 2,800-acre park, tucked between sharp Santa Cruz Mountains ridges, has a remote feeling.

While most of the redwoods in the park are second-growth, some grand old first-growth specimens remain.

On lower slopes, just above Butano Creek, the walker encounters the forest primeval: redwoods, trillium, sword ferns. Moss-draped Douglas fir, tangles of blackberry bushes, and meadowland, are some of the environments visited by the park's diverse trail system. Año Nuevo Lookout offers fine views of the elephant seal reserve, and of the San Mateo coastline.

DIRECTIONS TO TRAILHEAD From Highway 1, turn inland on Pescadero Road, and drive 2.5 miles to Cloverdale Road. Drive south three miles to Butano State Park Road and turn left into the park. Park near the entry kiosk.

THE HIKE Signed Jackson Flats Trail begins just across from the park entry kiosk. The path starts out in meadowland, but soon enters redwoods.

The trail follows the north slope of the canyon cut by Little Butano Creek, and junctions with Mill Ox Trail. Take Mill Ox Trail to the right, down to the canyon bottom. Cross Butano State Park Road, and join an unmarked (except for an authorized vehicles only sign) paved road. Ascend through redwoods on this access road. The route soon junctions with Goat Hill Trail, which you follow into a mixed forest of oak and madrone. Follow this trail to the next intersection: Goat Hill Trail heads left and melts into the woods, but you take the short connector path to Olmo Fire Trail. Turn right. Olmo Fire Trail leads to a junction with Año Nuevo Trail on your left. Take this path over fir- and blackberry bush-covered slopes to Año Nuevo Viewpoint, located in a clearing. On clear days, you can look south to Año Nuevo Island.

From the viewpoint, the trail descends with enough switchbacks to make a snake dizzy, back to the park entrance.

BURLEIGH-MURRAY RANCH STATE PARK

■ BURLEIGH-MURRAY RANCH TRAIL
To old barn is 2 miles round trip; to trail's end is
5 miles round trip

Rolling grassland, eucalyptus grove windbreaks, an old barn and a bunkhouse—this is ranch country, not the redwood country more typically associated with the Santa Cruz Mountains. For the hiker, Burleigh-Murray State Park offers a distinct change of pace from the trail systems of other nearby parks, most of which travel to, or within, stands of first- and second-generation redwoods.

Beginning in the 1860s, the valley of Mill Creek and surrounding slopes were used for hay-growing and cattle grazing. The state purchased the land in 1983 and the California state park system has been considering a historical emphasis for the state park. In the meantime, the park has remained almost completely undeveloped.

The park's prized historic structure is an old dairy barn, known as an English bank barn (because it's built into the hillside to facilitate loading from its upper heights); such barns are extremely rare in the U.S.

Some handsome stonework, rusted farm machinery and a 1930s ranch house (now the park ranger's residence) add to the rustic scene. The photo opportunities are many on the old ranch.

Meandering through the state park is Mills Creek, named not for the considerable number of Santa Cruz Mountains sawmills, but rather for the Mills family, first owners of the ranch.

The only park trail is the old ranch road that extends from the park entrance on Higgins Purisima Road some two miles northeast. The path follows Mill Creek to the old barn. Beyond the barn, the road narrows to a trail and then, beyond some water tanks, fades into oblivion. (The park service has not yet extended the trail to Skyline Boulevard.)

DIRECTIONS TO TRAILHEAD From Highway 1, just south of the town of Half Moon Bay, turn east on Higgins-Purisima Road and follow it 1.5 miles to the small parking lot for Burleigh-Murray Ranch State Park on the north side of the road.

THE HIKE The flat, brush-lined road follows Mill Creek for a half mile before crossing, then recrossing it. A mile out, the road passes a eucalyptus-shaded pic-

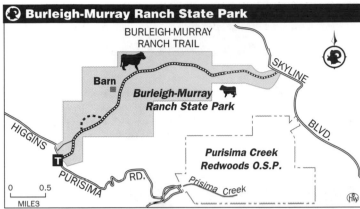

nic site, then angles left past the ranch house-turned-ranger's residence, crosses a bridge and brings you to the large dilapidated barn.

The route beyond the barn is an ever-narrowing footpath through Mill Creek Canyon. At two miles, it reaches a trio of leaky water tanks, then soon peters out in the thick coastal scrub.

FREMONT PEAK STATE PARK

■ FREMONT PEAK TRAIL
1 mile round trip

The view. That's the reason—really, just about the only reason— travelers go so far out of their way to visit Fremont Peak State Park.

From atop 3,169-foot Fremont Peak, hikers are treated to a tremendous panorama of San Benito Valley, Monterey Bay and the rugged Santa Lucia Mountains back of Big Sur. The park also offers two more views: One is a glimpse into history and the part Captain John Charles Frémont played in the drama of California's struggle for statehood.

Another view from the park is into the heavens. Fremont Peak Observatory houses a 30-inch reflecting telescope, one of the largest telescopes available for

Captain John Charles Frémont.

public use. Call the park for information about astronomy programs held during the spring, summer, and early fall viewing seasons.

In March of 1846, Captain Frémont and his men were camped near Monterey, then the capital of the Mexican province of Alta California. Mexican military leaders demanded that the Americans leave the territory. Frémont not only refused, but planted the American flag atop the tallest peak in the area and built a small fort nearby.

A war of nerves ensued before Frémont and his men finally broke camp. The incident reflects the kind of tension and jockeying for position between the rebellious Americans and the Mexican government in the years prior to the Bear Flag Revolt and California's entry into the Union.

Frémont ultimately returned to California as military governor for a short time. His colorful career included a short stint as a U.S. Senator from California, a run for the presidency in 1856 as the first presidential nominee of the infant Republican party, and service as a general in the Civil War.

Before Frémont's name was attached to the mountain, it was known as Gabilan Peak from the Spanish word for hawk. The state parks department acquired the peak in 1936.

Fremont Peak's northern slope is cloaked with manzanita, toyon and scrub oak, while the exposed southern slope is covered with knee-high grassland that is bright green and dotted with wildflowers in spring, golden brown in summer. Soaring above the tops of Coulter pine and madrone on the upper ridges are eagles, hawks and turkey vultures. More than a hundred birds have been sighted in the park.

In light of Frémont's talent as a wide-ranging explorer, trailblazer, naturalist and mapmaker (he was captain of the U.S. Topographic Engineers) the trail to the peak is all too bare. Nevertheless, the aforementioned grand view is reason enough for a walk in this off-the-beaten-path park. (Another good reason is the chance for motorists to stretch their legs while en route via Highway 101 from Los Angeles to San Francisco.) For a nice day, combine this short hike with a walking tour of San Juan Bautista State Historic Park, which features adobes, the original town plaza, Mission San Juan Bautista and the old Plaza Hotel, a stage stop.

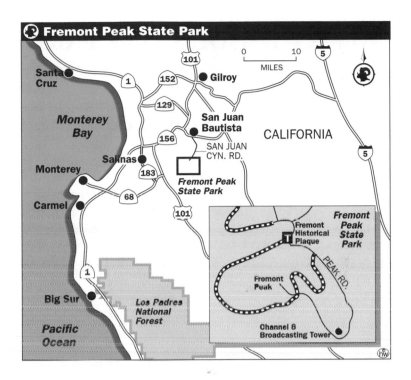

Fremont Peak State Park

DIRECTIONS TO TRAILHEAD From Highway 101 north of Salinas and south of Gilroy, exit on Highway 156 and travel 11 miles to the town of San Juan Bautista. From the outskirts of town, take the signed turnoff for the state park (San Juan Canyon Road) and travel 11 miles to road's end at Fremont Peak State Park. Park in the uppermost lot.

THE HIKE You'll see both a road and a trail beginning from the parking lot. The half mile trail, signed with a hiker's symbol, does not go to the peak but instead, dips into and then climbs out of a ravine, before switchbacking up to the park's observatory.

Walk up the road for a short distance and then join the signed Peak Trail, a footpath that contours around the mountain. Enjoy the view of Monterey Bay, as the path climbs to a saddle and meets a short summit trail that ascends to rocky Fremont Peak.

After taking in the view, return via the road, which passes by a communications facility before returning you back to the trailhead.

HENRY W. COE STATE PARK

■ MONUMENT, MIDDLE RIDGE, FISH TRAILS

6.2 mile loop, 9.5 mile loop

This part of the Diablo Range is heavenly for hikers. Henry W. Coe State Park, perched high above the Santa Clara Valley, preserves a cross-section of classic California Coast Range: ragged, rolling hills dotted with antiquarian oaks and strewn with wildflowers.

Geologists say the Diablo Range, which stretches from the Carniquez Strait to the Antelope Valley, and is bordered by the San Joaquin Valley on the east and, in part by the Santa Clara Valley to the west, has undergone a tumultuous history of uplift, folding and faulting. A part of the range—particularly the drier part—is a devilish landscape.

Henry W. Coe State Park, however, welcomes visitors with a diverse ecology: grasslands, conifer forests, oak woodlands. The park features some unusual flora, including magnificent manzanita, growing more than fifteen-feet high on Middle Ridge and on well-named Manzanita Point. Despite the area's long pre-park use as grazing land, assorted native grasses, including purple needle grass and Western rye, survive.

Henry Willard Coe, Jr. pioneered hereabouts in 1880, and over the years increased his holdings. His daughter, Sada Coe Robinson, gave 12,230 acres of the family ranch for a park in 1953. Subsequent additions have increased the park to 81,000 acres making Henry W. Coe California's second-largest state park.

Best times to visit the park are in spring when wildflowers—Mariposa lilies, poppies, fiddlenecks, buttercups, shooting starts and more—pop out all over, and in autumn when the black oaks glow golden and the temperature is just right for hiking.

Stop at the park visitor center, located next to an old ranch house,

Henry W. Coe State Park
Frog Lake
No Access
MONUMENT TRAIL
MIDDLE RIDGE TRAIL
FISH TRAIL
PACHECO
ROUTE
POVERTY FLAT
SPRINGS TRAIL
Park Headquarters

Little lakes and rolling hills—a cross-section of California's Coast Range preserved in the state park.

and view the natural and cultural history exhibits. Pick up a map and inquire about trail conditions here.

Old ranch roads, open to hikers, cyclists and equestrians, comprise most of the park's extensive trail system. Day hikers departing from the visitor center can fashion a trip from the more than 40 miles of trail emanating from the head-quarters' area through the original nucleus of the park.

The park visitor center, at about 2,600 feet in elevation, is one of the high-est parts of the park. In other words, most trails lead downhill, meaning return trips are an uphill climb.

I have two favorite loops through the main part of the park. One is a 6.2 mile jaunt to Middle Ridge, around Frog Lake, with a return on Fish Trail. A longer 9.5 mile loop takes off from the junction with Fish Trail and continues 2.5 miles to Poverty Flat; its oak- and sycamore-shaded trail camps are ideal sites for a midday picnic or taking a rest.

DIRECTIONS TO TRAILHEAD   From Highway 101 in Morgan Hill (south of San Jose, north of Gilroy), exit on East Dunne Avenue. Drive 13 miles east on the narrow winding road to the park visitor center and hiker parking lot.

THE HIKE   From the visitor center, walk a hundred yards back up the park entrance road and join Manzanita Point Road on your right. After a 0.1 mile climb on the paved road, you'll join signed Monument Trail, a footpath.

Monument Trail ascends fairly steeply over oak-dotted grasslands and soon reaches a signed junction. At this point, one may take a short spur trail to the west for a great view of the Santa Clara Valley, before returning to the main trail which leads leads a few hundred yards east to a monument to park namesake Henry W. Coe.

Here you are on the crest of Pine Ridge. Ponderosa pine—unusual in the Diablo Range—give the ridge its name.

Your path joins a major dirt road, known as Hobbs Road, and begins a descent down the back side of Pine Ridge into a black oak forest. The road crosses the Little Fork of Coyote Creek and you pass a side trail on your right leading to Frog Lake. There's fine picnicking on the shores of this little green reservoir.

Continue up the road to Middle Ridge or join Frog Lake Trail for the climb to the ridgetop and a meeting with Middle Ridge Trail.

Middle Ridge Trail descends, then ascends before entering a stand of truly gargantuan manzanita. A few pine trees grow up through the manzanita—a weird sight.

At the signed junction with Fish Trail, those ambitious hikers following the longer loop will continue descending on Middle Ridge Trail, cross the Middle Fork of Coyote Creek twice to Poverty Flat Road, following the road a short distance down to the Poverty Flat trail camps. Your return to the trailhead will be via Poverty Flat Road, the madrone- and laurel-shaded Forest Trail and the Corral Trail.

Those hikers on the shorter loop will descend through the woods to recross the Little Fork of Coyote Creek, then head across an inspiring valley oak-studded meadow. The trail meets, then crosses Manzanita Point Road. You link up very briefly with Springs Trail, then join Corral Trail for a westward walk over a buckwheat-covered slope and through an oak woodland back to the trailhead.

MT. DIABLO STATE PARK

≡ JUNIPER, NORTH PEAK TRAILS
"The Grand Loop" is 7 miles round trip with
500-foot elevation gain

From the Golden Gate to the Farallon Islands, from the High Sierra to the Central Valley—this is the sweeping panorama you can savor from atop Mt. Diablo. Geographers claim that hikers can see more of the earth's surface from the top of Mt. Diablo than from any other peak in the world with only one exception: Africa's legendary 19,340-foot Mt. Kilimanjaro.

The far-reaching panorama from Mt. Diablo is all the more impressive considering the mountain's relatively short (elevation 3,849 feet) height. Two reasons for the grand views: (1) the mountain rises solo very abruptly from its surroundings, and (2) the land surrounding the mountain—the San Franciso Bay and Central Valley—is nearly flat.

Hikers atop Mt. Diablo, 1915.

Geologically speaking, the mountain is a bit odd in that the hiker climbs over successively older and older rocks on the way to the summit; this is exactly the opposite of the usual progression. Much of Diablo's sedimentary rock, which long ago formed an ancient sea bed, has been tilted, turned upside down and pushed up by a plug of hard red Franciscan rock.

Even those hikers without any interest in geology will be impressed by the bizarre, wind-sculpted rock formations bordering a picnic area on the mountain called "Rock City." The mountain's rock show also includes the satanic-looking Devil's Pulpit, located just below the summit.

Several colorful yarns describe how the mountain got its name. The most popular account supposedly arose from an 1806 expedition of Spanish soldiers from San Francisco Presidio who marched into the area to do battle with the local Indians. In the midst of the fighting, a shaman clad in striking plumage appeared on the mountain. The Spaniards were convinced they saw El Diablo—The Devil—and quickly retreated.

In 1851, Mt. Diablo's summit, long a landmark for California explorers, was established as the official base point for California land surveys. Even today, Mt. Diablo's base line and meridian lines are used in legal descriptions of much California real estate.

Toll roads up the mountain were opened in the 1870s and a fancy hotel was built. In order to make their California holiday complete, tourists of the time just had to climb Mt. Diablo and take in the majestic view.

In 1931, the upper slopes of Mt. Diablo were preserved as a state park. In more recent years, the lower slopes were added to the park, thanks in a large measure to the efforts of Save Mt. Diablo, a local conservation organization.

Today the park consists of some 19,000 acres of oak woodland, grassland and chaparral. Stands of knobcone and Coulter pine, as well as scattered grey pine, are found all over the mountain.

Mt. Diablo boasts some fine trails but the state park is primarily oriented to the automobile. Something of the majesty of conquering Diablo is lost for hikers when they're joined at the top by dozens of visitors stepping from their cars.

Still, there are plenty of places on Diablo's flanks where cars can't go. And the road to the summit, while intrusive, does allow hikers to easily customize the length of their day hike.

Want an easy hike? Start walking just below the summit. Want a vigorous aerobic workout? Start hiking at the base of the mountain and trek all the way to the top.

A relatively easy way to the top is via two-mile-round-trip Juniper Trail. More ambitious hikers will tackle the 6 mile round-trip Summit Trail.

A great way to tour the park is to follow what park rangers call "The Grand Loop," a seven mile circuit that connects several trails and fire roads and offers views of—and from—Diablo in every direction.

DIRECTIONS TO TRAILHEAD   From Highway 680 in Danville, exit on Diablo Road and go east. After three miles, go north on Mt. Diablo Scenic Boulevard, which becomes South Gate Road, then Summit Road, and winds 8.5 miles to Laurel Nook Picnic Area. Park in the wide turnout (Diablo Valley Overlook), then join signed Juniper Trail, which departs from the picnic area.

THE HIKE   From the picnic area, the path ascends northeast over brushy slopes. After crossing paved Summit Road, the path climbs some more up to the lower summit parking lot.

Plan to spend some time on the summit enjoying the view. A couple handy locator maps help identify cities and natural features near and far.

After you've enjoyed the view, join the trail heading east from the south side of the parking lot. The path parallels the road for a short distance, then reach-

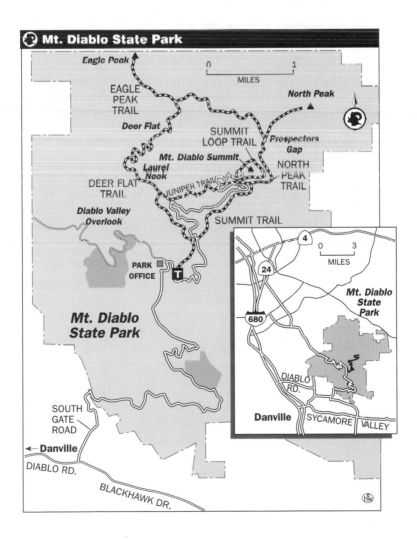

es a junction. Summit Trail heads southwest down the mountain, but you join the eastward-trending trail to North Peak.

Enjoy the awesome view of the Central Valley as you march over a rocky, juniper-dotted slope. The red-brown rock formation above looks more than a little diabolical; the most prominent rock formation is known as Devil's Pulpit. A half mile from the above-mentioned intersection, the trail, sometimes called Devil's Elbow Trail, sometimes called North Peak Trail, angles north and descends to a distinct saddle, Prospectors Gap. At the gap is a junction with the rugged 0.75-mile-long dirt road leading to North Peak.

Our path contours along the bald north slope of Diablo, passing junctions with Meridian Ridge Fire Road and Eagle Peak Trail, and arriving at Deer Flat, a pleasant rest stop shaded by blue oak.

Intersecting Deer Flat Trail, you'll switchback up to Juniper Campground, then continue a short distance farther to Laurel Nook Picnic Area, where you began your hike.

CHAPTER SIX

6

CENTRAL CALIFORNIA COAST

ighway 1, from Carmel south to the Monterey/San Luis Obispo County line, was designated California's first official Scenic Highway in 1965. "Scenic" would be the least of the superlatives used by those who get to know the Central Coast.

Dominating the seascape of San Luis Obispo County is the "Gibraltar of the Pacific," Morro Rock. The 50-million-year-old volcanic peak is now a wildlife preserve and part of the state park system. Morro Bay is a tremendously rich coastal ecosystems; a good bay view is available from the Morro Bay Sand Spit, part of Morro Bay State Park.

On the bluffs of Montaña de Oro State Park grow fields of mustard and poppies that give the park its "Mountain of Gold" name. Brightening the Pismo Dunes in springtime are yellow and magenta sand verbena, corcopsis and white

"Meet me on the boardwalk, mom," at the south access to the Oceano Dunes.

fringed aster. Part of the Pismo Dunes, California's most extensive dune system, is protected in a state preserve.

The Central Coast hosts two wildlife dramas that attract visitors from around the world. At Año Nuevo State Reserve, hikers on guided tours get close-up looks at a large population of elephant seals. During autumn, the eucalyptus grove in Natural Bridges State Beach hosts the largest gathering of monarch butterflies in America.

OCEANO DUNES
STATE RECREATION AREA

■ OCEANO DUNES PRESERVE TRAIL
2 or more miles round trip

Pismo Beach has a little something for everyone. Digging for the famed Pismo clam (now scarce) has long been a popular pastime. Two camp-grounds at the state beach are favorites of families looking for weekend getaways. Oceano Dunes State Vehicular Recreation Area is a sandy play-

Pismo, Oceano, Guadalupe—by whatever name, theses dunes are a sandscape to remember.

ground for street vehicles and off-highway vehicles.

For walkers, the attraction is Oceano Dunes Preserve, a region of tall sand hills where vehicles are prohibited, and you can wander for miles. Often referred to as the Nipomo Dunes these days, they extend 18 miles from the northern end of Oceano Dunes to Pt. Sal State Beach.

This walk explores the dune preserve inland from Oceano Dunes State Vehicular Recreation Area. The shoreline itself is often a traffic jam of cars, trucks and off-highway vehicles, filled with families, low-riders, and what seems to be half the population of Bakersfield.

A few hundred yards inland from this shoreline Sigalert, it's quiet, even lonely. Virtually no one bothers to walk into the dune preserve to see Nature's handiwork.

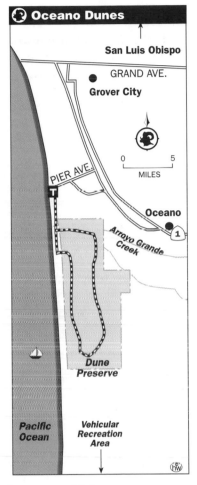

DIRECTIONS TO TRAILHEAD From Highway 101 in Arroyo Grande, exit on Grand Avenue and follow it westward to Highway 1. Head south a mile to the community of Oceano, just south of Grover Beach, and turn west on Pier Avenue. Oceano Dunes State Vehicular Recreation Area entrance station is a short distance ahead. If you have a four-wheel drive or high-clearance vehicle, you can pay a fee here and drive onto the beach. (Pismo boosters claim their beach is the only one in California where the sand is firm enough to support travel by standard automobiles, even low-slung family cars, but I have my doubts; I've seen a lot of cars stuck in the sand.)

If you're driving, head south about a half mile.

The beach is signed with numbered markers. Park near the first marker you see—Marker #1.

If you're not keen on driving the beach, park along Pier Avenue short of the entrance kiosk. You may then (1) walk a half mile south along water's edge (not as treacherous as it looks from the distance with all those vehicles on the beach) to the dune entrance; or (2) walk a quarter mile or so along Strand Way, a residential street paralleling the beach, then continue south along the banks of Arroyo Grande Creek, which near its mouth also parallels the beach, to the dune preserve entrance.

(If you park on Pier Avenue, add about another mile to your walk.)

THE HIKE Head inland to the fence that marks the boundary of the Oceano Dunes Natural Preserve. Take any of the meandering southbound trails that cross the dunes. A ridgeline of sand shields walkers from the sights and sounds of the busy beach below.

Continue southward along the shrub-dotted base of the dunes for a mile or so, then ascend out of the foredunes toward the crest of the great dunes to the east. You can then return north via the crest of the large dunes.

When you reach Arroyo Grande Creek, the northern boundary of the pre-serve, return to the beach. At this point, you're a couple hundred yards north of Marker #1, so head south back to the trailhead.

LOS OSOS OAKS STATE RESERVE

■ OAK TRAIL
1 to 2 miles round trip.

A ntiquarian California live oaks, estimated to be 600 to 800 years old, are the highlight of this state reserve in Los Osos Valley near San Luis Obispo. Two miles of trail meander through the old oaks which have, during their long life, contorted into some unusual shapes.

Botanists say the oak woodland is a culmination of thousands of years of plant succession that has transformed the area from sparsely vegetated sand

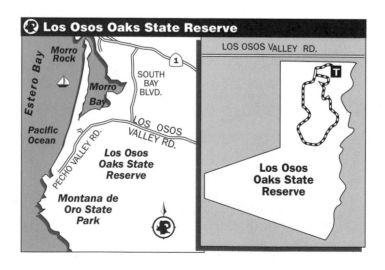

These graceful oaks have grown here for centuries—and are preserved for generations to come.

dunes into a landscape of California live oaks. Though many of the oaks are quite large, some oaks growing on the crest of the dunes are dwarfed.

Chumash Indians gathered acorns from the grove. Shell fragments and bits of charcoal are evidence of their frequent encampments.

Meandering along the eastern boundary of the reserve is Los Osos Creek, lined with bay laurel, sycamore and even some cottonwood trees.

The oaks are full of bird life. Several species perch in the crown of the trees, others hunt bugs and grubs in the piles of leaves beneath the trees. The chaparral that makes up one-fourth of the reserve is home to quail and many more birds.

Those piles of sticks you see, some several feet high, are wood rat nests. Judging by all those nests, the rarely seen rodent may be the most common animal in the reserve.

Docent-led walks are sometimes scheduled on the weekends. While walking in the reserve, stay on the trail; poison oak is abundant.

DIRECTIONS TO TRAILHEAD From Highway 101 on the southern outskirts of San Luis Obispo, exit on Los Osos Valley Road and travel eight miles to Los Osos Oaks State Reserve on the left side of the road.

THE HIKE The path crosses a bridge over a trickling creek, passes a plaque thanking, among others, the California State Parks Foundation for preserving this place, then begins a clockwise loop through the reserve.

The main path winds through the old oaks, wanders near Los Osos Creek, then leads to an overlook of a still pastoral part of Los Osos Valley. At a couple of trail junctions, you have the opportunity to shorten or extend your walk.

MONTAÑA DE ORO STATE PARK

■ BLUFF TRAIL
4 miles round trip.

Atop the Montaña de Oro State Park bluffs grow fields of mustard and poppies, which give the park its name, which means "mountain of gold."

At the turn of the century, the greater portion of what is now the state park was part of the Spooner Ranch. The most popular beach in the park is Spooner's Cove; its isolation made it an ideal landing spot for contrabandistas during the Spanish era, and for bootleggers during Prohibition.

Marching across a "mountain of gold."

While walking the bluffs, you may see harbor seals venturing ashore or otters diving for food beyond the surf line. Bird watchers delight at the pelicans, cormorants and crimson-billed black oyster catchers.

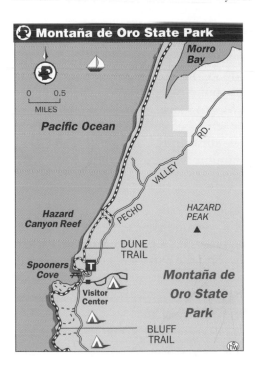

Inland areas of the park include Valencia Peak, which offers great Central Coast panoramas and Coon Canyon, where a stand of Bishop pine thrives. The park's campground occupies the bluffs above a small creek; the visitor center is the old Spooner ranch house.

DIRECTIONS TO TRAILHEAD
From Highway 101, exit on Los Osos Valley Road, continuing northwest for 12 miles until the road turns south to become Pecho Valley Road, which leads to Montaña de Oro State Park. There's parking at Spooner's Cove. The trail begins a hundred yards south of the turnoff for the campground on the west side of Pecho Valley Road.

THE HIKE The path crosses a dry creek on a footbridge and leads up to the bluffs overlooking Spooner's Cove.

A half mile from the trailhead, a short fork to the right leads to Coralina Cove, bedecked with sea-polished broken shells and beautiful beach pebbles. The crystal-clear tidepools are full of anemones, starfish, mussels and colorful snails.

Continuing on Bluffs Trail, you'll cross a wooden bridge. A mile from the trailhead is Quarry Cove, a fine tidepool site. The wide trail, lined with thistle and New Zealand spinach, eventually brings you to an overlook above some sea caves. Beyond is Grotto Rock.

You may return the same way, or cross Pecho Valley Road to the trailhead for Coon Creek Trail.

MORRO BAY STATE PARK

■ BLACK HILL TRAIL
To Black Hill summit is 3 miles round trip with
600-foot elevation gain

A series of nine peaks between San Luis Obispo and Morro Bay originated as volcanoes beneath the sea that covered this area some fifteen million years ago. After the sea and volcanic explosions subsided, erosion began dissolving the softer mountain material around the volcanic rock and left nine volcanic peaks standing high above the surrounding landscape. These volcanic plugs include Hollister Peak and famed Morro Rock.

Black Hill, the last peak in the volcanic series before Morro Rock, has a trail that tours a little of everything—chaparral, eucalyptus, oaks, pines, and coastal shrubs. From the mountain's 640-foot summit, you can view the Morro Bay Estuary, the sand spit, and the hills of nearby Montaña de Oro State Park.

DIRECTIONS TO TRAILHEAD Follow Coast Highway for 12 miles north of San Luis Obispo to the Los Osos-Baywood Park exit just before Morro Bay. Turn south on South Bay Boulevard and go 0.75 mile to Morro Bay State Park entrance. Bear left on the first fork beyond the entrance, heading one mile to the campground entrance directly across from the state park marina lot, where you should park. Park along the first crossroads inside the campground. Walk up the campground road to join the trail.

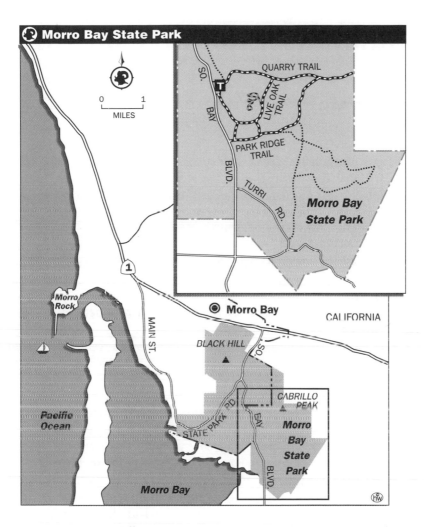

THE HIKE Walk up the group camp access road, past the group camp restroom. Follow the trail under the power lines between the golf course on the left and Chorro Group Camp on the right, cross a paved road and begin ascending the mountain. A mile from the trailhead, there's a junction. Bear left. The route becomes steeper, passing first through coastal shrubs then conifers. The trail passes a water tank, then switchbacks to the summit.

After enjoying the fine view, you may return the same way or return via the east fork of the old exercise trail by backtracking 0.5 mile to the trail junction, then heading straight (east). You'll discover a eucalyptus grove, where monarch butterflies cluster. Cross a golf course road and rejoin the eastern section of the Exercise Trail, which returns you to the trailhead.

MORRO STRAND STATE BEACH

■ MORRO STRAND TRAIL
From The Cloisters to Morro Rock is 3.2 miles round trip

Morro Rock could have served as inspiration for that old 1960s' Simon and Garfunkel tune with the "I am a rock, I am an island," refrain. Indeed, Morro Rock was an island located about 1,000 feet offshore until the late 1800s when harbor-makers started expanding Morro Bay's entrance and sand shoals began piling up between the rock and mainland.

As a result of such tidal tampering, Morro Rock became part of what geographers call a tombolo, a sand spit that connects an island to the mainland. (Pt. Sur Light Station on the rugged Big Sur coast is perched on the Central Coast's other famed tombolo.)

Morro is a slimmer and trimmer rock than the great rounded dome explorer Juan Rodríguez Cabrillo named "El Moro" when he sailed by in 1542. Morro is missing a million tons or so of basaltic rock—the result of quarrying operations that took place from the 1880s until 1969 when the rock was declared a state park preserve. Most of the rock removed from Morro was used to construct breakwaters at Morro Bay and San Luis Bay.

Morro Strand offers the beach hiker an altogether different perspective on Morro Rock than the usual postcard view from Morro Bay. As viewed from the south, Morro Rock is part of a busy scene that includes the harbor, a shoreline powerplant and the town of Morro Bay. From a viewpoint to the north, the "Gibraltar of the Pacific" appears much more solitary, more island-like. From this angle, it's easy to imagine Morro's past life as an undersea volcano.

Morro Bay attracts flocks of migratory waterfowl in the winter including ruddy ducks, widgeons, buffleheads, and pintails. Scores of grebes, loons, terns and black brants (small geese that fly in from northern Canada) also winter here.

This hike begins at a particularly intriguing trailhead called The Cloisters, a combination wetland, small housing development and city park that's sandwiched between Coast Highway and the low dunes back of Morro Strand State Beach. Wildlife experts, landscape architects and park officials teamed to create a pond and related "natural" habitats designed to attract a variety of birds. The developer of The Cloisters was required to make these unusual environmental efforts in order to build on adjacent property.

Learn more about The Cloisters via an asphalt trail that encircles the wetlands and some interpretive signs. Other trails link The Cloisters to the beach.

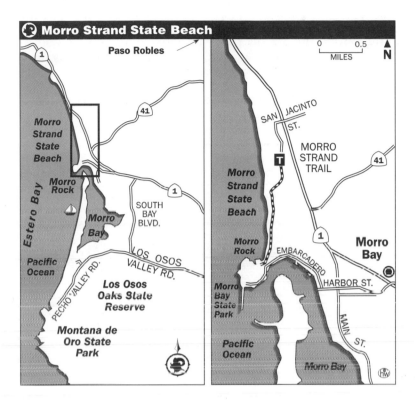

Morro Strand State Beach

Paso Robles

Morro Strand State Beach

Morro Rock

Estero Bay

Morro Bay

Pacific Ocean

SOUTH BAY BLVD.

LOS OSOS VALLEY RD.

PECHO VALLEY RD.

Los Osos Oaks State Reserve

Montana de Oro State Park

0   0.5 MILES   N

SAN JACINTO ST.

MORRO STRAND TRAIL

Morro Strand State Beach

Morro Rock

EMBARCADERO

HARBOR ST.

Morro Bay

MAIN ST.

Morro Bay State Park

Pacific Ocean

Morro Bay

DIRECTIONS TO TRAILHEAD From Highway 1, about two miles north of "downtown" Morro Bay, turn west on San Jacinto Street, then bear south through a small subdivision to the parking lot.

THE HIKE From the developed part of the park with the children's playground, walk oceanward toward the low dunes and join a boardwalk path. (Detour briefly north if you wish and learn about The Cloisters wetland from some interpretive signs.) This walk heads south alongside the dunes. The path, a boardwalk, curves through the dunes and deadends on the beach. Head south down the beach toward mighty Morro Rock.

When you're hiking down-coast, the massive Morro Bay Power Plant is nearly as dominating a presence as Morro Rock. When in operation, the plant, located just inland from Morro Rock, generates electricity with oil-fired turbines that convert ocean water to steam.

Your trail is a broad, sandy beach formerly called Atascadero ("the mudflats" in Spanish) State Beach. A few years back state park officials renamed it Morro Strand. The state beach is bisected into northern and southern sections by a campground located a half mile north of The Cloisters.

Some surf fishers, surfers and clammers know about this beach, but not many. You might find yourself accompanied only by your thoughts as you meander Morro Strand.

Trail's end is the base of Morro Rock. Coleman City Park, located just inland from the rock, offers some picnic tables.

On your return, savor the views of the Santa Lucia Mountains that seem to curve with the coast toward Big Sur.

SAN SIMEON STATE PARK

■ SAN SIMEON CREEK TRAIL

3.5 miles round trip

What's there to see in San Simeon besides the castle? It's a common question asked by thousands of travelers on their way to Hearst Castle.

The answer is found at San Simeon State Park, which boasts a diversity of scenery from shoreline to Monterey pine forest: a new trail, complete with interpretive displays, a boardwalk that crosses a wetland, and numerous benches that offer a place to rest and observe the tranquil surroundings. The pathway circles the park's San Simeon Creek and Washburn campgrounds. About 0.25 mile of the path is wheelchair accessible.

Back in the 1880s, the park's 500 acres of backcountry were part of Ira Whittaker's ranch and dairy operation. Eucalyptus was planted, both as a windbreak and for firewood to fuel the dairy's boiler to make cheese.

Botanical highlight is a stand of Monterey pine, part of the famed Cambria pines, and one of only four native groves left on earth. In winter, monarch butterflies, more often seen on the Central Coast in eucalyptus trees and other nonnative flora, cluster in the park's Monterey pines.

San Simeon Creek is habitat for the endangered red-legged frog and Western pond turtle. Many migratory birds can be counted at the park's seasonal wetland: cinnamon teal, mallards, egrets and herons.

DIRECTIONS TO TRAILHEAD From Highway 1, just south of the turnoff for San Simeon Creek Campground, turn inland and park at Washburn day-use area. Walk inland along the service road to the signed trailhead on your right. Campers can walk to the trailhead—just west of San Simeon Creek bridge—along the campground road.

THE HIKE The path tours the eastern fringe of the seasonal wetland and soon reaches a boardwalk that leads across it from one viewing area to another.

Beyond the boardwalk the trail junctions. The right fork leads southwest 0.2 mile to the Moonstone Gardens restaurant and Highway 1. Along this side trail, Eagle-eyed hikers might get a glimpse of Hearst Castle located five miles north.

The main trail climbs onto a flat-topped, Monterey pine-dotted ridge. A sometimes overgrown path detours left (north) two hundred yards to a scenic overlook.

Our route descends from the pines into lush riparian area and turns north. A boardwalk crosses a boggy lowland filled with willow, cottonwood and a thick understory of wax myrtle and blackberry bushes.

The path next ascends grassy slopes along the eastern boundary of the park. From the former grazing land, you look out over a scene from the California of a century ago: a windmill, pastoral slopes dotted with cows, the unspoiled beauty of the southern Santa Lucia Mountains.

The trail skirts the edge of the campground, then leads west. Savor the mountain vistas as the path heads southwest on the bluffs above San Simeon Creek.

About a quarter mile from its end the trail splits. The path you've been following continues above San Simeon Creek back to the day use area. A second branch crosses the campground road and leads toward the wetland boardwalk, where you turn right and retrace the first five minutes of your walk back to the trailhead.

WILLIAM RANDOLPH HEARST STATE BEACH

■ SAN SIMEON BAY TRAIL
To San Simeon Point is 2 miles round trip

A walk along San Simeon Bay is a nice diversion before or after a tour of La Cuesta Encantada, the Enchanted Hill—the name of the famous castle built by newspaper publisher William Randolph Hearst.

In the mid-1860s a severe drought wrecked the Central Coast cattle business and forced many debt-ridden Spanish rancheros to sell their land. Senator George Hearst bought out the rancheros and began developing his family estate.

After the death of William Randolph Hearst in 1951, his heirs donated the beach south of Sebastian General Store for a park. It's a tranquil place; San Simeon Bay provides fairly good refuge from northwest and west winds. San Simeon Store was established in 1873 and is still in operation.

The Hearst Corp. drew up plans in the 1960s to develop what would have been a town of 65,000 people, floated various resort proposals during the 1990s, and finally agreed to sell a significant length of privately held coastline and interior ranchland to the state in 2005.

William Randolph Hearst left us some sand, along with his castle.

As a result of the $95 million deal, Hearst is turning over a 13-mile strip of shoreline west of Highway 1 for use as state parkland. The company also agreed to relinquish rights to develop most of the Hearst Ranch's 80,000 acres of rolling hills east of the highway.

Coastal hikers cheered because the state received an easement to complete an 18-mile segment of the California Coastal Trail through the Hearst Ranch. Public access to, and trails through, the property will be phased in over the coming years as the state prepares and implements a management plan for the new parkland. Look for some exciting new hiking opportunities along this coast.

DIRECTIONS TO TRAILHEAD William R. Hearst Memorial State Beach is located on San Simeon Road west of Highway 1. Park in the state beach day use lot or along San Simeon Road south of Sebastian General Store. Park in designated areas and please respect private property signs.

THE HIKE Proceed through the picnic ground located in the eucalyptus grove just north of the fishing pier. When you reach the beach, turn up-coast. (Note that one of the development rights retained by the Hearst Corp. permits the company to build a 100-room hotel at San Simeon Point.)

When the beach begins to arc westward, ascend to a narrow dirt road leading atop the wooded bluffs. The road, which narrows to a trail, offers fine coastline and castle views as it curves toward San Simeon Point. From the point are additional breathtaking views to the south of the undeveloped San Luis Obispo County coast.

The path continues around the point on overgrown blufftop trails, then passes under the boughs of Monterey cypress on a dark tunnel-like trail for 0.25 mile before re-emerging back on the bluffs. The bluff trails grow more and more faint and erratic and you descend a low sand dune to the beach. You can follow the beach until tides and rocks prevent further progress and you meet the Coast Highway quite some distance north.

POINT LOBOS STATE RESERVE

■ CYPRESS GROVE TRAIL, NORTH SHORE TRAIL
0.75 mile to 3 miles or more round trip

Sometimes it's the tranquil moments at Point Lobos you remember: Black-tailed deer moving through the forest, the fog-wrapped cypress trees. And sometimes it's nature's more boisterous moments that you recall: the bark of seal lions at Sea Lion Point, the sea thundering against the cliffs.

A visit to Point Lobos State Reserve, in good weather and bad, is always memorable. Some of photographer Ansel Adams' greatest work was inspired by the wind-sculpted cypress, lonely sentinels perched at the edge of the continent. Landscape artist Francis McComas called Point Lobos "the greatest meeting of land and water in the world."

At Point Lobos, the Monterey cypress makes a last stand. Botanists believe that during Pleistocene times, some half-million years ago, when the climate was wetter and cooler than it is now, huge forests of cypress grew along the coast—indeed, throughout North America. When the world's climate warmed, the cypress retreated to a few damp spots. Nowadays, the grove at Point Lobos and another across Carmel Bay at Cypress Point are the only two native stands in existence.

The Monterey cypress, with the help of humans, can cross hot and dry regions and become established in cool areas elsewhere. In fact, this rare conifer is easily grown from seed and has been successfully distributed all over the world, so it's puzzling why the trees' natural range is so restricted.

DIRECTIONS TO TRAILHEAD Point Lobos State Reserve is located three miles south of Carmel just off Highway 1. Both Cypress Grove Trail and North Shore Trail depart from the northwest end of Cypress Grove parking area.

THE HIKE Cypress Grove Trail, a 0.75 mile loop, visits Allan Memorial Grove, which honors A.M. Allan, who helped preserve Point Lobos from resort developers in the early 1900s. When Point Lobos became a reserve in 1933, Allan's family gave the cypress grove to the state.

The trail passes near The Pinnacle, northernmost point in the reserve. Winds off the Pacific really batter this point and the exposed trees. To combat the wind, the trees adopt a survival response called buttressing: a narrow part of the trunk faces the wind while the trunk grows thicker on the other side in order to brace itself. The wind-sculpted trunks and wind-shaped foliage give the cypress their fantastic shapes.

Cypress Grove Trail offers great tree-framed views of Carmel Bay and Monterey peninsula. Offshore are the rocky islands off Sea Lion Point. The Spaniards called the domain of these creatures Punto de los Lobos Marinos— Point of the Sea Wolves. You'll probably hear the barking of the sea lions before you see them.

North Shore Trail meanders through groves of Monterey pine, less celebrated than the Monterey cypress, but nearly as rare. Native stands of the fog-loving, three-needled pine grow in only a few place in California.

North Shore Trail wanders through the pines and offers terrific coastal panoramas. Watchers of the late, late show and admirers of spooky beauty will enjoy the shrouds of pale-green lichen hanging from the dead branches of the Monterey pines. Lichen, which conducts the business of life as a limited partnership of algae and fungi, is not a parasite and does not hurt the tree. It's believed that the presence of lichen is an indication of extremely good air quality.

The trail also gives a bird's-eye view of Guillemot Island. A variety of birds nest atop this large offshore rock and others. Pigeon guillemots, cormorants and gulls are some of the birds you might see.

As you hike by Whalers Cove, you'll probably see divers entering the Point Lobos Underwater Reserve, America's first such reserve set aside in 1960. Divers explore the 100-foot-high kelp forests in Whalers and Blue Fish Cove. Mineral rich waters from the nearby 1,000-foot-deep Carmel Submarine Canyon upwell to join the more shallow waters of the coves.

The reserve has an excellent interpretive program. Docent-led walks explore the trails and tidepools. Ask rangers or visit the park's information station for scheduled nature walks.

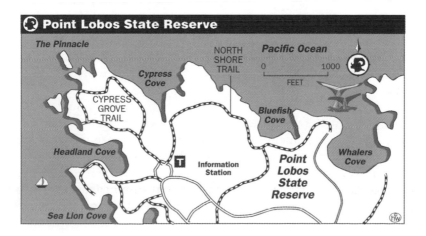

Point Lobos State Reserve

CARMEL RIVER STATE BEACH

■ CARMEL RIVER BEACH TRAIL
2 miles round trip

C armel River, which arises high on the eastern slopes of the Santa Lucia Mountains and empties into the sea just south of Carmel, is a river of many moods. Some of its forks, swollen by winter and spring rains, can be capricious, frothy waterways as they course through the Ventana Wilderness.

Tamed by Los Padres Dam on the northern boundary of the national forest, the river's descent through Carmel Valley is relatively peaceful. At its mouth, too, the Carmel River has differing moods and appearances. About May, a sand-bar forms, turning the river mouth into a tranquil lagoon. During winter, the river bursts through the berm and rushes to the sea. Steelhead trout swim upriver to spawn.

At the north end of Carmel River State Beach is a brackish lagoon, where shorebirds feed. Carmel River Lagoon and Wetlands Natural Reserve is here, and even the most casual bird-watcher will be impressed by the abundance of waterfowl. Ducks, mallards and coots patrol the lagoon. Egrets and herons stand amongst the reeds. Hawks hover overhead. Bring your binoculars.

This walk explores the river mouth, then travels the length of Carmel River State Beach to a point just north of Point Lobos named Monastery Beach, for the Carmelito Monastery located just across Highway 1 from the shore.

DIRECTIONS TO TRAILHEAD During the summer and autumn months, the sandy berm at the Carmel River mouth provides a fine path between river and sea. At this time of year, you can start this walk at the north end of Carmel River State Beach. From Highway 1, just south of the town of Carmel, turn west on Rio Road. When you reach Santa Lucia Street, turn left, then proceed five more blocks to Carmelo Street. Turn left and follow this road to the beach.

You can also start at the south end of Carmel River State Beach, easily accessible from Highway 1.

THE HIKE Follow the shoreline down coast over the sandy berm. In places, the route is rocky, the domain of nervous crabs who scatter at your approach. You'll surely notice the iceplant-lined path above the beach; save this path for the return trip.

After rounding a minor point and passing some wind-bent Monterey cypress, you'll arrive at Monastery Beach—also known as San Jose Creek Beach, for the creek that empties onto the northern end of the beach. With the chimes from the nearby monastery ringing in your ears, you might be lulled into think-ing that Monastery Beach is a tranquil place, but it's not; the surf is rough and the beach drops sharply off into the sea. Even the most experienced swimmers should be ultra-cautious.

For a little bit different return route, take the state beach service road, which farther north becomes a trail. This dirt road/trail, just before reaching the lagoon, climbs a small hill where a large cross is implanted. The cross was erect-ed by the Carmel Mission in 1944, and is similar to the one put here by the 1769 Portolá expedition in order to signal the Spanish ship that was to resup-ply them. Unfortunately, the expedition did not realize how close it was to its intended destination—Monterey Bay—and turned back south.

From the cross, follow a path down slope and intersect another path that leads along the south bank of the Carmel River. Follow the berm and beach back to the trailhead.

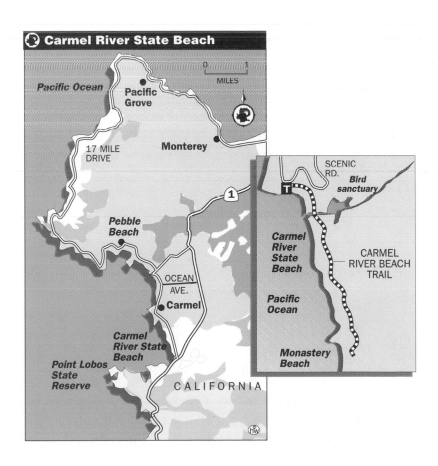

ASILOMAR STATE BEACH

■ ASILOMAR COAST TRAIL
0.5 to 2 miles round trip

Asilomar State Beach, located on the southwest shores of Pacific Grove, packs a lot of interest into a mile of coastline: a restored dune ecosystem, rocky coves, a broad sand beach. Add a visit to the historic Asilomar Conference Grounds and you have a walk to remember.

Bordering the west side of the conference center are white sand dunes, vegetatively restored with native plants. A boardwalk provides close-up views of this living example of plant succession. Just inland from the water, "pioneer" species of sand verbena and beach sagewort have taken hold; these colonizers created soil conditions acceptable for larger plants such as tree lupine and coyote bush to thrive; ultimately Monterey pine will succeed.

The conference center at Asilomar (pronounced Ah-seel-o-mar), derived from the Spanish to suggest "refuge by the sea," was originally founded by the YWCA for use as a summer retreat in 1913. Architect Julia Morgan, who would later gain worldwide fame as the designer of Hearst Castle, was commissioned to plan the original buildings.

Beach, bluff, and boardwalk trails offer tranquil hiking at this "refuge by the sea."

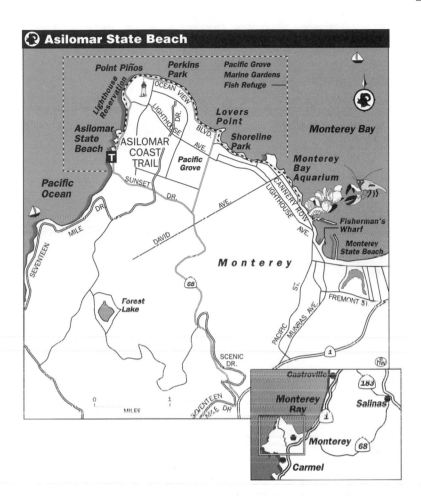

Asilomar State Beach

DIRECTIONS TO TRAILHEAD From Highway 1 between Carmel and Monterey, turn west on Highway 68 (which becomes Sunset Drive) and follow it to the beach. If you're in the Cannery Row area, follow Ocean View Boulevard west and south along the coast.

You can begin this walk opposite Asilomar Conference Center or at the north end of Asilomar State Beach just south of the Sunset Drive–Jewell Avenue intersection.

THE HIKE Asilomar Coast Trail extends a mile along the length of the state beach. From the trail, several side paths fork to tidepools and pocket beaches. Sea otters, sea lions, seals are sometimes seen from vantage points along the trail. In winter, scan the horizon for migrating California gray whales.

From the coast, walkers can follow the boardwalk across dunes to the Asilomar Conference Center, a national historic landmark set in the piney woods.

MARINA STATE BEACH

■ DUNE NATURE TRAIL
Nature trail with return via beach is 0.6 mile round trip

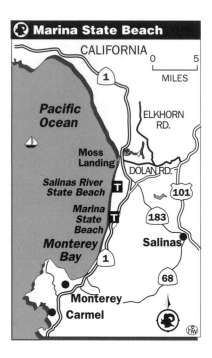

Providing a dramatic backdrop to Marina State Beach are some of the central coast's tallest dunes, handsomely shaped sand mounds that are habitat for a number of plants and animals. Rare native flowers such as Monterey paintbrush and the coast wallflower brighten the dunes, where the black legless lizard and the ornate shrew skitter about. These dune creatures and their habitat are threatened by the encroachment of nonnative iceplant and, of course, human developments.

Marina State Beach is popular with hanglider enthusiasts and with locals who flock to the shore at day's end to watch the often colorful sunsets.

DIRECTIONS TO TRAILHEAD From Highway 1 in Marina, exit on Reservation Road and drive west 0.25 mile to the Marina State Beach parking lot.

THE HIKE Dune Nature Trail, a 0.3 mile interpretive pathway, explores the dune ecosystem. The trail is mostly a wooden boardwalk linked with "sand ladders." Signs identifying the flora and a great view of the Monterey Peninsula add to the walk's enjoyment.

Ambitious walkers can walk the shoreline 3.5 miles north to Salinas River Wildlife Refuge.

SALINAS RIVER STATE BEACH

■ DUNE TRAIL
2 miles round trip

Mile-long Dune Trail explores some of Monterey Bay's intriguing sand dunes and links two coastal access points of Salinas River State Beach. The dunes back the state beach, a popular fishing spot.

East of the dunes are croplands and wetlands in the former Salinas River channel, which extends south from Moss Landing to the Salinas River Wildlife Area; in 1908, farmers diverted its course in order to create additional farmland.

DIRECTIONS TO TRAILHEAD From Highway 1 at Moss Landing, exit on Portero Road and follow it 0.5 mile to the parking lot at Salinas River State Beach.

The other trailhead is off Molera Road. Follow signed Monterey Dunes Way 0.5 mile to the beach.

Warning: Both trailheads have been the site of vehicle break-ins. Lock your car and take your valuables with you.

THE HIKE Dune Trail begins south of the harbor of Moss Landing, often a surprisingly good place to watch for wildlife: sea otters paddle here and there, sea lions bask on a narrow finger of sand, pelicans are abundant on air and land and sea.

From the harbor, walkers can follow a 0.5 mile dirt road (closed to vehicles) south to the Salinas River State Beach access and parking area off Potrero Road, where Dune Trail officially begins.

The path is over soft sand, seasonally colored by lupine, Indian paintbrush and California poppy. Hikers get mostly inland views, though the path does crest a rise for a peek at the coast. A mile out, you have the choice of retracing your steps or returning via the beach.

Please heed all posted warnings and don't walk over those areas of the dunes' complex undergoing environmental restoration.

NEW BRIGHTON AND SEACLIFF STATE BEACHES

■ SEACLIFF TRAIL

From New Brighton State Beach to Seacliff State Beach
is 3 miles round trip; longer beach walks possible

Just south of Santa Cruz, two lovely strands with British-sounding names located on Monterey Bay beckon the beach-walker. Both New Brighton and Seacliff State Beaches host lots of swimmers, surfers and campers.

New Brighton's half-mile-long beach is backed by bluffs forested with cypress and Monterey pine. Raccoons, deer and other animals inhabit this wooded upland as well as the park's grassy coastal terrace where the campground and picnic area are situated. Migrating monarch butterflies winter in the park's groves.

Seacliff's most obvious attraction is its odd pier. This pier begins traditionally enough with a 500-foot long wooden structure protruding into Monterey Bay; its extension, however, is something to behold. The wood pier connects to the scuttled *Palo Alto*, a World War I-era supply ship. A group of coastal entrepreneurs purchased the vessel in 1929, then sank the ship at the end of the pier. The *Palo Alto* was then remodeled into an amusement center complete with carnival booths, dance hall, restaurant and swimming pool.

The renovated plank part of the pier is popular with anglers hoping to hook halibut, perch, flounder and more. The pier's far end is reserved for resting and

Seacliff's odd pier: pilings plus an old cement boat.

roosting seabirds, including pelicans and cormorants. Migrating California gray whales can frequently be glimpsed from the pier.

Seacliff State Beach has a small visitors center (open Wednesday through Sunday) featuring exhibits that interpret Monterey Bay's natural history.

DIRECTIONS TO TRAILHEAD From Highway 1 in Santa Cruz, drive four miles south and exit at Park Avenue. Head south 0.1 mile, turn left, then after another 0.1 mile turn right into New Brighton State Beach.

You can begin this walk up on the bluffs by the picnic area or from the day-use parking area just above the beach at New Brighton's west end. An access road leads under a train trestle to China Cove, the site of a 19th-century Chinese-American fishing camp.

THE HIKE If you begin from the bluffs, join the 0.2 mile beach access trail (stairs and a path) that drops to the beach. Those embarking from the China Cove trailhead will simply descend a flight of stairs or the park's access road to the beach.

Walk down-coast (that's east along this section of Monterey Bay). After a half mile or so, you'll beach-comb beyond the New Brighton State Beach boundary, then soon traipse onto Seacliff State Beach. Private residences line the cliffs above.

The near-view is dominated by the Seacliff Pier while more distant vistas, on fog-free days, encompass the Monterey Peninsula. What looks like a motor home sales lot above the beach is actually a state park "En Route" Campground.

Walk onto the curious Seacliff Pier and gaze down-coast. If you're in the mood for a longer walk, hit the beach. Otherwise, return the way you came.

NATURAL BRIDGES STATE BEACH

■ MONARCH TRAIL
0.75 mile round trip

Until October 1989, when the devastating Loma Prieta Earthquake shook Santa Cruz, it was easy to see why the beach here was named Natural Bridges. Alas, this strong temblor doomed the last remaining natural bridge.

While its offshore bridges are but a memory, this park on the outskirts of Santa Cruz nevertheless offers plenty of other natural attractions. A eucalyptus grove in the center of the park hosts the largest concentration of monarch butterflies in America. The park has an extensive interpretive program from October through March, when the monarchs winter at the grove.

Another park highlight is a superb rocky tidepool area, habitat for mussels, limpets, barnacles and sea urchins. After you explore the park, visit nearby Long Marine Laboratory, located just up-coast at the end of Delaware Avenue. University of California Santa Cruz faculty and students use the research facility, which studies coastal ecology. The Lab's Marine Aquarium is open to the public by docent tours.

DIRECTIONS TO TRAILHEAD Natural Bridges State Beach is located off Highway 1 in Santa Cruz at 2531 W. Cliff Drive. Follow the signs from Highway 1.

The last Natural Bridge fell down in the great quake of 1989.

THE HIKE Signed Monarch Trail begins near the park's small interpretive center. Soon the trail splits; the leftward fork leads to a monarch observation platform. Sometimes on cold mornings, the butterflies look like small, brown, fluttering leaves. As the sun warms the tropical insects, the "leaves" come to life bobbing and darting. As many as 200,000 monarchs cluster in the state park on a "good" butterfly year. The other branch of the trail is a self-guided nature trail. It ends in a grove of Monterey pine.

When you head back to the visitor center, detour down to the beach. Just up the beach is Secret Lagoon, the domain of ducks and great blue herons. Up the beach is one of the Central Coast's truly superb tidepool areas.

WILDER RANCH STATE HISTORIC PARK

■ OLD LANDING COVE TRAIL, OHLONE BLUFF TRAIL

From Wilder Ranch to Old Landing Cove is 2 miles round trip; to Four Mile Beach is 10.5 miles round trip

At Wilder Ranch State Historic Park, located on the coast just north of Santa Cruz, you get the feeling that not one stone has gone unpreserved.

The Brussels sprouts fields are in an agricultural preserve, the former Wilder Ranch is in a cultural preserve, and Wilder Beach is now a natural preserve for the benefit of nesting snowy plovers. All these preserves are found within Wilder Ranch State Historic Park, which in turn preserves some 4,000 acres of beach, bluffs, and inland canyons.

Rancho del Matadero was started here by Mission Santa Cruz in 1791. The Wilder family operated what was by all accounts a very successful and innovative dairy for nearly 100 years. The California Department of Parks and Recreation acquired the land in 1974.

The Wilders' ranch buildings, barn, gardens and Victorian house still stand, and are open to public tours. The parks department is slowly restoring the area to reflect its historic use as a dairy.

In addition to the guided historic walks, the park boasts Old Landing Cove Trail, a blufftop path that as its name suggests leads to a historic cove. From the

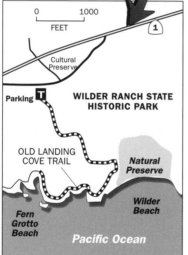

1850s to the 1890s, schooners dropped anchor in this cove to load lumber. Observant hikers can spot iron rings, which supported landing chutes, still embedded in the cliffs.

Fans of Brussels sprouts will see more of this vegetable than they ever dreamed possible; fully 12 percent of our nation's production is grown in the state park.

DIRECTIONS TO TRAILHEAD   From Santa Cruz, head north on Coast Highway four miles to the signed turnoff for Wilder Ranch State Park on the ocean side of the highway. Follow the park road to its end at the large parking lot, where the signed trail begins.

THE HIKE The path, an old ranch road, heads coastward. Signs warn you not to head left to Wilder Beach (where the snowy plovers dwell) and discourage you from heading right, where pesticides are used on the fields of Brussels sprouts.

The trail offers a bird's-eye view of the surf surging into a sea cave, then turns north and follows the cliff edge.

Old Landing Cove is smaller than you imagine, and you wonder how the coastal schooners of old managed to maneuver into such small confines. If it's low tide, you might see harbor seals resting atop the flat rocks located offshore.

One more natural attraction at the cove: a fern-filled sea cave. The ferns are watered by an underground spring.

The trail continues another half mile along the bluffs, offering vistas at seals basking on the rocks below the sandy beach. This is a good turnaround point (for a 3.5 mile round trip).

Ambitious hikers will continue north another 3.5 miles along land's end, following footpaths and ranch roads past Strawberry Beach, and Three Mile Beach, retreating inland now and then to bypass deep gullies, and finally arriving at the park's north boundary at Four Mile Beach. A splendid coastal hike!

AÑO NUEVO STATE RESERVE

■ AÑO NUEVO TRAIL
3 miles round trip

One of the best new year's resolutions a walker could make is to plan a winter trip to Año Nuevo State Reserve. Here you'll be treated to a wildlife drama that attracts visitors from all over the world—a close-up look at the largest mainland population of elephant seals.

From December through April, a colony of the huge creatures visits Año Nuevo island and point in order to breed and bear young. To protect the elephant seals (and the humans who hike out to see them), the reserve is open only through naturalist-guided tours during these months.

Slaughtered for their oil-rich blubber, the elephant seal population numbered fewer than 100 by the early 1900s. Placed under government protection, the huge mammals rebounded rapidly from the brink of extinction. Año Nuevo State Reserve was created in 1958 to protect the seals.

Male elephant seals, some reaching lengths of 16 feet and weighing three tons, arrive in December and begin battling for dominance. Only a very small percentage of males actually get to inseminate a female; most remain lifelong bachelors. The females, relatively svelte at 1,200 to 2,000 pounds, come ashore in January and join the harems of the dominant males.

La Punta de Año Nuevo (The Point of the New Year) was named by the Spanish explorer Sebastián Vizcaíno on January 3, 1603. It's one of the oldest place-names in California.

At the time of its discovery, the Point was occupied by the Ohlone, who lived off the bounty of sea. Judging from kitchen midden sites—shell mounds—found in the nearby dunes, it was a rich bounty indeed.

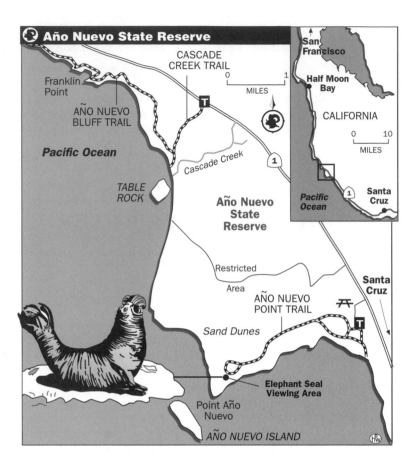

The Año Nuevo area later hosted a variety of enterprises. From the 1850s to 1920, redwood cut from the slopes of the nearby Santa Cruz Mountains was shipped from Año Nuevo Bay. A dairy industry flourished on the coastal bluffs. The reserve's visitor center is a restored century-old dairy barn.

While the elephant seals are clearly the main attraction when they come ashore during the winter to breed and during the spring and summer to molt, the reserve is even fascinating when the big creatures are not in residence; in fact, Año Nuevo is a year-round destination.

Bird-watchers may glimpse a cliff swallow, Western gull, red-tailed hawk and many other inland and shore birds. The beautiful sand dunes of the Reserve are covered with beach grass, morning glory and extensive patches of beach strawberry.

Joining the elephant seals on Año Nuevo Island are Steller sea lions, California sea lions and harbor seals. Seals inhabit Año Nuevo year-round. Viewing is great in the spring and summer months—on the beaches. Autumn brings one- to three-year-old "yearling" seals ashore to rest on the beaches.

Guided walks are conducted daily and consist of a 2.5-hour, three-mile-long walk. Advance reservations for the guided walks are strongly recommended. Reservations can be made through tfhe state park system's reservation contractor.

From April through November, acccess to the Año Nuevo Point Wildlife Protection Area is by permit only. Permits are issued free of charge daily at the reserve, on a first-come–first-served basis.

DIRECTIONS TO TRAILHEAD Año Nuevo State Reserve is located just west of Highway 1, 22 miles north of Santa Cruz and 30 miles south of Half Moon Bay.

RESERVATIONS/INFORMATION
Año Nuevo Point, where the elephant seals reside, is open only to visitors on guided walks, conducted by state park volunteer naturalists, from December through March.

BEAN HOLLOW STATE BEACH

■ ARROYO DE LOS FRIJOLES TRAIL
From Pebble Beach to Bean Hollow State Beach is 2 miles round trip

Pebble Beach—not to be confused with the Pebble Beach of 18-hole renown near Carmel, the Pebble Beach in Tomales Bay State Park, or the Pebble Beach near Crescent City—is one of those enchanting San Mateo County beaches that extend from Año Nuevo State Reserve to Thornton State Beach, a bit south of San Francisco. The pebbles on the beach are quartz chipped from an offshore reef, tumbled ashore, then wave-polished and rounded into beautifully hued small stones.

The one mile walk between Pebble Beach and Bean Hollow Beach offers a close-up look at tidepools, wildflowers (in season), and colonies of harbor seals and shorebirds. Some walkers say that the San Mateo County beaches and bluffs remind them of the British coast near Cornwall: the beginning of the trail crosses a moor-like environment bedecked with iris and daisies.

The rocky intertidal area is habitat for sea slugs and snails, anenomes and urchins. Bird-watchers will sight cormorants, pelicans and red-billed oyster

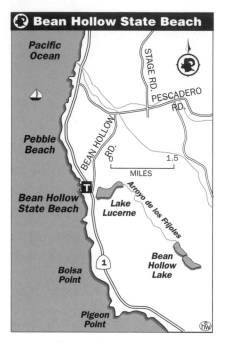

catchers flying over the water. The sandy beach is patrolled by gulls, sandpipers and sanderlings.

DIRECTIONS TO TRAILHEAD Pebble Beach is located some 40 miles south of San Francisco. The beach is off Highway 1, about 2.5 miles south of Pescadero. The trail begins at the south end of the parking lot.

THE HIKE The first part of the walk is along a nature trail. Waves crashing over the offshore reef are a dramatic sight. Keep an eye out for harbor seals swimming just offshore.

A couple of small footbridges aid your crossing of rivulets that carve the coastal bluffs. To the south, you'll get a glimpse of Pigeon Point Lighthouse, now part of a hostel. If the tide is low when you approach Bean Hollow State Beach, head down to the sand.

The state beach originally had the Spanish name of Arroyo de los Frijoles, "Creek of the Beans," before being Americanized to Bean Hollow. Picnic tables at the beach suggest a lunch or rest stop.

PESCADERO STATE BEACH

■ SEQUOIA AUDUBON TRAIL

From Pescadero State Beach to North Marsh is 2.5 miles round trip; to North Pond is 2.5 miles round trip; Precautions: North Pond area closed 3/15 to 9/1.

Bring a pair of binoculars to Pescadero Marsh Natural Preserve, the largest marsh between Monterey Bay and San Francisco. Pescadero Creek and Butano Creek pool resources to form a lagoon and estuary that is a haven for birds, and a heaven for bird-watchers.

Peer through willows, tules and cattails, and you might spot diving ducks, great egrets, or yellow-throated warblers. More than 180 species of birds have been sighted in the preserve.

Best bird-watching is in late fall and early spring. To protect the birds during breeding season, the northernmost preserve trail is closed. You may take one of the walks described below, or simply wander the perimeter of the marsh to one of the wooden observation decks, and begin your bird-watching.

DIRECTIONS TO TRAILHEAD Pescadero State Beach and Pescadero Marsh Natural Preserve are located off Highway 1, some 15 miles south of Half Moon Bay. The state beach has three parking areas. The largest area is at the south end of the beach, where Pescadero Road junctions Highway 1.

THE HIKE From the southernmost beach parking area, follow the beach north. If it's low tide, you'll get a good look at some fascinating tidepools. A half mile of travel brings you to the mouth of Butano Creek. You may have to hike inland a bit to find a good place to ford the creek.

Turn inland and pass under the highway bridge. You'll join Sequoia Audubon Trail, which meanders between the south shore of North Marsh and the north bank of Butano Creek. Take the first fork to the left and loop toward North Marsh. A right turn, as you near the marsh, will allow you to loop back to the Sequoia Audubon Trail.

To North Pond: Walk north on Pescadero Beach. A half mile beyond Butano Creek, you'll come to the massive cliff faces of San Mateo Coast State Beaches. (With a low tide, you could walk along the base of the cliffs to San Gregorio Beach.) Turn inland to

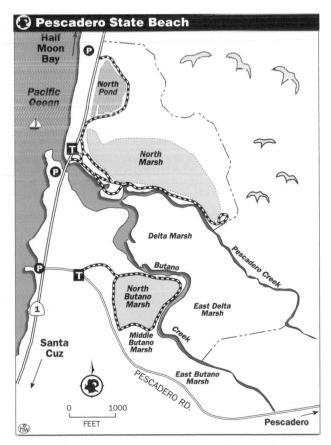

Pescadero State Beach

Half Moon Bay

Pacific Ocean

North Pond

North Marsh

Delta Marsh

Pescadero Creek

Butano

North Butano Marsh

East Delta Marsh

Middle Butano Marsh

Creek

East Butano Marsh

Santa Cuz

PESCADERO RD.

Pescadero

0   1000
FEET

the northern Pescadero State Beach parking area. Directly across the road from the entrance to the parking lot is the trailhead for North Marsh Trail.

Follow the half mile path as it loops around North Pond. Cattle graze the slopes above the pond, and abundant birdlife populates the surrounding thickets. The path climbs a small hill where a wooden observation deck affords a grand view of the large North Marsh.

You can return by taking the trail south and to the left. It leads to Sequoia Audubon Trail, which in turn takes you under the Butano Creek Bridge. You then follow the beach back to your starting point.

West Butano Loop: For another fine bird walk, transport yourself 0.5 mile up Pescadero Road. Entry to the small, dirt parking area is almost directly opposite the San Mateo County road maintenance station.

The unsigned trail leads north from the parking area, and winds through a wide, lush meadow. When you get to the creek, follow the trail east (rightward). As you follow Butano Creek, you'll be walking the tops of dikes which once allowed coastal farmers to use this rich bottom land for growing artichokes, brussels sprouts, and beans. Adjacent lands are still carefully cultivated by local farmers.

Watch for blue herons and snowy egrets. Perhaps you'll even spot the San Francisco garter snake, an endangered species. After following Butano Creek through the marsh, you'll join the trail to the right to return to the starting point.

HALF MOON BAY STATE PARK

■ COASTSIDE TRAIL
From Francis Beach to Roosevelt Beach is 6 miles round trip

From East Breakwater, Half Moon Bay arcs southward, backed by a long sandy beach. Forming a backdrop to the beach are eroded cliffs and low dunes.

Three miles of shoreline and four beaches—Roosevelt, Dunes, Venice and Francis—comprise Half Moon Bay State Park. Extending north of the park is more accessible—and walkable—shoreline.

Coastside Trail, extending along the park's eastern boundary, is a multi-use pathway open to cyclists and walkers. Depending on the tide, you can return via the beach. Coastside Trail is a better bike ride than walk; its function is to link

Half Moon Bay State Park

Pacific Ocean

Montara

Montara Lighthouse

Montara Mountain

Moss Beach

James Fitzgerald Marine Reserve

Pillar Point Harbor

Pillar Point

Dunes Beach

Half Moon Bay

Venice Beach

Half Moon Bay

Francis Beach

92

0   1
MILES

the various state beaches and it does that quite well but it isn't all that interesting of a saunter. It does, however, bring some marvelous beaches within reach, and for that reason is worth the walk.

DIRECTIONS TO TRAILHEAD From Highway 1 in the town of Half Moon Bay (0.25 mile north of the intersection with Highway 92) turn west on Kelly Avenue and drive to Francis Beach. There is a state park day use fee.

THE HIKE The trail winds past low sandy hills, dotted by clumps of cordgrass. At trail's end you can extend your walk by beachcombing northward toward Pillar Harbor by way of Miramar Beach and El Granada Beach.

MCNEE RANCH STATE PARK

■ MONTARA MOUNTAIN TRAIL
7.5 miles round trip with 2,000-foot elevation gain

Not even a sign welcomes you to McNee Ranch State Park, located on the San Mateo County coast 25 miles south of San Francisco.

But what the park lacks in signs and facilities, it makes up in grand views and wide open spaces. And oh, what a view! The coastline from Half Moon Bay to the Golden Gate National Recreation Area is at your feet.

The panoramic view is a hiker's reward for the rigorous ascent of Montara Mountain, whose slopes form the bulk of the state park. Montara Mountain, geologists say, is a 90-million-year-old chunk of granite (largely quartz diorite) that forms the northernmost extension of the Santa Cruz Mountains.

Alas, what is a beautiful park to hikers is an ideal location for a multi-lane highway to the California Department of Transportation. Caltrans wants to build a Highway 1 bypass through the park to replace the existing landslide-prone stretch of highway known as the Devil's Slide that begins about two miles south of Pacifica.

Caltrans and its building plans have been fiercely contested by environmentalists, who fear the highway bypass would completely destroy the ambiance of the park and lead to further development in the area. The two sides have been battling it out in court for several years.

At the moment, it's not cement, but the coastal scrub community—ceanothus, sage and monkeyflower—that predominates on the mountain. The park also boasts several flower-strewn grasslands. Meandering down Montara Mountain is willow- and alder-lined Martini Creek, which forms the southern boundary of the state park.

The park's trail system includes footpaths as well as Old San Pedro Road, a dirt road that's popular with mountain bikers. Little hiker symbols keep walkers on the trail, but since all routes climb Montara Mountain and more or less meet at the top, don't be overly concerned about staying on the "right" trail.

Opposite the state park, across Coast Highway, is Montara State Beach. This half mile sand strand is a popular surfing, fishing and picnicking spot.

Hikers will note that the nearest spot for provisions is the hamlet of Montara, where there's a café and grocery store. Good accommodations for a hiker on a budget is the Point Montara Lighthouse Hostel right on the coast. The thirty-bed hostel, which is located right next to a working lighthouse, has kitchen facilities, a volleyball court, and even an outdoor hot tub.

DIRECTIONS TO TRAILHEAD Take Highway 1 to Montara and park in the fair-sized lot at the north end of Montara State Beach. Walk carefully 150 yards up-coast and cross the highway. The unsigned trail begins at a pipe gate across a fire road on the inland side of Coast Highway.

THE HIKE Head up the fire road a short distance and join the trail on your left, which swings north, up-coast, over a seasonally flowered grassy slope. The path drops to join a dirt road, then begins ascending once more.

As you climb, you pass two benches, strategically placed for you to catch your breath. The dirt road eventually swings south, but you join a footpath and ascend to a saddle. Two trails lead left to the peak and terrific views.

Below you, up-coast, is the town of Pacifica and beyond that the Golden Gate Bridge and San Francisco Bay. To the east is Mount Diablo, and way out to sea on the far horizon are the Farallon Islands.

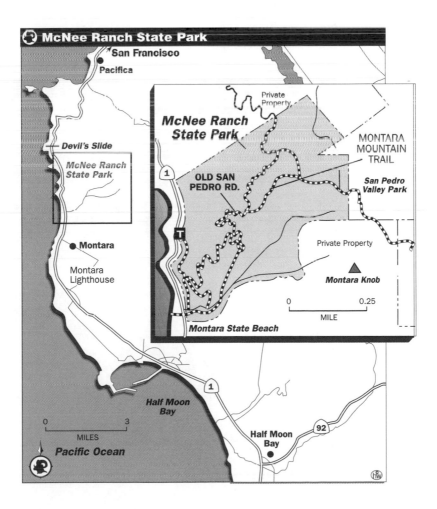

Top: Barkhouses at Indian Grinding Rock State Historic Park.

Middle: The granite spires of Castle Crags State Park.

Bottom: Snow on the tufa formations in Mono Lake Tufa State Reserve.

CHAPTER SEVEN

NORTHERN CALIFORNIA MOUNTAINS

The High Sierra extends along the eastern edge of California. The rugged "Range of Light" is a magnificent backdrop for Lake Tahoe, as well as the state parks along its shore—Emerald Bay, D.L. Bliss, and Sugar Pine Point. A reminder of just how rugged the Sierra can be is found at Donner Lake, where a state park remembers the ill-fated journey and encampment of the pioneers of the Donner Party.

In the Sierra foothills lies the Gold Country, where the fabled Mother Lode lured hundreds of thousands of settlers to California. Highway 49 pays tribute to that era: Marshall Gold Discovery, Empire Mine, Malakoff Diggins. These parks preserve tunnels, trails, mines and mountains made famous by the '49ers.

Also on the western slope of the Sierra Nevada are the famed giant sequoia groves of Calaveras Big Trees State Park. The "Big" in the park name is no exaggeration; sequoias are the largest living things on earth.

Classic California: oak-dotted hills and a pastoral scene that's easy on the eye.

The environment that contributes to the making of fine wine—rolling hills, fertile valleys, warm days and cool nights—also adds up to some beautiful countryside, known to visitors from around the world as "California's wine country." Several inviting parks are nestled in the land of grape. It's easy to see why famed writer Jack London found inspiration at his Beauty Ranch, now preserved as Jack London State Historic Park. Robert Louis Stevenson was similarly inspired by the environs around Mt. Saint Helena.

In that "other wine country" north of Napa-Sonoma, walkers can gain insight into Native American life at Anderson Marsh State Historic Park and take in (or jump in) California's largest body of water—Clear Lake.

JACK LONDON STATE HISTORIC PARK

■ BEAUTY RANCH, LAKE, MOUNTAIN TRAILS

To lake is 2 miles round trip; to top of Sonoma Mountain is 8.25 miles round trip with 1,800-foot elevation gain

There have been few more colorful, individualistic, and, ultimately more tragic figures in American literature than Jack London. Born in San Francisco in 1876, London struggled to release himself from the stifling burdens of illegitimacy and poverty.

His quest led him on a succession of rugged adventures in far-flung locales. He was an oyster pirate in San Francisco Bay, a gold prospector in the frozen Klondike, a sailor in the South Seas. He drew largely on his rough and tumble experiences throughout his prolific career as a writer of novels, short stories, and magazine articles.

London, who by most accounts was the most successful writer of his time—in terms of financial earnings, fame and popularity—is today best-known for his outdoor adventure stories. White Fang, The Call of the Wild, and To Build a Fire, his most popular works, have stereotyped the writer as one who depicts the theme of the individual's struggle to survive, using nature's harshness as a backdrop. But London's message was more complex than that, yet through time it's been largely ignored.

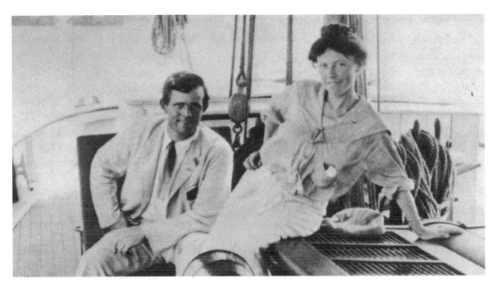

Jack London and his wife, Charmian.

A passionate humanist, London was deeply committed to the cause of socialism. In his day, before the Russian Revolution skewed the promise of utopian socialism, London viewed socialism as the way to restore human dignity and respect for the individual. He raged against the oppressive social conditions of the Industrial Age in The People of the Abyss, Martin Eden, and The Iron Heel.

London's life was a mass of contradictions. He was a wealthy socialist, a he-man who was plagued with ill health, an imaginative writer who feared he would one day run out of ideas. He and his wife Charmian lived in the bucolic setting of Glen Ellen, far from the crowded city conditions he decried.

London first purchased land in the Sonoma Valley in 1905, and continued to add to his holdings until he owned 1,350 acres. As he described the setting: "...there are great redwoods on it...also there are great firs, tanbark oaks, live oaks, white oaks, black oaks, madrone and manzanita galore. There are canyons, several streams of water, many springs...I have been riding all over these hills, looking for just such a place, and I must say that I have never seen anything like it."

The Jack London Ranch is now the site of Jack London State Historic Park, established in 1960 in accordance with the wishes of his wife.

Among the attractions to be found in the park are the House of Happy Walls Museum, built by Charmian London as a memorial to her husband's life and work and the remains of the Wolf House mansion, suspiciously burned to the ground shortly before the Londons were scheduled to move in.

Before or after this walk, be sure to make the 1.5 mile pilgrimage to Jack London's gravesite and to the Wolf House ruins.

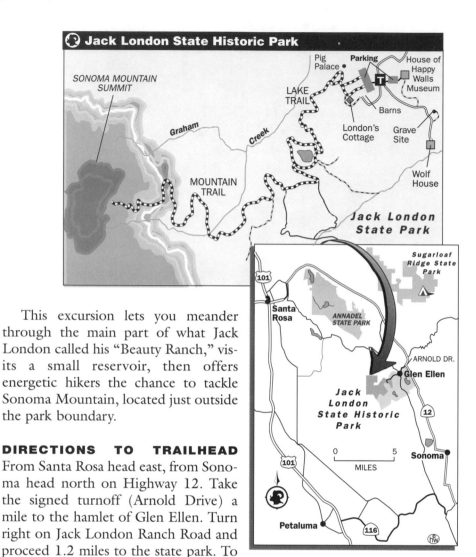

This excursion lets you meander through the main part of what Jack London called his "Beauty Ranch," visits a small reservoir, then offers energetic hikers the chance to tackle Sonoma Mountain, located just outside the park boundary.

DIRECTIONS TO TRAILHEAD From Santa Rosa head east, from Sonoma head north on Highway 12. Take the signed turnoff (Arnold Drive) a mile to the hamlet of Glen Ellen. Turn right on Jack London Ranch Road and proceed 1.2 miles to the state park. To visit the museum, turn left; for trailhead parking, angle right.

THE HIKE The path ascends a hundred yards southwest through a eucalyptus grove to a trail map and picnic area. Proceed straight ahead, past an old barn to a dirt road, where you go right.

A side trail leads to the cottage where London worked in his final years. The dirt road forks. You head right along a vineyard, meandering past "Pig Palace," London's hog pen deluxe, as well as assorted silos.

About a half mile from the trailhead, you'll crest a hill and get your first great view of the Valley of the Moon. The trail soon splits: equestrians go left, hikers go right on a narrow footpath through a forest of Douglas fir, bay laurel and madrone that ascends past some good-sized redwoods.

Lake Trail loops around the Londons' little lake, where the couple swam and enjoyed entertaining friends. This is a good turnaround point for families with young children.

Sonoma Mountain-bound hikers will join the dirt road, Mountain Trail, which curves east to Mays Clearing, another fine vista point offering Valley of the Moon panoramas.

Mountain Trail climbs steadily, crosses two forks of fern-lined Graham Creek, and ascends to what was once Jack London's hunting camp (Deer Camp), tucked in a grove of redwoods. It's marked "Rest Area" on the park map.

Mountain Trail resumes climbing, steeper now, beneath big black oaks, for another mile, ascending to the headwaters of Middle Graham Creek and up to the park boundary.

The park map shows the path ending here; actually, it continues another 0.25 mile to the crest of Sonoma Mountain's east ridge. Enjoy the superb views from this, the park's summit. (The actual mountaintop, eighty feet higher in elevation than the east summit, is forested with antennae and microwave relays and is located another 0.25 mile to the west.)

ANNADEL STATE PARK

■ WARREN RICHARDSON, STEVE'S "S" TRAILS
To Lake Ilsanjo is 5 miles round trip with 500-foot elevation gain; circling the lake adds an additional 2 miles

Thirty-five miles of hiking trail plus good black bass and bluegill fishing are the highlights of Annadel State Park. Tucked away in the heart of the park, Lake Ilsanjo, where the fish bite and hikers hike, is a pleasant destination for day hike. Bring meal worms to tempt the bluegill to bite, or purple plastic worms for the bass, or simply bring your own picnic and let the fish feed themselves.

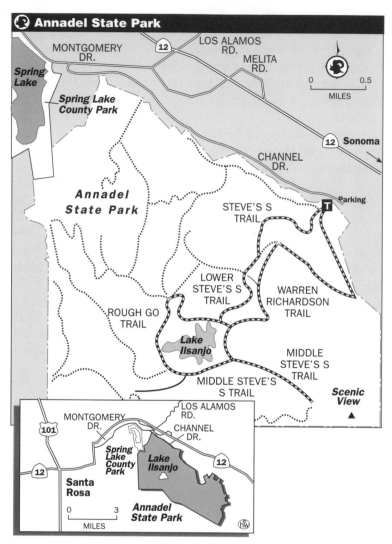

The lake's Spanish-sounding name does not date from the days of the ranchos and rancheros, as one might guess; it's actually a composite formed from the first names of two former landowners, Ilsa and Joe Coney, who built the lake in 1956.

It was not the tranquil shores of Lake Ilsanjo, but the rocky hills around it that brought the first humans to the area. Pomo and Wappo gathered obsidian, using the shiny black rock to fashion knife blades, arrowheads and spearheads.

Settlers, too, came for the rocks. Basalt was quarried here at the turn of the century to build San Francisco; after the great 1906 earthquake, the rock was used to rebuild the city. Also quarried, for city streets, was cobblestone, though in no time such paving fell into disfavor with drivers of the new horseless carriages.

Once part of the 1837 Mexican land grant, Rancho Los Guilicos, the Annadel area was owned by a series of farmers and gentlemen ranchers. Annadel became a state park in 1971.

A favorite way to Lake Ilsanjo is via Warren Richardson Trail, a wide path that honors a prominent Sonoma County cattle rancher and avid horseman with a love for trails. Warren Richardson Trail winds through a cool forest and crosses an open meadow on the way to the lake. For a fun return trip, loop back on steep, fern- and fir-lined Steve's S Trail.

DIRECTIONS TO TRAILHEAD From Highway 101 in Santa Rosa, exit on Highway 12 (toward Sonoma) and follow it east through town. Turn right on Montgomery Drive, then right again on Channel Drive and follow it a mile into the park. The park office (where you'll find water, maps for sale) is at the entrance; trailhead parking is a mile farther down the road.

THE HIKE From the parking lot, join the trail leading south, which in no time at all delivers you to a dirt road—Warren Richardson Trail. You'll pause to view an interpretive display about how the Indians used acorns, then spot Steve's S Trail (your return route) on the right.

About 0.75 mile of easy walking from the trailhead brings you to a hairpin turn and a junction with Two Quarry Trail. Swing northwest on Warren Richardson Trail and begin ascending through a forest of redwoods and Douglas fir. Sword ferns seem to point the way uphill.

The dirt road turns south again, passes a junction with Louis Trail, then begins descending. You get your first glimpse of Lake Ilsanjo. Emerging from the woods, you cross a meadow to the lakeshore.

To circle the lake, continue on Warren Richardson Trail, then join Rough Go Trail and Middle Steve's S Trail. Parts of the lakeshore are carpeted with blue-eyed grass.

Your return route joins Steve's S Trail, which skirts the east end of the meadow as it begins to ascend. Topping a hill, the path joins up with the North Burma Trail for a brief descent; then Steve's S Trail forks left and descends through a Douglas fir forest. A mile's descent deposits you on Warren Richardson Trail, very close to where you began this hike.

SUGARLOAF RIDGE STATE PARK

■ BALD MOUNTAIN, VISTA, GRAY PINE, MEADOW TRAILS

6 mile loop through park with 700-foot elevation gain; shorter and longer loops possible

Today we buy granulated sugar in sacks, but grocers of years ago sold crystallized sugar in a sugarloaf—a conical shape that resembled an upside-down ice cream cone.

Among the more prominent sugarloaves in Southern California are 9,952-foot Sugarloaf Peak in the San Bernardino Mountains and Sugarloaf Mountain in the Santa Monica Mountains—reportedly inspiration for the Paramount Pictures logo.

In Northern California, a distinguished sugarloaf rising above the wine country is the highlight of Sugarloaf Ridge State Park. Sugarloaf Ridge is part of a length of Coastal Range called the Mayacamas Mountains, which border Sonoma and Napa Valleys. The distinct ridge, volcanic in origin, is impressive—and just a little bit spooky when wrapped in mist or when turkey vultures circle.

The state park is laced with 25 miles of trail, leading through three distinct ecosystems. Chaparral blankets the high ridges, except for the park's aptly named high point, Bald Mountain. Your reward for climbing this mountain is a terrific view stretching from the Napa Valley vineyards to the snowy peaks of the Sierra Nevada.

The park's grassy meadows are bedecked in spring with a multitude of colorful wildflowers from Indian pinks to blue dicks. Also look for lupine, California poppy, cream cups, buttercups and Mariposa lily.

In the canyons watered by Sonoma Creek and its tributaries grow Douglas fir, oak, big-leaf maple, and even a grove of redwood. Swollen by winter rains, Sonoma Creek generates a handsome, 25-foot waterfall that cascades below the park campground.

Depending on time, energy, and inclination, the hiker can fashion several four- to eight-mile loops through the state park. For a good introduction to local flora, join the 0.75 mile Creekside Nature Trail. Numbered posts along the trail correspond to park brochure nature descriptions.

DIRECTIONS TO TRAILHEAD From Highway 101 in Santa Rosa, exit on Highway 12 and travel east 11 miles to Adobe Canyon Road. Turn left and follow it four miles to the hikers' parking lot a bit before road's end.

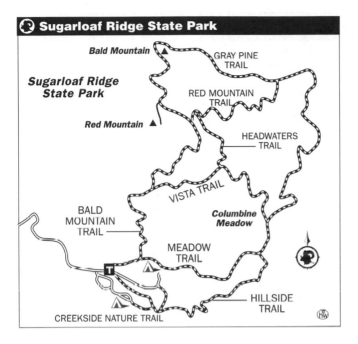

Sugarloaf Ridge State Park

Bald Mountain ▲

GRAY PINE TRAIL

Sugarloaf Ridge State Park

RED MOUNTAIN TRAIL

Red Mountain ▲

HEADWATERS TRAIL

VISTA TRAIL

BALD MOUNTAIN TRAIL

Columbine Meadow

MEADOW TRAIL

T

HILLSIDE TRAIL

CREEKSIDE NATURE TRAIL

THE HIKE From the east end of the parking lot, hit the trail which leads into a meadow and soon splits. Join Lower Bald Mountain Trail, which crosses a meadow, then ascends through an oak and madrone woodland. After a mile's brisk climb, the path intersects paved Bald Mountain Trail. A strategically placed bench allows you to catch your breath and to gaze out over the park

Proceed right on the road, ascending steeply 0.25 mile to signed Vista Trail. The intrepid will continue marching up the road, past the turnoff to Red Mountain (2,548 feet) to the summit of Bald Mountain 2,729 feet. From Bald Mountain, enjoy the view of the Napa Valley below, Mt. Saint Helena above. On especially clear days, the panorama includes the High Sierra and San Francisco Bay.

Those forsaking the peak, will join Vista Trail, which drops into a couple of ravines watered by seasonal Sonoma Creek tributaries. Vista Trail serves up promised vistas of Sugarloaf Ridge, then descends through Columbine Meadow. Cross Sonoma Creek, join Gray Pine Trail and cross a meadow. Bordering the meadow is quite a mixture of trees: maples, black oaks, alders and bays.

At a signed trail junction, you can select Meadow Trail, which crosses a meadow and returns you to trailhead.

A less direct way back is to join Hillside Trail, which climbs above Sonoma Creek and gives you another perspective —a northern view—of the state park, then descends to join Creekside Nature Trail near the campground and trailhead.

BOTHE-NAPA VALLEY STATE PARK

■ REDWOOD, RITCHEY CANYON TRAILS

6.5 miles round trip with 1,200-foot elevation gain;
longer and shorter options possible

First-time visitors to this park typically arrive by accident, not design; they've just completed a tour of one of the renowned Napa Valley wineries and are looking for a place to picnic.

But if it's the park's proximity to wineries (just down the road are Beringer Vineyards, Charles Krug Winery and a dozen more) that first lures travelers, it's the park's beauty that brings them back: year-round Ritchey Creek shaded by redwoods and Douglas fir, plus inspiring wine country views from Coyote Peak. The park is a particularly pleasant refuge in summer, because it stays cool when Napa Valley temperatures soar into the 90s.

During the 1800s, this land belonged to Dr. Charles M. Hitchcock of San Francisco, who built a second home called "Lonely" in 1872.

Life in the country seemed to have resulted in the fierce independence of Hitchcock's daughter, Lillie. An early feminist, she scandalized her social set by riding horseback astride, forcing her way into an exclusive men's club, and winning poker games.

As a child, Lillie Hitchcock was rescued from a fire that killed two of her playmates. As an adult, she was an enthusiastic booster of San Francisco's firemen. When she died in 1929, Lillie Hitchcock Coit left the city of San Francisco the money to build Coit Tower, a memorial to the city's firemen.

Reinhold Bothe acquired part of the Hitchcock/Coit estate and developed a resort, Paradise Park, with cabins and a swimming pool. The resort was popular during the 1930s, much less so after World War II. The state park system purchased Paradise Park from Bothe in 1960.

Best hike in the 1,900-acre park is an exploration of three mile long, fern-lined, redwood-shaded Ritchey Canyon. The redwoods sprouted from the roots of trees felled in the 1850s during the settlement of Napa Valley. The second-generation trees are thriving. Adding a magical touch to the forest scene are redwood orchids and trillium growing at the base of the redwoods.

DIRECTIONS TO TRAILHEAD Bothe-Napa Valley State Park is located on the west side of Highway 29 in the Napa Valley, five miles north of St. Helena, four miles south of Calistoga. Leave your car by the visitor center or at the horse

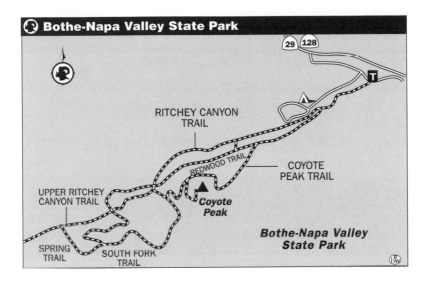

Bothe-Napa Valley State Park

RITCHEY CANYON TRAIL

REDWOOD TRAIL

COYOTE PEAK TRAIL

UPPER RITCHEY CANYON TRAIL

Coyote Peak

Bothe-Napa Valley State Park

SPRING TRAIL SOUTH FORK TRAIL

trailer parking area just past the campground road turnoff where the trail begins.

THE HIKE The trail, which travels west beneath big leaf maple, madrone and oaks soon crosses a paved road and begins paralleling the road to the campground, as well as Ritchey Creek.

Beneath the tall Douglas firs and redwoods grows a tangle of ferns, bay laurel and wild grape. After 0.5 mile, you'll pass a trail on your right leading to the campground. A mile out, the forest thins and you intersect Coyote Peak Trail on your left.

Recently re-worked and re-routed Coyote Peak Trail climbs high and dry terrain and offers good views of Upper Ritchey Canyon, plus glimpses of the wine country and mighty Mt. Saint Helena.

As the path steepens, you'll pass more big redwoods and firs. About 1.5 miles along, you cross Ritchey Creek (usually an easy crossing except when rains swell the creek). This is a good turnaround point for the leg-weary or families with small children.

The trail continues up-canyon, crossing Ritchey Creek again and linking up with Upper Ritchey Canyon Trail. After passing a junction with Spring Trail, you climb above the forest into a brushy environment of manzanita and scrub oak, then dip back into the redwoods.

Three miles from the trailhead, your path forks. The main trail angles left, then climbs south to the park boundary.

A better bet is the right fork, which leads over an old bridge to an 1885 homestead site, where plum and apple trees grow in a picnic-perfect clearing.

Return the same way, or take a slightly longer route back via either Spring Trail or Coyote Peak Trail.

ROBERT LOUIS STEVENSON STATE PARK

■ STEVENSON MEMORIAL TRAIL

To Stevenson Memorial is 2 miles round trip; to summit of Mt. Saint Helena is 10 miles round trip with 1,300-foot elevation gain

You can see the imposing mountain towering above the wineries. Mt. Saint Helena is a landmark, a wild backdrop behind the neatly cultivated vineyards of Napa Valley.

The best view of the wine country is from the top of 4,343-foot Mt. Saint Helena, reached by a five-mile trail that winds through stands of knobcone pine to deliver summit panoramas of not only Napa Valley but the High Sierra and San Francisco Bay as well.

While winter is not the most popular of seasons for touring the wine country, it is the best time for looking down at it from the top of Mt. Saint Helena. Crisp, clear winter days mean breathtaking views from the summit. Local Sierra Club members schedule an annual New Year's Day hike up the mountain—surely an invigorating way to celebrate the year past and welcome the year ahead.

Most of the summit and broad shoulders of Mt. Saint Helena are protected by Robert Louis Stevenson State Park. Stevenson, best remembered for his imaginative novels, Dr. Jekyll and Mr. Hyde and Treasure Island, honeymooned in a cabin tucked in one of Mt. Saint Helena's ravines in the summer of 1880.

Quite the world traveler, Stevenson, constantly seeking relief from chronic tuberculosis, globe-trotted from Switzerland to the south of France to Samoa. The native Scot followed his heart to California to marry an American woman, Fanny Osbourne.

Short of money, the newlyweds honeymooned in the abandoned mining camp of Silverado, moving into an old cabin and using hay for a bed. While so encamped, Stevenson filled a diary with local color and later penned an account of his experience, *The Silverado Squatters,* which introduced him to American readers.

Stevenson filled his notebooks with descriptions of the many colorful Napa Valley denizens—from stage drivers to winemakers—he met. Perhaps the biggest influence upon Stevenson during his stay on Mt. Saint Helena was the mountain itself; it became the model for Spyglass Hill in his novel Treasure Island.

Today you can take a short (one mile) hike into California literary history by joining the trail leading to the secluded site of the Stevensons' honeymoon. Wrote Stevenson: "At sunrise, and again later at night, the scent of sweet bays filled the canyon." A memorial in the form of an open book commemorates the author's stay on the mountain and marks the site of his cabin.

Travelers interested in learning more about Robert Louis Stevenson and his work should head for the Silverado Museum in St. Helena, located seven miles south of Calistoga. The museum features books, letters, and other memorabilia of Stevenson's life.

Stevenson Memorial Trail is particularly enjoyable for the first interesting mile as it winds through the forest to the memorial. The next four miles of trail—a well-graded fire road leading to the summit—are frankly a bit monotonous; however, the grand vistas, becoming better and better as you climb, more than compensate.

Robert Louis Stevenson at the time of his wedding, 1880.

DIRECTIONS TO TRAILHEAD From downtown Calistoga, at the junction of Highways 128 and 29, head north on the latter road. Highway 29 ascends 8.2 miles to a summit, where you'll find parking at turnouts on both sides of the highway for Robert Louis Stevenson State Park. The trail departs from the west side of the highway. Hint. The not very-well-signed state park is easy to miss. If you find yourself rapidly descending on Highway 29, you overshot the summit and the state park. Carefully turn around and return to the summit.

THE HIKE Just above the parking is a picnic area. During Stevenson's day, a stage stop and the Toll House Hotel were located here. The Stevensons came down the hill from their honeymoon cabin to buy provisions.

Signed "Stevenson Memorial Trail" switchbacks up a shady slope forested with oak, madrone, bay and Douglas fir. A pleasant mile's walk brings you face-to-face with the granite Stevenson memorial, itself something of a historical curiosity, having been erected by "The Club Women of Napa County" in 1911.

To continue to the peak, scramble up a badly eroded hundred-yard-long stretch of trail to the fire road and turn left. The road soon brings you to a hairpin turn and the first grand view en route. You can admire part of the Napa Valley and surrounding ridges, San Francisco high-rises, and two distinct and aptly named nearby peaks: Turk's Head to the west and Red Hill to the south.

The road continues climbing moderately, but doggedly, up the mountain. Wind-battered, but unbowed, knobcone pines dot the middle slopes of Mt. Saint Helena. Three miles from the trailhead, you'll pass under some power

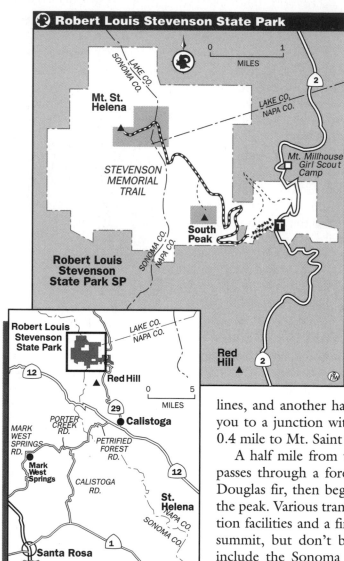

Robert Louis Stevenson State Park

lines, and another half mile's travel brings you to a junction with a spur trail leading 0.4 mile to Mt. Saint Helena's South Peak.

A half mile from the summit, the road passes through a forest of sugar pine and Douglas fir, then begins the final climb to the peak. Various transmitters, communication facilities and a fire lookout clutter the summit, but don't block the view. Vistas include the Sonoma County coast to the west, Santa Rosa due south, San Francisco and the Bay to the southwest, and the High Sierra north of Yosemite to the east. On the clearest of days, you might be able to glimpse Mt. Shasta, nearly 200 miles northeast.

ANDERSON MARSH
STATE HISTORIC PARK

■ CACHE CREEK, ANDERSON FLATS, RIDGE, MARSH TRAILS

2 to 3 miles round trip

One of the most populous Native American groups in California, the Pomo occupied the Anderson Marsh area as far back as 10,000 years ago. The Pomo, known as some of the best basket-makers on the continent, found an ample supply of raw material in the marsh.

Pomo elders construct a village in the park every year. This village of tule huts also serves as a picnic area, an odd but somehow fitting mixture of the ancient and modern uses of nature.

Anderson Marsh is also a nature preserve, which protects the habitat of a tule marsh, itself an integral part of the Clear Lake ecosystem. The marsh, located on the southeast shore of Clear Lake, offers food and breeding habitat for mammals, fish, birds and amphibians. The crappie, catfish, bass and blue gill spend parts of their life cycles amidst the tules.

Anderson Marsh is a remnant (about 8 percent) of a once-vast tule marsh that nourishes Clear Lake, California's largest natural lake. Marsh and park are named for Scottish immigrant John Still Anderson, who started a cattle ranch here in 1885. Anderson's descendants continued to live on and work the ranch until the late 1960s. Some of the original ranch buildings are open for tours on weekends.

Two trails lead along the wetter parts of the park—Cache Creek and the marsh. Two other trails—Ridge (which ascends through an oak woodland) and Anderson Flats (which crosses a grassland) explore drier parts of the park. It's less than a mile's walk to the reconstructed Pomo village.

DIRECTIONS TO TRAILHEAD Anderson Marsh SHP is located just off Highway 53 between the hamlet of Lower Lake and the town of Clear Lake. The park is a short distance north of Lower Lake and the Highway 29/53 junction. Leave your car in the lot by the visitor center or, if the park gate is closed, in a turnout across the highway from the park entrance. The park is open Wednesday through Sunday, 9 a.m. to 5 p.m.

THE HIKE Head west through the meadow along the park's southern boundary fence. The flat path through the Anderson pastureland forks: Anderson Flats

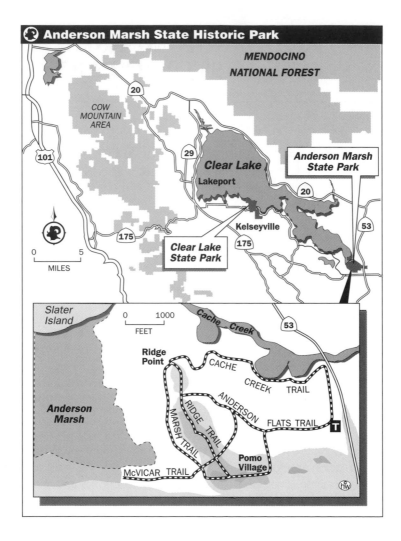

Trail (a possible return route) is on your right, but you bear left, angling with the fence line to what is (sometimes) the site of a reconstructed Pomo village.

The path ascends through a blue-oak woodland, passes a junction with Ridge Trail, then turns left to an interpretive display about bald eagles that drop in on the marsh during winter months. (Those seeking an up-close look at the marsh will join McVicar Trail, which heads into the Audubon Sanctuary.)

Otherwise, join Marsh Trail, which offers a good view of the marsh as it descends from the oak woodland toward the marsh. A bit more than a mile from the start, you'll top a low ridge and meet up with Cache Creek Trail. Atop this ridge, amidst plenty of poison oak, are Pomo grinding holes and petro-glyphs. For a moment, you're able to imagine Pomo life, at least until you look into the distance and spot the vacation homes fringing the marsh.

The quick way back—a straight line across the meadow— is Anderson Flats Trail. A more interesting return is along Cache Creek, Clear Lake's main outlet, and a watercourse that eventually empties into the Sacramento River.

Cache Creek Trail meanders across meadowland, then turns east to follow the cottonwood-lined creek. The path nears the highway, then veers right and returns to the ranch house.

CLEAR LAKE STATE PARK

■ DORN NATURE TRAIL
1.5 mile loop

Clear Lake is the largest lake located entirely within the state. (Tahoe is a larger lake, but it's partly in Nevada.) Around the lake are mountains and beyond a fruited plain of vineyards, walnut groves and, as locals boast, "the world's largest Bartlett pear growing area."

Clear Lake, earth scientists estimate, is 2.5 million years old; some claim it's the oldest lake in North America. At the very least, it's considerably older than such 5,000-year-old "infants" as Lakes Tahoe and Superior.

Clear Lake is a natural lake, meaning that it has a set-in-nature feeling, and gives an altogether more tranquil vibe than state mega-reservoirs such as Folsom Lake or Lake Oroville.

Clear Lake State Park offers much-needed public access to the lake and preserves about two miles of lakeshore. Swimming, water skiing and hiking are popular at the park, but fishing is as big as the lake itself. "Wall to wall" catfish, bluegill, crappie and black bass lure fishermen to the lake.

Located on the lake's south shore, the state park includes some terrific lakeshore campsites at Kelsey Creek Campground. A modern visitor center features exhibits about the lake, as well as Native America lore. Dorn Nature Trail samples the slopes above Clear Lake and offers fine Lake County vistas.

DIRECTIONS TO TRAILHEAD From Highway 29 in Kelseyville (just south of Lakeport) turn east on signed Soda Bay Road and follow the signs to Clear Lake State Park and the day-use parking area near the visitor center.

THE HIKE From the visitor center, walk back up the day-use access road to the main park road; here you'll see signed Dorn Nature Trail. The path joining Dorn Nature Trail from the left is the return leg of the loop.

The path ascends into a woodland of California buckeye and valley oak, switchbacks a bit, and soon serves up the first view of the lake.

A quarter-mile climb brings you to the crest of a minor ridge and a junction with a side trail splitting to the right and leading to Upper Bayview Campground. Stay left and continue on Dorn Trail to an overlook.

Oak and manzanita frame a grand view of the lake, backdropped by vineyards, orchards, and the Mendocino Coast Range.

A bit farther down the trail, a second overlook offers another vista of the lake, as well as towering Mount Konocti.

Three-quarters of a mile out, about halfway through this walk, the path descends and passes a right-forking trail leading to Lower Bayview Campground. The descent continues over fern-covered slopes, contours west, and then drops to the park road back at the trailhead.

CALAVERAS BIG TREES STATE PARK

■ SOUTH GROVE TRAIL
5 miles round trip with 400-foot elevation gain

The "Big Trees" in the park name is a tip-off: two groves of giant sequoia redwoods are the highlights of Calaveras Big Trees State Park.

The trees became world famous in the 1850s, thanks in part to some circus-style promoters, who chopped down "Discovery Tree" and took it on tour. Another set of profiteers stripped the bark off the "Mother of the Forest" and exhibited the "reassembled" tree in New York and in England's famed Crystal Palace.

Fortunately, for the trees, anyway, most of the truly curious came to visit the Sierra redwoods rather than expecting the trees to "visit" them. Scientists, celebrities, and thousands of just plain fascinated folks made their way to Calaveras County, often staying in the Mammoth Grove Hotel built close to the big trees.

For a time, scientists believed the giant sequoias in North Grove were the only ones on earth. With the discovery of other, greater groves in the Yosemite-

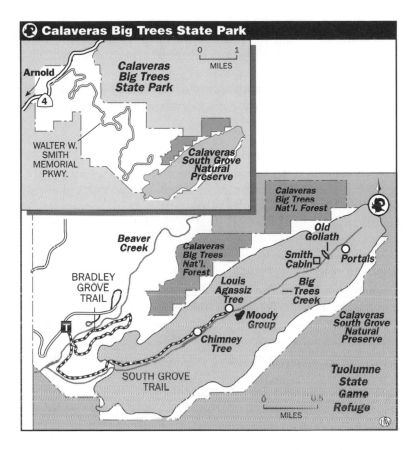

Sequoia National Park areas, the Calaveras Big Trees declined somewhat in importance as a tourist attraction.

The biggest trees are truly big—250 to 300 feet tall and 25 to 30 feet across. And they're ancient—2,000 to 3,000 years old. The trees are relics from a warmer and wetter clime and time, the Mesozoic Era, some 180 million years ago, when dinosaurs roamed the earth. Once much more numerous, the big trees survive now only in 75 groves on the western slope of the High Sierra.

"A flowering glade in the very heart of the woods, forming a fine center for the student, and a delicious resting place for the weary," is how the great naturalist John Muir described the forest of giant sequoia, ponderosa pine and incense cedar now protected by Calaveras Big Trees State Park.

The park has some great campgrounds and picnic areas, as well as an opportunity for trout fishing and a dip in the Stanislaus River. Most visitors, however, come to see the big trees, particularly those found in North Grove. A gentle one mile trail meanders through the grove, leading to such grand sequoia specimens as Abraham Lincoln, Siamese Twins, Empire State and Father of the Forest.

Much, much less visited is the park's more remote South Grove, which offers a chance for solitude among the giants. The grove is protected in a "Natural Preserve," the highest category of environmental protection offered by the state park system.

Interpretive pamphlets for both South Grove and North Grove trails are available for a small donation at their respective trailheads or at the park's museum and visitor center.

DIRECTIONS TO TRAILHEAD   The park is located off Highway 4, four miles northeast of Arnold, and some 21 miles from Angels Camp and the junction with Highway 49. Once in the park, continue nine miles along the scenic park road (Walter W. Smith Memorial Parkway) to South Grove trailhead. Snow closes the road to South Grove; call the park for latest road and weather conditions.

THE HIKE   South Grove Trail soon crosses Beaver Creek on a footbridge and reaches a junction with Bradley Trail. (This 2.5-mile-long path loops through land logged in the early 1950s. After the loggers left, park caretaker Owen Bradley planted sequoia seedlings and today about 150 young Sierra redwoods thrive in Bradley Grove, a testament to forest regeneration and to the future.)

South Grove Trail climbs moderately through tall sugar and ponderosa pines and rises out of the Beaver Creek drainage. After crossing a fire road, the path meanders upstream alongside Big Trees Creek.

Bear right at the trail junction and continue hiking among the Sierra redwoods, incense cedars and occasional big leaf maple. Just past a large hollow redwood lying across the creek, you'll reach another junction. You can bear left to complete the loop trail, but better yet, head right to visit Agassiz Tree, largest in the park. One of the more curious Sierra redwoods encountered en route is aptly named Chimney Tree; its insides were long ago consumed by fire, forming a "chimney" in a still-living tree.

Agassiz Tree, one of the "Top Ten" Sierra redwoods in size, honors nineteenth century naturalist Louis Agassiz, last of the scientific creationists and a pioneer in Ice Age theory and plant and animal classification.

While the trail ends here at this biggest of the big trees, the adventurous can continue another mile along Big Trees Creek and get up-close looks at other magnificent South Grove specimens: The Moody Group, named for a nineteenth-century evangelist, storied Old Goliath, felled by a windstorm in 1861, and three mammoth trees called The Portals.

Retrace your steps back to loop trail junction, this time branching right and descending back to the trailhead.

INDIAN GRINDING ROCK
STATE HISTORIC PARK

■ SOUTH NATURE TRAIL
0.5 to 1 mile round trip

The grinding rock—a 173-foot length of bedrock with 1,185 mortar cups is something to behold. If you let your imagination go a bit, you can conjure a whole village at work.

The Miwok gathered acorns when they ripened in autumn and stored them in large granaries. The acorns were cracked and shelled, then ground with stone pestles in the mortar holes, or chaw'se, into flour. The acorn meal was then cooked on hot rocks.

Evidence of the Miwok, whose ancestral territory centered on the western slope of the Sierra Nevada, and ranged over to the San Francisco Bay area, has been discovered in numerous locales—and in such state parks as China Camp and Olompali—but here around the grinding rock, in the Sierra foothills, it's easiest to imagine their way of life.

Miwok crafts are on display in the park's excellent Chaw'se Regional Indian Museum. On the grounds are replicas of the Miwok's sturdy barkhouses and a

The grinding rock here is the largest collection of bedrock mortar holes in N

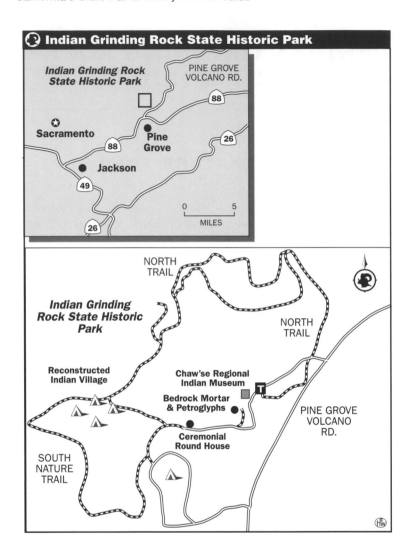

roundhouse, a traditional ceremonial gathering spot of old as well as a meeting place for several different Native American groups today.

DIRECTIONS TO TRAILHEAD From Highway 49 in Jackson, head east nine miles to the hamlet of Pine Grove. Turn left and travel 1.5 miles to Indian Grinding Rock State Historic Park. There's ample parking near the trailhead and museum-visitor center.

THE HIKE Two short trails explore the park. North Trail (one mile round trip) begins near the museum. It follows a low ridge and loops back to the reconstructed Miwok village. At the village, you can join South Nature Trail or return to the museum via a more direct route past the ceremonial roundhouse.

South Nature Trail (0.5 mile loop) is a self-guided interpretive path keyed to a park pamphlct. As you tour meadowland, oak woods, and stands of sugar pine and ponderosa pine, you'll learn how the Miwok collected and used the bountiful local vegetation.

MARSHALL GOLD DISCOVERY STATE HISTORIC PARK

■ DISCOVERY, MONUMENT, MONROE RIDGE TRAILS
4 mile loop

It was here in 1848 James Marshall discovered gold; a year later, the world discovered California.

Marshall, a carpenter, was constructing a sawmill in partnership with John Sutter when he spotted some golden flecks in the American River. He went to Sutter's Fort to share his news with his employer. The two tried to keep the gold news secret but word leaked out and the world rushed in.

The population of the hamlet of Coloma swelled to ten thousand in 1849. Two years later, the gold gave out and most of the miners left.

Today, Coloma, birthplace of the Gold Rush, is a tiny village within the boundaries of Marshall Gold Discovery State Historic Park. Several historic buildings line Highway 49, as well as narrow back streets. Park highlights include an operating replica of Sutter's Mill and the Gold Discovery Museum, with its mining exhibits and videos telling the story of Marshall's discovery.

A walking tour takes in a number of '49er-era buildings, as well as structures dating from later in the nineteenth century. Step into the Wah Hop Store, a Chinese general store. Visit Marshall Cabin, where Marshall, who benefited little from his great discovery, died bitter and penniless.

Other walks into history include a stroll down Main Street Coloma and a visit to the Pioneer Cemetery and Coloma Winery.

Monument Trail climbs to James Marshall Monument, where a bigger-than-life figure holds a bigger-than-life gold nugget and points to the spot where he made his discovery. Monroe Ridge Trail extends 2.3 miles from North Beach

picnic area to the Marshall Monument; it offers more of a workout than the historical walks.

The trail honors a pioneering African-American family who first settled here during the Gold Rush era. Family matriarch Nancy Gooch was brought to California as a slave but was soon freed when California entered the Union as a free state. She earned her living by doing laundry and domestic chores for miners and earned enough to purchase the freedom of her son Andrew Monroe and his wife Sara Ellen, who were still enslaved in Missouri.

The Monroes had a successful fruit orchard, prospered, and bought land. Family holdings included the famed gold discovery site, which the parks department purchased from the Monroe family in the 1940s.

DIRECTIONS TO TRAILHEAD Marshall Gold Discovery State Historic Park is located on Highway 49 in the town of Coloma, some 6.5 miles north of Placerville on Highway 50; some 17 miles south of Auburn and Highway 49's junction with Interstate 80. On the southern outskirts of Coloma, Highway 49 bends sharply east; you should bear south here onto Springs Road and in a short distance turn right on Monument Road, following it to a parking area near the

Marshall Monument, which occupies the top of a hill. Walk back down the hill along the road a short ways to the signed trailhead on your right.

Don't even think you'll find a free parking place anywhere in the state park. Leave your car only in the designated areas.

THE HIKE Monroe Trail (a fire road for a short distance) leads first to an old spring house, surrounded by ferns. You then begin a stiff half mile northern ascent via a series of switchbacks that brings you to Vista Point. Rest a moment at a picnic table and admire the vista—the hamlet of Coloma and the South Fork of the American River.

The path descends gently, following the ridgetop, then more abruptly as it switchbacks down to the old Monroe fruit orchard. Stop at the brass plaque honoring the Monroe family, then carefully cross Highway 49 to the North Beach Picnic Area. Cross the parking lot and join the riverside path, which leads to the gold discovery site and mill site, then to the sawmill replica.

Cross the highway again to the park visitor center and join signed Monument Trail. A half mile climb over forested slopes brings you to the top of a hill and to James Marshall Monument, built in 1890. The trailhead is just below the monument.

SOUTH YUBA RIVER STATE PARK

■ INDEPENDENCE TRAIL
2 miles round trip; longer walks possible

Wheelchair access to the forest primeval has fortunately become more common over the years, but longer, truly challenging trails for the physically disabled, remain in short supply. South Yuba Independence Trail offers delightful passage through California's Gold Country for adventurers of all abilities.

Today's Independence Trail had its origins as the Excelsior Canal, built in 1859 to carry water from the South Yuba to hydraulic gold mining operations in Smartsville, 25 miles away. While the five-foot wide aqueduct crossed very steep country, it followed the contours of hillsides and thus was almost completely level.

This relative flatness of the trail, combined with some ingenious bridgework, adds up to what was an admirable engineering feat for its time, as well as a terrific

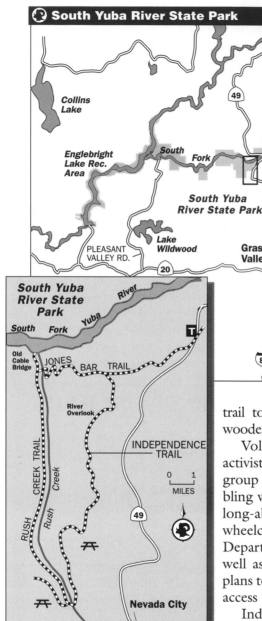

South Yuba River State Park

trail today. Particularly impressive are the wooden flumes that bridge steep ravines.

Volunteer efforts, spearheaded by activist John Olmsted and the nonprofit group Sequoya Challenge, rebuilt crumbling wooden flumes and transformed the long-abandoned water ditch into a scenic, wheelchair-accessible trail. The California Department of Parks and Recreation, as well as volunteer groups, have ambitious plans to complete a full ten miles of whole-access trail along the South Yuba River.

Independence Trail is a major, but by no means the only, highlight of a state park-in-the-making called the South Yuba River Project. Other highlights include the world's largest single-span covered bridge, and miles of dramatic canyon of the South Yuba River.

The project is an exciting—and large—undertaking for the state park system. When completed, the park will extend some 20 miles from Malakoff Diggins

State Historic Park to the confluence of the South and main forks of the Yuba River.

A trail extends along parts of the twenty mile stretch of river.One length of trail begins at the park visitor center and famed covered bridge, reached by driving eight miles north on Pleasant Valley Road from Highway 20.

DIRECTIONS TO TRAILHEAD   The main entrance to the Independence Trail is just off Highway 49, seven miles north of Nevada City, and one mile past the Yuba River crossing.

THE HIKE   From the signed trailhead, the path uses an underpass to dip under Highway 49, then begins contouring along the south bluff of the river. You can walk in the old water ditch or on a parallel path above it.

The pleasant path crosses ravines by way of several wooden flumes. A bit more than a mile of woodsy walking brings you to Flume 28 over Rush Creek. Here you'll find a vista point, fishing platform, picnic deck and an outhouse.

Independence Trail continues another 0.5 mile (as a wheelchair accessible route) to Jones Ravine. From the ravine, a hiking trail continues westward.

EMPIRE MINE
STATE HISTORIC PARK

■ HARDROCK, OSBORN HILL TRAILS
2 to 3 miles round trip

E mpire Mine, one of California's richest, produced more than six million ounces of gold during its 100 years of operation. The gold mine, along with 784 acres of gold country, is preserved in Empire Mine State Historic Park.

Shortly after the great gold rush of 1849, logger George Roberts discovered an outcropping of gold-bearing quartz about where today's visitors park their cars. Miners swarmed these hills to lay claim to the riches below. Trouble was, the gold was way below the surface, which pretty well thwarted most of the low-tech, low-budget prospectors. The miners dug 20- to 40-foot "coyote holes," tunneled and blasted, only to see their efforts fall victim to cave-ins or floods.

Around 1851, George Roberts and his fellow gold-seekers sold their claims to a consortium that consolidated them and dubbed the operation the Empire Mine. San Francisco businessman William Bourn and his son William Jr. took over in 1870 and, after investing more money and digging deeper than many thought possible, eventually turned a profit in the 1880s and beyond.

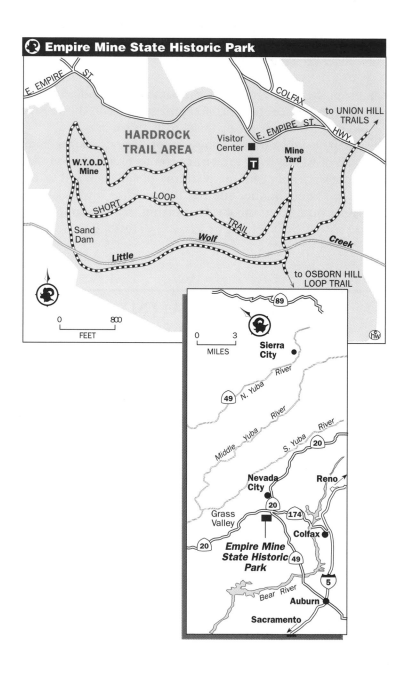

Much of the Empire's success can be attributed to the experienced hard-rock miners from Cornwall, England who came here. By some accounts, the 1890 population of Grass Valley was 85 percent Cornish.

Park visitors can get a look at the main mine shaft from an observation platform. At the visitor center are interpretive exhibits and gold samples displayed in an open vault.

The advantages of owning a gold mine are evident when one sees Empire Cottage, an English manor-style home designed by famed San Francisco architect Willis Polk for William Bourn, Jr. in 1898. Quite a "cottage!"

Join one of the park's scheduled tours of the Empire Cottage and/or Empire Mine. Or take a 16-stop walking tour on your own past structures, building foundations and mining machinery.

DIRECTIONS TO TRAILHEAD Empire Mine State Historic Park is located in Grass Valley, just east of Highway 49 on East Empire Street. Follow the signs from the highway to the park.

THE HIKE The park has ten miles of pathways—above ground that is. Below the earth is honeycombed with some 367 miles of tunnels, some nearly a mile deep.

Across the highway from the visitor center is the Union Hill section of the park. This part of the park is wooded (sugar pine, ponderosa pine, incense cedar and Douglas fir), along with some oaks and big leaf maple. A few fruit trees—apple, pear, cherry—are reminders of early settlers in the area.

Three trails, one to three miles long, explore Union Hill. Along Pipeline Trail are remains of a waterpipe that carried water from a reservoir to the north and generated power to operate mining machinery. Indian Ridge Trail is a historic pathway used by the Nisenan tribe of Maidu. Union Hill Trail skirts the fringe of the fast-growing community of Grass Valley.

Two-mile-long Hardrock Trail is a 20-stop interpretive trail that visits mines, machinery, a mule corral, a stamp mill and much more. Pick up the park's "Walking Trails of Empire Mine" brochure to get all the details of the complexities of hard-rock mining. Osborn Hill Loop Trail, a mile-long side trail splitting off from Hardrock Trail, ascends to a couple more mine sites and offers a great view of the Sacramento Valley.

MALAKOFF DIGGINS
STATE HISTORIC PARK

■ DIGGINS LOOP TRAIL
3 mile loop down into giant mining pit with
600-foot elevation loss

Bordered by colorful cliffs, the Malakoff mine pit is more than a mile long, a half mile wide and nearly 600 feet deep. In the right light, it resembles a Bryce Canyon in miniature.

Malakoff Diggins State Historic Park is the site of what was once the world's largest hydraulic gold mine. As the story goes, an Irish prospector thought he discovered gold by the Yuba River; despite his best efforts at subterfuge, he was unable to keep his secret from his fellow miners in the nearby town of Nevada City, 16 miles away. The miners tried their luck, found nothing, and declared the site a "humbug," a name that stuck to the adjacent hamlet and creek.

Several years later, when gold was really discovered, residents of Humbug deemed the name inappropriate and unrespectable so they changed it to Bloomfield. Alas, Bloomfield already existed farther south in California so the town's name changed again—this time to North Bloomfield. (Historians have yet to figure why the miners chose the name Bloomfield.)

The change in the town's name, accompanied by a change in technology— hydraulic mining—led to a dramatic change in fortune. Spraying vast amounts of water under high pressure onto the gold-laden gravels of the Malakoff area, the miners created quite a pit—and profit—for the mine owners. During its operation, between 1866 and 1884, some 41 million cubic yards of earth were excavated, yielding several million dollars worth of gold.

The amount of erosion and subsequent environmental damage caused by hydraulic mining was astonishing. Debris dumped into the Yuba River was carried all the way to the Central Valley; silt clogged up the river and caused floods, leading to loss of life and property. Silt was flushed all the way to San Francisco Bay. Navigation of the Sacramento River was imperiled.

In one of the great landmark cases in early conservation history, Woodruff (a Central Valley property owner) vs. the North Bloomfield Gravel Mining Company, Judge Lorenzo Sawyer issued a permanent injunction in 1884 against dumping tailings into the Yuba River. Other injunctions soon followed, all but ending hydraulic mining.

Learn more about hydraulic mining and the life of a miner at the state park's excellent museum. On summer weekends, rangers lead tours of the park's historic sites and the restored buildings—drug store, general store, Skidmore House, livery stable and more—of North Bloomfield.

You can also tour the small mining town on your own with the aid of the pamphlet "A Walking Tour of North Bloomfield." Pick up a copy at the park office. The park's Humbug Trail descends 2.5 miles along Humbug Creek to the Yuba River, where there are some U.S. Bureau of Land Management campsites.

Choose from a variety of pathways. Rim Trail is a fairly level 3.5 mile jaunt overlooking the great mining pit. The path offers close-up views of the spectacular erosion, both human and natural, that shaped this land. You'll pass grassy flats bedecked with lupine, buttercups and other wildflowers, thickets of manzanita, as well as slopes forested with sugar and ponderosa pine. Highlighting the trail are panoramas of the pit and its surrounding colorful cliffs.

DIRECTIONS TO TRAILHEAD Malakoff Diggins State Historic Park is located 16 miles northeast of Nevada City on North Bloomfield Road.

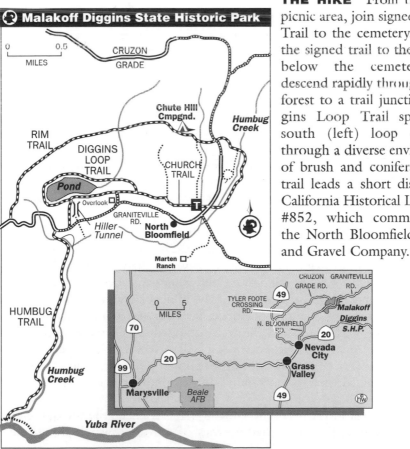

THE HIKE From the park's picnic area, join signed Church Trail to the cemetery. Pick up the signed trail to the Diggins below the cemetery and descend rapidly through mixed forest to a trail junction. Diggins Loop Trail splits; the south (left) loop descends through a diverse environment of brush and conifers. A side trail leads a short distance to California Historical Landmark #852, which commemorates the North Bloomfield Mining and Gravel Company.

Another side trail leads to the dark and dank Hiller Tunnel, a quarter mile spur (you need a flashlight to explore this). The tunnel is a segment of a much larger drainage tunnel that sent lots of muck and sediment down Humbug Creek and then on down to the South Yuba River.

Diggins Loop Trail circles Diggins Pond, which at first looks lifeless, but it's not. Watch for sandpipers at water's edge. Cattails crowd the shoreline in places, while just above the lakeshore slopes grow alder and willows.

Diggins Trail, somewhat overgrown with brush, continues its loop around the north side of the pond, then reaches a junction with the Church Trail, which you'll join and return to the trailhead.

PLUMAS-EUREKA STATE PARK

■ EUREKA PEAK LOOP TRAIL
6 miles round trip; 1,800-foot elevation gain; if ski lift road open, 3 miles round trip with 1,000-foot gain

Most California gold discoveries began with a flash in the pan; this one began with a hike. The year was 1851. An exploratory party of miners dispatched two members to climb Eureka Peak. The two found a quartz outcropping, rich in gold, silver and lead. "Gold Mountain" the miners promptly dubbed the peak. Their discovery became known as the Eureka Chimney, a mammoth deposit of ore-bearing rock that would yield more than two million dollars in gold in a fourteen-year period.

From 1872 through 1890, the highly efficient British firm, Sierra Buttes Mining Company, worked Eureka Peak and extracted many more millions of dollars worth of gold from the mountain. Seventy shafts were sunk into the peak, and more than seventy miles of tunnels were constructed in the area.

Hard-rock mining was hard work, but the miners knew how to have fun as well. Winter fun meant skiing, with Eureka Peak serving as a popular downhill run. Hitting the slopes in 1870, the well-equipped skier strapped on twelve-foot long, four-inch wide wooden skis. All skiers carried their favorite "dope"—various concoctions of tallow, turpentine, pine pitch and castor oil—that they applied to their skis. Primitive the equipment may have been, but winners reached speeds exceeding eighty miles per hour.

Eureka Peak has another claim to fame: it may have been the site of the first-ever ski lift. One of the mines had a series of gravity-powered trams which carried ore down in buckets. The miners hopped aboard, caught a lift up the slope, then skied down.

Today Plumas-Eureka (the name comes from an early mine) State Park emphasizes hard-rock mining history with a museum and several historic structures. You can visit a blacksmith shop, a stable, a stamp mill, the Moriarity House (a typical residence of a miner's family, circa 1890), and miners' bunkhouse, now the park museum/visitor center.

The trail to Eureka Peak begins at the park's ski area, which features a ski lift operated on winter weekends. Cross-country skiing is particularly popular on the state park's trails. For the hiker, the route to Eureka Lake and Eureka Peak offers grand High Sierra views. The peak's reflection in the deep blue waters of the lake is a majestic sight.

DIRECTIONS TO TRAILHEAD From the visitor center, follow the park road (County Road A-14) a mile through the historic hamlet of Johnsville to road's end at the ski area. From the parking lot, a dirt fire road ascends to Eureka Lake, where Eureka Peak Loop Trail begins. Monday through

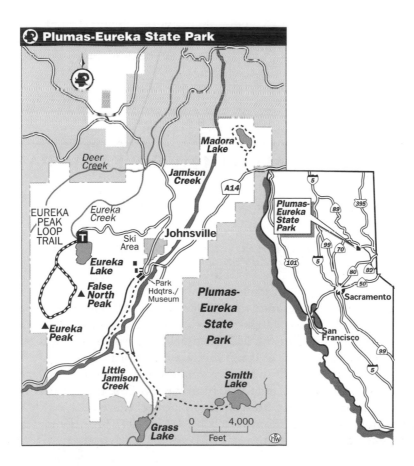

Thursday, vehicles are permitted to travel the road between the ski area and the lake; beginning your hike at the lake effectively halves the six mile distance. Friday through Sunday, only foot-traffic is permitted on the dirt road.

THE HIKE You'll get an up-close look at the ski lift and ski bowl as you ascend the fire road. The mostly westward-traveling road bends briefly east just before it reaches Eureka Lake.

The road ends at the lake and you join the trail, which crosses over Eureka Lake's earth fill dam, dips in and out of a ravine, then begins a steep ascent of a white pine- and red fir-forested Eureka Peak.

A long 0.5 mile ascent brings you to a junction, where you veer left, ascending to False Peak (sometimes called North Peak), elevation 7,286 feet. Truly the best views are from Eureka's "False" Peak. Look for Beckwourth Peak to the east, the pointed Sierra Buttes to the southeast and snow-topped Lassen Peak (10,457 feet) on the northwest horizon.

Miners and hikers have carved their initials in the rock on the northwest side of False Peak for 120 years. (Don't add yours to the collection; defacing park features is illegal.)

Continue past wind-bowed pine and hemlock, circling around the south side of the actual Eureka Peak, and following the trail as it abruptly drops off the peak and descends steeply back to the loop trail junction. Retrace your steps back to Eureka Lake and the trailhead.

WASHOE MEADOWS STATE PARK

■ WASHOE MEADOWS TRAIL
2 to 4 miles round trip

Washoe Meadows State Park, located on the outskirts of South Lake Tahoe, is a completely undeveloped park. Like Burton Creek State Park on the other end of the lake, its use—even its whereabouts—is virtually unknown except by local walkers, runners and Nordic skiers.

Lake Tahoe has long been the center of Washoe territory. The lake and environs are the geographical, indeed, spiritual focus of the tribe. As tribal elders put it: "We did not travel here from another place. We have been on this land since the beginning and have always lived here." In fact, anthropological evidence suggests at least ten thousand years of Washoe occupation.

A shoreline saunter by Lake Tahoe.

During an 1844 expedition, Captain John C. Frémont reported meeting a peaceful people, who used snow shoes and caught rabbits with nets. A flood of miners and settlers displaced and devastated the Washoe people. (For a moving account of Washoe life and their tragic collision with western frontier culture, read the Thomas Sanchez novel, *Rabbit Boss.*)

Washoe ancestral land centered around Da ow a ga (Lake Tahoe), sacred giver of life; the land included fertile valleys, the desert, and snow covered mountains. And, it included meadows as well—so it's altogether fitting that a park be named after this long-neglected group of native Americans.

The meadow's trail system is not way-marked, so try to stay oriented. Fortunately because it's a meadow, you can see where you're going, where you've come from.

DIRECTIONS TO TRAILHEAD Best place to start your walk is at the trailhead off Lake Tahoe Boulevard. Follow Lake Tahoe Boulevard 0.4 mile past its intersection with Sawmill Road. You'll see a gated dirt road on your left. Park nearby and walk down this dirt road.

The park also extends 1.5 miles along Sawmill Road, which leads to Highway 50; entering the park from this direction can be confusing.

D.L. BLISS AND EMERALD BAY STATE PARKS

■ RUBICON TRAIL

To Old Lighthouse is 0.75 mile round trip; to Emerald Point
is 6 miles round trip; to Vikingsholm is 9 miles round trip

Adjoining state parks D.L. Bliss and Emerald Bay protect six miles of Lake Tahoe's shore. Rubicon Trail, a superb shoreline pathway, contours over shady slopes, linking the two parks and offering grand views of what Indians called the "Lake in the Sky."

Even if the parks themselves weren't so splendidly scenic, they would still attract lots of visitors because they offer something in short supply around Lake Tahoe: public access to the lake.

For the tree-loving hiker, Rubicon Trail offers plenty of arboreal companionship. You get the Christmas spirit when you wander through stands of red and white fir. Joining the stately firs are ponderosa pine, Jeffrey pine and incense cedar. "Leaf peepers," or homesick New Englanders, will enjoy how autumn colors Tahoe's aspen and maple trees.

Not all park flora is a hundred feet tall. Monkeyflower, columbine, lupine and leopard lily are among the wildflowers splashing spring and summer color on park slopes.

Most park visitors come not to see flora's handiwork, but Lora's handiwork—Lora Knight, that is. In 1928, Knight commissioned Swede Lennart Palme to build her a ninth-century Norse Castle. A year later, Vikingsholm—turrets, towers and 38 rooms—was completed. Knight, a Santa Barbaran, spent summers in her authentically furnished fortress until her death in 1945.

During the summer months, guides give tours of Vikingsholm. (Tours are conducted 10 a.m. to 4 p.m., daily, every half-hour, through Labor Day, then only on the weekends for a few more weeks.

Even if you can't schedule a holm tour, the two-mile round-trip hike on Vikingsholm Trail (a road closed to vehicle traffic) to view the curious structure is well worth the effort. Just looking at the exterior of the castle (not a single tree was disturbed when it was constructed) in its lakeside setting is impressive.

Another reward at trail's end is Emerald Bay itself, one of Tahoe's best beaches. Swimmers can brave the bay's chilly waters, which warm only to the low 60s, even in mid-summer.

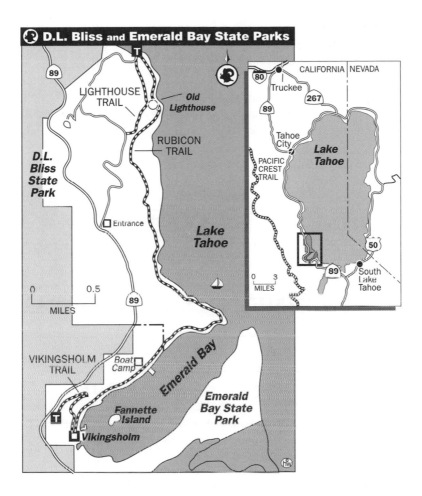

D.L. Bliss and Emerald Bay State Parks

DIRECTIONS TO TRAILHEAD From South Lake Tahoe, drive 11 miles north on Highway 89 to the D.L. Bliss State Park entrance. If you're coming from Tahoe City, you'll drive sixteen miles south on 89 to the park entrance. Follow the park road 2.5 miles to its end at the parking area for Calawee Cove Beach.

To reach the trailhead for Vikingsholm from South Lake Tahoe, drive north nine miles on Highway 89 to the Vikingsholm Overlook, a large parking area on your right. If you're coming from Tahoe City, drive 18 miles south on 89.

Emerald Bay/Vikingsholm is also the terminus for the Rubicon Trail, described below.

THE HIKE Sunbathers hit the beach while hikers choose between two paths— an upper and a lower trail—looping south. Take either; they rejoin in a bit more than a 0.25 mile at the Old Lighthouse. Take the short spur trail leading to the recently restored lighthouse.

Rubicon Trail climbs gently south, soon offering much better views of Lake Tahoe, then ascending into a white fir forest. Emerging from the trees, the path begins a one mile descent to the lakeshore, then meanders lakeside to Emerald Point. Here the trail splits: one branch visits Emerald Point, the other bypasses the point. The trails soon rejoin, you cross the boundary from D.L. Bliss State Park into Emerald Bay State Park, and you hike another 0.5 mile among pine, fir and incense cedar to the park's boat camp. This camp is an ideal lakeside picnic spot.

For its last mile, Rubicon Trail sticks close to shore with only a single foray inland to climb around Parson Rock. Vikingsholm is your turnaround point, unless you've arranged to have transportation waiting for you at Vikingsholm parking lot, a one mile ascent up Vikingsholm Trail.

SUGAR PINE POINT STATE PARK

■ GENERAL CREEK TRAIL
4.5 mile loop with 300-foot elevation gain; to Lily Pond is 6.5 miles round trip with 500-foot gain; to Duck Lake is 14 miles round trip and to Lost Lake is 14.5 miles with 1,300-foot gain

Sugar Pine Point names a forested promontory perched above the western shore of Lake Tahoe, as well as a state park that offers ten terrific miles of trail.

Sugar pines are, alas, a bit scarce these days. In the 1870s, there was lots of logging in this part of the Tahoe Basin in order to supply Comstock Lode miners with lumber and firewood.

One of Lake Tahoe's first permanent residents was "General" William Phipps, who homesteaded the land we now call Sugar Pine Point in 1860. Phipps protected his 160 acres from being logged.

Turn-of-the-century banker Isaias Hellman built "the finest High Sierra summer house in California," a rustic yet elegant three-story mansion overlooking the lake. Now known as the Ehrman Mansion (for a later owner) the house is open for guided tours during the summer months. Exhibits about the natural history of the Tahoe Basin can be viewed in the nature center, located in the Ehrman Mansion's former power-generating plant.

While the state park has about two miles of lakefront, most of the park—and the best hiking—is inland along General Creek. Trails lead along the creek through a forested valley to the state park boundary, then into the El Dorado National Forest. The park is often used by long-distance hikers to gain access to the northerly part of the Desolation Wilderness, as well as to intersect the Pacific Crest Trail and other paths leading into the High Sierra backcountry west of Lake Tahoe.

Trees are one attraction of a hike through the state park. Besides the sugar pine, look for Jeffrey pine and stately white fir. In autumn, the black cottonwood and quaking aspen are something to behold.

DIRECTIONS TO TRAILHEAD From Tahoe City, drive nine miles south on Highway 89 to Sugar Pine Point State Park. The state park is located some eighteen miles north of the community of South Lake Tahoe. Once inside the park, rangers recommend that hikers park in the campground overflow lot near

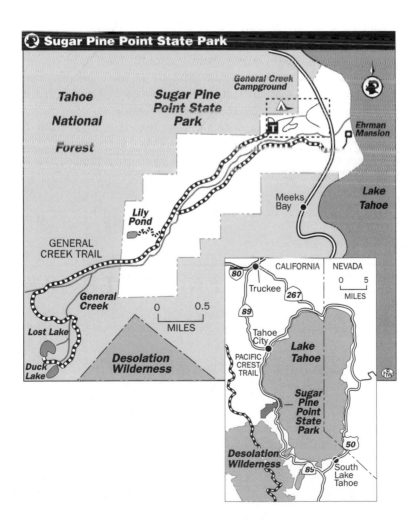

the entrance to General Creek Campground. The trail, a dirt road closed to vehicles, begins at Campsite 150.

THE HIKE The wide path leads west along the north bank of General Creek. At a signed junction you'll spot a trail leading down to a bridge crossing the creek. This bridge and another two miles farther along General Creek Trail allow a pleasant loop trip without getting your feet wet.

The trail meanders through well-spaced stands of Jeffrey and lodgepole pine and across meadowland seasonally sprinkled with lupine and aster. Those granite boulders you see looking so out of place in the sylvan scene were left behind ages ago by a retreating glacier. Hikers with an interest in geology will enjoy glimpses of the two large lateral moraines that border the valley of General Creek.

A bit more than two miles along, when you reach a second footbridge, you can loop back to the trailhead via a path on the opposite side of General Creek.

Soon after passing this bridge, General Creek Trail dwindles to a footpath and another half mile's travel brings you to a signed junction with a side trail leading to Lily Pond; it's a 0.75 mile, heart-pounding ascent to the little pond.

General Creek Trail continues meandering above the creek. About 3.5 miles from the trailhead, you'll exit the state park and enter El Dorado National Forest. After more meandering, the trail crosses General Creek (no bridge this time), turns south, then east, and after a mile crosses the creek fed by Lost Lake and Duck Lake.

Now the trail turns south again and climbs to shallow Duck Lake, ringed by lodgepole pine. Lost Lake, another quarter mile along the trail, is a bit more dramatic than neighboring Duck, and offers good swimming.

BURTON CREEK STATE PARK

■ BURTON CREEK TRAIL
2 to 8 miles round trip

Lake Tahoe's secret state park is Burton Creek, more than 2,000 acres of forest and meadowland, located just across the highway from the tiny but well-known lakeshore campground at Tahoe State Recreation Area. (The Tahoe SRA entry kiosk is a good place to ask questions about Burton Creek.)

The park has a great deal of potential to become a favorite of trail users—cross-country skiers, mountain bicyclists, and hikers—as soon as access problems are resolved and some signs are erected.

Bisecting the park, from its northwest to its southwest corner, is Burton Creek. The creek has been dammed, but two natural preserves have been established in the creek corridor. Above the dam is Antone Meadows Natural Preserve; from the dam to the highway is Burton Creek Natural Preserve.

The park is completely undeveloped except for some six miles of dirt roads. Chief users of the trail system are cross-country skiers. During the winter, Tahoe Nordic Center grooms the park trails. (To reach the center, take Village Road off Highway 28.)

The hiking is strictly improvisational; wander the dirt roads for as long or short a hike as you please. Numbers posted at road junctions aid your navigation of the tangle of roads. Keep track of those numbers!

A section of the new Tahoe Rim Trail leads through the western part of the park. Best walking is along Burton Creek and through the surrounding meadows.

DIRECTIONS TO TRAILHEAD The park has two entrances from Tahoe City. The Bunker Drive entrance has parking; the Tamarack Lodge entrance presents both access and parking difficulties.

MONO LAKE TUFA STATE RESERVE

■ SOUTH TUFA TRAIL
1 to 2 miles round trip

It's one of the grand landscapes of the American West—an ancient lake cradled by volcanoes, glacier-carved canyons and snowy peaks. Visitors marvel at the 8-mile-long (north to south) and 13-mile-wide (east to west) lake and its unusual tufa towers, remarkable limestone creations that rise from the lake in magnificent knobs and spires.

Mono Lake has been called "California's Dead Sea," but it's actually a life-support system for great numbers of birds. California gulls fly in from the coast to nest on the lake's isles. An estimated 90 percent of the state's population of this gull is born at Mono Lake.

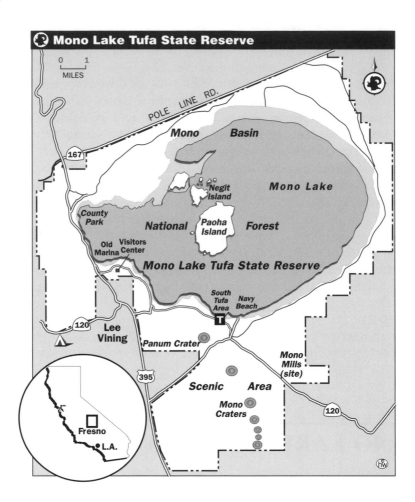

Some 800,000 eared grebes, duck-like diving birds, have been tallied. Mono's summertime winged visitors include Wilson's and red-necked phalaropes, species that commute from wintering grounds in South America.

Primary bird food is the brine shrimp, which, like other organisms dependent on Mono's waters, has evolved over the last million years or so to adapt to an extremely saline habitat.

While Mono is anything but a dead sea, it was, until recently, a dying lake. Beginning in 1941 and continuing for more than a half-century, the Los Angeles Department of Water and Power diverted most of the major creeks and rivers that had sustained Mono Lake for centuries. Such diversions caused the lake level to drop 40 feet and its waters to double in salinity.

The resultant damage to the lake's ecological integrity and to Mono Basin's wildlife habitat prompted the Mono Lake Committee and the National Audubon Society to take legal action to stop this drastic drain. After 16 years of conservation efforts and legal challenges by citizen activists in numerous courts and forums, the State Water Resources Control Board agreed to raise the lake level in 1994.

Theoretically and legally at least, Mono Lake has been "saved." Much shoreline and wildlife habitat restoration will be necessary, however, to return the lake to ideal environmental health. Learn more about the lake and conservation efforts at the Mono Basin National Forest Scenic Area Visitor Center located on the outskirts of Lee Vining. The Mono Lake Committee maintains an information center and gift/bookstore in "downtown" Lee Vining.

Travelers with limited time can get a quick look at the lake and some tufa formations with the help of two boardwalk trails located at Old Marina on the west shore and Mono Lake County Park on the northwest shore.

DIRECTIONS TO TRAILHEAD From Highway 395, about 5 miles south of the hamlet of Lee Vining, turn east on Highway 120 and drive 5 miles to the signed turnoff for the South Tufa Area/Mono Lake Tufa State Reserve. Turn left and proceed a mile on good gravel road to a parking area near the trailhead.

THE HIKE The best place to observe Mono's most compelling natural attraction—its tufa towers—is the South Tufa Area, explored by a short interpretive trail. The trail's shoreline segments will no doubt need to be relocated periodically as the lake rises and reclaims its ancient bed.

Tufa towers are formed when calcium-rich freshwater springs bubble up into the carbonate saturated alkaline lake water. This calcium-carbonate co-mingling results in limestone formations—the magnificent tufa spires.

Trailside interpretive signs explain more than most hikers will want to know about the lake's food chain of algae, billions of brine flies, trillions of shrimp, as well as gulls, grebes and other migratory birds. Some visitors, overwhelmed by the lake's majesty, might be disappointed to learn that Mono is the native Yokut word for "brine fly."

South Tufa Trail leads past some landlocked tufa formations, then skirts the lakeshore for a look at those protruding from the middle of Mono. Loop back to the parking area if you wish, or extend your hike by continuing on to Navy Beach, the lake's best swimming area.

GROVER HOT SPRINGS STATE PARK

■ BURNSIDE TRAIL
To waterfall is 3 miles round trip; to Burnside Lake is 10 miles round trip with 2,100-foot elevation gain

Nothing like a soothing soak in a hot spring after a long day on the trail. For the High Sierra visitor who wants to take a hike and "take the cure" in the same day, Grover Hot Springs State Park, located a bit south of Lake Tahoe, is the perfect destination.

Don't expect a deluxe Euro-resort; Grover Hot Springs offers your basic soak, nothing more, nothing less. Bathers can sit in one hot pool (102 to 105 degrees) fed by six mineral springs, and one cool pool. The two pools and the changing rooms are the extent of the state park facilities.

No, it's not the concrete pools, surrounded by a wooden fence (the effect is rather like a backyard swimming pool installed in the 1950s) but the setting that's inspiring at Grover Hot Springs.

Tucked in Hot Springs Valley, surrounded on three sides by Sierra Nevada peaks, Grover Hot Springs offers a soak in a setting as soothing as its waters. The granite peaks, including 10,023-foot Hawkins Peak to the northwest and 9,419-foot Markleeville Peak to the southwest, form an inspiring backdrop to an area that's been attracting visitors since the 1850s.

At the park, true hot springs aficionados can read up on the exact mineral content of Grover Hot Springs and find out just how many grams per gallon of magnesium carbonate and sodium sulfate the waters hold. Most bathers, even those without any interest in chemistry, will be happy to know that Grover, unlike most other hot springs, contains almost none of that nose-wrinkling sulphur.

Most visitors come to this out-of-the way park for the waters, not the walking. Too bad, because the state park and surrounding national forest boast some inspiring footpaths.

Easy family hikes include a nature trail called Transition Walk that loops around the park's alpine meadow and a three-mile round-trip walk to a waterfall on Hot Springs Creek. A more ambitious jaunt is the hike to Burnside Lake located in the adjacent Toiyabe National Forest. Burnside Trail crosses the state park, then ascends through a pine forest to the alpine lake.

DIRECTIONS TO TRAILHEAD From Highway 89 in Markleeville (a half-hour drive from South Lake Tahoe), turn west on Hot Springs Road and travel

3.5 miles to Grover Hot Springs State Park. You can park at the pool (then walk a footpath and the park road to the trailhead) or proceed past the park entrance station to the overflow parking area and the signed trailhead at the north end of Quaking Aspen Campground.

If you want to make the trip to Burnside Lake a one-way trip, you can drive to the lake. From the signed turnoff on Highway 88, drive 5.5 miles down bumpy, dirt Burnside Road to road's end at the lake.

THE HIKE The path parallels Hot Springs Creek, a year-round watercourse that flows through the park's large meadow. Some of the catchable trout planted in the creek are caught by campers for their suppers, though more serious anglers head for the nearby Carson River. The quaking aspen fringing the meadow are showy in autumn, when the fluttering leaves turn orange and gold.

A short mile's walk from the trailhead brings you to a signed junction. (The trail to the waterfall branches left, leading along Hot Springs Creek. Some minor rock climbing leads to an overlook above the small, but vigorous falls.)

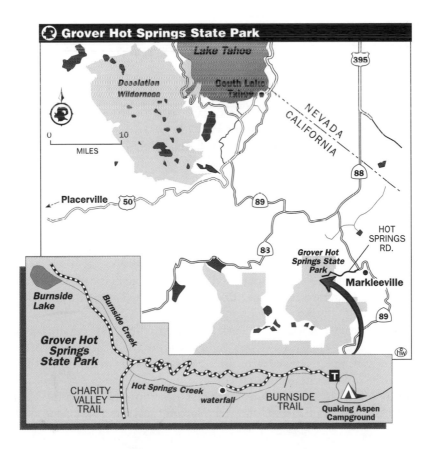

Burnside Trail enters the forest and ascends a mile to another junction, this one with Charity Valley Trail, which heads south along Charity Valley Creek. Soon thereafter, Burnside Trail crosses Burnside Creek and climbs northwest, switchbacking up steep Jeffrey pine- and white fir-cloaked slopes. Near the top, you'll get a grand, over-the-shoulder view of Hot Springs Valley.

The last mile of this hike resembles the first mile—a walk through meadowland. The meadow below Burnside Lake is much wetter than the one in the state park, however, so take care to stay on the trail; you won't get your boots so wet, and you'll help protect the fragile meadow ecology.

Boulders perched above the lakeshore suggest fine picnic spots, and inspiring places from which to contemplate pretty Burnside Lake.

DONNER MEMORIAL STATE PARK

■ LAKESHORE INTERPRETIVE TRAIL
2.5 miles round trip

It's the dark side of the California dream, one of the most gruesome stories of the Old West: The Donner Party.

In April 1846, a group of Midwestern families left Independence, Missouri, bound for California. Their wagon train rolled over the Great Plains and through the Rockies, but was seriously delayed when a "shortcut" leading southwest was anything but. A breakdown in civilized behavior followed: the emigrants quarreled constantly; one man killed another; an old man was left on the trail to die.

An early and severe snowstorm that prevented passage over the High Sierra forced the ill-fated party to spend the winter near present-day Truckee. Forty-one of the 89 would-be settlers perished. After their provisions and oxen were consumed, the desperate emigrants finally cannibalized their dead friends and relatives.

Today, Donner Memorial State Park is located where many members of the Donner Party spent their final days. Rangers report that about two hundred thousand visitors, most very curious about the cannibalism aspect of the Donner story, stop at the state park each year.

The state park's surprise is that it displays not only the dark side of human nature but the beautiful side of Mother Nature. Anything but gruesome, the

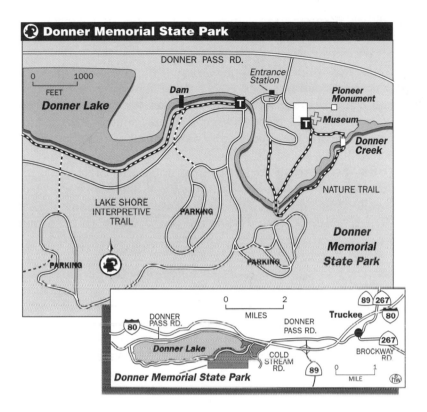

Donner Memorial State Park

DONNER PASS RD.

0   1000
FEET

Donner Lake

Dam

Entrance
Station

Pioneer
Monument

Museum

Donner
Creek

NATURE TRAIL

LAKE SHORE
INTERPRETIVE
TRAIL

PARKING

PARKING

**Donner
Memorial
State Park**

PARKING

0   2
MILES

DONNER
PASS RD.

80

DONNER
PASS RD.

Truckee

89 267

80

Donner Lake

COLD
STREAM
RD.

267

BROCKWAY
RD.

Donner Memorial State Park

89

0   1
MILE

state park and surrounding Sierra Nevada is a major recreation center, featuring camping, hiking, fishing and boating.

Donner Lake is a mellow place for a hike, a picnic or a little trout fishing. The state park, located on the east side of the lake, has 2.5 miles of lake frontage.

Outside the park visitor center is the tall Pioneer Monument; its base measures 22 feet high, the height of the snow during that terrible winter of 1846-47. Inside the park visitor center is the Emigrant Trail Museum, which depicts the demise of the Donner Party, plus more positive aspects of the region's history. The museum also offers a nice introduction to the natural history of the Sierra Nevada.

To see some of this natural history for yourself, take a hike. One of the most dramatic (and obvious) workings of nature is the

Pioneer Monument honoring the Donner party and other 19th century pioneers.

evidence left behind of recent glaciation. The great sheet of ice that slid through the region thousands of years ago left behind huge boulders and other rock debris.

Jeffrey pine and white fir cloak park slopes; the woods are home to deer, squirrels, chipmunks and raccoons.

The state park doesn't have an extensive trail system, but does offer two enjoyable family hikes. When snow covers the park, rangers link park roads and trails into a good beginners' cross-country ski route.

DIRECTIONS TO TRAILHEAD Donner Memorial State Park is located south of Interstate 80, and west of Truckee. From downtown Truckee, follow Donner Pass Road two miles to a stop sign. Turn left and follow the signs into the park. Truckee itself is located 33 miles west of Reno, thirteen miles from Lake Tahoe.

THE HIKE The park's Nature Trail (0.5 mile round trip) begins just south of the museum. It meanders by a pine and fir forest to Donner Creek. An interpretive booklet, explaining flora and fauna, is available at the museum.

Lakeshore Interpretive Trail (2.5 miles round trip) is even more educational. Eighteen trailside exhibits illustrate the history of the Emigrant Trail and tell of the area's geology and ecology, Washoe culture, and the local recreational possibilities. The path leads to, and along, Donner Lake. At trail's end at the lake is some fine picnicking.

MCARTHUR-BURNEY FALLS MEMORIAL STATE PARK

■ FALLS, BURNEY CREEK, RIM TRAILS
3.5 miles round trip

President Theodore Roosevelt once proclaimed Burney Falls "the eighth wonder of the world." High praise indeed, for the twin, thundering 129-foot falls, accompanied by numerous plumes of water, is a spectacular sight.

Burney Falls is protected by McArthur-Burney Falls Memorial State Park, one of the more off-the-beaten-track units of the California state park system. The park is sometimes described as being located in "Pit River Country," "the Shasta-Cascade Wonderland," or "halfway between Mt. Shasta and Lassen Peak." Geologists describe the park's location as on the edge of the Modoc Plateau or on the far south end of the Cascade Range.

Volcanic action was the dominant force shaping the landscape in this part of California. This vulcanism is evident not only around nearby Shasta and Lassen peaks, but in more subtle ways in the state park itself.

Sometimes water percolates through the porous surface of the lava rock and is trapped in huge subterranean rivers and reservoirs. One of these underground aquifers feeds Burney Creek—and in turn, Burney Falls. The falls flows all year, even though a half mile above the falls Burney Creek is often absolutely dry.

Present-day park flora illustrate the aftereffects of vulcanism, too. Notice the scarcity of bushes—what botanists call "understory"—beneath the trees. This lack of ground cover is due to the composition of the ground itself; what moisture falls onto the porous basalt rock percolates deep into the ground and is thus unavailable to many shallow-rooted plants that would normally grow in this type of climate and ecosystem.

Several Native American groups, particularly the Ilmawi, had villages near the present-day park. They dug deep pits nearby in order to trap big game. Nineteenth-century explorers and settlers referred to these people as Pit River Indians. The falls was considered a "power spot" by the native people.

To some early 20th-century Californians, the falls was a power spot too—for hydroelectric power that is. One dam, Pit River Number Three, resulted in the formation of Lake Britton, located a mile down-canyon from Burney Falls. For a time, the falls was threatened by dam builders but their preservation was assured in 1922 when Frank McArthur donated the falls, along with some surrounding land, to the state park system. The park honors McArthur's pioneer parents, John and Catherine McArthur.

Burney Falls is a spectacular year-round sight.

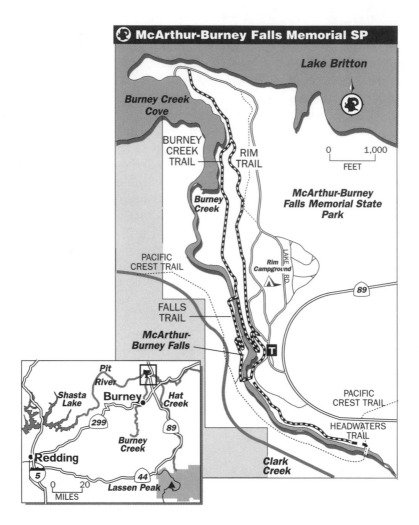

Park trails serve up several different views of the falls and the 200 million gallons of water that tumble into Burney Creek Gorge. A one mile nature trail with 24 stops introduces visitors to geological and botanical features. Pick up an interpretive pamphlet at the park visitor center or at the camp store.

DIRECTIONS TO TRAILHEAD The state park is located off Highway 89, eleven miles north of the little town of Burney. Falls Trail begins at a viewpoint on the west side of the park entrance opposite a little camp store.

THE HIKE Follow Falls Trail, paved for a couple hundred yards, which switchbacks down toward the falls. Falls Trail is also the park's nature trail, with a number of interpreted stops en route.

Most park visitors aren't hikers, so most venture only as far as the base of the falls. The spray from the falls is terrific natural air-conditioning; it's always quite cool in the canyon, even on a summer's day.

I recommend following Falls Trail along the east side of Burney Creek to the first footbridge over Burney Creek, then heading up-creek along the west side of Falls Trail. After you ascend the gorge wall and get an eye-level view of the falls, retrace your steps.

Burney Creek elbows west, then north, while you continue due north on Burney Creek Trail into a mixed forest of ponderosa pine, incense cedar and Douglas fir. A mile's walk brings you to a signed junction: Burney Creek Trail continues north to its end at a peninsula separating Burney Creek Cove from the main body of Lake Britton. You'll find a boat launch facility at the cove, a sandy beach and swimming area on the lake.

From the junction, Rim Trail ascends moderately up the rim of Burney Creek Canyon, then skirts the park's campground before petering out just short of the viewpoint where you began this walk.

AHJUMAWI LAVA SPRINGS STATE PARK

■ LAVA SPRINGS, SPATTER CONE LOOP TRAILS

From Big Lake Landing Site to Crystal Springs is 4.2 miles round trip; Spatter Cone Trail is 5 mile loop

Here the California landscape is revealed at its most elemental level: fire in the form of black volcanic basalt, and water in many forms—lakes, rivers, creeks and springs.

Ahjumawi Lava Springs State Park, located on the edge of the Modoc Plateau in the Fall River Valley in northeastern Shasta County, may very well be the most remote of California's 300 state parks. Ahjumawi is likely to remain in obscurity because visitors must boat over (and cannot drive to) the park.

While Ahjumawi is difficult to find, difficult to visit, and even difficult to pronounce (Ah-joo-maw-we), it's nevertheless easy to admire. Imagine a classic California Cascade range postcard. Then add water, lots of it. Ahjumawi is a particular lure for canoeists, who can paddle many miles of interconnected waterways.

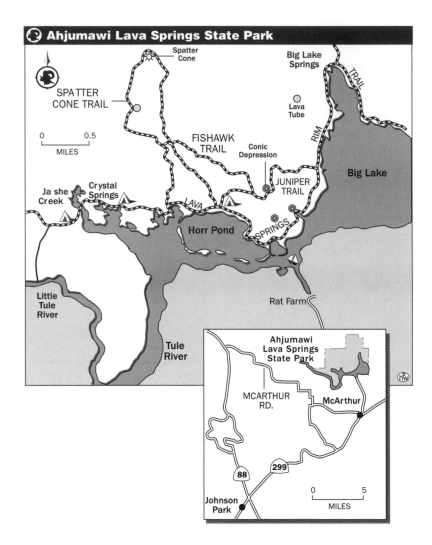

Hikers discover the area's obvious volcanic origins from 20 miles of park trails. Paths lead past basalt outcroppings, lava tubes, cold springs bubbling up at the edge of lava fields, and even a spatter cone.

However intriguing, mixing and mingling with the lava is only part of the Ahjumawi hiking experience. Trails explore a jumble of environments (located in close proximity to one another) including a soggy, tule-fringed marsh, hot and dry brush, wildflower-strewn hillsides and ponderosa pine forests.

Geologists believe that most of the lava in the park originated from nearby Timbered Crater, a small volcanic summit that last flowed lava Ahjumawi's way about 2,000 years ago (relatively recently in geologic time).

The park is named for the native Ahjumawi, who have lived in the area for thousands of years. Ahjumawi ("where the waters come together") fishermen have constructed stone fish traps in the shallows since prehistoric times. The tribe still maintains traps along the park's shoreline

Migratory birds flock to the chain of lakes comprising the park's southern boundary. Gaggles of geese, grebes and ducks nest here in summer. White pelicans, great blue herons, bald eagles and sandhill cranes are among the larger birds commonly sighted in the park.

The park's animal inhabitants include coyote, porcupine, squirrel and yellow-bellied marmot.

The park is mostly BYOB (Bring Your Own Boat). Call the park to inquire about any boat rental possibilities. Sometimes local businesses rent watercraft.

THE HIKE The hiking experience varies greatly with one's choice of boat landings. If you leave from Rat Farm Launch and boat over to near the park campground at Horr Pond, you'll land about in the middle of the park's trail system.

Lava Springs Trail is the lakeshore path. Hike west from the Horr Pond Camp to Crystal Springs Camp (2.4 miles round trip) or head east on an even more remote length of shoreline trail.

Spatter Cone Loop Trail (4.8 miles) tours the park's lava flows, then visits a lava tube and its namesake spatter cone.

CASTLE CRAGS STATE PARK

■ CRAGS TRAIL
5.5 miles round trip with 2,200-foot elevation gain

Soaring above the upper Sacramento River Valley are the sky-scraping spires of granite called the Castle Crags. From the lofty ramparts, the hiker can look down on forested slopes and up at magnificent snow-covered Mt. Shasta.

The Castle Crags were formed in much the same manner as nearby Mt. Shasta and the other peaks of the Cascade Range—by volcanic activity some 200 million years ago. For the last million years, the Crags have been subjected to the forces of wind, rain, ice and even some small glaciers, which have shaped the granite into its distinctive shapes. Rising beside the spikey peaks is a round one, Castle Dome, which many mountaineers liken to Yosemite's Half Dome.

In 1855, the territory below the Crags was the site of a struggle between local native people and settlers. The locals, armed only with bows and arrows,

The granitic spires of Castle Crags are a well-known landmark in far northern California.

were driven from their land in a one-sided battle that was chronicled by Joaquin Miller, "poet of the High Sierra."

Mining—first gold, later mercury and chromite—and logging, were the chief industries around the Crags for a hundred years. During the 1920s and 1930s, conservationists worked to protect the Castle Crags; they circulated news of the scenic spot and promoted the idea of a comprehensive California state park system.

Crags Trail, with its steep elevation gain, is a real workout. Rewarding your effort are postcard views of the Crags and of Mt. Shasta. The trail crosses Kettlebelly Ridge, part of the old California-Oregon Toll Road used by settlers on their way west.

DIRECTIONS TO TRAILHEAD   Castle Crags State Park is located some 25 miles north of Lake Shasta (6 miles south of Dunsmuir) off Interstate 5. Take the Castella exit and follow signs to the park. Follow the entrance road to the Vista Point parking area. The signed trail begins just down the road from the Point.

THE HIKE   From the signed trailhead, the trail climbs west through a mixed forest of pine, fir and cedar. After a short time, you'll pass a junction with Root Creek Trail, a mile-long path leading through the forest to its namesake creek. A little more climbing brings you to a four-way intersection. Here you meet the famous Pacific Crest Trail, seven miles of which leads through the state park. Your quiet contemplation of the notion of walking some 2650 miles from Mexico to Canada will undoubtedly be interrupted by the sizzle of electricity passing through the high-voltage lines strung above the trail junction.

You continue on Crags Trail on an ever-more-earnest ascent for another half mile to a short connector trail known as Bob's Hat Trail, which drops a quarter mile back to PCT. (Keep this trail in mind as a return trip option.)

Crags Trail turns north, and in another 0.5 mile splits again. The left fork goes to Indian Springs, where cold water bubbles from the depths of the Crags. Your path climbs even more steeply, winding among boulders and over flat rocks. Trees become more sparse with the gain in elevation, opening up ever-grander views over the manzanita and hardy heather of the Crags. Trail's end is at the base of roundish Castle Dome.

You can climb rocks to your heart's content around here, but use caution and don't exceed your abilities.

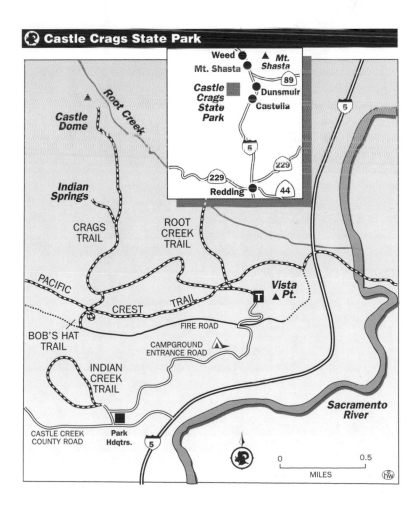

Delicate ferns and towering redwoods beckon the hiker to explore California's grand stands.

CHAPTER EIGHT

NORTHERN CALIFORNIA REDWOODS

Long considered the "gems" of the state park system, the redwood parks preserve both small and large groves of California's official state tree. The coastal redwoods were a rallying point during the 1920s, and in earlier decades, for such conservation groups as the Save-the-Redwoods League; concern over the fate of the redwoods helped launch the state parks movement.

The famed Sequoia sempervirens grow in a long belt on the western side of the Coast Range from Big Sur to the Oregon border. The characteristic long, lingering fogs and heavy winter rains found in this belt provide the ideal climatic conditions for the coastal redwoods.

The best old-growth redwoods remain in Del Norte, Humboldt and Mendocino counties. Along Highway 101, Prairie Creek, Jedediah Smith and Del Norte state parks lie between the Pacific and the Klamath Range; these parks are included in loose confederation with Redwood National Park.

Jedediah Smith features the 5,000-acre National Tribute Grove, At Prairie Creek, the redwoods are sprinkled with open meadows, roamed by the unusual Roosevelt elk.

A hundred miles south of these far-north redwoods is another string of state parks along the South Fork of the Eel River. Largest is Humboldt Redwoods State Park, bisected by the Avenue of the Giants, the famed scenic highway Heart of the park is the Rockefeller Forest, the most impressive ancient redwoods left on earth.

ARMSTRONG REDWOODS STATE RESERVE / AUSTIN CREEK STATE RECREATION AREA

■ GILLIAM CREEK, AUSTIN CREEK TRAILS

4 mile loop with 800-foot elevation gain or 8 mile loop with 1,000-foot gain; longer options possible

Armstrong Redwoods State Reserve/Austin Creek State Recreation Area is one place on the map, but two distinct environments on the ground. Armstrong Redwoods is a 700-acre tall-tree preserve, a cool and dark forest. Austin Creek, in contrast, offers open sun-drenched, grassy hillsides dotted with oaks. Both parks are a welcome respite from the Russian River resort traffic and all those wine country tourists in the flatlands below.

Both parks offer good hiking: a gentle saunter through Armstrong Redwoods, a moderate to vigorous hike through the Austin Creek foothills. Armstrong Redwoods is a place to cool off in the summer. Austin Creek's exposed slopes are a bit too hot in summer; hiking here is far more pleasant in spring and fall.

Armstrong Redwoods was set aside as a preserve by mega-logger Colonel James Armstrong, surely one of the few 19th-century timber barons who recognized both the beauty and the board feet in California's redwood groves. The park has some excellent picnic grounds and features the Redwood Forest Theater, a 1,200-seat outdoor amphitheater, a popular site for concerts and plays.

Best hike through the redwoods is the self-guided nature trail. As you wander among the virgin trees past interpretive displays, you'll visit the 310-foot Parson Jones tree and the old (1,400-plus years) Colonel Armstrong tree. After you walk the short mile along Fife Creek to the picnic area, you can loop back to the trailhead via East Ridge Trail.

Austin Creek's twenty miles of trail for the most part follow creeks—East Austin, as well as Gilliam, Schoolhouse and Fife—through an environment of alder, big leaf maple and Oregon ash. Paths also traverse slopes forested with Douglas fir, oak and madrone. Three backcountry camps—Tom King, Manning Flat and Gilliam Creek—suggest Austin Creek State Recreation would be an ideal location for a weekend getaway or a family backpacking trip.

This hike offers both short and long loops that head down Gilliam Creek and ascend back to the trailhead along Austin Creek. Whichever loop you choose, it's downhill first, uphill last; save some energy for the return trip.

DIRECTIONS TO TRAILHEAD From Highway 101, four miles north of Santa Rosa, exit on River Road and drive west some 16 miles to Guerneville. Turn north on Armstrong Woods Road and drive two miles to Armstrong Redwoods State Reserve. Continue up the steep park road to a fork; the main park road continues to Bullfrog Pond, but you veer left to parking for the signed Gilliam Creek Trail.

THE HIKE Descend north into mixed forest of oak, Douglas fir and redwood. A half mile out, you'll climb a bit and see some coastward views of the multiple ridges rolling to the west.

The trail turns west and descends through woods, then grassland, to Schoolhouse Creek, about a mile from the trailhead. You'll cross a fork of the creek as well as Schoolhouse Creek itself as you descend another mile to a trail junction located near the meeting of waters of Gilliam and Schoolhouse creeks.

Those opting for the four mile hike will go right at this trail junction, cross Schoolhouse Creek, then follow the banks of Gilliam up-creek a short distance to meet Austin Creek Trail (a fire road). You'll hike the fire road back toward the trailhead.

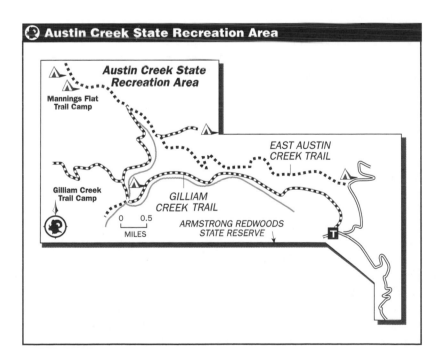

Those in the mood for a longer hike will continue following Gilliam Creek, crossing and re-crossing the creek a couple of times as the path leads past ferns, flowers (in spring), cascading water and quiet pools.

Three miles out you cross Gilliam Creek for the last time, climb gently above the north bank of the creek, and descend again. A short side trail leads to Gilliam Creek Camp. Near the confluence of Gilliam and East Austin creeks, you'll ford the latter and climb briefly, but steeply, to meet a fire road. Turn right on the fire road, which climbs gradually north through a forest of oak, madrone and fir.

Five miles out, you descend to cross East Austin Creek and meet East Austin Creek Trail (another fire road). To visit Manning Flat Trail Camp, head left to the shady camp perched on the west bank of the creek.)

Turn right on the road, which follows its namesake East Austin Creek and soon passes a great swimming hole. All too soon, you think (especially on a hot day), your path begins an earnest half mile ascent, passes the side trail leading to Tom King Trail Camp, and leaves Austin Creek behind.

Next comes a half mile descent and a meeting with the short spur connecting to Gilliam Creek Trail. One way back to the trailhead is to take the spur, then retrace your steps on the Gilliam Creek Trail. It's a stiff climb back.

An equally stiff climb (some choice, huh?) is to continue on East Austin Creek Trail. The killer climb toward Bullfrog Pond Campground is a long mile, with a thousand-foot elevation gain.

When you reach the paved park road (carefully, walk on the shoulder) 0.5 mile, then pick up a short footpath on your right that leads back to the trailhead.

HENDY WOODS STATE PARK

■ GENTLE GIANTS, DISCOVERY, NAVARRO RIVER TRAILS
3 miles round trip

Drive inland a bit from the forever-foggy Mendocino County coast and you'll find sunny meadows, a pastoral valley of apple orchards, vineyards and farm houses, plus tall redwoods that escaped the logger's ax.

Hendy Woods, a twenty mile drive from the coast, is warmer, and has an altogether different vibe than the other coastal redwood parks.

The land now comprising the state park was purchased a century ago by foundry owner Joseph Hendy, who later sold his land to the Masonite Corporation; the corporation, in cooperation with the Save-the-Redwoods League, donated 405 acres to the state parks system in 1958.

While Hendy Woods, with two old-growth redwood groves, is rightly cate-gorized as a "redwood park," some locals are quick to point out that it could also be considered a "wine country park." Anderson Valley, where the park is situated, is an emerging wine-making center.

Getting to the park is part of the fun: Highway 128, winds from Cloverdale on Highway 101 to the Mendocino coast, following the Navarro River. Along the way are farmhouses, apple orchards, sheep, cows, vineyards, and the drowsy hamlets of Yorkville, Boonville, and Philo.

The Navarro River, which runs the length of the park, offers swimming (wading, really) in summer, canoeing and kayaking during late winter and early spring. Redwoods grow tall along the banks of the Navarro.

Hikers will enjoy the half mile Discovery Trail, plus another nature trail, wheelchair accessible, that explores the redwoods.

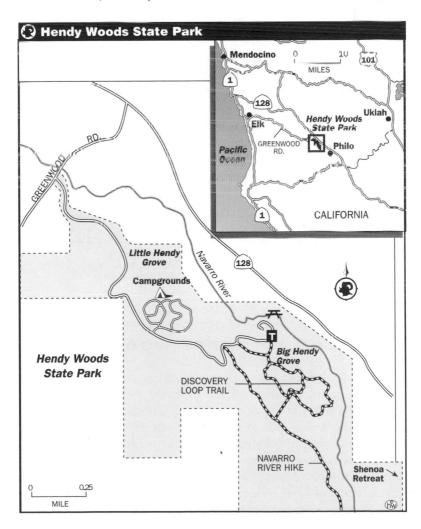

This walk begins with a loop or two through the redwoods, then continues along the Navarro River.

DIRECTIONS TO TRAILHEAD From Highway 1, about ten miles south of Mendocino, turn inland on Highway 128 and travel twenty miles to Philo Greenwood Road. Turn right and drive a half mile to the entrance of Hendy Woods State Park. Follow the park road 1.75 miles to its end at the picnic area.

(If you're traveling Highway 128 northwest from Cloverdale/ Highway 101, you'll proceed some eight miles past Boonville to the state park turnoff.)

Those New Age hikers staying at Shenoa Retreat or those folks staying at one of the other private resorts might want to begin this walk from the vicinity of Shenoa Retreat, located off Ray's Road, 2.5 miles from Highway 128. However, this area is private property; unless you're a guest at one of these facilities, you should start your walk at the state park.

THE HIKE From the picnic area, follow the path into the redwoods. You'll wind through the old-growth redwoods and their neighboring trees— madrone, Douglas fir, bay laurel and more. Join the two-looped Discovery Trail, then take a right-forking trail that ascends to a gravel fire road.

After crossing a creek, travel through an area filled with impressive redwoods. You'll pass two signed "Horse Trails" that lead down to some inviting swimming holes on the Navarro River.

Your turnaround point, about 1.5 miles from the trailhead, could be at the state park boundary or a mile farther near Shenoa Retreat on the far outskirts of Philo.

MONTGOMERY WOODS
STATE RESERVE

■ MONTGOMERY WOODS TRAIL
2 mile loop

Redwood admirers know Montgomery Woods State Reserve as a little gem with big trees: 300-foot tall giants in a series of impressive memorial groves. The reserve's location (the most geographically isolated of California's redwood state parks) makes a visit here seem all the more special.

Getting to the remote park, hidden away along the headwaters of Big River in the Coast Range of Mendocino County, can be an adventure in itself. Curvy two-lanes lead from the coast and Ukiah over oak-dotted rolling hills and past Orr Hot Springs, an off-the-beaten-path, rustic hot springs resort.

Thanks to the efforts of the Save-the-Redwood League, the reserve has expanded greatly from an initial nine acres donated in 1945 to some 1323 acres today.

A tranquil trail links the reserve's five memorial groves that tower above Montgomery Creek. The path gives hikers up-close looks at the grand stands, whose trees are not only tall, but broad (up to 14 feet in diameter), as well.

Montgomery Woods is known as a climax forest, where a small congregation of understory plants gathered around the redwoods lives in a harmonious, fairly stable environment. Beneath the redwoods, ferns, wild iris, miners lettuce, poison oak and redwood sorrel flourish.

DIRECTIONS TO TRAILHEAD From Highway 101 just north of Ukiah, exit on North State Street and head briefly north (away from downtown) to Orr Springs Road. Turn west and travel 13.5 miles to Montgomery Woods State Reserve. Look for the trailhead and small parking area near a road bridge.

From Highway 1, just south of Mendocino, turn east onto Comptche-Ukiah Road and travel 30 miles to the state reserve.

THE HIKE Follow the path along Montgomery Creek past laurel and tan oak. The trail soon leads across a footbridge to join an old road on the opposite side of the creek. Here you'll find the first memorial grove—Elizabeth M. Orr Memorial Grove—en route, as well as the reserve's small picnic area.

A 0.25 mile ascent on the road, then a brief descent brings you to the splendid Grubbs Memorial Grove. About 0.5 mile from the trailhead, the road gives way to a footpath and crosses the creek at the mile-mark via a long log with steps carved into it.

The return leg has a wilder, more-isolated feeling. After traveling over a length of boardwalk, the fern-lined path heads down-creek before returning to Grubbs Memorial Grove and the trailhead.

STANDISH-HICKEY
STATE RECREATION AREA

■ BIG TREE, MILL CREEK TRAILS
2 mile loop via Big Tree Trail; 6 mile loop via Mill Creek Trail

The redwood groves (mostly second-growth) are pleasant enough, but it's not the trees that attract visitors year after year, it's the river.

The Eel River, that is.

Occupying both banks of the Eel's South Fork, the recreation area offers a swimming hole, three campgrounds, steelhead and salmon fishing in winter, and some good hiking.

The Eel passes through some inspiring scenery on its long journey from its headwaters in the Yolla Bolly Wilderness to its mouth at Eureka's Humboldt Bay. In redwood country, the Eel has sculpted some impressive towering bluffs, particularly along the two mile stretch within Standish-Hickey.

The park's premier arboreal attraction is the Captain Miles Standish Tree, a scarred 225-foot tall, 13-feet-in-diameter giant, estimated to be 1,200 years old. The tree honors one of the early Pilgrims; his descendants, the Standish family, along with the Hickey family, donated much of the acreage to form the park.

Because the rain-swollen Eel River floods so often, its banks, bottom and swimming holes change each year. All the park's Eel-spanning footbridges are removed during the winter, effectively making most of the trail system inaccessible. In fact, sometimes high water knocks out the bridge in late spring and early summer as well.

Standish-Hickey's three mile round trip Lookout Trail offers a pretty good look down at the Eel, but I prefer the more intimate view of the park offered by two loop trails—Big Tree and Mill Creek.

DIRECTIONS TO THE TRAILHEAD From Highway 101, a mile north of Leggett, take the Standish-Hickey State Recreation Area exit. Once inside the park, continue straight past the entrance station, taking the very steep road down to the seasonal bridge across the Eel River and over to Redwood Campground. Bear right after campsite #108 to the day use parking lot.

THE HIKE Join signed Big Tree Trail for a short distance to a fork and bear left. The path soon leaves the banks of the Eel and begins a mellow ascent through the redwoods.

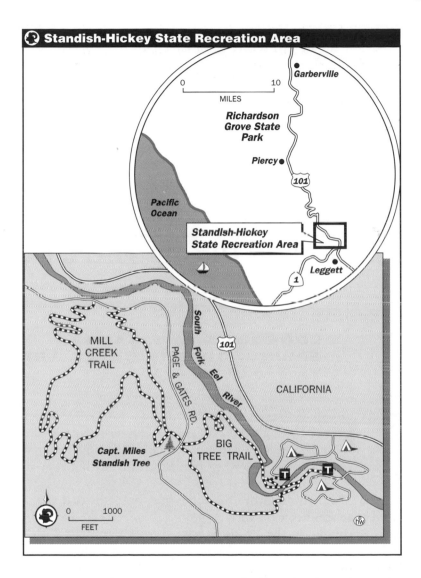

Standish-Hickey State Recreation Area

A mile out, the trail passes a junction with the other leg of Big Tree Trail, crosses Page & Gates Road, and arrives at the impressive Captain Miles Standish Tree. While admiring the redwood, you can choose whether to return via the other branch of Big Tree Trail and complete your hike, or join Mill Creek Loop Trail.

The latter path crosses meadowland and ascends through the woods to a slightly scary-looking landslide area above Mill Creek. The trail descends to cross the creek, then climbs again, traveling along a ridge, then descending again toward the Eel River.

The path meets Page & Gates Road, very close to the mouth of Mill Creek where it flows into the Eel River. Go right on the road for a short distance.

Follow the trail signs which take you back into the creekbed for a short detour around the now-unsafe bridge over Mill Creek, then resume walking on Mill Creek Loop Trail, which ascends a bit at first before leveling out through lovely Big Tree Meadow.

Back at Miles Standish Tree, you'll join Big Tree Trail's left fork on the other side of Page & Gates Road, descending to the river and crossing Cabin Meadow. When you reach the banks of the Eel, near the park's swimming area, you'll cross a little log bridge, then follow the trail over the opposite gravel bar to a second wooden bridge to Redwood Campground and the trailhead.

RICHARDSON GROVE STATE PARK

■ LOOKOUT POINT, TANOAK SPRING, DURPHY CREEK TRAILS
4 miles round trip

You can't miss viewing the redwoods in Richardson Grove State Park; the highway lobby had Highway 101 built right through the heart of the park. But if you really want to experience the magic and majesty of "The Grove," as it's affectionately known, you must get off the highway and hit the trail.

Fortunately, Richardson Grove has some fine footpaths that visit quiet redwood groves and Eel River beaches.

The park, acquired in the 1920s, is named for California's 25th governor, William Friend Richardson, though it's any park lover's guess why. The ultra-conservative Richardson was completely unsympathetic to the state park system, then in its infancy, and vetoed all expenditure bills.

Start your visit to Richardson Grove with a look at the natural history exhibits and history displays at the visitor center. Check out the arboreal curiosities: a walk-through tree, and a dawn redwood, the coastal redwood's Chinese cousin, located in the group camp. The park features a full schedule of interpretive programs during the summer months.

This loop trip offers an enjoyable jaunt through the redwoods growing above the South Fork of the Eel River. The Eel's frequent floods in years past have deposited thick layers of rich soil—ideal for growing especially tall redwoods.

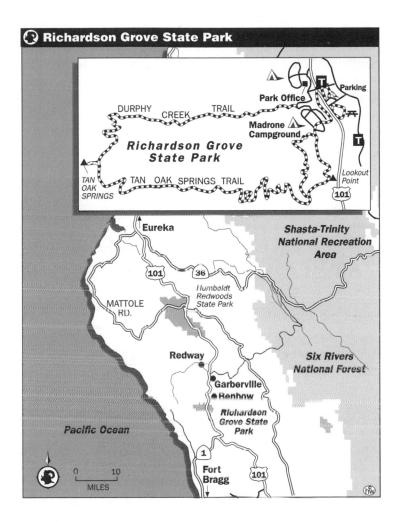

DIRECTIONS TO TRAILHEAD From Highway 101, eight miles south of Garberville, take the Richardson Grove State Park exit.

Once inside the park, getting to either of the trailheads is a bit tricky, unless you happen to have reserved a site in Madrone Campground. If you're not camping, best bet is to park at the picnic ground near the visitor center, follow the short path to the Highway 101 underpass, emerging on the other side and picking up the path leading to and through Madrone Campground.

THE HIKE From the signed trailhead in Madrone Campground, begin your climb to Lookout Point Trail, which almost immediately forks. Stay left and begin ascending thorough redwoods and Douglas firs to Lookout Point. The so-so vista is of the Eel River Canyon and Highway 101. From the lookout, the path steepens. You briefly join the trail to Hartsook Inn before meeting up with Tan Oak Springs Trail and switchbacking up a forested ridge.

After cresting the ridge, about 1.5 miles from the trailhead, the path descends a short distance to Tan Oak Springs. The cattail- and tule-surrounded spring isn't much to behold, but it's a nice place to take a breather.

Past the spring, the trail continues descending to the south bank of Durphy Creek, then levels off to follow the creek eastward on a more level course through the redwoods.

The trail ends at the park road, where you'll turn left to return to the trailhead.

BENBOW LAKE
STATE RECREATION AREA

■ PIONEER MEADOW,
PRATT MILL TRAILS
2.5 mile loop with 400-foot elevation gain

Benbow Lake is a summer-only attraction: the Eel River is dammed from Memorial Day to Labor Day, creating a lake that's very popular with swimmers and canoeists. During this time, park staff offers guided "canoe hikes"—fun and educational excursions on the lake.

In the 1920s, the Pratt family constructed a steam-driven sawmill on one side of the Eel River, while the Benbow family constructed a hotel/resort. Fortunately, not all the scenery went through the mill, so that in 1926 when the large Tudor-style Benbow Inn opened for business, its setting on the South Fork of the Eel River was still beautiful. Hollywood celebs frequented the inn back then, as did Herbert Hoover and Eleanor Roosevelt.

Benbow Lake State Recreation Area today consists of 1,200 acres of riverfront, meadows and redwood groves. The park, fast becoming a cultural center, hosts a summer arts festival, a Shakespeare Festival, and concerts.

A couple of trails sample the recreation area, offering some great views of the lake. If a 2.5 mile hike isn't enough exercise, try swimming or canoeing on the lake or tackling the park's par exercise course.

DIRECTIONS TO TRAILHEAD From Highway 101, two miles south of Garberville, take the Benbow exit, following the frontage road to the park. Turn into the campground and drive to its north end. The trail leaves from

The matchless grove at Bull Creek Flat forms the heart of Humboldt Redwoods, one of the first state parks established in the 1920s.

campsite 73. During the off-season, when the upper campground loop is closed, begin this walk at campsite 11 and hike an extra 0.25 mile.

THE HIKE From campsite 73, join Pratt Mill Trail and begin ascending through redwoods. The path dips into, then switchbacks out of, a ravine and, a half mile from the trailhead, comes to a junction. Go left to meet Pioneer Trail, which ascends west for a quarter mile to a junction with Ridge Trail; this path loops a mile (rejoining Pioneer Trail) to a peak for great views of South Fork country.

Pioneer Trail levels out a bit, passes the other branch of Ridge Trail, then descends to Pioneer Meadow. The path continues descending, offering views of Benbow Lake, to a junction with Pratt Mill Trail (an old road).

Bear right and hike along the lakeshore a quarter mile to a short side trail leading to Pratt Mill. A rusted boiler located among tall redwoods marks the site of the old mill.

Your trail continues southeast, ascending briefly to a lookout high above the lake's and the park's picnic area. A bit more climbing brings you back to close the loop and a left turn returns you to campsite 73 and the trailhead.

HUMBOLDT REDWOODS STATE PARK

■ BULL CREEK FLATS LOOP TRAIL
From Rockefeller Forest to Big Trees Area via 8.5 mile loop;
several shorter options possible

Famed Avenue of the Giants offers a good look at Humboldt County's redwoods. More than a dozen short paths meander through Avenue-adjacent groves named for the famous, the rich and famous, and the just plain rich.

The 32 mile parkway, the parallel scenic alternate to Highway 101, runs the length of Humboldt Redwoods State Park. This park was one of California's first to be preserved when the state park system was established in the 1920s. Today it protects about one-eighth of all remaining old-growth coast redwoods.

Just off the Avenue of the Giants in Weott is the park visitor center. Stop to pick up maps, inquire about trail conditions and check out the nature exhibits, including an excellent one about the importance of ancient forests.

The matchless old-growth forest along Bull Creek was an early cause célèbre with early California conservationists, who struggled to save the redwoods from the mill. Out of this struggle to save Humboldt County's tall trees came the formation of the Save-the-Redwoods League in 1918.

Thanks to John D. Rockefeller, Jr. quietly funnelling two million dollars to the League, matching state funds, conservationists were able to purchase some 10,000 acres along Bull Creek from the Pacific Lumber Company in 1930.

Today the Bull Creek backcountry forms the heart of the park. Thriving along this creek is more than a redwood grove; it's truly a forest. The Rockefeller Forest is, without resorting to too many superlatives, the most impressive stand of redwoods found anywhere in the world.

A five mile long road winds through the Bull Creek area, as do several hiking trails. My favorite is the route along Bull Creek itself. This path offers curiosities (Flatiron Tree, Giant Tree and more), as well as swimming in and sunning beside Bull Creek. And, of course, there are the spectacular redwoods—explored by a trail that stretches not only the legs but the imagination as well.

If you're pressed for time, both ends of the above-described Bull Creek Flats Loop Trail have shorter, inviting explorations. You can easily walk from the Big

Trees parking area to Giant Tree, then stroll along Bull Creek. The half mile Rockefeller Forest Loop Trail is a gem.

From the Avenue of the Giants, there's easy access to many short trails into the redwoods. Favorites include Children's Forest Loop Trail, Founders Grove Trail, Drury-Chaney Trail, and Franklin K. Lane Grove Trail.

DIRECTIONS TO TRAILHEAD From the north-central part of the Avenue of the Giants, four miles north of the park visitor center and just south of the hamlet of Redcrest, turn west on Mattole Road and drive 1.5 miles to the parking area for the Rockefeller Forest Loop Trail. (If you want to make this a one-way hike and make car shuttle arrangements, a second trailhead is located at the Big Trees Parking Area, another three miles west on Mattole Road.)

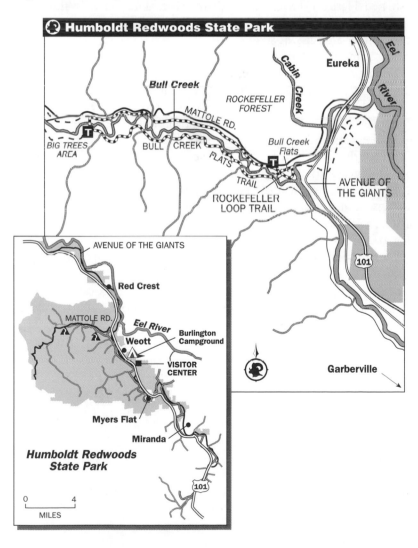

THE HIKE Begin your walk on the right branch of the Rockefeller Loop (a very pleasant family hike in its own right) and follow it for a short 0.25 mile or so to a junction, bearing right onto Bull Creek Flats Loop Trail.

The route heads up-creek, along a path crowded in places by rushes and horsetail. A mile out, the trail breaks into a clearing and 0.5 mile farther crosses a tributary creek on a bridge; in another mile more, a log bench beckons you to take a break.

About a mile from the Big Trees Parking Area, the path climbs to closely parallel Mattole Road. After crossing a couple side creeks on wooden bridges, you arrive at the parking lot.

From here, cross the bridge over Bull Creek and follow the signs to the oddly shaped Flatiron Tree and to Giant Tree. The Giant is not the world's tallest redwood, but it is the biggest—the champion by virtue of its combined height, diameter and crown size.

Leaving behind the Giant Tree, the path travels through a fern-filled forest, crosses Squaw Creek on a bridge, and soon passes a junction with the right-forking Johnson Camp Trail. Not only do the ancient trees towering above make you feel small, their fallen cousins, which require a 75-yard zig and a 75-yard zag by trail to get around, are also humbling to the hiker.

The trail enters and exits a hollow, hike-through log, then meanders a bit, north and south, with Bull Creek. A mile-and-a-half from the Big Trees area, the path plunges into the fern-filled canyon of Connick Creek, emerging to travel past awesome redwoods, including the so-called Giant Braid, a trio of redwoods twisted together.

For the most part, as you hike along, you'll hear but not see Bull Creek, until 0.5 mile or so from the Rockefeller Loop, when the path drops close to the creek. The trail explores some more magnificent redwoods on the flats above the creek.

Your redwood journey ends when you cross Bull Creek on a seasonal bridge and reconnect with Rockefeller Loop Trail for the short walk back to the parking area.

GRIZZLY CREEK REDWOODS STATE PARK

■ MEMORIAL, BAIRD TRAILS
1.5 miles round trip; longer hikes possible

One of the smallest of California's coast redwoods state parks, Grizzly Creek is also farthest from the coast—nearly 30 miles. Its location, far from Highway 101/Avenue of The Giants tourist route means few visitors discover the park's 300-foot redwoods or the six short trails that visit them.

The park is tucked in the Van Duzen River Valley, where Grizzly Creek meets the Van Duzen River. This locale may be remote, but filmmaker George Lucas found one of the park's virgin redwood groves so appealing he used the location in his Star Wars sequel, *Return of the Jedi.*

The park is located on Highway 36, a remote byway that links such out-of-the-way places as Mad River, Forest Glen, Wildwood and Beegum as it winds through the forest from Highway 101 to Interstate 5. So remote is this road that it's difficult to believe that until 1918, before the completion of 101, this little road was the major route of travel between San Francisco and Eureka.

Worth a stop is Cheatham Grove, a stand of virgin redwoods located three miles west of the main part of the state park. A short loop trail explores the grove where six wonderful environmental campsites are located. (They are more tranquil than those at Grizzly Creek Campground.)

The park's fern-lined trails meander among the old-growth and second-growth redwoods. A nature trail interprets local flora.

During summer, the low water level permits installation of a footbridge across the Van Duzen River. The bridge gives access to 1.25-mile-long Memorial Trail which loops through the forest. From Devil's Elbow, a bend in the river, hikers get a good view of the river and the park.

DIRECTIONS TO TRAILHEAD From Highway 101 in Alton, exit on Highway 36 and drive 17 miles east to Grizzly Creek State Park. Turn right past the entrance station and park in the picnic area lot.

THE HIKE Cross the Van Duzen River on the summer bridge and follow a dirt road for a short distance to Memorial Trail on your left.

Memorial Trail heads into the redwoods—a drier, less fern-filled forest than those found closer to the coast, and drier even than other groves in the park. After 0.25 mile, the path splits: Go right, meandering into a tanoak, maple and bay laurel woodland. At the eastern end of Memorial Trail, take the short Baird Trail looping through the old-growth redwood forest thriving on the banks of the Van Duzen River. After you've enjoyed the redwoods, finish Memorial Loop Trail, which returns you to the picnic area.

PRAIRIE CREEK REDWOODS STATE PARK

■ FERN CANYON, JAMES IRVINE, CLINTONIA, MINERS RIDGE TRAILS

Loop through Fern Canyon 1 mile round trip; via Gold Bluffs, Gold Bluffs Beach is 6.5 miles round trip with 500-foot elevation gain

Dim and quiet, wrapped in mist and silence, the redwoods roof a moist and mysterious world. Park trails meander over lush ground and the walker is treated to the cool feeling and fragrance of wood and water.

A couple beautiful "fern canyons" are found along the north coast, but the Fern Canyon in Prairie Creek Redwoods State Park is undoubtedly the most awe-inspiring. Five-finger, deer, lady, sword, and chain ferns smother the precipitous walls of the canyon. Bright yellow monkeyflowers abound, as well as fairy lanterns, those creamy white or greenish bell-shaped flowers that hang in clusters. Ferns are descendants of an ancient group of plants which were much more numerous 200 million years ago. Ferns have roots and stems similar to flowering plants, but are considered to be a primitive form of plant life because they reproduce by spores, not seeds.

Gold Bluffs was named in 1850 when prospectors found some gold flakes in the beach sand. The discovery caused a minor gold rush. A tent city sprang up on the beach but little gold was extracted.

Gold Bluffs Beach is a beauty—eleven miles of wild, driftwood-littered shore, backed by extensive dunes. Sand verbena, bush lupine, and wild strawberry splash color on the sand.

This walk explores some of the highlights of Prairie Creek Redwoods State Park—Fern Canyon, magnificent redwood groves, and Gold Bluffs Beach.

DIRECTIONS TO TRAILHEAD From Highway 101, three miles north of Orick, turn west on Davison Road. The dirt, washboard road (suitable only for vehicles under 24 feet in length) descends logged slopes and through second-growth redwoods to the beach. The road heads north along Gold Bluffs Beach. One and a half miles past the campground, the road dead-ends at the Fern Canyon Trailhead.

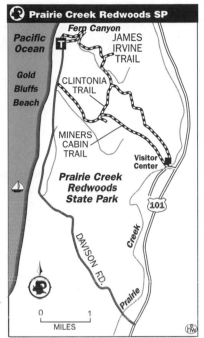

THE HIKE The path leads along the pebbled floor of Fern Canyon. In the wettest places, the route follows wooden planks across Home Creek. With sword and five-finger ferns pointing the way, you pass through marshy areas covered with wetlands grass and dotted with a bit of skunk cabbage. Lurking about are Pacific giant salamanders.

A half mile from the trailhead, the path climbs out of the canyon to intersect James Irvine Trail, named for a man who contributed much to the formation of redwood parks.

The James Irvine Trail crosses to the south side of the canyon and proceeds southeast with Home Creek. The trail reaches the upper neck of Fern Canyon and junctions with Clintonia Trail. (James Irvine Trail continues ascending through dense redwood forest to a trailhead near the park visitors center.) Clintonia Trail leads a mile through virgin redwood groves to a junction with Miners Ridge Trail. Bear right.

Part of Miners Ridge Trail is an old logging road, once used by mule-drawn wagons. The trail was also a pack train route for the Gold Bluffs miners. You'll descend with Squashan Creek to the ocean.

It's a 1.5 mile beach walk along Gold Bluffs Beach back to the trailhead.

Lucky walkers might catch a glimpse of the herd of Roosevelt elk that roam the park. These graceful animals look like a cross between a South American llama and a deer, and convince walkers that they have, indeed, entered an enchanted land.

DEL NORTE COAST REDWOODS STATE PARK

■ DAMNATION CREEK TRAIL
From Highway 101 to Damnation Cove is 5 miles round trip
with 1,000-foot elevation gain

Del Norte Coast Redwoods State Park delivers the scenery in its name: an impressive coastline, as well as magnificent old-growth redwoods. The combination of redwoods—and a mixed forest of Sitka spruce, Douglas fir and red alder—along with the coast, adds up to some terrific hiking.

The majority of the state park is located on the ocean side of Highway 101; in fact, what is now a splendid hiking trail used to be the Redwood Highway (101). The old highway was abandoned in 1935 for its present route.

Steep Damnation Creek Trail plunges through a virgin redwood forest to a hidden rocky beach. Giant ferns, and the pink and purple rhododendron blossoms climbing 30 feet overhead, contribute to the impression that one has strayed into a tropical rain forest.

The creek name, as the story goes, was proffered by early settlers who had a devil of a time making their way through the thick forest near the creek banks. Even trailblazer Jedediah Smith, whose expedition camped alongside Damnation Creek in June of 1828, found it very rough going.

No, this isn't your basic mellow walk in a redwood park, on level trails. However, if you hike here, you're sure to find a measure of solitude.

Allow extra time for this hike; it's a strenuous journey back to the highway from Damnation Cove. An additional precautionary note: the final length of trail down to the beach is a tricky descent from the sometimes muddy and slippery bluffs and should be undertaken only by those confident in their abilities. Also, rocky Damnation Cove is best explored at low tide when you can view the tidepools.

DIRECTIONS TO TRAILHEAD From Highway 101 in Crescent City, head 8 miles south to the signed turnout on the coast side of the highway at mile-marker 16.

THE HIKE The trail soon leaves the sights and sounds of the highway behind as it climbs through redwood forest for 0.25 mile, crests a ridge, and begins its oceanward descent. Joining the redwoods on the wet and wild coastal slope are

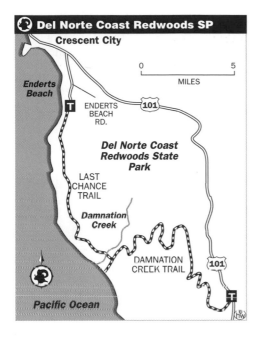

Del Norte Coast Redwoods SP

other big trees—Sitka spruce and Douglas fir—as well as a carpet of oxalis.

As you descend, you'll walk in the footsteps of the native Yurok, who used this trail to reach the beach, where they gathered seaweed and shellfish. At 0.6 mile, you'll junction a stretch of pavement—a retired length of the old Coast Highway, now part of Coastal Trail, which connects the redwood parks.

Steep switchbacks carry you ever downward. About halfway to the beach, you'll be treated to tree-framed views of the Pacific as the trail angles along with Damnation Creek. Wooden bridges facilitate crossing of two branches of Damnation Creek.

Near trail's end you'll reach a clifftop perch above the mouth of Damnation Creek. It's an inspiring view: the creek flowing into the surging Pacific, sea stacks and rocky Damnation Cove.

You be the judge of the sketchy trail and the level of the tide as you decide whether or not to descend to the shore.

JEDEDIAH SMITH REDWOODS STATE PARK

■ BOY SCOUT TRAIL
7.5 miles round trip to Fern Falls

Northernmost of California's redwood state parks, Jedediah Smith beckons the hiker with both a redwood forest primeval and the banks of the Smith River, the state's only major river without a dam.

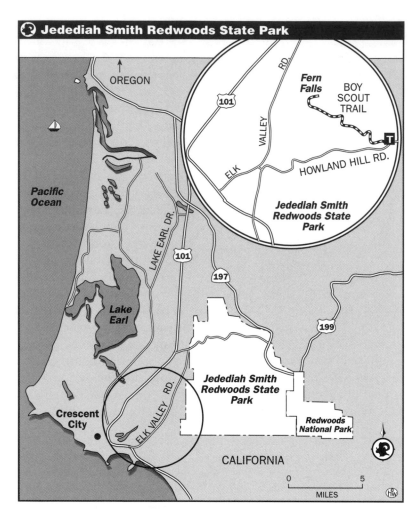

Jedediah Smith Redwoods State Park

The park honors mountain man/pathfinder Jedediah Smith, credited with discovering (for west-bound travelers) the Rocky Mountains pass through which most California- and Oregon-bound emigrants traveled.

Smith was also the first to journey (by land, anyway) to what was to become the west coast of the continental United States—from San Diego to just short of the Canadian border. The Smith River was named for the dogged adventurer, who crossed the wild watercourse in 1828.

Centerpiece of the state park is Stout Memorial Grove. Among the magnificent 5,000 acres of nearby National Tribute Grove is one of the world's largest trees: Stout Tree, named not for its considerable girth, as you might suspect, but for Frank D. Stout, whose family donated the grove to the Save-the-Redwoods League.

Another towering redwood is Boy Scout Tree, visited by a trail constructed by the scouts of Crescent City's Troop 10 in the 1930s.

DIRECTIONS TO TRAILHEAD From Highway 101, at the south end of Crescent City, turn east on Elk Valley Road. After 1.5 miles, fork right on Howland Hill Road and continue east about four more miles to the signed trailhead located on the north side of the road.

THE HIKE Stroll the fern-lined path, the 300-foot-tall trees towering above you. After a mile, the trail follows a redwood-topped ridge, with tall sword ferns pointing the way.

About two miles along, the path descends a series of wooden steps to a lush, lovely creek. Another mile of quiet forest walking brings you to a fork: the right branch goes to Boy Scout Tree while the other leads to Fern Falls.

State parks preserve some of the most beautiful portions of California's North Coast.

CHAPTER NINE

NORTHERN CALIFORNIA COAST

Extending almost 400 miles from San Francisco to the Oregon border, California's North Coast is a land of rugged shores and pounding surf.

San Francisco is known as a city of walkers; favorite destinations of weekend hikers include China Camp, Angel Island and Mt. Tamalpais state parks, which offer great vistas of the bay and the city.

North Coast state parks pay tribute to a variety of cultures: Chinese fishermen at China Camp, the Russian outpost at Fort Ross. Olompali State Historic Park celebrates thousands of years of uniquely Californian history from ancestors of the native Miwok people to Spanish missionaries.

Few coastal locales are as photographed at the town of Mendocino and its bold headlands. The headlands are laced with pathways that offer postcard views of wave tunnels and tidepools, sea stacks and blowholes.

Accenting the coast is a variety of flora, from the towering Sitka spruce at Patrick's Point State Park to the delicate blossoms in Kruse Rhododendron State Preserve. Five-finger and bird's foot, lady and licorice are ferns growing in Van Damme State Park's well-named Fern Canyon.

Wildest of the north coast parks is Sinkyone Wilderness State Park, part of California's "Lost Coast," where the hearty explorer discovers dense forests, prairies and black sand beaches.

CANDLESTICK POINT
STATE RECREATION AREA

■ CANDLESTICK POINT TRAIL
2 miles round trip

To San Francisco baseball fans, 3Com Park, formerly known as Candlestick Park, was long the windy home stadium of their beloved Giants. The team relocated to more upscale digs at the new Pac Bell (now SBC) Park in 2001, leaving behind San Francisco's football team, the '49ers, as the sole tenants..

In the shadow of "The Stick" is a state recreation area that beckons other sports-minded visitors. Advanced board-sailers relish the challenge of the wind tunnel off the south shore of the park. Afternoon winds funnelling through Alemany Gap to the Bay often create rides to remember.

Kayakers like to put-in and take-out on the park's sandy beach. Fishermen enjoy the two fishing piers. Some of the best winter bird-watching on the Bay is found at Candlestick Point. And there are plenty of facilities for picnics and barbecues.

The California State Parks Foundation is assisting in the restoration of the point's tidal areas.

DIRECTIONS TO TRAILHEAD From Highway 101, south of San Francisco, take the Candlestick Park exit. Follow the Hunters Point Expressway around the stadium to the state recreation area. There's limited parking along the road, plentiful parking near the main picnic/day use area.

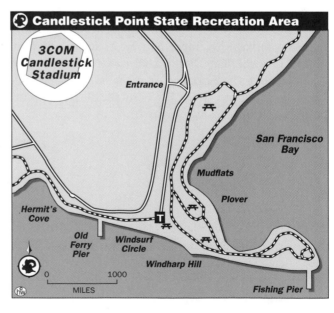

Candlestick Point State Recreation Area

THE HIKE   For the walker, a multi-use trail extends a mile or so along the shoreline from the fishing pier to the picnic areas.

Expect a windy walk. Those infamous winds that have long plagued outfielders, turning even routine fly balls into a challenge to catch, once even blowing a pitcher off the mound, can really slow down a walker.

ANGEL ISLAND STATE PARK

■ ANGEL ISLAND LOOP TRAIL
5 miles round trip with 400-foot elevation gain

For an island barely a square mile in size, Angel Island has an extremely diverse history. Over the last two centuries, the island has seen use as a Mexican land grant, an Army artillery post, and an immigration station. Now it's a state park, attracting hikers, history buffs, and islophiles of all persuasions.

A hundred years of U.S. military occupation began in 1863 when the first gun batteries were installed. The military used the island until 1962, when its Nike missile station was deactivated. During wartime periods, particularly during the Spanish-American War, Angel Island was one of the busiest outposts in America. The island served as a processing center for men about to be dispatched to the Philippines, and as a reception/quarantine center for soldiers who returned with tropical diseases.

Not all of the island's attractions are historical. Rocky coves and sandy beaches, grassy slopes and forested ridges, plus a fine trail network, add up to a walker's delight. Perimeter Road takes the walker on a five mile tour of the island and offers a different bay view from every turn. From atop Mt. Livermore, a terrific 360-degree panorama unfolds of San Franciso Bay and the Golden Gate.

DIRECTIONS TO TRAILHEAD   For information about ferry service to island from Tiburon, call Tiburon Ferry at (415) 435-2131. There is limited ferry service from San Francisco via Blue and Gold Fleet; call (415) 773-1188. The ferries land at Ayala Cove on the northwest side of the island.

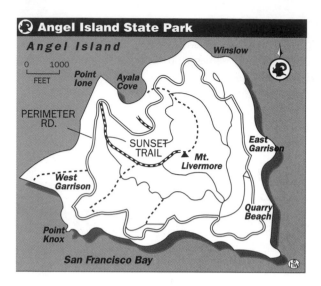

Angel Island State Park

Angel Island

Winslow

0   1000
FEET

Point Ione

Ayala Cove

PERIMETER RD.

SUNSET TRAIL

Mt. Livermore

East Garrison

West Garrison

Quarry Beach

Point Knox

San Francisco Bay

Park your car—for a fee—in one of Tiburon's parking lots near the waterfront, or attempt to find some of the scarce free parking.

THE HIKE When you disembark, pick up a park map and head for the park visitor center, located in a yellow building that once served as bachelor quarters for unmarried officers assigned to the U.S. Quarantine Station that operated here from 1892 to 1949. At that time, Ayala Cove was named Hospital Cove. At the visitor center, check out the interpretive exhibits.

Walk uphill on the road to the left of the visitor center. You'll intersect Perimeter Road and the Sunset trailhead at the top of the hill.

Sunset Trail switchbacks up steep, coastal-scrub-covered slopes, to the top of 788-foot Mt. Caroline Livermore. Picnic tables have replaced the helicopter pad and radio antennae that once stood on the summit. Views of Ayala Cove, Tiburon, and the Golden Gate, are memorable.

Continuing right (west) on Perimeter Road, you'll soon overlook Camp Reynolds (West Garrison). A side road leads down to the island's first military fortifications. You can walk the parade ground and see the brick hospital built in 1908. Still standing are the chapel, mule barn, officers quarters, and several more structures.

Perimeter Road turns eastward, contouring around chaparral-covered slopes and offering a view down to Point Blunt. You may hear and see the harbor seals gathered around the point. The road curves north and soon arrives at East Garrison, where a collection of utilitarian-looking buildings are a reminder of the many thousands of men who were processed here. East Garrison trained about 30,000 men a year for overseas duty. The hospital, barracks, mess hall, and officers' homes still stand.

Continue north. You'll soon come to the Immigration Station, the so called "Ellis Island of the West." From 1910 to 1940, 175,000 immigrants, mostly Asians, were detained and processed. During World War II, German, Italian, and Japanese prisoners of war were confined here.

Perimeter Road rounds Point Campbell, northernmost part of the island, and you'll get a glimpse of the Richmond-San Rafael Bridge, and then a view of Tiburon, before the road descends to Ayala Cove.

MT. TAMALPAIS STATE PARK

■ RAILROAD GRADE, FERN CREEK TRAILS

From Mountain Home Inn to East Peak summit is 6 miles round trip with 1,300-foot elevation gain

For more than a century, Bay Area walkers and visitors from around the world have enjoyed rambling the slopes of Mt. Tamalpais. Glorious panoramas of the Pacific coastline and San Francisco Bay were attracting walkers to the mountaintop well before Mt. Tam was preserved as a state park in 1928.

If you're lucky, perhaps you'll experience what some Bay Area walkers call "a Farallons Day"—one of those clear days when visibility is greater than 25 miles, thus allowing a glimpse of the sharp peaks of the Farallon Islands.

The Mt. Tamalpais and Muir Woods Railroad, known as "the crookedest railroad in the world," was constructed in 1896; it brought passengers from Mill Valley to the summit via 281 curves. Atop Mt. Tam, the Tavern of Tamalpais welcomed diners and dancers.

Redwood lined creeks, stands of Douglas fir, and oak-dotted potreros are just a few of the great mountain's delightful environments. Thanks to the early trail-building efforts of the Tamalpais Conservation Club, as well as later efforts by the CCC during the 1930s, more than fifty miles of trail explore the state park. These trails connect to two hundred more miles of trail that lead through the wooded watershed of the Marin Municipal Water District, and over to Muir Woods National Monument and Golden Gate National Recreation Area.

Mt. Tam's top, with its fire lookout tower ringed with barbed wire, itself isn't quite as nice as the top-of-the-world views it offers. Motorists can drive to within 0.3 mile of the top, which often means a crowd at the summit.

Ah, but getting there is more than half the fun, particularly on trails like Railroad Grade and Fern Creek, which offer a little bit of everything: dense stands of laurel, open grassland, oak-dotted knolls, a canyon full of redwoods and ferns.

If you want to stay on the Railroad Grade all the way to the top of Mt. Tam, add 2.5 miles to the ascent plus 2.5 miles to the descent.

DIRECTIONS TO TRAILHEAD From Highway 1 in Mill Valley, veer right on Panoramic Highway, ascending a few miles to Mountain Home Inn and a parking area. The trail begins across Panoramic Highway. A bus stops at Mountain Home Inn, so by all means consider the bus a way to the trailhead.

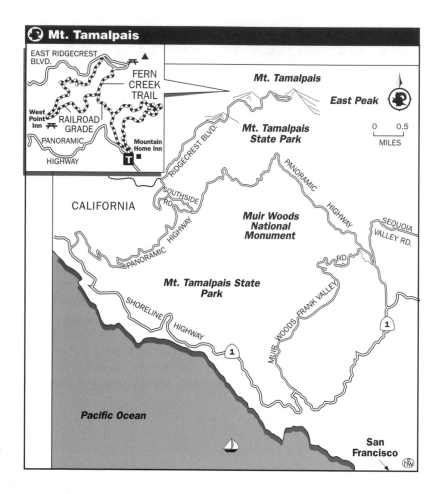

THE HIKE Begin your steady ascent (7 percent grade all the way) on the Old Railroad Grade. An occasional view opens up among the brush.

Almost two miles out, you'll reach a junction with the east fork of Fern Canyon. Take this very steep shortcut a long half mile to Ridgecrest Boulevard just below the East Peak parking lot.

(Dogged railroad buffs will ignore such shortcuts and stay on the Railroad Grade, which visits the West Point Inn, originally built by the railroad and now owned by the Marin Water District and run by the West Point Inn Association. Hikers may pause on the veranda and buy some liquid refreshment. You'll circle clockwise around West Point, heading north another two miles up the railroad grade).

Once you reach the summit parking lot and picnic area, catch your breath and join the 0.3 mile summit trail to the top of Mt. Tam.

CHINA CAMP STATE PARK

■ SHORELINE, BAY VIEW TRAILS
4.5 miles round trip with 400-foot elevation gain

On Point San Pedro Peninsula, only a few ramshackle buildings remain of the once-thriving shrimp fishing village of China Camp. During the 1800s, more than thirty such camps were established on the shores of San Francisco Bay.

The fishermen were mostly Chinese, primarily natives of Kwantung Province. The fishermen staked nets on the shallow bay bottom, in order to capture tiny grass shrimp. The shrimp were dried, then the meat separated from the shell. It was a labor-intensive process, but a ready market for the shrimp existed in China and Japan.

In the early 20th century, competing fishermen helped push through legislation that banned the use of bag nets, and in 1905, the export of dried shrimp

Take a fascinating hike into history at China Camp.

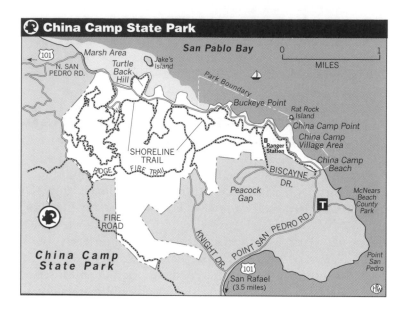

was banned entirely, thus ending the San Francisco Bay and San Pablo Bay shrimping business.

In 1977, the state acquired 1,500 acres of bay shore to form China Camp State Park. Some 1890s-era buildings still stand at China Camp Village, and interpretive exhibits tell of the difficult life in this fishing village.

The park's ridge separates the 1890s from the 21st century. While the view south has changed immeasurably, the view down to China Camp on San Pablo Bay is almost exactly what it was in the early 1900s.

Shoreline Trail is a mellow path that meanders through the forest and grassland above the miles of marshland that border China Camp. For a grand tour of the park, follow Shoreline Trail to the west boundary of the park. An optional return route could be on Bay View Trail, which travels through redwoods and stands of bay through the higher (750 feet or so) elevations of the park. Views of upper San Francisco Bay are outstanding. Returning via Bay View and Ridge trails adds up to 6.5 miles; all together that's a 12-mile tour of the park.

A more modest loop, described on the next page, uses parts of Shoreline and Ridge trails for a fine family outing.

DIRECTIONS TO TRAILHEAD From Highway 101 in San Rafael, take the North San Pedro Road exit and head east through a residential area to China Camp State Park. After entering the park, proceed approximately 3 miles to China Camp Village and park in the village lot.

THE HIKE Cross North San Pedro Road and head uphill on the Village Trail. Bear right on the Village Trail where it intersects with Shoreline Trail. As you follow San Pablo Bay from east to west, you'll stay at about a one hundred foot elevation.

Enjoy views of the park's four distinct shoreline hills—Jake's Island, Turtle Back, Bullet Hill and Chicken Coop Hill. When the bay water was higher, these hills were islands.

Two miles out, you'll reach the dirt road leading to Miwok Meadows, a day use area. (Ambitious hikers will continue on Shoreline Trail.) Those opting for a shorter loop will head uphill on the Miwok Fire Trail and join up with the Oak Ridge Trail. Head east on the Oak Ridge Trail, gaining a different perspective with a little elevation compared to the view from Shoreline Trail. When you meet Peacock Gap Trail, turn left, descending briefly back to Shoreline Trail and returning to the trailhead.

Those choosing the longer hike will head left (south) down the Miwok Fire Trail and cross the Miwok Meadows gravel parking lot. At the southwest corner of the lot, you'll find a wooden bridge spanning an intermittent creek. Shoreline Trail picks up again here and you'll continue east until it meets up with Back Ranch Fire Trail. Join this trail and head uphill across slopes forested with oak, madrone and bay laurel. Proceed right (west) at the intersection with Ridge Fire Trail and head to a former Nike missile station to savor terrific views of San Pablo Bay.

For a great loop hike, backtrack on the Ridge Fire Trail and descend on the Back Ranch Fire Trail until it meets up with the Bay View Trail. Follow Ridge Fire Trail left (east) and when it meets up with Miwok Fire Trail, follow this path downhill for a short distance. Miwok Fire Trail meets Oak Ridge Trail, which you'll join heading east. When you reach Peacock Gap Trail, turn left, descend to Shoreline Trail and return to the trailhead.

BENICIA STATE RECREATION AREA

■ DILLON POINT TRAIL
3 miles round trip

A good slogan for Benicia State Recreation Area might be "Where the waters meet."

Flowing from the east are no less than the combined waters of fourteen tributaries of the Sacramento and San Joaquin rivers; the waters surge through the

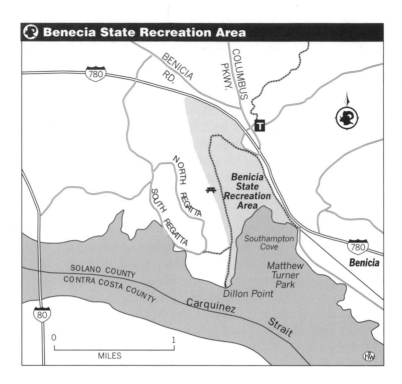

Carniquez Strait, creating quite a spectacle. Nowhere else is San Francisco Bay more narrow than at Dillon Point in the state recreation area.

DIRECTIONS TO TRAILHEAD From Highway 780, exit on Columbia Parkway and follow the signs to Benicia State Recreation Area.

THE HIKE For the hiker, Benicia offers a couple different bay-side strolls. The trail system is part of that ambitious path-in-the-making, the Bay Area Ridge Trail. Most popular is the 1.5-mile-long walk out to Dillon Point on the park road. The road is open to vehicles (fee charged), but auto traffic is usually very light and far outnumbered by walkers, runners and cyclists. At Dillon Point is a popular fishing area where local anglers cast for starry flounder, sturgeon and striped bass.

Another path, beginning near the park entrance, features an exercise parcourse, so you can make your walk a real workout. Paths lead from the exercise trail through the adjacent marshland to water's edge. Bird-watching is particularly good in the marsh.

SAMUEL P. TAYLOR STATE PARK

■ RIDGE TRAIL, BARNABE TRAILS

To Barnabe Peak via 6 mile loop with 1,300-foot elevation gain

From Barnabe Peak, you get a fire lookout's view: Point Reyes National Seashore, Mt. Tamalpais, as well as lots more of central Marin County.

Samuel P. Taylor State Park preserves 2,700 acres of oak, tan oak and madrone woodlands, creekside redwoods, and open grassland. The park is a pleasure to view and hike.

Samuel P. Taylor, an entrepreneur, came to California with the Gold Rush, making enough to capitalize construction of a paper mill on Lagunitas Creek, the first such mill west of the Mississippi. Taylor's Mill produced newsprint for the big San Francisco dailies, as well as better quality paper used in Sacramento for documents issued by the new state of California.

Eventually Taylor went into the resort business. During the 1870s and 1880s, Taylorville offered a new form of recreation: camping. Those preferring not to rough-it could stay in a three-story hotel. A narrow-gauge railroad came through Taylor's property, making it easy for city folk to reach his retreat, which became one of the most popular weekend getaways in northern California. Taylorville is long gone, but the natural setting that made the resort so attractive to the city-weary of the 19th century remains equally attractive today.

Barnabe Peak honors explorer John C. Frémont's mule. Barnabe lived out his days as the Taylor family pet. The view from 1,466-foot Barnabe Peak is not as grand as that from Fremont Peak (see Fremont Peak State Park hike) but does provide an inspiring Marin County panorama. And the view is fairly unobstructed; Barnabe Peak along with famed Mt. Tam are the only Marin County peaks with fire lookouts. This loop trip offers a pleasant riverside stroll, plus a good workout to the peak.

Don't miss visiting the park's anything-but-satanic Devil's Gulch, heavenly shaded by oak, madrone and Douglas fir, with slopes brightened in spring with milkmaids, Indian paintbrush and buttercups. Add Devil's Gulch to your hike with a two mile or so extension, or simply visit it separately from the trailhead located off Sir Francis Drake Highway.

DIRECTIONS TO TRAILHEAD From Highway 101 in San Rafael, exit on Sir Francis Drake Boulevard and travel some fifteen miles to the park. The park entrance is about two miles past the tiny hamlet of Lagunitas. Leave your car in the picnic area lot.

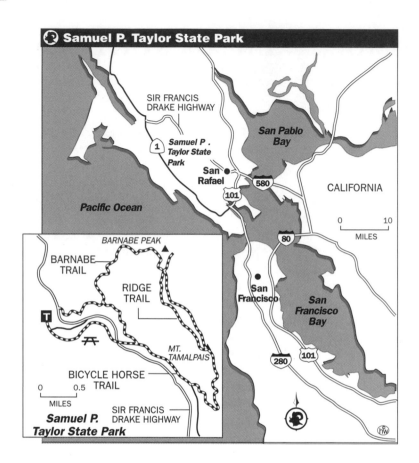

THE HIKE From the picnic area, cross the bridge over Lagunitas Creek and turn left onto the bike/horse trail. This wide, pleasant trail, the former railway bed of the North Pacific Coast Railroad, travels creekside in the shade of bay, maple and redwoods. It soon re-crosses the creek, and crosses Sir Francis Drake Highway on a hiker/cyclist bridge.

The level path continues along the north bank of Lagunitas Creek, and is soon joined by a riding/hiking trail. A half mile from this junction you'll come to another—with signed Ridge Trail. The riding/hiking trail, also known as Cross-Marin Trail, continues 13 more miles to Mount Tamalpais, but you go left, and begin a steady ascent on the aptly named Ridge Trail, gaining good vistas of central Marin County.

A bit more than a mile from the summit, the fire road you've been following offers a parallel trail alternative; the trail is your best bet for spring wildflower watching while the road serves up better vistas. Both trail and road climb briskly, but not too steeply, to the summit.

Enjoy the views west of Bolinas Ridge and Golden Gate National Recreation Area, Mt. Tamalpais to the southeast.

Join Barnabe Trail for a steep descent of a bit over a mile to meet the park's horse trail. Detour a short distance to the right to visit Samuel P. Taylor's gravesite. Otherwise turn left, continue a short ways, and then turn right again on the path leading to Madrone Group Campground.

Follow the campground road out to the highway, cross it, and pick up North Creek Trail. Head left (south) back to the main picnic area.

OLOMPALI STATE HISTORIC PARK

■ OLOMPALI AND MT. BURDELL TRAILS

2.75 miles round trip with 600-foot elevation gain

Olompali State Historic Park in Marin County embraces thousands of years of a history that is uniquely Californian—from the native Miwok to the Chosen Family Commune of the 1960s, from Spanish missionaries to the Grateful Dead rock band.

For the hiker, Olompali offers a colorful history lesson and a great walk in the park. "You can walk through a couple thousand years of history and get a feel for what the land looked like when the Miwok lived here," explains state park ranger Fred Lew.

From what anthropologists surmise (they've surmised a lot because limited excavation at the park has turned up thousands of artifacts), the Coast Miwok lived in shelters made of sticks, tules and grass. They enjoyed lives, by all evidence, of abundance: they gathered acorns, hunted game in the mountains, fished from the shores of the nearby bay. Olompali (pronounced O-lum-pa-lee) was one of the largest villages in the San Francisco Bay area.

The arrival of Spanish missionaries and soldiers ended the Miwok's way of life, though at Olompali they made a valiant effort to adapt. The Miwok learned to make adobe bricks at nearby missions and replaced their tule huts with adobe shelters. They planted crops and raised livestock. In 1843 Franciscan-educated Miwok leader Camillo Ynitia was given Olompali by the Mexican government; he was one of the very few native people to ever receive a land grant, and one later honored by the U.S. government.

A decade later, Ynitia sold his land. By 1865, Rancho Olompali, as it was now known, belonged to San Francisco's first dentist Galen Burdell and his wife, Mary. The Burdells raised cattle and developed a fabulous estate, complete with imposing mansion and a huge formal garden.

During the 1950s, University of San Francisco Jesuits used the property as a religious retreat. The Chosen Family Commune leased the estate in 1967. The Grateful Dead played here, and one of their album covers of that era features a view of the Olompali hills. After hosting a nude wedding ceremony and celebration that attracted nationwide media coverage, the commune disbanded when a fire destroyed much of the old Burdell mansion.

The state purchased the land in 1977, and opened Olompali State Historic Park in 1990. Take a walk through Olompali history and you'll see Camillo Ynitia's adobe, the ruins of the Burdell mansion, and what's left of Mary Burdell's grand garden, where daffodils, planted here more than a century ago, still bloom each year. A barn, a blacksmith shop, the ranch foreman's house and much more can be visited on this history walk.

DIRECTIONS TO TRAILHEAD   From Highway 101, a half hour's drive or so north of San Francisco, and two miles north of Novato, get in the left turn lane for San Antonio Creek Road. Make a U-turn and drive south to the park entrance. If you're heading south on 101, it's a simple and clearly marked exit to the park.

THE HIKE   Begin your exploration of the park's historic structures. After wandering among the buildings and viewing interpretive panels, visit what's left of the estate's once fabulous formal garden, and hit the trail.

The trail's a loop, so it doesn't matter which way you want to hike it. Near the crest of the loop, you'll get glimpses of San Pablo Bay. During spring, such

A family-friendly history walk is a great introduction to Olompali.

wildflowers as purple iris, pink shooting stars, white milkmaids and orange monkeyflowers brighten park slopes. Keep an eye on the sky for golden eagles.

Olompali is now more than a walk through a historic park. A trail extension allows hikers to ascend the eastern slope of 1,558-foot Mt. Burdell. The path connects the 700-acre park with another 2,000 acres of Marin County parkland.

TOMALES BAY STATE PARK

■ JOHNSTONE TRAIL

From Heart's Desire Beach to Jepson Memorial Grove is 3 miles round trip with 300-foot elevation gain; to Shell Beach Is 8 miles round trip

Two lovely trails, named for a professor and a planner, explore Tomales Bay State Park. Jepson Trail honors Botanist Willis Jepson, founder of the School of Forestry at the University of California, Berkeley, and author of the authoritative *Manual of the Flowering Plants of California.* Conservationist Bruce Johnstone, Marin County planner, and his wife, Elsie, worked hard to preserve Tomales Bay and place part of it in a state park. Johnstone Trail leads bayside from Heart's Desire Beach to Shell Beach.

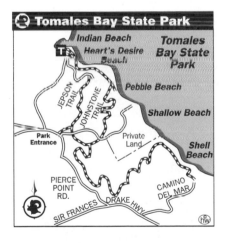

Bay Area walkers have a little secret: When fog smothers Point Reyes and San Francisco Bay, try heading for Tomales Bay State Park. The park has a microclimate, and often has sunny days and pleasant temperatures when neighboring coastal locales are damp and cold.

DIRECTIONS TO TRAILHEAD From the town of Inverness, follow Sir Francis Drake Boulevard to Pierce Point Road. Turn right and drive a half mile to the entrance to Tomales Bay State Park. Follow signs to the large parking lot at Heart's Desire Beach.

Harvesting oysters from Tomales Bay—a time-honored activity.

THE HIKE Near the trailhead are some interpretive displays that tell of clams and Bishop pine. Signed Johnstone Trail departs from the south end of Heart's Desire Beach and immediately climbs into a moss-draped forest of oak, bay, madrone, and wax myrtle.

A half mile of travel brings you to Pebble Beach. At a trail junction, a short side trail goes straight down to Pebble Beach, but Johnstone Trail swings southwest and begins switchbacking up forested slopes. Some wetter areas of the coastal slope are dotted with ferns. The trail crosses a paved road and soon junctions.

To continue to Shell Beach, you'll bear left on Johnstone Trail. The trail detours around some private property, and contours over the coastal slope at an elevation of about 500 feet. Some strategically placed benches allow walkers to savor the fine bay views afforded by Johnstone Trail. The path leads through Bishop pine and a lush understory of salal and huckleberry bushes. After a few miles, the trail descends through madrone and oak forest to Shell Beach.

Walkers content with looping back to Heart's Desire Beach via Jepson Trail will continue straight at the above-mentioned junction. Bishop pine, along with its similar-looking piney cousins, the Monterey and knobcone, are known as fire pines because they require the heat of fire to crack open their cones and release their seeds. Bishop pines are slow to propagate and are relatively rare in coastal California. (Another nice stand of Bishop pine is located in Montaña de Oro State Park in San Luis Obispo County.) The surest way to distinguish a Bishop pine from its look-alike, the Monterey pine, is by counting the needles: Monterey pines have three needles to a bunch, Bishop pines have two needles to a cluster.

SONOMA COAST STATE BEACH

■ SONOMA COAST TRAIL
From Blind Beach to Shell Beach is 4 miles round trip;
to Wright's Beach is 6.5 miles round trip

The names alone are intriguing: Blind Beach and Schoolhouse Beach, Arched Rock and Goat Rock, Penny Island and Bodega Head.

These colorfully named locales are some of the highlights of Sonoma Coast State Beach, thirteen miles of coastline stretching from the Russian River to Bodega Bay.

Sonoma Coast State Beach is not one beach, but many. You could easily overlook them, because most aren't visible from Highway 1. The beaches are tucked away in rocky coves, and hidden by tall bluffs.

Sonoma Coast Trail is a pretty blufftop route that connects some of these secret beaches. During spring, wildflowers brighten the bluff: blue lupine, Indian paintbrush and sea fig.

Sonoma Coast Trail begins on the bluffs above Blind Beach, but the walker can also begin at Goat Rock, located a half mile north of the trailhead. The rock is connected to the mainland by a causeway. During the 1920s, Goat Rock was quarried, and used to build a jetty at the mouth of the Russian River.

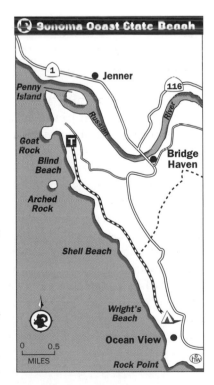

A mile north of the trailhead, and 0.5 mile north of Goat Rock is the mouth of the Russian River. The 110 mile-long river is one of the largest on the North Coast. At the river mouth, you can observe ospreys nesting in the treetops. The California brown pelican is one of several species of birds that breed and nest on Penny Island, located in the river mouth.

DIRECTIONS TO TRAILHEAD From Highway 1, ten miles north of the town of Bodega Bay, turn west on Goat Rock Road. Signed Sonoma Coast Trail begins at a small parking lot on the left of the road. If you'd

Dramatic beaches characterize 13-mile-long Sonoma State Beach.

like to begin this walk at Goat Rock, continue to road's end at a large parking area.

THE HIKE Sonoma Coast Trail heads south along the edge of the bluffs. Soon, you'll step over a stile and head across a pasture. The trail climbs to a saddle on the shoulder of Peaked Hill (elevation 376 feet).

You then descend to the flat blufftops, and cross a bridge over a fern-lined ravine. It's a pastoral scene with grassy bluffs and a weathered old barn in the distance.

After crossing another ravine, the path reaches the Shell Beach parking area. A short trail descends the bluffs to Shell Beach. Another trail extends northwest, crosses the highway, and reaches redwood-shaded Pomo Canyon. Picnic tables and walk-in (environmental) campsites are located near the creek.

Sonoma Coast Trail continues south, detouring inland around a private home, then doubling back seaward. The trail plunges into Furlong Gulch, then switchbacks back up to the bluffs. You can follow the trail or the beach to Wright's Beach Campground.

FORT ROSS STATE HISTORIC PARK

■ FORT ROSS TRAIL

To Fort Ross Cove is 0.5 mile round trip; to Reef Point
Campground is 4 miles round trip; you can extend the walk
north along park bluffs and south along the coast

Fort Ross, the last remnant of czarist Russia's foothold in California, is today a walker's delight. Near the fort, sinuous Highway 1 suddenly straightens. You look out upon a handsome, windswept bluff, and spy a redwood stockade and a Russian Orthodox chapel. For the first-time visitor, it's a startling sight.

Napoleon was beginning his 1812 invasion of Russia when Fort Ross—named for Rossiya itself—was built. The fort's location ideally suited the purposes of the colony. The site was easily defensible. Tall trees, necessary for the fort's construction and the shipbuilding that would take place in the nearby cove, covered the coastal slopes. The waters were full of sea otters—an attraction for the Russian American Fur Company, which would soon hunt the animals to near-extinction. Wheat, potatoes, and vegetables were grown on the coastal terrace, and shipped to Russian settlements in Alaska. All in all, the fort was nearly self-sufficient.

Thanks to the state's replication and restoration efforts, the fort's building brings back the flavor of the Russians' foray into North America. The high stockade, built entirely of hand-hewn redwood timber, looks particularly formidable.

Also of interest are the seven-sided blockhouse, with its interpretive exhibits, and the small, wooden Orthodox chapel. And be sure to stop at the Fort Ross Visitor Center, an excellent facility with Russian, Pomo and natural history exhibits.

When you've completed your walk through history, another surprise awaits: a hike out on the lonely, beautiful headlands.

In 1990, the state park tripled in size; the addition was the former Call Ranch, more than two thousand acres of wooded canyons and dramatic coastline. From the old fort, you can walk two miles north along the coast via old logging roads dipping into Kolmer Gulch, where there's a picnic area, and continuing to a stand of redwood and Douglas fir.

You can also walk two miles (or more) south along the coast, as detailed below. North- or south-bound hikers will enjoy grand views of the fort and up-close looks at the result of earthquake action along the San Andreas Fault.

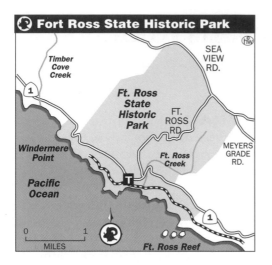

Fort Ross State Historic Park

Fort Ross State Historic Park is located off of Highway 1, some twelve miles north of the hamlet of Jenner.

THE HIKE Exit the fort's main gate, follow the stockade walls to the left, and join the downhill path. It's a short walk to secluded Fort Ross Cove, one of California's first shipyards. You'll find an interpretive display and picnic tables here.

Cross Fort Ross Creek on a small footbridge. Earthquake action along the mighty San Andreas Fault has altered the course of the creek by more than a half mile. Follow the path inland along the creek, which is lined with bay laurel, willow, alder and Douglas iris. After a hundred yards of travel, look to your right for an unmarked, narrow path leading south.

The indistinct path travels onto an open coastal terrace. You'll no doubt see some sheep eating the pastoral vegetation. Follow the undulations of the rye grass- and barley-covered headland, and meander first southeast, then southwest. Continue down-coast until you spot a path descending to a dirt road. (Don't try to climb the sheep fence; use the stile located where the road dead-ends.)

Descend the dirt road to Reef Campground, formerly a private campground, and now a state park facility. It's a good place for a picnic.

Across the road, another stile beckons to the entrance of Sonoma County's "lost coast," so named because high cliffs and high tides keep this seven miles of beach remote from most hikers.

Should you continue, a mile of walking across boulder-strewn beaches brings you to Fort Ross Reef, which discourages further progress.

SALT POINT STATE PARK

■ SALT POINT TRAIL

From Salt Point, Stump Beach Cove is 2.5 miles round trip; to Fish Mill Cove is 6 miles round trip; to Horseshoe Cove is 10 miles round trip

Sheer, sandstone cliffs, and sandy coves highlight Salt Point State Park's seven miles of coastline. Tidepools, sea stacks, and sea caves add to the coastal drama.

Marine life is abundant in tidepools. One of the first underwater reserves to be set aside in California—Gerstle Cove—is popular with divers.

Several midden sites found within park boundaries suggest that Pomo and Coast Yuki spent many summers camped on this coast. They gathered abalone and salt to preserve seafood.

DIRECTIONS TO TRAILHEAD Salt Point State Park is located about 90 miles north of San Francisco (or 18 miles north of Jenner, seven miles north of Fort Ross) on Highway 1. From Highway 1, turn west into the state park's campground and follow signs to Marine Terrace Parking Area.

THE HIKE Hike north atop the dramatic bluffs of Salt Point. In 0.25 mile, you'll cross Warren Creek. At the creek mouth is a little cove, one of about a dozen you'll encounter along the state park's coastline.

The coves are quiet now, but in the last century there was much activity. Aleut hunters, brought to nearby Fort Ross by the Russian American Fur Company, hunted otters and seals. Lumber schooners maneuvered into the coves to load redwoods logged from nearby slopes.

The path reaches the bluffs above Stump Beach Cove, which is not, as you might suspect, named for the remains of redwoods logged nearby; the name honors Sheriff Stump, one-time law-and-order man for Salt Point township.

An old farm road leads down to the cove, where there's a picnic area. Sit a while and watch the terns, cormorants, gulls, osprey and brown pelicans.

If you return to the trailhead from Stump Beach Cove, you'll have hiked a total of 2.5 miles. To continue this hike, follow the trail up the north slope above Stump Creek. Rejoining the bluffs, you dip in and out of Phillips Gulch, Chinese Gulch, and other little gullies.

The path is not particularly distinct, and you must devise your own route in places along the edge of the grassy headlands. Photographers will marvel at the spectacle of surf meeting rock. Waterfalls spill into picturesque coves at the mouths of Chinese and Phillips Gulches.

After a time, the trail becomes easier to follow, and alternates between open meadowland and wind-sculpted stands of Bishop pine and Douglas fir.

A good destination is the picnic area south of Fisk Mill Cove, which is about three miles from the trailhead. Or you can even continue another two miles north to Horseshoe Cove at the northern end of the state park.

KRUSE RHODODENDRON STATE RESERVE

■ KRUSE RHODODENDRON LOOP TRAIL

2.25 miles round trip with 200-foot elevation gain

One of the annual rites, and fine sights, of spring is a walk amongst the pale pink blossoms of Kruse Rhododendron State Reserve. California rhododendrons festoon the forest floor from about mid-April to mid-June.

The rhododendron's success depends on its struggle for light in a dark world dominated by the tanbark oak, Douglas fir and redwood. A severe forest fire that scorched the slopes of Kruse Ranch was responsible for the sudden emer-

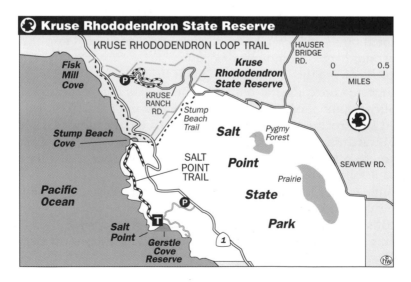

gence of the rhododendrons here. Now, as the tall tree forest regenerates, it restricts the light available to the rhododendrons, thereby diminishing their grand display.

The Kruse family established a ranch here in 1880, raised sheep, and extensively logged the coastal slopes. Edward Kruse donated the land to the state in 1933, in memory of his father.

DIRECTIONS TO TRAILHEAD Kruse Rhododendron State Reserve adjoins Salt Point State Park. Turn east off Highway 1 onto steep Kruse Ranch Road and travel 0.5 mile to the trailhead.

THE HIKE This is a loop trail; begin from the leg north of Kruse Ranch Road or from the leg to the south.

The trail crosses two gulches—Chinese and Phillips. (You'll explore the mouths of these gulches if you take the Salt Point Trail through the state park.)

For a longer hike, leave the loop trail a mile from the trailhead at the point where the path crosses Kruse Ranch Road. It's possible to follow this dirt road for a mile to Stump Beach Trail, then follow this latter path 1.25 mile back to Highway 1, where it rounds Stump Beach Cove.

MANCHESTER STATE BEACH

■ MANCHESTER BEACH, ALDER CREEK TRAILS
To Alder Creek is 5 miles round trip

The elements that comprise a wild beach—wind, waves, and wood, seem just a little bit bigger than life at Manchester State Beach.

The Monterey cypress windbreaks on the bluffs and driftwood wind shelters visitors have constructed on the beach hint at the high winds in this area. So strong are the breezes that blow over this beach, the prudent hiker is advised to call ahead for a "wind report."

If a prize were awarded to the state beach with the most impressive driftwood collection, Manchester might just be the one to win. Huge logs tossed up by the sea lie in jumbled piles at the foot of sand dunes. Like cannons defending a coastal fortification, other large logs aim seaward from the base of the bluffs.

Wave-tossed driftwood decorates this wild beach.

The state beach extends five miles from just above the mouth of Garcia Creek to the mouth of Alder Creek. Steelhead spawn in Alder Creek, which offers resting and nesting habitat for wintering waterfowl.

Near Manchester's south boundary is the landmark Pt. Arena Lighthouse. Docents lead tours of the lighthouse, first built in 1870, then rebuilt after the 1906 earthquake. The tower still holds the original Fresnel Lens, which cast a beam visible to ships 20 miles out to sea.

Manchester's beach is complemented by a sizeable upland area. Instead of the usual out-and-back beach walk characteristic of most state and county beaches, Manchester offers the hiker a loop-trail tour of dark sand, ponds, bluffs and dunes.

DIRECTIONS TO TRAILHEAD From Highway 1 in the hamlet of Pt. Arena, drive north 7 miles to Kinney Road and the signed Manchester State Beach turnoff. Turn left and follow the signs to the lot at road's end beyond the park's campground.

THE HIKE Cross the low dunes to the beach and head north. Great logs lie in heaps at the base of the dunes. Beach-goers have fashioned some intriguing wind shelters from material tossed up by the restless sea.

A mile out, you'll pass the outlet of a pond. Soon the low dunes bordering the beach give way to tall bluffs. Almost two miles along, you'll reach the mouth of Alder Creek and a connector trail that leads up to paved Alder Creek Road. Walk the road about 150 yards to the gated trail taking off from the west side of the road. A half mile of hiking brings you to a condemned wreck of a beach house. A bit farther is Osprey, one of the park's environmental campsites.

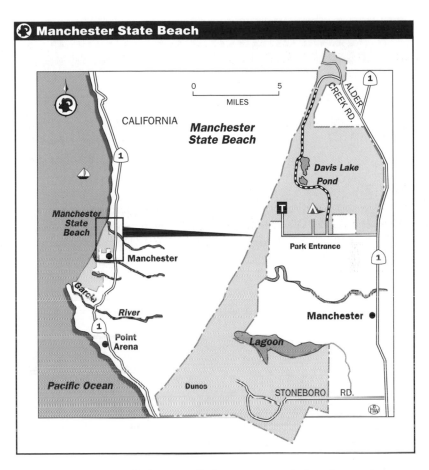

Manchester State Beach

The route passes more of these walk-in camps as it heads south across the dunes.

From the last camp, improvise a route oceanward toward the above-mentioned pond outlet and join the south-trending trail over the low bluffs. When the trail turns inland, head for the coast and walk a mile along the beach back to the trailhead.

VAN DAMME STATE PARK

■ FERN CANYON TRAIL

From Van Damme State Park Campground to Fern Canyon is
5 miles round trip with 200-foot gain; to Pygmy Forest is 7
miles round trip with 400-foot gain

Five-finger and bird's-foot, lady and licorice, stamp, sword and deer—
these are some of the colorful names of the ferns growing in well-named
Fern Canyon. This lush canyon, the heart of Van Damme State Park, is also
rich with young redwoods, red alder, big leaf maple and Douglas fir, as well
as a tangled understory of wild cucumber and berry bushes.

Little River meanders through Fern Canyon, as does a lovely trail which
crosses the river nine times. Fern Canyon Trail, paved along its lower stretch,

Fern-filled Fern Canyon.

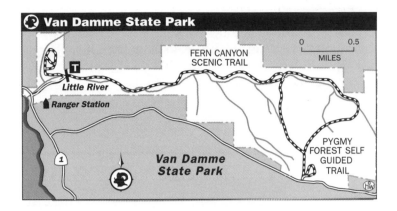

follows the route of an old logging skid road. For three decades, beginning in 1864, ox teams hauled timber through the canyon.

A lumber mill once stood at the mouth of Little River. During the late 19th century, schooners, used for shipping logs and lumber, were constructed at a boatworks located at the river mouth. Lumberman and San Francisco business-man Charles F. Van Damme was born in the hamlet of Little River. He purchased land on the site of the former sawmill and bequeathed the river mouth and canyon to the state park system.

In Van Damme State Park, another very special environment awaits the walker: the Pygmy Forest. A nutrient-poor, highly acidic topsoil, combined with a dense hardpan beneath the surface that resists root penetration, has severely restricted the growth of trees in certain areas of the coastal shelf between Salt Point and Fort Bragg.

The Pygmy Forest in Van Damme State Park is truly Lilliputian. Sixty-year-old cypress trees are but a few feet tall and measure a half-inch in diameter. The walker has a choice of two trails that lead to the Pygmy Forest. One route loops 3.5 miles through Fern Canyon; another, the one-mile-long Logging Road Trail leads more directly to the forest. A self-guided nature trail, built upon an elevated wooden walkway, loops through the Pygmy Forest.

DIRECTIONS TO TRAILHEAD Van Damme State Park is located off High-way 1, three miles south of Mendocino. Turn inland on the main park road, and follow it through the canyon to a parking area at the beginning of signed Fern Canyon Trail.

THE HIKE The first and second crossings of Little River give you an inkling of what lies ahead. During summer, the river is easily forded; in winter, expect to get your feet wet.

The wide path brings you close to elderberry, salmonberry and a multitude of ferns. Two miles and eight river crossings later, you'll pass the state park's environmental campsites—reserved for walkers and bicyclists.

The road splits into a short loop and the two forks rejoin at the end of the paved road. Both trails lead to Pygmy Forest. To the left, the longer loop continues east through Fern Canyon before joining the old logging road and traveling to Pygmy Forest. For a shorter walk to Pygmy Forest, cross Little River and follow the Old Logging Road Trail a mile.

GREENWOOD CREEK STATE BEACH

■ GREENWOOD TRAIL
To beach is 1 mile round trip

Sea stacks, sea caves and a short sandy beach beckon the sojourner to Greenwood Creek State Beach. Picnic sites strategically placed on the bluffs and a coastal trail offer visitors two ways to partake of the inspiring tableau.

The pretty picture also includes a grassy marine terrace accented by a few cypress trees. Park namesake Greenwood Creek carves a course through the bluffs and empties into the sea. In summer, a sand bar closes the mouth of Greenwood Creek; winter rains open it, allowing steelhead to spawn upstream. Migratory ducks and geese winter along the creek.

Greenwood Cove was one of many 19th-century doghole ports on the Mendocino coast. Schooners slipped cautiously alongside the grimly named Casket Wharf while timber was hoisted aboard. A steel cable lifted a slings-full of locally cut and milled lumber onto the ships.

It was a tricky, often treacherous, operation, but the only transport option available in a region lacking good roads or a natural harbor. Greenwood's cable operation continued until the 1920s.

The town of Elk was originally named Greenwood in honor of Caleb Greenwood and family, who settled here in the 1850s. Caleb's father was an organizer of the ill-fated Donner Party; Caleb organized an expedition to Donner Lake to rescue survivors of that unspeakable winter ordeal.

The once-sleepy hamlet of Elk now boasts a number of fine restaurants and upscale inns. A state park visitor center is located in Elk in a historic lumber mill office. Exhibits interpret the region's environment, logging industry and Native American traditions.

DIRECTIONS TO TRAILHEAD Greenwood Creek State Beach is located just west of Highway 1 in Elk, some 17 miles south of Mendocino. The visitor center is a very short walk north of the state beach parking lot.

THE HIKE Descending from the bluffs, the trail soon forks. The right fork leads to a picnic site. The left (main) trail continues downhill to a picnic site as well, then reaches the beach.

You can walk down-coast 0.2 mile to the mouth of Greenwood Creek and to a cliff beyond that blocks further passage. Hikers can travel about 0.2 mile up-coast before cliffs thwart northward progress.

MENDOCINO HEADLANDS STATE PARK

■ MENDOCINO HEADLANDS TRAIL
2 to 5 miles round trip

Few coastal locales are as photographed as the town of Mendocino and its bold headlands. The town itself, which lies just north of the mouth of Big River, resembles a New England village, no doubt by design of its Yankee founders. Mendocino may be familiar to fans of the once-popular television series "Murder She Wrote"; it served as the fictional Cabot Cove, sleuth Jessica Fletcher's hometown. Now protected by a state park, the headlands are laced with paths that offer postcard views of wave tunnels and tidepools, beaches and blowholes.

Once the most cosmopolitan of little ports, Mendocino declined in economic and cultural importance as the logging industry came to a halt in the 1930s. The town revived in the 1950s when a number of San Francisco artists established the Mendocino Art Center. What was bohemian and cheap in the 1950s and 1960s is now upscale and pricey, but the town's Maine village look has been preserved.

Mendocino's citizenry not only preserved the town in a historical district, but succeeded in placing a portion of the majestic bluffs, threatened with a modern subdivision, under the protection of Mendocino Headlands State Park in 1972.

Mendocino is a great town for the walker to explore. Grand Victorian houses and simple New England saltboxes mingle with a downtown that includes several fascinating 19th-century buildings. Among the architectural gems are the Masonic Hall, built in 1866 and topped with a redwood sculpture of Father Time, the Mendocino Hotel with its antique decor and the Presbyterian Church, constructed in 1867 and now a state historical landmark.

Be sure to check out the historic Ford House perched above the bay on the south side of town. Inside the house are exhibits interpreting the human and natural history of the Mendocino coast, as well as the state park visitor center.

A summer or weekend walk onto the headlands allows you to escape the crowds, while a winter walk, perhaps when a storm is brewing offshore, is a special experience indeed. From the end of town you can walk down-coast to Big River or up-coast to a blowhole.

DIRECTIONS TO TRAILHEAD From "downtown" Mendocino, follow Main Street up-coast past the Mendocino Hotel to Heeser Street. Park wherever you can find a space.

THE HIKE The unsigned trail leads southwest through a fence and soon forks; the route down-coast to Big River beach is described first.

Heading east, the trail delivers you to some blufftop benches and a coastal accessway leading down to Portuguese Beach, known as Point Beach by locals. Wooden steps cross a gully and the trail soon forks again—offering both a route along the edge of the bluffs and another heading on a straighter course toward Big River.

Notice the cross-ties, remains of the old oxen-powered railway that hauled lumber to the bluff edge, where it was then sent by chute to waiting ships.

Wildflowers seasonally brightening the grassy headlands include lupine and Mendocino Coast paintbrush. More noticeable are non-native species gone wild—nasturtiums, calla lilies, hedge rose—as well as Scotch broom, an unwelcome pest that thrives along the north coast.

After meandering past some Bishop pines, the path descends moderately to steeply to the beach where Big River empties into Mendocino Bay. The quarter -mile-long beach is also part of Mendocino Headlands State Park. Upriver is a marsh, Big River Estuary, a winter stopover for ducks and geese. Salmon and steelhead spawn upriver.

Return the same way or detour through town to admire some of Mendocino's historical buildings.

To the Blowhole and beyond: Bearing right at the first trail junction from the trailhead leads to the blowhole. While no aqueous Vesuvius, the blowhole can at times be a frothy and picturesque cauldron.

The path continues north along the edge of the headlands for another mile. You'll pass a plaque dedicated by the sister cities of Mendocino and Miasa, Japan, "to the peaceful pursuit of the peoples of the Pacific and to the protection of the environment that all living things therein may exist in perpetual harmony."

BIG RIVER STATE PARK

■ BIG RIVER HAUL ROAD
From Big River Beach to trailhead is 8.3 miles one way

Big River wasn't named for its length or breadth, but for the size of the redwoods that once grew along the banks. Big (second-growth) redwoods and a big estuary are among the compelling natural attractions of Big River State Park, a big (7,334 acres) unit added to California's park system in 2002.

For a century and a half, the Big River region was owned by various timber companies and very much off-limits to recreation. State funds, federal funds and donations secured by the Mendocino Land Trust, along with the dedicated work by many conservationists, helped create the state park. The park preserves the only major undeveloped estuary in northern California.

Big River is big on biological diversity: freshwater and brackish marshland, mudflats, plus stands of redwoods, hardwoods, bishop pine and pygmy cypress. The new park is big on birds, too, and offers critical habitat for more than two dozen rare, endangered and threatened species, including northern spotted owl, bald eagle and California brown pelican. Big River's estuary is ideal spawning habitat and nursery waters for coho and steelhead.

Kayaking and canoeing Big River are popular activities. Paddling Big River's forested canyon is a delight—provided paddlers time their travels with the tides.

Some proud locals claim the world's best blackberries grow in the new park. To verify this claim, go berry picking in late summer.

Big River State Park is all but surrounded by public land. Jackson Demonstration State Forest borders the park on the north, Van Damme State Park (with a brief interruption by Comptche-Ukiah Road and a corridor of private land) borders the park on the south.

DIRECTIONS TO THE TRAILHEAD From Highway 1 at the south edge of Mendocino, turn inland on the Big River beach access road. The old haul road (closed to vehicles) begins at the east (most inland) end of the parking area.

To reach the trailhead for the little Southside Trail, you'll turn inland on Comptche-Ukiah Road and drive 0.25 mile to a small (parking for just a couple of cars) turnout by an old logging road on the left.

Explore Big River with a beautiful wooden outrigger canoe.

THE HIKE Hikers can ramble through the park and onto adjacent parkland, connecting to a far-flung trail network that totals more than one hundred miles of trail. Old logging roads lead to Jackson State Forest and Mendocino Woodlands State Park.

Numerous dead-end logging roads and skid trails crisscross the park, rangers caution, meaning it's easy to get frustrated, disoriented or lost if you venture off the main road. The main road, in this case, is the Big River Haul Road, which loosely parallels the north side of Big River, and winds 8.3 miles to its end at the edge of the estuary. A multi-use path, it's open to hiking, cycling and horseback riding. Many of the confusing old logging roads will be "decommissioned," as park planners put it.

Wander the haul road for as long as you wish. For a mellow introduction to the park, hike to the two- or three-mile mark (posted on trees).

Southwide Trail leads along the south side of Big River. It's not a maintained route and may soon be too washed out and overgrown for use. Impressive redwoods and river vistas are the highlights of this two-mile round trip hike. First you head east on a retired logging road and walk amidst some tall redwoods. Views soon open up to reveal the park's namesake river and the town of Mendocino. Farther along, you'll cross well-watered, fern-filled hillsides.

MENDOCINO WOODLANDS STATE PARK

■ MENDOCINO WOODLANDS TRAILS
1-5 miles round trip from camps

It was a noble idea that arose in the 1930s when many Americans had fallen on very hard times: create large campgrounds across America, inspired settings for introducing the public to the wonders of nature. Forty-six camps (including famed Camp David in Maryland) were built. Today, only Mendocino Woodlands has retained its historical integrity and is still used for its original purpose.

Located in the redwood forest, seven miles inland from the Mendocino coast, Mendocino Woodlands State Park is a kind of living monument to the Depression-era workers of the Federal Works Progress Administration and the

Civilian Conservation Corps. The camps, along with some 200 structures, are preserved as they were in the 1930s. In recognition of its contribution to U.S. history, Mendocino Woodlands was honored with National Historical Landmark status in 1997.

The camps are far more than historical curiosities and are used today by church, youth, arts, music and nature study organizations, which set up "camps" within three large campgrounds. Family and group recreation and environmental education are other uses of the facilities.

The nonprofit Mendocino Woodlands Camp Association has been the steward and concessionaire for the state park since 1949. Association staff offers nature programs to students and campers.

DIRECTIONS TO TRAILHEAD The park is located 7 miles from the Mendocino Coast. From Highway 1 in Mendocino, drive miles inland on Little Lake Road to the signed turnoff for Mendocino Woodlands State Park.

THE HIKE Some 25 miles of trail loop through and around the park, an attractive mix of redwood forest, riverside and meadowland environments. The park, which totals a respectable 700 acres is bordered by the huge Jackson State Forest to the north and the big new Big River State Park to the south. Mendocino Woodlands trails connect to the far-flung trail systems of the state forest and state park.

Day use is permitted, but not particularly encouraged. Park staff has the concern that day hikers (at least more than a few of them at a time) might detract from the camping experience. Most of the paths begin in the camps and signage is sporadic at best.

RUSSIAN GULCH STATE PARK

■ RUSSIAN GULCH TRAIL
From Campground to Falls is 6.5 miles round trip
with 200-foot elevation gain

Russian Gulch is a lush coastal range canyon filled with second generation redwoods, Douglas fir and California laurel. Beneath the tall trees grows an understory of ferns, berry bushes, azaleas and rhododendrons. The mouth of the canyon is framed, as if in a photograph, by a handsome Coast Highway bridge.

Above the river mouth, the park head-lands offer great north and south coastal views. Out on the headlands is The Punch-bowl, a collapsed wave tunnel that forms a 100-foot-diameter hole. This blowhole is an inspiring sight when the surf wells up inside the hole.

Take a direct or a more roundabout route through the canyon and either a longer or shorter route to the waterfall. It's possible to combine all trails into a delight-ful nine mile tour of the park.

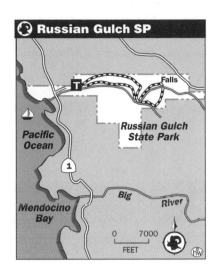

DIRECTIONS TO TRAILHEAD Russian Gulch State Park is located just off High-way 1, two miles north of the town of Mendocino. Fern Canyon Trail, a continuation of the park road closed to vehi-cle traffic, departs from the east end of the campground.

THE HIKE The paved trail, suitable for bicycles, is nearly flat for the first mile as it winds along with the stream. Along the bottom of the gulch grow alder, willow and big-leaf maple. On higher canyon slopes are western hemlock, Dou-glas fir and second-growth redwoods.

One and a half miles of travel brings you to a couple of picnic tables beneath the redwoods. A short distance past the picnic area, you'll spot signed North Trail, which leads northwest back to the park campground; consider this path as an alternate return route. Hikers may continue about 100 feet past this trail junction to the signed beginning of the waterfall loop.

Russian Gulch forks here and so does the trail. Take the left, shorter, route and climb by trail, wooden steps and footbridges 0.75 mile to the falls.

If you continue on the loop trail (this adds 2.3 more miles to your walk), you'll climb stone steps above the falls, then switchback away from the creek through tanoak forest. After topping a ridge, the trail drops into the south fork of Russian Gulch and returns you to the lower trail junction and the return route to the trailhead.

JUG HANDLE STATE RESERVE

■ JUG HANDLE ECOLOGICAL STAIRCASE TRAIL
5 miles round trip with 300-foot elevation gain

The watershed of Jug Handle Creek holds a rare natural phenomenon— an "ecological staircase"—that attracts scientists and nature lovers from all over the world. The staircase is composed of five terraces, each about 100,000 years older and about 100 feet higher than the one below it.

The terraces were sculpted into the sandstone cliffs by wave action. As a result of tectonic action—our North American plate crunching against the offshore Pacific plate—the terraces were uplifted. In fact, today the terraces continue their inexorable uplift at the rate of an inch per century.

Terraces, and the forces forming them, are by no means unique to Jug Handle Creek; however, in most California coastal locales, the terraces are eroded and indistinct. Only at the state reserve are the evolutionary sequences so distinguishable, and so well preserved.

DIRECTIONS TO TRAILHEAD Five miles south of Fort Bragg, turn west off Highway 1 into the Jug Handle Reserve parking area.

THE HIKE Head west on the signed trail out onto the grassy blufftops. The trail loops toward the edge of the bluffs, offers a view of Jug Handle Cove, then returns east to dip under the highway bridge.

The first terrace supports native grassland. and wind-sculpted Sitka spruce. Second-growth redwoods are the most noticeable feature of the second terrace.The upper terraces are the site of the Mendocino Pygmy Forest. Cypress and pine are but five to ten feet tall, and shrubs such as rhododendron, manzanita and huckleberry, are also dwarf-sized.

Adding to the somewhat bizarre natural world of upper Jug Handle Creek, are a couple of sphagnum bogs—layers of peat standing in water— which support mosses and an insectivorous plant called sundew that uses its sticky leaves to capture its victims.

When you reach the end of the trail, you can rejoin Gibney Fire Road for a quick return to the main trail leading back to the parking area.

MACKERRICHER STATE PARK

■ TEN MILE BEACH TRAIL
From Laguna Point to Ten Mile River is 10 miles round trip; shorter hikes possible

Ten Mile Dunes and Inglenook Fen, Laguna Point and Cleone Lake. These are some of the intriguing names on an intriguing land—MacKerricher State Park. Extending from just north of the Fort Bragg city limits to Ten Mile River, this park offers the walker a chance to explore headlands and wetlands, sand dunes, forest and meadowland.

In 1868, Scottish immigrant Duncan MacKerricher paid $1.25 an acre for a former Indian reservation, El Rancho de la Laguna. MacKerricher and his heirs worked the land until 1949 when they gift-deeded it to the state. The vast redwood forests of the coast range in the areas bordering Ten Mile River were heavily logged. An early coast railroad connected the mills of the town of Cleone with a landing at Laguna Point. Lumber was loaded onto flatcars which rolled by gravity to waiting schooners; horses hauled the cars back to the mill. At the point, anchor pins and other signs of the old landing can be seen.

A more obvious reminder of this coast's logging history is the old haul road that crosses the park. In 1949, the road replaced a railway, which for three decades carried timber from the Ten Mile River area to the Union Lumber Company in Fort Bragg. In 1982, winter storms washed out sections of the road, closing the five mile stretch from Cleone Lake to Ten Mile River. The road is closed to motor vehicles and is a superb path for walkers.

The old haul road travels the length of Ten Mile Beach to the mouth of Ten Mile River, so named because it's ten miles north of Noyo River. The beach is backed by one of the California coast's longest dune systems.

DIRECTIONS TO TRAILHEAD From Highway 1, three miles north of Fort Bragg, turn west into the main entrance of MacKerricher State Park. Follow the signs to the Laguna Point parking area.

MacKerricher State Park

THE HIKE Immediately west of the underpass, a short gravel road leads up to the paved ex-logging road. Walk north on the high embankment. You'll soon observe Cleone Lake, a tidal lagoon cut off from the sea by the road. Many shore and water birds visit the lake. Mill Creek, which feeds the lake, is a winter stopover for ducks and geese. Bird-watchers will enjoy the mile-long walk around the lake.

Soon you'll pass some squat shore pines—a coastal form of the much better-known lodgepole pine. You'll also walk past a side trail leading to the state park campground. A quarter mile later another side trail beckons; this one leads over the dunes, which are covered with grasses, sand verbena and beach morning glory.

About 1.5 miles north of the trailhead, you'll encounter a washed-out section of road and, a few hundred yards farther, another bad section.

Two miles north of Laguna Point, tucked in the dunes, lies Inglenook Fen; it's a sensitive area and not open to the public. A botanist studying this unique ecosystem gave it the Old English word fen—meaning something like a bog or marsh. Sandhill Lake and the marshy area around it support many rare plants such as marsh pennywort and rein orchid, as well as many endemic varieties of spiders and insects.

After walking three miles, you'll pass a couple of small creeks and begin crossing the widest part of the sand dunes, which at this point are about a mile wide and more than one hundred feet high. About 4.5 miles from the trailhead, the road turns inland with Ten Mile River. You can continue walking north a short distance if you wish, down to the mouth of Ten Mile River. The marsh area is inhabited by lots of waterfowl.

The main route travels inland above the east bank of Ten Mile River. A side trail leads southeast to a parking area beside Highway 1, while the paved road continues under the highway bridge.

SINKYONE WILDERNESS STATE PARK

■ LOST COAST TRAIL

To Jones Beach is 2 miles round trip; to Whale Gulch is 4.5 miles round trip

The land we now call Sinkyone Wilderness State Park, located about 225 miles north of San Francisco, has long been recognized as something special. During the late 1960s, the great Catholic theologian Thomas Merton believed that the Needle Rock area would be an ideal place for a life of prayer and contemplation, and talked of establishing a monastic community there.

The state park, along with the U.S. Bureau of Land Management's King Range National Conservation Area to the north, comprise California's Lost Coast, 60 miles of wild shoreline located in northern Mendocino and southern Humboldt counties. One reason the coast is "lost" is because no highways cross it. So rugged is this country, highway engineers were forced to route Highway 1 many miles inland from this coast—and the region has remained sparsely settled and unspoiled. Its grand vistas and varied terrain—dense forests, prairies, coastal bluffs, beaches—reward the hardy explorer.

The sea is an overwhelming presence here, and its rhythmic sounds provide a thunderous background for a walk along land's end. The sky is filled with gulls and pelicans, sea lions and harbor seals gather at Little Jackass Cove, and the California gray whale migration passes near shore during winter and early spring.

A herd of Roosevelt elk roams the park. These magnificent creatures were once common here and in the King Range, but were exterminated in the last century. The Roosevelt elk that lucky visitors see today are "extras" relocated from Prairie Creek State Park.

Lost Coast Trail travels the length of Sinkyone State Park north through King Range National Conservation Area. The sixty mile trail would make an ideal week-long backpacking adventure. The portion of the Lost Coast Trail detailed here explores the northernmost, and most easily accessible, portion of the state park. It's a relatively easy introduction to a challenging trail.

DIRECTIONS TO TRAILHEAD From Highway 101, take either the Garberville or Redway exit and proceed to "downtown" Redway, located 3 miles north of Garberville on Business 101. Turn west on Briceland Road. After 12 miles of travel, fork left to Whitethorn. A mile or so past the hamlet of Whitethorn (don't blink or you'll miss it), the pavement ends, and you continue on a potholed dirt/mud road for 3.5 miles to a junction called Four

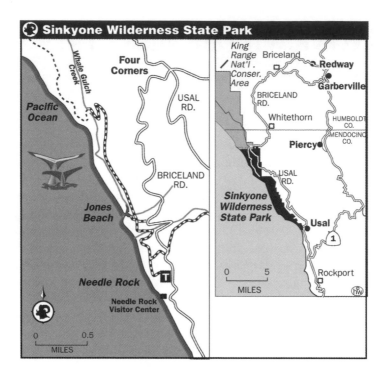

Corners. Leftward is Usal Road, rightward is a road climbing into the King Range National Conservation Area. Proceed straight ahead 3.5 miles to the Sinkyone Wilderness State Park Visitor Center.

The park road is steep, winding, and only one lane wide. Maps and information are available at the visitor center.

THE HIKE   Begin at the Needle Rock Visitor Center. During the 1920s, a small settlement and shipping point were established at Needle Rock. The Calvin Cooper Stewart family were the main residents of Needle Rock, and today their ranch house serves as the park visitor center.

Walk up the park road toward the old barn. Notice a trail leading to the bluff edge, then down to the beach. Famed Needle Rock is a short distance up the dark sand beach.

Join Lost Coast Trail, which leads behind the barn and dips in and out of a gully. You'll pass Barn Camp, one of the state park's primitive, or walk-in, campsites. A quarter mile of travel brings you to Streamside Camp, another of the park's primitive, but superb, camps.

You'll soon reach a junction with a trail climbing to the east. This is Low Gap Trail, which ascends the coastal bluffs and crosses the park road. The trail plunges into the forest, travels along Low Gap Creek, and, after a stiff climb, reaches Usal Road. Lost Coast Trail, your route, continues along the lovely bluffs to Low Gap Creek, heads inland briefly, then crosses a bridge over the creek. The path heads toward a stand of eucalyptus, which shelters the Jones Beach campsites.

The trail forks. The left fork leads 0.2 mile to Jones Beach. If it's low tide, you can walk back to the trailhead via the beach.

Lost Coast Trail proceeds with the right fork and soon descends into a canyon. You cross two creeks, which drain an area that can be very marshy during the rainy season. You walk near the edge of a cattail-lined pond, climb to higher ground, and pass a second pond.

Soon you are treated to a bird's-eye view of Whale Gulch. A rough, unmaintained path descends to the mouth of Whale Gulch, where there's a small lagoon and piles of driftwood logs. After sitting on a driftwood log for a while and contemplating the Lost Coast, return to the trailhead the way you came.

AZALEA STATE RESERVE

■ EAST AND WEST LOOP TRAILS
0.5 and 0.75 mile loops

The wondrous western azalea lights up this reserve located on the north bank of the Mad River. During May and June, pink and white blossoms burst forth to perfume the air and delight the eye.

Wild azaleas are typically a come-and-go phenomenon; the flowers often appear en masse after a major environmental disturbance, such as a fire. In the wild, azaleas are naturally replaced by other flora as the woodland matures in a process called forest succession.

Azaleas flourish in open areas where there is ample space and plenty of access to light. To ensure that the state reserve remains to the azalea's liking, park resource managers control competing vegetation, sometimes even using controlled burns to create the appropriate environmental conditions. (Most parks revere trees; this one considers them competitive species.)

The azalea reserve is one of many special environments along the Mad River, which flows some 110 miles northwest from its headwaters in the Coast Range to empty into the Pacific near McKinleyville. The reserve's azaleas are bordered by such Mad River-typical conifers as Sitka spruce and Douglas fir.

DIRECTIONS TO TRAILHEAD   From Highway 101, a few miles north of Arcata, exit on North Bank Road. Head inland (east) 0.75 mile to the turnoff for Azalea State Reserve.

You can also reach the park by way of Highway 299.

West loop trails begin from the small parking area; east loop trails start on the opposite side of North Bank Road.

THE HIKE   East Loop Trail, a trio of interconnecting loops, begins by plunging right into thickets of azaleas. Continue on a counterclockwise loop by ascending some stairs, then a trail up a wooded slope, and gain a great view of the azalea show.

West Loop (0.5 mile) first tours an intriguing collection of north coast flora, including ferns (licorice and sword), salmonberry, elderberry, myrtle and Sitka spruce. Halfway along, the path delivers hikers to the azaleas.

TRINIDAD STATE BEACH

■ MILL CREEK, ELK HEAD TRAILS
From Mill Creek Access to beach is 0.5 mile round trip; to Trinidad Head is 2.5 miles round trip with 300-foot elevation gain; to Elk Head is 2.5 miles round trip

Two heads are better than one. That's one way of looking at Trinidad State Beach and the two dramatic heads—Elk and Trinidad—that overlook a picturesque cove, harbor and island.

Trinidad Head, a commanding, 362-foot-high promontory, is the commanding backdrop of the town of Trinidad, a picturesque harbor and a historic lighthouse. Sitka-spruce-spiked Elk Head, located just north of Trinidad, is more of a secret, its scenic trails used mainly by locals.

Located in the waters between the heads is tree-topped Pewetoll Island, the domain of thousands of black oyster catchers. Farther offshore are Flatiron Rock and other surf-battered rocks that serve as resting places for seals and sea lions.

The park's 159 acres are spread over a marine terrace cloaked in beach pine and Sitka spruce. And consider the lilies of the field: the Columbia lily and endangered western lily grow atop the steep bluffs.

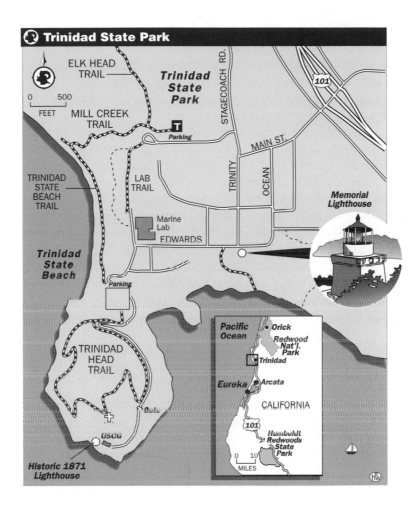

Trinidad State Park

ELK HEAD TRAIL

Trinidad State Park

STAGECOACH RD.

101

0 500 FEET

MILL CREEK TRAIL

Parking

MAIN ST.

TRINITY

OCEAN

TRINIDAD STATE BEACH TRAIL

LAB TRAIL

Memorial Lighthouse

Marine Lab

EDWARDS

Trinidad State Beach

Parking

TRINIDAD HEAD TRAIL

USCG

Historic 1871 Lighthouse

Pacific Ocean

Orick

Redwood Nat'l. Park

Trinidad

Eureka

Arcata

CALIFORNIA

101

Humboldt Redwoods State Park

0 10 MILES

Trinidad's beaches and bluffs offer hikers a wild and isolated experience despite their location so close to town. Actually, there's not much town to get away from: Trinidad, with a population of 350, is one of California's smallest incorporated cities.

You can begin your exploration of Trinidad Head at the main state beach access, the Elk Head access, or from Edwards Street at the edge of town.

DIRECTIONS TO TRAILHEAD From Highway 101, take the Trinidad exit and drive 0.25 mile west through town to Stagecoach Road. Turn right (north) and pull into the main Trinidad State Beach parking area on the left.

Elk Head access is located another 0.75 mile up Stagecoach Road.

THE HIKE From the picnic area, Mill Creek Trail descends amongst sword ferns and Sitka spruce. After 0.25 mile, the path splits. A short walk left leads to a sandy beach at the mouth of Mill Creek. Saunter along the surf south 0.5 mile to the base of Trinidad Head.

At the end of the ruggedly beautiful beach you'll encounter an ugly repository of junk. Be not discouraged and join a signed spur trail that soon leads to a paved road. Go right 100 yards to the beginning of the footpath and start your counter-clockwise tour of Trinidad Head.

Numerous benches en route invite hikers to sit and contemplate the inspiring seascape. The path ascends south, then west, to a cross atop Trinidad Head. Descend on the gravel road to a paved one and bear left. Enjoy views of Trinidad Harbor as the road leads north, then west. Close the loop and retrace your steps back to the beach via the connector trail.

Walk up the paved road away from the harbor and into town. You can't miss the Humboldt State University Marine Lab. Join signed Marine Lab Trail for the short walk across the bluffs back to the trailhead.

The right fork is an equestrian trail that extends to Elk Head. Follow the path across the Mill Creek footbridge, continuing north over the wooded headlands to the west end of the Elk Head parking area.

Join Elk Head Trail at the north end of the parking lot and walk northwest, then west across the grassy promontory of Elk Head. Soon a path and steps branching left off the main trail beckon you to descend to College Cove Beach.

Elk Head Trail continues west and serves up magnificent vistas of Trinidad Head and Pewetole Island. About a half mile from the trailhead, near the tip of Elk Head, a short side trail leads to Meguil Point (superb tidepools are exposed at very low tide).

The path bends east, looping through stands of cypress, shore pine and Sitka spruce before returning to the trailhead.

PATRICK'S POINT STATE PARK

■ RIM TRAIL
From Palmer's Point to Agate Beach Campground is 4 miles round trip

Though Patrick's Point State Park is positioned in the heart of the redwoods, other trees—Sitka spruce, Douglas fir, and red alder—predominate on the park's rocky promontories. The state park takes its name from Patrick Beegan, who homesteaded this dramatic, densely forested headland in 1851.

For hundreds of years the Yurok spent their summers in the Abalone Point area of the headlands. The Yurok gathered shellfish and hunted sea lions. A variety of game and a multitude of berries that were plentiful in the surrounding forest.

The area now called Patrick's Point also had some spiritual significance to the native people. According to the Yurok belief, Sumig, the spirit of the porpoises, retired to Patrick's Point when humans began populating the world.

Rim Trail follows an old Indian pathway over the park's bluffs. Spur trails lead to rocky points

Agate Beach vista from Patrick's Point.

that jut into the Pacific and offer commanding views of Trinidad Head to the south and Big Lagoon to the north.

DIRECTIONS TO TRAILHEAD Patrick's Point State Park is located thirty miles north of Eureka and five miles north of Trinidad. Exit Highway 101 on Patrick's Point Drive and follow this road to the park. Once past the park entrance station, follow the signs to Palmer Point.

THE HIKE The trail plunges into a lush community of ferns, salmonberry, and salal. The scolding krrrack-krrrack of the Steller jay is the only note of dissent heard along the trail.

Abalone Point is the first of a half-dozen spur trails that lead from Rim Trail to Rocky Point, Patrick's Point, Wedding Rock, Mussel Rocks, and Agate Beach. Take any or all of them. (These side trails can sometimes be confused with Rim Trail; generally speaking, the spurs are much more steep than Rim Trail, which contours along without much elevation change.)

From Patrick's Point and the other promontories, admire the precipitous cliffs and rock-walled inlets. Gaze offshore at the sea stacks, a line of soldiers battered by the surging sea. Seals and sea lions haul out on the offshore rocks, which also double as rookeries for gulls, cormorants and pigeon guillemots.

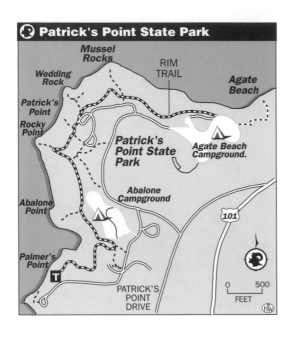

Rim Trail meanders through a tapestry of trillium and moss, rhododendron and azalea. Sword ferns point the way to a grove of red alder.

Rim Trail ends at the north loop of the Agate Beach Campground road.

Hikers wishing to explore Agate Beach should continue a short distance along the road to the signed trailhead for Agate Beach Trail. This short, steep trail switchbacks down to the beach.

In marked contrast to the park's rocky shore that you observed from Rim Trail, Agate Beach is a wide swath of dark sand stretching north to the state parks at Big Lagoon.

Beachcombers prospect for agates in the gravel bars and right at the surf line. These agates are a nearly transparent variety of quartz, polished by sand and the restless sea. Jade, jasper and other semiprecious stones are sometimes found here. One more noteworthy sight is the huge quantity and unique sea-sculpted quality of the driftwood on this beach.

HUMBOLDT LAGOONS STATE PARK

■ BIG LAGOON BEACH TRAIL

Along sandspit is 6 miles round trip; to Big Lagoon County Park is 8.5 miles round trip; to Patrick's Point State Park is 10 miles round trip

Big Big Lagoon is 3.5 miles long, walled off from the power of the Pacific by a 600 to 700-foot-wide strip of sand. The lagoon's marshy habitat is an important rest stop for migratory birds on the Pacific flyway.

Long, sandy Big Lagoon Beach, along with Dry Lagoon and portions of Stone Lagoon, comprise Humboldt Lagoons State Park. The park appeals to hikers and fishermen, who enjoy the lonely beauty of the sandspits and wetlands.

The park is much more than marshlands. Sitka spruce thrive on the north and southwest shores, and even some wind-blown old-growth redwoods cling tenaciously to life on the east shore.

Gold-seekers swarmed into the area in 1849 when discoveries were made along the Klamath and Trinity rivers. Prospectors attempted to mine the sandspits along Big and Stone lagoons, but managed to extract very little gold despite considerable effort.

Dry Lagoon State Park was established in 1931. The park expanded over the next half-century to more than 1,000 acres, added a couple more lagoons, and in 1981 its name was changed to Humboldt Lagoons State Park. Land acquisitions by the Save-the-Redwoods League further enlarged the park.

Walking Big Lagoon Beach means paying attention to the tides. Several times each winter, Big Lagoon's barrier beach is breached by waves; the beach at these times is impassable. During other seasons, best hiking is at lower tides. Consult a local tide table.

(More about the local lagoons: Dry Lagoon offers a mile-long beach hike north of the lagoon, plus a one mile loop trail around the environmental campsites. You can take a two- to three mile hike along the barrier beach fronting Stone Lagoon.)

Experience the lonely beauty of the lagoons.

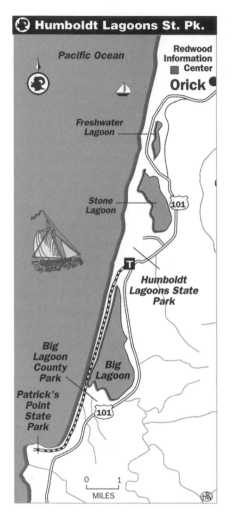

Humboldt Lagoons St. Pk.

Pacific Ocean

Redwood Information Center

Orick

Freshwater Lagoon

Stone Lagoon 101

T

Humboldt Lagoons State Park

Big Lagoon County Park

Big Lagoon

Patrick's Point State Park 101

0   1
MILES

DIRECTIONS TO TRAILHEAD From Highway 101, some seven miles south of Orick, turn west onto the signed state park road and travel a mile to road's end at a beach parking lot.

THE HIKE From the parking lot, follow the beach south. Atop the nearby wooded bluffs are some excellent environmental campsites. About a half mile along, the mixed black-and-white sand beach broadens. You'll reach the north end of Big Lagoon about 0.75 mile from the trailhead.

Now you'll walk the crest of the barrier beach, dotted with sea rocket, dune tansy and sand verbena. Two miles out, you'll notice a couple of low spots in the sandspit. During very high tides, waves crest the sandspit, spilling into the lagoon.

Three miles along, you'll get a good view of Big Lagoon at its widest—more than a mile across. On the east side grows a forest of Sitka spruce and some wind-sculpted redwoods.

Rest awhile on the driftwood logs scattered on the beach. Down-coast is a nice view of Agate Beach and the dramatic, wooded bluffs of Patrick's Point State Park; it's another two mile walk, if you're in the mood.

Return the same way, or, if you want to extend your walk a bit more, curve around the lagoon to the south shore, where you'll find Big Lagoon County Park.

TOLOWA DUNES STATE PARK

■ DEAD LAKE TRAIL
From Sand Hill Road to Dead Lake is 2 miles round trip;
to Tolowa Dunes is 3.5 miles round trip

Ancient sand dunes, a dramatic, driftwood-strewn beach, wooded ridges and one of the California coast's finest wetlands comprise Tolowa Dunes State Park, located just south of the Oregon border.

Long known as the Lake Earl State Park Project, the 5,000-acre park was renamed in 2001 for the Tolowa, the most recent of the Native Americans who lived in the Lake Earl area for thousands of years. Attracted by the ocean's abundant harvest, the Tolowa camped in the Pelican Bay area, fished salmon from the Smith River mouth, gathered mussels and clams, and hunted sea lions.

For the Tolowa, Yontocket (the northern section of the park) is the center of the world, the place where the first redwood grew. Today's Tolowa visit the site and hold ceremonies there.

Two coastal lagoons—lakes Earl and Tolowa—are separated from Pelican Bay by a sandbar. The mostly freshwater Lake Earl and the more saline Lake Tolowa host more than 250 species of birds. The lakes are a crucial stopover for birds traveling the Pacific Flyway, the west coast bird migration route. Sometimes as many as 100,000 birds can be sighted here. Surrounding the lakes are saltwater marshland and freshwater wetlands, as well as far-reaching sand dunes.

The park has two sections: a northern one that extends up-coast from Kellogg Road and a southern one that spreads down-coast from Lake Tolowa. Between the state park segments lies land under the stewardship of the California Department of Fish and Game.

Opportunities for exploration of Lake Tolowa and its larger neighbor, Lake Earl, are limited by the marshy terrain and mudflats, which are better suited to the needs of soft-shelled clams than hikers. Nevertheless, the park does have a pretty good trail system that visits the lakes and dunes.

Some 20 miles of hiking trail wind through the park. Many of the paths are sandy, which make them slow-going. Spring, when the ponds are full and the wildflowers are in bloom, and autumn, with crisp, clear days, are good seasons for hikes in the state park. Guided nature walks are offered in the summer. The weather is pleasant enough for a summer hike, but oh, those bugs! The mosquitoes are very aggressive!

Your reward for reaching the lakeshores is excellent bird-watching opportunities, including the chance to observe a multitude of waterfowl, including canvasbacks and the endangered Aleutian goose.

DIRECTIONS TO TRAILHEAD   Travel north on Highway 101 through Crescent City. At the north end of Crescent City, bear left on Northcrest Drive and follow it a half mile to Old Mill Road. Turn left and drive a mile to Sand Hill Road, turn left and continue a short distance to road's end at the parking lot.

THE HIKE   The path begins as a gravel road, then heads into the woods. A mile out, you'll find Dead Lake, a small freshwater lake that, like so many bodies of water along the redwood coast, was formerly a lumber mill pond. The lake is now habitat for wood ducks and bass and crappie.

Continue toward the ocean on the path, which reaches the sand dunes about 0.75 mile from the lake.

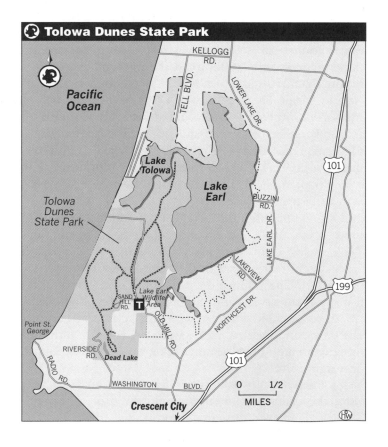

HIKES INTO HISTORY

CALIFORNIA STATE HISTORIC PARKS

Weaverville Joss House, Malakoff Diggins, San Pasqual Battlefield, William B. Ide Adobe. The names alone are intriguing and beckon us from the well-traveled highways to the remote byways where these state historic parks are located.

When hikers think of state parks, most think of the treasures of nature they preserve. Fewer hikers realize that state parks also preserve and interpret California's history. These State Historic Parks, as they're called, offer some great family walks, as well as relief for the road warrior and a learning experience for young and old.

While some historic parks consist of but a single building in a remote locale, others include blocks—or even districts—full of significant structures in the midst of such cities as Sonoma, Sacramento and Santa Barbara. Forty or so State Historic Parks preserve structures and lands of historic interest. These parks may also commemorate a person or historic event.

With six million visitors a year, Old Town San Diego State Historic Park is San Diego's leading tourist attraction and California's most popular state park. Park rangers note that even the most casual visitors to Old Town San Diego come away knowing more about California history than when they came in—a primary goal of the rangers who staff state historic parks

The walking in these historic parks is easy—a few blocks, a half mile, a mile at most. Many parks offer food and refreshment, either inside or just outside the park.

1. Old Town San Diego State Historic Park, built around a central plaza, offers a chance to stroll through California history, San Diego-style, during the Mexican and early American periods. Walkers can view La Casa de Bandini, built in 1829 as a hotel/stagecoach station, and now a restaurant; La Casa de Estudillo, the finest of the original adobe buildings—a mansion with a lovely courtyard; Casa de Altamirano, Old Town's first frame building, restored as the newspaper office it was in 1868 when it housed the San Diego Union. Other historic buildings include a schoolhouse and a stable with a carriage collection.

Shoppers enjoy poking around the specialty shops, while diners can select from several Mexican restaurants or an Italian or Greek eatery. And Old Town San Diego has two more attractions: a convenient location near the junction of Interstate 5 and Interstate 8, plus free parking.

Neptune Pool, Hearst Castle.

2. El Presidio de Santa Bárbara State Historic Park, located in downtown Santa Barbara, preserves a bit of the old military fortress built by the Spanish in 1782 to guard the central coast. A walking tour (pamphlet available) tours El Cuartel, the old guardhouse and Santa Barbara's oldest adobe. A must-see is the recently restored Presidio Chapel, a re-creation of the city's first church. The Spanish artifacts on the altar and colorful wall paintings provide an interesting contrast to the building's simple exterior. Park headquarters, located in a historic adobe on Canon Perdido Street, displays artifacts found on the presidio site. Several adobes and historical buildings nearby, as well as the famed Santa Barbara Courthouse, entice the walker to further exploration.

3. Hearst San Simeon State Historic Monument (Hearst Castle) offers five fabulous walking tours of the palatial estate of the late William Randolph Hearst. More than one million visitors arrive annually to see the collection of world treasures on display in the 130-room palace. Tour No. 1, recommended for first-time visitors, includes the major rooms of the mansion, swimming pools and gardens.

Other tours, restricted to much smaller groups (12 to 15 people) cover the upper levels of the castle, the castle's guest wing, as well as the gardens, pools, wine cellar and guest house. There's also an evening tour.

4. Monterey State Historic Park beckons California history enthusiasts, architects and city strollers to spend a day walking Monterey's "Path of History." After Mexico obtained its independence from Spain in 1821, the Mexican

flag flew over Monterey; it is this era and the early American that are empha-
sized by the park. Guide maps and pamphlets are available at the Old Custom
House, oldest government building on the Pacific Coast. The building now
houses a collection of clothing, leather goods and china items typical of what
was imported through the port of Old Monterey.

The Robert Louis Stevenson House, Pacific House (where there's a museum of California History), California's First Theater (still in use) plus many
more old adobes are part of the park. A walking path leads a few blocks south
to Fisherman's Wharf and a few blocks north to Cannery Row and Monterey
Bay Aquarium.

5. San Juan Bautista State Historic Park preserves the original town
plaza, the old Plaza Hotel, and the Mexican-era home of leading citizen José
Castro. The park is located in the modern-day, but not modern, town of San
Juan Bautista, located a few miles off Highway 101 between Salinas and Gilroy.

Visit the well-preserved carriage and coach collection on display at the old
stable. Also beckoning the walker is Mission San Juan Bautista, founded in
1797 and now a parish church where mass is still held. Next to the church is a
small history museum. Some inviting shops and restaurants adjacent to the park
suggest further exploration.

6. Sonoma State Historic Park, located in downtown Sonoma, preserves
Mission San Francisco Solano, last of the California missions. The mission,
founded in 1823, is now a museum. A self-guided walking tour (pick up a map
at the park visitor center) winds through the streets surrounding a central plaza
and visits more than a dozen buildings built between 1823 and 1855.

In 1834, General Mariano Vallejo arrived in Sonoma with instructions to
secularize the mission and lay out a town. On the north side of the plaza is the
site of the general's first home, Casa Grande. The General Vallejo home, his
1852 residence, is located 0.5 mile from the plaza on Third Street. After admiring all that adobe architecture around Sonoma Plaza, you're surprised to
discover that Vallejo's home is built in New England-style. Vallejo's storehouse
is now a museum about Vallejo, who, after the Americanization of California,
served as mayor of Sonoma as well as a state senator, and who greatly influenced
California politics.

Sonoma's shady, open, Mediterranean-style plaza is a good spot for picnics
or relaxation. Near the plaza are numerous shops and restaurants.

7. Bodie State Historic Park preserves a one-time gold rush boomtown
of the 1870s-80s in a state of "arrested decay." A park brochure details a
lengthy 69-stop walking tour of Bodie, which has a remarkably diverse collection of buildings in various states of decrepitude.

Bodie is a step back in time; it is a boomtown gone bust, a curious, isolated
world that at first glance appears to be far removed from the present. But there
is also a perceptible sense of peace, a comfortable familiarity about the place that
was once home to nearly 10,000 people.

Access to the abandoned town, located in the eastern Sierra southeast of the small town of Bridgeport, can be tricky; only one of the roads leading to Bodie is paved and even that ends up as three miles of dirt and rocks. The rugged, time-consuming drive up to town is quite fitting—one could hardly expect to approach it via a superhighway off-ramp.

Nearly 90 percent of the visitors to Bodie arrive during the summer months. The weather from October through April is unpredictable; although the park is open year-round, once the winter snows hit, the roads are not plowed, leaving Bodie virtually inaccessible during the notoriously long and brutal winters. Intrepid souls still manage to get through—on mountain bikes, cross-country skis and four-wheel drive vehicles.

The remote location, the ramshackle buildings, the cemetery at the edge of town—the entire place appears to be constructed like a Hollywood film set. But there's no fakery here; part of Bodie's appeal is the dignity with which it's been allowed to age without insensitive restoration or commercialism. The Old Miners' Union Hall is today the park museum for Bodie, considered by many to be the very best ghost town in the West.

8. Columbia State Historic Park, located on Highway 49 north of Sonora, offers an excellent self-guided walk through one of the best preserved towns of the Mother Lode. (It's well preserved because after a couple fires, the business district was rebuilt with fireproof brick.)

Ride into town astride a horse or upon the hard wooden seat of a stagecoach, then start walking into California's Gold Rush history. Visit a blacksmith shop where a smithy labors at his forge; cringe at a dentist office displaying some truly scary tools of the trade; indulge your sweet tooth at a candy store with a sack of horehound.

10 Historic Walks

Sonoma State Historic Park

Shasta State Historic Park

Old Sacramento

Columbia State Historic Park

Bodie State Historic Park

Monterey State Historic Park

San Juan Bautista State Historic Park

Hearst San Simeon State Historic Monument

CALIFORNIA

El Presido de Santa Barbara State Historic Park

Old Town San Diego State Historic Park

When gold was discovered here in 1850, the hamlet of Hildreth's Diggins mushroomed into the metropolis of Columbia (population 6,000), making it for a short time the second-largest city in California. Columbia boomed for 20 years as more than a billion dollars worth of gold was mined from the surrounding Sierra foothills.

Columbia is now a booming tourist town, complete with dozens of shops and businesses—divided about evenly between walk-in mini-museums and modern-day merchants operating in Mother Lode-mode. This is a historic town that offers full immersion into the sights, sounds, smells and tastes of the Gold Rush.

Grizzled prospectors are on hand to show pilgrims how to pan for gold. Wranglers rent horses for rides through town or into the surrounding Sierra foothills. Two Victorian-era hotels beckon those weary travelers choosing to overnight in Columbia.

Park rangers recently began a new guided walk program. Rangers lead visitors on an hour-long walk that really evokes the flavor of the Gold Rush era and allows walkers into some historic buildings that the general public is normally not permitted to enter.

9. Old Sacramento State Historic Park offers a wonderful, 20 stop-or-so self-guided walking tour, which begins at the visitor center (pick up a map here) on Second Street. Stroll along the balcony-covered boardwalk and relive the early days of California's state capital, while simultaneously enjoying the shops and restaurants in the historic buildings.

The Big Four Building (an operating replica of the 1880s hardware store once located here), the first theater to be built in California, the building that was the western terminus of the Pony Express in 1860 and a meeting place of the California Supreme Court are among the landmarks along the tour. Guided tours are conducted on weekends.

Another highlight is the California State Railroad Museum, the finest and most popular interpretive railroad museum in North America. You'll view some lovingly restored steam engines, including the C.P. Huntington, as well as a variety of other California rolling stock. Some of the show-stopper pieces are placed in dramatic settings such as a bridge high above the museum floor. More cars and locomotives are on display at a reconstructed 1876 passenger depot located a block from the museum.

10. Shasta State Historic Park, located in the "other" Gold Country in the Klamath Mountains of northwest California, preserves the business district of Shasta, known in the 1850s as the "Queen City" of the northern mines.

Many of the buildings are in ruins, but the park boasts two major structures—the Shasta County Courthouse and Litsch General Store, now museums. A self-guided walk (brochure available from the park visitor center) takes in the historic business district, and the ruins of "Brick Row" which, during the prosperous 1850s, was once one of California's largest communities. Footpaths lead to a pioneer cemetery and to various ruins scattered about the park.

STATE PARK DISTRICT OFFICES

Angeles District
1925 Las Virgenes
Calabasas , CA 91302
818-880-0350

Capital District
704 O Street
Sacramento, CA 95814
916-445-7373

Central Valley District
22708 Broadway
Columbia, CA 95310
209-536-5930

Channel Coast District
911 San Pedro Street
Ventura, CA 93001
805-585-1850
Park Information: 805-968-1033

Colorado Desert Office
200 Palm Canyon Drive
Borrego Springs, CA 92004
760-767-4037

Diablo Vista District
363 3rd Street West
Sonoma, CA 95476
707-938-1519

Gold Fields District
c/o Folsom Lake SRA
7806 Folsom-Auburn Road
Folsom, CA 95630
916-988-0205

Inland Empire District
17801 Lake Perris Drive
Perris, CA 92571
909-657-0676

Mendocino District
P.O. Box 440
Mendocino, CA 95460
707-937-5804

Monterey District
2211 Garden Road
Monterey, CA 93940
831-649-2836

North Bay and Russian River Districts
P.O. Box 123
Duncan Mills, CA 95430
707-865-2391

Marin Sector
P.O. Box 1016
Novato, CA 94948
415-898-4362

North Coast Redwoods District
P.O. Box 2006
Eureka, CA 95503
707-445-6547

Northern Buttes District
400 Glen Drive
Oroville, CA 95966-9222
530-538-2200

Orange Coast District
3030 Avenida del Presidente
San Clemente, CA 92672
949-492-0802

San Diego Coast District
8885 Rio San Diego Drive, Suite 270
San Diego, CA 92108
619-688-3260

San Luis Obispo Coast District
750 Hearst Castle Road
San Simeon, CA 93452
805-927-2065

Santa Cruz District
303 Big Trees Park Road
Felton, CA 95018
831-335-6318

Sierra District
P.O. Box 266
Tahoma, CA 96142
530-525-7232

CSP PHONE NUMBERS

Admiral William Standley SRA	(707) 247-3318	Cayucos SB	(805)781-5200/781-5930
Ahjumawi Lava Springs SP	(530)335-2777/225-2065	China Camp SP	(415)456-0766/898-4362
Anderson Marsh SHP	(707)994-0688/279-4293	Chino Hills SP	(909)780-6222
Andrew Molera SP	(831)667-2315	Chumash Painted Cave SHP	(805)968-1033
Angel Island SP	(415)435-1915	Clear Lake SP	(707)279-4293/1519
Annadel SP	(707)539-3911/938-1519	Columbia SHP	(209)532-0150/4301
Ano Nuevo SR	(650)879-0227/2025	Colusa-Sacramento River SRA	(530)458-4927
Antelope Valley California Poppy Reserve	(661)942-0662	Corona del Mar SB	(949)492-0802
Anza-Borrego Desert SP	(760)767-5311	Cowell Beach Ranch	(650)726-8819/(831)335-6318
Armstrong Redwoods SR	(707)869-2015/865-2391	Crystal Cove SP	(949)494-3539/492-0802
Asilomar SB	(831)372-8016	Cuyamaca Rancho SP	(760)765-0755/742-3462
Auburn SRA	(530)885-4527	D.L. Bliss/Emerald Bay SPs	(530)525-7277/7232
Austin Creek SRA	(707)869-2015/865-2391	Del Norte Coast Redwoods SP	(707)464-6101
Azalea SR	(488-2041/677-3570	Delta Meadows River Park	(916)777-7701
Bale Grist Mill SHP	(707)963-2236/942-4575	Dockweiler SB	(213)738-2961
Benbow Lake SRA	(707)923-3238/247-3318	Doheny SB	(949)496-6171/492-0802
Benicia Capitol SHP	(707)745-3385	Donner Memorial SP	(530)582-7892/525-7232
Benicia SRA	(707)648-1911	El Capitan SB	(805)968-1033/968-1711
Bethany Reservoir SRA	(209)874-2056	El Presidio de Santa Barbara SHP	(805) 965-0093
Bidwell Mansion SHP	(530)895-6144	Emerald Bay SP	(530)273-8522
Bidwell-Sacramento River SP	(530)342-5185	Emma Wood SB	(805)648-4807/585-1850
Big Basin Redwoods SP	(831)338-8860/335-6318	Empire Mine SHP	(530)273-8522
Bodie SHP	(760)647-6445	Folsom Lake SRA	(916)988-0205
Bolsa Chica SB	(714)846-3460	Folsom Powerhouse SHP	(916)985-4843/988-0205
Border Field SP	(619)575-3613	Forest of Nisene Marks SP	(831)335-6318/763-7062
Bothe-Napa Valley SP	(707)942-4575	Fort Humbold SHP	(707)445-6567
Brannan Island SRA	(916) 777-6671/7701	Fort Ross SHP	(707)847-3286/865-2391
Burleigh Murray Ranch SP	(650) 726-8819	Fort Tejon SHP	(661)248-6692
Burton Creek SP	(530)525-7232	Franks Tract SRA	(916)777-6671/777-7701
Butano SP	(650) 879-2040	Fremont Peak SP	(831)623-4255
Calaveras Big Trees SP	(209)795-2334	Garrapata SP	(831)624-4909
CA State Mining and Mineral Museum	(209)742-7625	Gaviota SP	(805)968-1033/968-1711
CA State Capitol Museum	(916)324-0333	George J. Hatfield SRA	(209)826-1197
California State Railroad Museum	(916)445-7387/7373	Governor's Mansion SHP	(916)323-3047
California Citrus SHP	(909)780-6222	Gray Whale Cove SB	(650)726-8819
Candlestick Point SRA	(415)671-0145	Great Valley Grasslands SP	(209)874-2056/826-1197
Cardiff SB	(760)753-5091	Greenwood SB	(707)937-5804
Carlsbad SB	(760)438-3143	Grizzly Creek Redwoods SP	(707)777-3683/946-2409
Carmel River	(831)624-4909	Grover Hot Springs SP	(530)694-2248/525-7232
Carnegie SVRA	(925)447-9027	Half Moon Bay SB	(650)726-8819
Carpinteria SB	(805)684-2811/585-1850	Hearst San Simeon SHM (Hearst Castle)	(805)927-2000
Caspar Headlands SB/SR	(707)937-5804		(800)445-4445
Castaic Lake SRA	(213)798-2961	Hendy Woods SP	(707)895-3141/937-5804
Castle Crags SP	(530)235-2684	Henry W. Coe SP	(831)779-2728
Castle Rock SP	(408)867-2952	Henry Cowell Redwoods SP	(831)335-4598/429-2850
Caswell Memorial SP	(209)599-3810	Humboldt Lagoons SP	(707)488-2041

Humboldt Redwoods State Park	(707)946-2409/2015	Patrick's Point SP	(707)677-3570/488-2041
Hungry Valley SVRA	(661)248-7007	Pelican SB	(707)464-6101
Huntington SB	(714)536-1454/(949)494-3539	Pescadero SB	(650)726-8819/(831)335-6318
Indian Grinding Rock SHP	(209)296-7488	Pfeiffer Big Sur SP	(831)667-2315
Jack London SHP	(707)938-5216/1519	Picacho SRA	(760)996-2963
Jedediah Smith Redwoods SP	(707)464-6101	Pigeon Point Light Station	(650)879-2120
Jug Handle SR	(707)937-5804	Pico Pio SHP	(562)695-1217
Julia Pfeiffer Burns State Park	(831)667-2315	Pismo SB	(805)489-2684
Kruse Rhododenron SR	(707)847-3221/865-2391	Plumas-Eureka SP	(530)836-2380
La Purisima Mission SHP	(805)733-3713	Point Lobos SR	(831)624-4909
Lake Oroville SRA	(538)538-2219/2200	Point Montara Light Station	(650)728-7177
Lake Perris SRA	(909)940-5608/5603	Point Mugu SP	(805)488-5223/(818)880-0350
Lake Valley SRA	(530)525-7277	Point Sal SB	(805)773-3713
Leo Carrillo SP	(805)488-5223/(818)880-0350	Point Sur SHP	(831)625-4419/667-2316
Limekiln SP	(831)667-2403	Pomponio SB	(650)726-8819/(831)335-6318
Los Encinos SHP	(310)454-8212/(818)784-4849	Portola Redwoods SP	(650)948-9098
Los Osos Oaks SR	(805) 549-7434	Prairie Creek Redwoods SP	(707)464-6101
MacKerricher SP	(707) 964-9112/ 937-5804	Providence Mountains SRA	(760)928-2586/(661)942-0662
Malakoff Diggins SHP	(530) 265-2740	Railtown 1897 SHP	(209)984-3953
Malibu Creek SP	(818) 880-0367	Red Rock Canyon SP	(661)942-0662/(818)880-0350
Malibu Lagoon SB	(818) 880-0350	Refugio SB	(805)968-1033/968-1711
Manchester SP	(707) 937-5804	Richardson Grove SP	(707)247-3318
Marina SB	(831)384-7695	Robert Louis Stevenson SP	(707)942-4575
Marshall Gold Discovery SHP	(530)622-3470	Russian Gulch SP	(707)937-0497/5804
McArthur-Burney Falls Memorial SP	(530) 335-2777	Saddleback Butte SP	(661)942-0662
McConnell SRA	(209)394-7755/826-1196	Salinas River SB	(831)384-7695
McGrath SB	(805) 654-4744/648-3918/585-1850	Salt Point SP	(707)847-3221/865-2391
Mendocino Headlands SP	(707)937-5804	Salton Sea SRA	(760)393-3059
Mendocino Woodlands SP	(707)937-5755	Samuel P. Taylor SP	(415)488-9897/898-4362
Millerton Lake SRA	(559) 822-2332/2225	San Buenaventura SB	(805)648-4127
Mitchell Caverns	(760)928-2586	San Clemente SB	(949)492-3156/0802
Mono Lake Tufa SR	(760)647-6331/3044	San Elijo SB	(760)753-5091/(619)688-3260
Montaña de Oro SP	(805)528-0513/772-7434	San Gregorio SB	(650)726-8819/(831)335-6318
Montara SB	(650)726-8819	San Juan Bautista SHP	(831)623-4881/4526
Monterey SHP	(831)649-7118	San Luis Reservoir SRA	(209)826-1196/800-346-2711
Montgomery Woods SR	(707)937-5804	San Onofre SB	(949)492-4872/0802
Morro Bay SP	(805)772-7434	San Pasqual Battlefield SHP	(760)737-2201
Morro Strand SB	(805)772-7434	San Simeon SP	(805)927-2065/2020
Moss Landing SB	(831)384-7695	Santa Susana Pass SHP	(310) 454-8212
Mount Diablo SP	(925)837-2525/ 673-2891	Schooner Gulch SB	(707)937-5804
Mount San Jacinto SP	(909)659-2607/767-4037	Seacliff SB	(831)685-6442/335-6318
Mt. Tamalpais SP	(415)388-2070	Shasta SHP	(530)243-8194
Natural Bridges SB	(831)423-4609/335-6318	Silver Strand SB	(619)435-5184/(619)688-3260
New Brighton SB	(831)464-6330/335-6318	Silverwood Lake SRA	(760)389-2303
Oceano (Pismo) Dunes SVRA	(805) 473-7223	Sinkyone Wilderness SP	(707)986-7711/247-3318
Old Sacramento SHP	(916)442-7644	Sonoma Coast SB	(707)875-3483
Old Town San Diego SHP	(619)220-5422	Sonoma SHP	(707)938-1519
Olompali SHP	(415)892-3383/898-4362	South Carlsbad SB	(760)438-3143/(619)688-3260
Pacheco SP	(209)826-6283	South Yuba River SP	(530)273-3884/432-2546
Palomar Mountain SP	(760)742-3462	Standish-Hickey SRA	(707)925-6482/247-3319

State Indian Museum	(916)324-0971	Turlock Lake SRA	(209)874-2008/874-2056
Sugar Pine Point SP	(530)525-7982/7232	Van Damme SP	(707)937-0851/937-5804
Sugarloaf Ridge SP	(707)833-5712/938-1519	Washoe Meadows SP	(530)525-7232
Sunset SB	(831)763-7062/335-6318	Weaverville Joss House SHP	(530)623-5284/225-2065
Sutter's Fort SHP	(916)445-4422	Westport-Union Landing SB	(707)937-5804
Tahoe SRA	(530)583-3074/525-3345	Wilder Ranch SHP	(831)423-9703/335-6318
Thornton SB	(831)335-6318	Wildwood Canyon Ranch	(909)657-0676
Tolawa Dunes SP	(415)669-1140/898-4362	Will Rogers SB	(213)305-9503/(213)485-2433
Tomales Bay SP	(415)669-1140/898-4362	Will Rogers SHP	(310)454-8212/(818)880-0350
Tomo-Kahni Village Site	(661)942-0662	William B. Ide Adobe SHP	(530)529-8599
Topanga SP	(310)454-8212/455-2465	William R. Hearst Memorial SB	(805)927-2068/2035
Torrey Pines SB	(619)755-2063	Woodland Opera House SHP	(916)666-9617
Torrey Pines SR	(619)755-2063	Woodson Bridge SRA	(530)839-2112
Trinidad SB	(707) 677-3570/488-2041	Zmudowski SB	(831)384-7695
Tule Elk SR	(661)764-6881/(559)822-2332		

INDEX

CALIFORNIA STATE PARKS FOUNDATION

California State Parks need your help!

Your membership in the California State Parks Foundation helps to protect California's natural, cultural, and historic treasures—your state parks! Benefits for all categories of membership include free park day-use passes, a large fold-out map listing all state parks, and the California Parklands newsletter featuring information you can use to enhance your park visits. Consider a gift member-ship for that special friend or relative. Please call (800) 963-7275 or email the foundation at members@calparks.org and join today!

John McKinney is the author of a dozen books about walking, hiking, and nature, including *The Joy of Hiking: Hiking the Trailmaster Way.* The Trailmaster writes articles and commentaries about walking for national publications, promotes hiking and conservation on radio and television, and serves as a consultant to a hiking vacation company. Contact him at: www.thetrailmaster.com.

For more information about California State Parks,
visit www.parks.ca.gov

California Parks Books from Wilderness Press

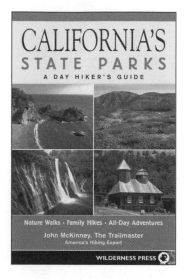

ISBN 0-89997-386-8

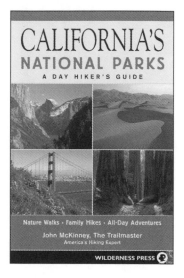

ISBN 0-89997-387-6

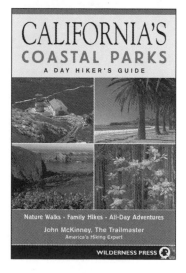

ISBN 0-89997-388-4

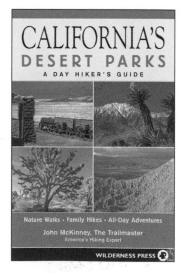

ISBN 0-89997-389-2